T0168726

LOW-WAGE WORK
IN GERMANY

LOW-WAGE WORK IN GERMANY

Gerhard Bosch and Claudia Weinkopf
editors

The Russell Sage Foundation Case Studies of Job Quality in Advanced Economies

Russell Sage Foundation • New York

The Russell Sage Foundation

The Russell Sage Foundation, one of the oldest of America's general purpose foundations, was established in 1907 by Mrs. Margaret Olivia Sage for "the improvement of social and living conditions in the United States." The Foundation seeks to fulfill this mandate by fostering the development and dissemination of knowledge about the country's political, social, and economic problems. While the Foundation endeavors to assure the accuracy and objectivity of each book it publishes, the conclusions and interpretations in Russell Sage Foundation publications are those of the authors and not of the Foundation, its Trustees, or its staff. Publication by Russell Sage, therefore, does not imply Foundation endorsement.

Library of Congress Cataloging-in-Publication Data
Low-wage work in Germany / Gerhard Bosch and Claudia Weinkopf, editors.
    p. cm. — (The Russell Sage Foundation case studies of job quality in
    advanced economies)
    Includes index.
    ISBN 978-0-87154-062-1
    1. Unskilled labor—Germany.   2. Wages—Germany.   3. Minimum wage—
Germany.   4. Labor market—Germany.   I. Bosch, Gerhard.   II. Weinkopf,
Claudia.
    HD8451.L69   2008
    331.7'980944—dc22   2007045931

Text design by Suzanne Nichols.

RUSSELL SAGE FOUNDATION
112 East 64th Street, New York, New York 10021
10 9 8 7 6 5 4 3 2 1

Contents

About the Authors

GERHARD BOSCH is professor of sociology and executive director of the Institute for Work, Skills and Training (IAQ) at the University of Duisburg-Essen.

CLAUDIA WEINKOPF is deputy director of the Institute for Work, Skills and Training (IAQ) at the University of Duisburg-Essen and head of the research department "Flexibility and Security."

LARS CZOMMER was a senior researcher at the Institute for Work and Technology (IAT) and currently runs the Office for Social Scientist Work.

KAREN JAEHRLING is senior researcher at the Institute for Work, Skills and Training (IAQ) at the University of Duisburg-Essen, working in the research department "Flexibility and Security."

THORSTEN KALINA is senior researcher at the Institute for Work, Skills and Training (IAQ) at the University of Duisburg-Essen, working as senior researcher in the research department "Flexibility and Security."

ROBERT SOLOW is Institute Professor Emeritus at the Massachusetts Institute of Technology and a Nobel laureate in economics.

ACHIM VANSELOW is senior researcher at the Institute for Work, Skills and Training (IAQ) at the University of Duisburg-Essen, working in the research department "Flexibility and Security."

DOROTHEA VOSS-DAHM is senior researcher at the Institute for Work, Skills, and Training at the University of Duisberg-Essen, working in the research department "Working Time and Work Organization."

INTRODUCTION

The German Story

Robert Solow

By any reasonable standard definition of "low-wage work," about a quarter of American wage earners are low-wage workers. The corresponding figure is smaller, sometimes much smaller, in other comparable advanced capitalist countries. This fact is not very good for the self-image of Americans. It does not seem to be what is meant by "crown(ing) thy good with brotherhood, from sea to shining sea." The paradox, if that is the right word, is the starting point for the extensive study of which this book is an important part. What are the comparative facts, what do they mean, and why do they turn out that way?

A foundation dedicated from its beginning to "the improvement of social and living conditions in the United States of America" has to be interested in the nature of poverty, its causes, changes, consequences and possible reduction. Low-wage work is not the same thing as poverty, still less lifelong poverty. Some low-wage workers live in families with several earners, and share a common standard of living, so they may not be poor even while working such jobs. Some low-wage workers are on a reasonably secure track that will eventually move them to better paid jobs, so they are not poor in a lifetime sense. But some low-wage workers are stuck with very low income for a meaningful length of time. For them, low-wage work does mean poverty in the midst of plenty.

Of course, the incidence of poverty can be reduced by transfer payments outside the labor market. Nevertheless, in a society that values self-reliance, and in which productive work confers identity and self-respect as well as the respect of others, income redistribution unconnected or wrongly connected with work is not the best solution except in special cases. In that kind of society, ours for instance, the persistence of low-wage work is felt as a social problem on its own. It first has to be understood if we are to find satisfactory ways to diminish its incidence or alleviate its effects.

One obvious basis for low-wage work is low productivity, which may be primarily a characteristic of the worker, as is often simply assumed, or may be primarily a characteristic of the job. If it inheres in the job, equity could be achieved by passing the job around, so to speak, like boring committee assignments or military service, but that would have no aggregate effect. Wherever low pay originates, however, raising productivity provides a double benefit: it diminishes the amount of low-wage work to be done, and it increases the useful output of the whole economy.

Low productivity, and therefore low-wage work, tends to reproduce itself from generation to generation. This is an important additional reason why a high incidence of low-wage work is a "social condition" that needs to be improved. Growing up in a chronically low-wage family limits access to good education, good health care, and to other ladders to social mobility. So a persistent high incidence of low-wage work, when confined to a relatively small group, contravenes the widely accepted social goal of equal opportunity.

These are among the reasons why, in 1994, the Russell Sage Foundation inaugurated a major program of research on the nature, causes, and consequences of low-wage work and the prospects of low-wage workers. This initiative replaced a successful but more conventional program of research on poverty. It was called, rather grandly, *The Future of Work*. One of its key motivations was the need to understand how poorly educated, unskilled workers could cope with an economy in which most jobs were becoming technologically advanced, and therefore more demanding of cognitive power and refined skills.

This formulation was intended to call attention both to workers and to jobs, the natural subtext being that low-end jobs might be disappearing faster than low-skilled workers. This potential disparity presented the danger that low-wage workers could be stranded in an economy that had no use for them. The research mandate was interpreted quite broadly.

The Future of Work program was, as a matter of course, focused on the United States. It produced a large body of useful and original research, some of which was collected and summarized in the 2003 volume *Low-Wage America: How Employers Are Reshaping Opportunity in the Workplace*, edited by Eileen Appelbaum, Annette Bernhardt, and Richard Murnane. One of the refreshing aspects of these studies was precisely that the needs and capacities of employers shared the stage in the low-wage labor market with the abilities and motivations of workers.

One interesting hypothesis that emerged from this work was the notion that employers have significant discretion about the way they organize their use of low-skilled workers and the value they put on the continuity and productivity of their work force. The extreme versions came to be labeled "low-road" and "high-road" modes of organization. At the low-road extreme lie employers such as the typical car-wash, whose workers are regarded as casual labor, interchangeable parts that can be picked up off the street freely under normal labor-market conditions. There is no advantage in doing otherwise. At the other extreme are employers who regard their unskilled workers as an asset whose productive value can be increased by more training and longer attachment to the firm.

The point of this distinction was the belief that in some market situations both styles can be viable. An employer's place on the continuum is not uniquely determined by technology and the intensity of competition in the product market. Satisfactory profits can be earned by somewhat higher- and somewhat lower-road modes of organization; in some industries, examples of both can be found coexisting.

Of course, the nature of the technology and the competitive intensity in the industry are important determinants of labor-market outcomes. That is not in doubt. In some situations, however, there may be scope for several levels of wages and job quality for unskilled workers. It is important here to note that job quality covers much more than the current wage and benefits paid; it includes the length and slope of the internal wage scale, the degree of job security, the training offered and the possibilities of promotion within the firm, small creature comforts, the pace of the work itself, the autonomy and ergonomic character of the work, and so on. Each of these has a cost to the firm and a value to the workers, and the two are not always the same.

It hardly needs arguing that these elements of job quality can be important for the satisfaction and self-respect attached to a job. It then becomes important to the researcher to understand the broad factors that govern the typical choices made by employers. These may include historical precedents, legislation, the working of the educational system, collective bargaining, and other "institutional" biases.

At this stage of the argument, the advantages of a comparative cross-country study stand out. Most of those broadly institutional factors cannot be studied empirically within the United States because they change so slowly in time, and because there is not much locational variation. One cannot actually see them at work in a still snapshot. One can speculate and make thought-experiments, but that is not the same thing. So the idea sprouted within the Russell Sage Foundation in 2003 that it might be very useful to observe systematically how the fate of low-wage labor differs across a sample of European countries. Not any countries will do: one wants countries with somewhat different but not radically different political and institutional histories; but they must be at the same level of economic development as the United States if lessons are to be learned that could be useful in the United States. In the end, the countries chosen included the three indispensable large countries—France, Germany, and the United Kingdom—and two small northern European countries—Denmark and the Netherlands. The choice was consciously limited to Europe in order to avoid the complication of drastically different sociopolitical systems. A competition was held, and a local team selected for each of these five countries.

The planners of the project framed it in such a way that would sharpen the inferences that could be made from cross-country comparisons. Most centrally, five target jobs were chosen as objects of close study, the same five in each country. They were nurses' assistants and cleaners in hospitals, housekeepers in hotels, checkout clerks and related occupations in supermarkets and retail stores specializing in electrical goods, packagers, machine tenders and other unskilled occupations in two branches of food processing, namely confectionary and meat products, and low-skilled operators in call centers. (This last choice took advantage of an already ongoing international study of the call-center industry.) These are all low-wage jobs in the United States. The fact that some of them are not low-wage jobs in some of the five countries is an example of the value of cross-country comparisons. The simple fact invites, or rather compels, the question: Why not?

Each national team was asked to compile a statistical overview of low-wage work in its country, with special but not exclusive attention to the five target jobs. The team was also asked to complement the routine data with a survey of the historical, legislative, educational and other institutional infrastructure that is believed to underlie its own particular ways of dealing with low-end jobs and low-skilled workers. The final part of each country report is a series of case studies of each of the target jobs, including interviews with employers, managers, workers, union representatives and other participants. (When temporary work agencies were used to provide some or all of the relevant workers, they were included in the interviews wherever possible.) The national teams met and coordinated their work in the course of the research. This book is the report of the Germany team.

There will be one more stage to complete the project. A six-country group of participants, including Americans, will prepare an explicitly comparative volume, job by job. They will try to fathom what deeper attitudinal, institutional, and circumstantial factors might explain the sometimes dramatic differences in the way these six modern nations engage with the problem of low-wage work.

One big, somewhat unexpected, finding is the one mentioned in the first paragraph of this introduction. The six countries differ substantially in the incidence of low-wage work. ("Incidence" is defined as the fraction of all workers, in the country or in a specific sector, who fall into the low-wage category.)

There is an interesting and important definitional issue that arises immediately. Uniformly in Europe (and elsewhere), a low-wage worker is anyone who earns less than two-thirds of the national median wage (usually the gross hourly wage, if only for data-availability reasons). This obviously makes the incidence of low-wage work an index of the inequality or dispersion of the wage distribution: multiplying or dividing everyone's wage by ten leaves the number of low-wage workers unchanged. The same applies to the measurement of poverty. In the United States, the poverty line is an absolute income. It was initially chosen as an empirical compromise, never entirely appropriate and less so as time passes, but nevertheless an absolute income. The United States has no corresponding definition for low-wage work, but the same approach could be taken. There are arguments to be made on both sides of this issue; for the purposes of this project, the choice of a low-wage threshold makes little practical difference. We use the European definition because that is the way their data are collected.

There is yet another practical reason to use the European definition. As noted, the two-thirds-of-median index simply reflects the degree of wage dispersion: a low incidence of low-wage work means a relatively compressed wage distribution, at least in the lower tail. This measure makes international comparisons more meaningful.

Comparing absolute real wages between the United States and other countries is problematic because pensions, health care, payroll taxes, employer contributions and other such benefits and deductions are handled differently in different systems. Relative comparisons are subject to similar distortions, but considerably less so.

Here are the basic facts. In 2005, the incidence of low-wage work was 25 percent in the United States, 22.1 percent in the United Kingdom, 20.8 percent in Germany (2004), 18.2 percent in the Netherlands (2004), 12.7 percent in France (2002) and 8.5 percent in Denmark. The range is obviously very wide.

In a way, that is helpful, because figures like this cannot be interpreted to the last decimal. Here is one interesting example of an unexpected twist. It turns out that the Dutch are the part-time champions among these countries, with a significantly larger fraction of part-time workers than elsewhere. This appears to be a voluntary choice, not something compelled by the unavailability of full-time work. Part-time workers tend to be paid lower hourly wages than full-time workers in the same or similar jobs, even in countries where it is against the law to discriminate against part-timers. The incidence measures given in the preceding paragraph are based on a headcount: 18 percent of all Dutch workers earn less than the low-wage threshold. One could with reason ask instead what fraction of the hours worked in the Netherlands falls into the low-wage category; the answer is about 16 percent. The fact that the hours-based incidence is lower would be common in all countries, but the difference is particularly large in the Netherlands.

A key issue is the degree of mobility out of low-wage work that characterizes each country's system. The seriousness of the "problem" turns almost entirely on the transitory nature of low-wage work. It is impossible to be precise about inter-country differences, because the data are sketchy and definitions vary. It is clear, however, that there are substantial differences among the countries, although mobility is fairly substantial everywhere, if only because younger workers eventually propel themselves into better jobs. The Danes appear to have the shortest residence times in low-wage work. For Americans the take-away lesson is that the self-image of an extremely mobile society is not valid, at least not in this respect.

Of course, there are many uniformities—often just what you would expect—among these countries in the pattern of low-wage work. The "concentration" of low-wage work in any subgroup of the population is defined as the incidence in that subgroup divided by the incidence among all workers. For instance, any subgroup with a higher incidence than the country at large will have a concentration index bigger than 1. This is the case for workers in the service sector of the economy, for women, for young people, for part-timers, and for those with little education. In most instances, the particular sectors we have picked out for study have a high concentration index; together, retail trade and "hotels and catering" have a concentration ratio of about 3 in the Netherlands. The categories mentioned obviously overlap, but the data do not permit us to zero in statistically on young part-time secondary-school-only women working in supermarkets. Nevertheless, the odds are very high that they fall into the low-wage category.

The cross-country differences are more interesting, however, because they at least offer the possibility that we can find explanations for them in the circumstances, institutions, attitudes and policies of these basically similar economies. It is important that these are basically similar economic systems with broadly similar labor markets. They differ in certain historically established social norms, institutions and policies. One can hope to figure out which of these fairly small differences underlie the observed variation in the conditions of low-wage work. This would be difficult or even meaningless if we were comparing radically different economic systems.

Here is one example of commonality that illustrates the point. In some of the target jobs, in several instances and several countries, there has been a noticeable increase in the intensity of competition in the relevant product market. Low-cost German chains compete with Dutch food retailers. Large food retailers, domestic and foreign, put pressure on meat processing and confectionary prices in every country. The spread of international hotel chains—along with the availability of exhaustive price comparisons on the internet—has made the hotel business more competitive. In all such instances, business firms respond to intensified competition by trying to lower their own unit costs (as well as by product differentiation, quality improvement, and other devices).

The urgent need to reduce costs seems almost invariably—though not exclusively—to involve particular pressure on the wages of low-skilled workers. It is not hard to understand why this should happen in every country, precisely because they are all advanced capitalist market economies. The main reason is that low-wage workers usually have very little "firm-specific human capital." That is to say, since they have few skills of any kind, they have few skills that are difficult to replace for the firm that employs them. If they quit in response to wage reductions, they can be replaced with little cost, especially in a slack labor market. Low-wage workers have few alternatives, so they cannot defend themselves well. For similar reasons, they have little political power and usually little clout with their trade unions, if they have any union protection at all. Firms seeking profit will respond similarly, though not identically in every detail. Country-specific institutions can modify the response, but not entirely.

A closely related common factor has to do with "flexibility." Partly because technology now permits it, and partly because a globalized market now demands it, business firms find that their level of production has to fluctuate seasonally, cyclically and erratically. Sometimes it is not so much the total but the composition of production that has to change, often with short notice. Under those circumstances, it is an advantage if the firm can vary its employment more or less at will; otherwise, underutilized labor constitutes an unproductive cost. The low-end labor force is likely to bear the brunt of this adjustment, for the same reasons already mentioned in connection with wage pressure. Low-wage workers cannot do much to defend themselves against or prepare themselves for these vicissitudes, other than to try for even lower-wage part-time jobs or to resort to public assistance.

There is always a possibility that observed cross-country variation in low-wage employment practices are somehow "natural," in the sense that they can be traced to underlying differences that were not chosen and could not be changed, such as geographical or topographical characteristics, resource availability, or perhaps even some irreversible bit of historical evolution. That does not seem to be what is happening in these six countries. In many instances, cross-country differences are the result of legislation, with minimum wage laws being an obvious example. A more unusual example, at least to Americans, is the fact that many European governments, such as those in France and the Netherlands, can and do extend certain collective bargaining agreements to cover employers and workers in the industry who were not parties to the bargaining itself. In this way, even comparatively small union density can lead to much broader coverage by union agreements.

This need not be an unalloyed benefit to workers. Companies have been known to arrange to bargain with a small, weak union and then press for the resulting favorable agreement to be generalized. But the practice may also reflect a desire by employers to eliminate large wage differentials as a factor in inter-firm competition. It is interesting that when the abolition of this practice of extending collective bargaining agreements was proposed in the Netherlands, the employers' federation opposed the proposal. It is a toss-up which event seems more outlandish to an American: the practice of mandatory extension or that employers should oppose abolishing it.

Explicit legislation is not the only source of institutional differences that affect the low-wage labor market. All sorts of behavioral norms, attitudes, and traditions on both sides of the labor market can have persistent effects. The country narratives describe many such influences. For example, the German report outlines a distinctive system of wage determination and labor relations, based on diversified high-quality, high-value-added industrial production, along with "patient," mostly bank-provided, capital, and participation of employee representatives in company supervisory boards.

This system may be coming to an end, undermined by international competition—especially from the ex-communist countries of eastern Europe, including the reunification of Germany—and shifts in public opinion and political power. It is still a matter of controversy among specialists whether the traditional system had become unsustainable or simply unsustained. The German "mini-job," low wage, frequently incurring lower non-wage employment costs in practice, and limited to very short hours per month, is an example of a device to encourage both demand and supply for certain kinds of low-wage work.

This introduction is not the place for a detailed description of each national system. The individual country narratives will provide that. It is important, however, to underline the fact that the components of each national system often hang together in some way. It may not be possible to single out one component and think: "That looks clever; why don't we try it in our country?" The German mini-job, for example, is occupied mostly by women, and may work the way it does because the social welfare apparatus in Germany is still organized around the notion of the single-breadwinner family. The concept of a labor relations "system" may suggest tighter-fitting than the facts justify; a word like "pattern" might be more accurate. But the basic point remains.

The four continental countries in the study correspond in a general way to the common notion of a "European social model" in contrast with the more individual-responsibility oriented approach of the United States. The post-Thatcher United Kingdom probably falls somewhere in between. It would be a bad mistake, however, to ignore the differences among Denmark, France, Germany, and the Netherlands. To do so would be to miss the variety of conditions for low-wage labor that is possible for advanced capitalist market economies. Only the briefest characterization is possible here, but the individual reports are quite complete.

The Danish "flexicurity" system has achieved the status of a buzzword. The idea is to allow wages and job quality to be determined in an unregulated labor market (except for considerations of health and safety, of course) but to combine this flexibility with a very generous safety net, so that "no Dane should suffer economic hardship." For this system to be workable, the rules of the safety net have to push most recipients into whatever jobs are available. Even so, the system is likely to be expensive. Apparently the *lowest* marginal income tax rate is 44 percent (which is higher than the *highest* rate in the U.S.). One would need to know more about the details of the tax system in order to understand the content of any such comparison, but the details are unlikely to reverse the presumption that Danes are less tax-averse than some others.

To describe the Danish labor market as "unregulated" means only that there is very little intervention by the government. In fact, the labor market is regulated through centralized negotiations between representatives of employers and employees, who have very wide scope. For example, there is no statutory minimum wage, but a minimum labor scale is negotiated by the "social partners." It (almost) goes without saying that there is some evasion of this scale in traditional low-wage sectors, including some covered in the case studies. One reason why this is tolerated is that many of the affected workers are young people, especially students, who are only engaged in low-wage part-time work as a transitory phase. Denmark is a country that is low on university enrollments but high on vocationally-oriented post-secondary, non-university education.

There is a neat contrast here with France, which lives up to its reputation as a rather bureaucratically organized society. As the French report says, "Low hourly wages are fixed in France—perhaps more than in any other country—at the political level, not through collective bargaining agreements, and these wages are set in a centralized, not a decentralized, manner. Thus, the legal minimum wage plays a crucial role in France." Since 1970, the SMIC (minimum inter-branch growth wage) is indexed not only to inflation but also to the growth of overall productivity and wages. The intent was specifically to resist what was felt to be a tendency in the market toward excessive wage inequality.

The SMIC has been set at a fairly high level, and one consequence of this has been the disappearance of some unskilled jobs, to be replaced by unemployment (especially long-term unemployment), participation in active labor market policies, and withdrawal from the labor force. Other forces have been at work, however—urban land-use regulation in food retailing, for example—so the simpleminded causal connection between the SMIC and high unemployment is not exact. France is also distinguished by having a trade union movement that is rather strong at the national level, but has very little presence on the shop floor. This may account for some evasion of labor market regulations at the low end.

The low-wage labor market in the United Kingdom is especially interesting because it is an example of changes in institutions and outcomes brought about in a relatively short time by deliberate acts of policy. The Thatcher government chose as a matter of principle to weaken or eliminate preexisting supports for the occupants of low-quality jobs, and to undermine the ability of the trade union movement to compress the wage distribution. As a result, the incidence of low-wage work increased in the late 1970s and after. The Blair government, looking for a work-based solution to the problem of poverty, undertook measures to increase the supply of low-wage workers, but it also introduced a (fairly low) National Minimum Wage in 1999. The net outcome appears to have been a steady increase in the incidence of low-wage work from the late 1970s until the mid-1990s, and a leveling-off since then.

In effect, the United Kingdom has changed from a system rather like the other continental European countries to something much closer to the United States. The incidence of low-wage work has then followed the same trajectory. Of course, other economic factors, common to many countries, were also at work.

The Netherlands occupies a position somewhere between the Nordic model and the United States model, but not in a simple average sense. Many of the institutions are peculiarly Dutch; together they are described as the "Polder" model. One of its features is the important extent to which organizations representing employers, the government, and labor act jointly to regulate the labor market and much else, sometimes in a very detailed way. For instance, the minimum wage for young workers is substantially lower than for adults. The proliferation of part-time jobs, many of them occupied by students and young people, may be a consequence of this in part, though it may have other roots as well.

It is striking to an outsider that these tripartite institutions are more than merely regulatory. They are described as "deliberative," and apparently much of the serious public discussion of issues underlying socioeconomic policy takes place within them. This fact may make fairly tight regulation palatable to the Dutch public. The system has had considerable success; for example, the national unemployment rate fell from over 10 percent in 1984 to under 4 percent in 2001, when the widespread recession supervened. As will be seen in the Dutch report, however, it has its problems.

The purpose of these brief vignettes is definitely not to provide a summary of the pattern evolved in each of these countries with respect to low-wage job quality. That information is to be found in each of the separate country studies. The goal of this introduction is to illustrate the important general point that there are several viable systems of labor-market governance, including the mode of management of the low-wage labor market. The issue is not uniquely determined by the needs of a functioning market economy, or by technology, or by the imperatives of efficient organization. The system in place in each country has evolved in response to historical circumstances, cultural preferences, political styles and fashion in economic and social ideas. One cannot avoid noticing that relatively small countries, like Denmark and the Netherlands in our sample, and the other Nordic countries, Austria and perhaps Ireland outside it, seem more able than large countries to create and maintain the amount of trust that is needed for tripartite cooperation. This observation begs the question as to whether successful policy aimed at improving the relative status of low-wage workers may require a degree of social solidarity and trust that may be beyond larger, more diverse populations.

There are certainly many common influences as well: the response to intensified competition; the role of women, immigrants, and minorities; limitations on productivity; and so on. But there is no unique or best pattern. It even seems likely that the same "principles" of organization, applied in different institutional contexts, would eventuate in quite different practices. Some of this may emerge in the detailed comparative volume that is still to come.

Putting together a coherent story about low-wage work in Germany is complicated by the reunification of the country after the fall of communism. East Germany was (and is) at a significantly lower level of productivity and real wages than West Germany. To group them together even now would distort the picture by classifying very many workers in the East as earning less than two-thirds of the combined national median wage. The report makes the distinction wherever necessary.

The general picture is that from 1980 to about 1995, the incidence of low-wage work among full-time employees in West Germany trended very slightly downward, from just above 15 percent to a bit above 14 percent. Since 1995, incidence has gone up, reaching 17 percent in 2003. (In East Germany, using its own median wage as a reference point, the incidence of low-wage work is even higher, and has been increasing more steeply.)

The German team relates this groundswell to incipient changes in the broad German industrial system. During the postwar *Wirtschaftswunder*, West Germany adopted a system often described as "diversified high-quality production" and became one of the world's leading manufacturing producers and exporters. Two important attributes of this system should be mentioned. First, the large capital investment needed to reconstruct the German economy was in large measure provided by big banks, who were prepared to focus on modest long-term returns rather than immediate profit, and whose representation on managing boards allowed them to enforce their long-term objectives. Second, the large labor unions in the manufacturing sector also had some quasi-management positions—on works councils and advisory boards—in a system of corporate governance known as "co-determination." This system was able to produce rising productivity and a comfortable and fairly compressed wage distribution, at least within the manufacturing sector; pensions and health care were financed by a broad tax wedge levied on payrolls. The trade union movement was able to diffuse many of the advantages of "diversified quality production" outside the core, mostly export-oriented, sectors.

This system has now come under stress from a number of sources: the inevitable growth of the service sector, which is less suitable for this style of governance and whose lower wages tend to discourage the supply of labor; a gradual weakening of union power and a tendency to shift collective bargaining from the national to the local level; intensified competition, especially from Eastern Europe, including the easy possibility of outsourcing and, after accession to the European Union, the importing of very low-paid "posted" workers working according to their home-country rules; and a general waning of belief in corporatist ideas. An additional source of problems is that the German welfare state still retains relics of its Bismarckian organization around the single (male) breadwinner household. The German team discusses the underlying question as to whether this system can be (and ought to be) preserved under contemporary conditions. They conclude that the choice is still open, and the likely outcome turns not only on upcoming developments in the German economy, but also on choices made in the rest of the European Union. This is a very big question.

As of 2004 the incidence of low-wage work in Germany (referred to the German median wage) was 20.8 percent, somewhat higher than the other continental countries in the study. The concentration was greatest in the expected groups: the service sector (especially in small firms), the unskilled, women, the young, and non-nationals. The discrepancy between men and women working full-time is especially marked: incidences of 10 percent and 31 percent, to such an extent that women, who are 36.8 percent of the total work force, make up 64.1 percent of all low-paid workers.

A particular feature of the current German scene is the recently created category of "mini-jobs." These are very part-time, low-paid, almost casual jobs, mostly occupied by women with family responsibilities and the young. They are made attractive to employees because they are exempt from the substantial tax wedge. Standard requirements with respect to non-wage benefits are not enforced. The dual motivation was presumably to increase the supply of low-wage labor and simultaneously to provide an easy entry for women into paid work, even if low-paid work. There is obviously a question as to whether this institution is a viable long-term solution in a modern economy.

The report contains an interesting discussion of the current state and future prospects of the distinctive German dual vocational training system, usually involving both schooling and an apprenticeship. This system began in manufacturing; some of the current strains on it may relate to the shift to services. In any case there is now a shortage of training places, despite attempts to adapt the system to current industrial conditions. Apparently a further problem may arise in the wake of plans to expand university education. The fear is that this would attract the best potential participants in the dual vocational system. The result might be a deterioration in the skill level of the industrial labor force, which would present an obvious challenge to the system of diversified quality production. This issue of the best balance between vocational training and university education should be of great interest to Americans, who have moved generally to the university side.

Preface

Gerhard Bosch and Claudia Weinkopf

Surely not in Germany!" one may be tempted to answer when asked about low pay in Germany. And indeed, Germany was for many years regarded as a country that by international standards had a particularly low wage spread—that is, relatively small differences between very low and very high wages, between poor and rich. This was due above all to a high level of coverage by collective agreements and strong trade unions, particularly in industries with high shares of exports; their collective agreements acted as benchmarks for other industries. Even in its heyday, however, the German model had areas in which workers could not earn a living wage, particularly service industries with high shares of women workers. In the old family model, low pay for women workers was largely seen as unproblematic—if women were economically active at all, they were either young and looking for a partner with whom to start a family or already married and seeking at most to top up their husband's earnings, which was the main source of household income.

It is only since the 1990s that low-wage work has increasingly become a topic for debate in Germany. Employment policy issues played a key role in triggering this debate, and two questions have dominated it: Should wages at the lower end of the labor market be even further reduced in order to boost employment levels and reduce unemployment, particularly among low-skill workers? And should such a strategy be supported or promoted by the state—for example, by subsidizing social security contributions in the low-wage segment or through other forms of wage subsidy? Approaches of this kind have been tried since the late 1990s as part of various pilot projects and programs, and the results have generally been disappointing, as the evaluations show. Also, model calculations and simulations of the effects of across-the-board subsidies in the low-wage segment have overwhelmingly concluded that the employment effects are slight and the costs very high.

Surprisingly, the debate has scarcely addressed the question of how large the low-wage sector in Germany already was and how it developed even without political intervention. The talk has centered on the "introduction" of a low-wage sector, although the model calculations of the costs of wage subsidies indicate that such a sector has existed for a long time, since a not inconsiderable number of workers already employed would be entitled to financial support on the introduction of low-wage subsidies. However, virtually nobody has bothered to take a close look at this low-wage sector and, particularly, its rapid growth. Such analyses would only interfere with the alleged need to "introduce" a low-wage sector and, if anything, draw attention to the new social problems created by low-wage work. The question of the quality of such jobs has also not been raised—"whatever creates jobs is what is in society's interest" not only was the political watchword during the 2005 federal elections but also has been the central theme in most debates in Germany.

Against this background, it was with great interest that, in the late summer of 2003, we received the call for tenders issued by the Russell Sage Foundation for an international comparative research project on low-wage work. The purpose of the project was to investigate the extent, evolution, and structure of low-wage work in five European countries—Denmark, France, the United Kingdom, the Netherlands, and Germany. The focus of the study was not to be the employment effects of low-wage work but rather the quality of low-paid jobs and the factors that influence them. What role is played by the institutional environment, which differs from country to country? How much freedom do employers have to create jobs at the bottom end of the wage and skill spectrum? To answer these questions, the quantitative analyses were to be supplemented by qualitative studies of selected activities in a number of industries. The call for tenders listed call centers, retailing, the food industry, hotels, hospitals, and agency work—all of these being industries in which low pay is widespread in the United States, as studies carried out as part of the Russell Sage Foundation's previous *Future of Work* research program had shown.

We hesitated only momentarily before deciding to respond to the call for tenders. It was not only the research questions that captured our interest but also the foundation's intention of closely coordinating the work of the national teams in Europe to ensure that their results achieved as high a level of comparability as possible. The decision on the awarding of the contracts for the country studies in Germany, France, the United Kingdom, the Netherlands, and Denmark was taken at the beginning of 2004 after an exhaustive evaluation process. The European teams and officials from the Russell Sage Foundation and their advisers held a number of meetings at which the research questions and approach were specified more precisely and harmonized with each other and interim results were discussed.

In this book, we present the results of the German country study. Our analysis shows that low-wage work has increased significantly in Germany since the mid-1990s and its incidence is now considerable. The share of low-wage work in Germany is almost as high as in the United States and the United Kingdom, whereas the share of low-wage work is considerably lower in France and Denmark. In none of the other countries in recent years have wages at the lower end been under such pressure as in Germany, nor has downward wage differentiation been so pronounced. Around 5 percent of all employees in Germany earn less than five euros per hour, which equates to about one-third of the country's median wage. In none of the other European countries under investigation do so many employees have to work for so little money, because such low pay is eliminated by statutory minimum wages (in France, the United Kingdom, and the Netherlands) or a high level of coverage by collective agreements and strong trade unions (in Denmark). Even the state minimum wages in the United States, which are very low by international standards, set a clear lower limit on pay. Furthermore, Germany offers very limited opportunities to climb out of low-wage work into better-paid employment or to overcome poverty.

We had not expected our results to be so unflattering to Germany's social market economy. We are aware that any international comparative evaluation must also take account of differences in national social security systems and benefits, as well as living costs. Nevertheless, some of the other results of our analyses further underline the need for action in Germany. Thus, for example, the share of economically active individuals living in poverty in Germany is above the European average.

In the three years during which we have been working intensively on low-wage work as part of this project, there has been a radical shift in public and political perceptions of this topic and in the debates around it. In Germany it is now almost universally accepted that low-paid work and, to some extent, demeaning working and employment conditions are relatively widespread. What continues to be hotly debated, however, is whether action should be taken to combat the problem and, if so, what form that action should take. This is reflected very clearly in the vigorous debates on whether a minimum wage is necessary in Germany or whether it would simply cause considerable damage to the labor market. The good labor market performance in Denmark, the United Kingdom, and the Netherlands shows that arduous work in the low-wage sector can be decently paid without jeopardizing employment.

This book is organized as follows. In chapter 1, we survey the evolution of low-wage work and its incidence and structure and analyze which changes in the German employment model have facilitated the increase in such work in Germany. The following chapters focus on the results of the sector and company case studies, and in particular on the target occupations: customer service in call centers operating in the energy supply and financial services sectors (chapter 2), production and packaging occupations in the meat and confectionary subsectors of the food industry (chapter 3), nursing and cleaning occupations in hospitals (chapter 4), room cleaning in hotels (chapter 5), and checkout and sales occupations in food and electrical retailing (chapter 6). In chapter 7, we summarize the results of our study and draw conclusions about the need for political action.

We would like to thank the Russell Sage Foundation for the generous financial support for the project and especially Eric Wanner and Aixa Cintron-Velez for working with us in a spirit of trust and cooperation. We would like to make special mention of the foundation's academic advisers, whose astute questions and valuable suggestions contributed considerably to the European country studies. Ann Carter and Chris Tilly, as well as another anonymous referee, reviewed the first drafts of our final report in English and made many valuable suggestions for revisions. We also benefited considerably from the close cooperation with the teams from Denmark, France, the United Kingdom, and the Netherlands and the excellent advice offered by various team members.

CHAPTER 1

Low-Wage Work in Germany: An Overview

Gerhard Bosch and Thorsten Kalina

G ermany was long regarded as a country with relatively low income inequality. According to studies by the Organization for
Economic Cooperation and Development (OECD 1996, 1997), income inequality in Germany was still declining between 1980 and
1995, bucking the global trend. Only the Scandinavian countries had
a narrower income spread and lower shares of low-paid workers than
Germany. Furthermore, the opportunities for low-paid workers in
Germany to move up to more highly paid jobs were considerably
greater than in the United States or the United Kingdom (OECD
1997, 31). This rosy picture of Germany has now changed. The share
of low-paid workers has been growing since the mid-1990s and now
exceeds the European Union (EU) average. Clearly, the German employment system has lost its historic capacity to prevent an expansion of low-wage work.

In the extensive literature on the old German employment and
productive system, the low income inequality up to the 1990s was attributed to the German economy's particular product portfolio—the
so-called diversified quality production (Streeck 1991)—and to the
country's high productivity levels. David Finegold and David Soskice
(1988) spoke of a "high skill equilibrium" that, in contrast to countries with "low skill equilibriums" (such as the United Kingdom),
provided good rates of pay even in the middle and lower wage brackets. In this literature, Germany was characterized as an example of a
coordinated market economy or a corporatist model in which the
various actors had been able to implement long-term innovation
strategies. One precondition for this coordination was the existence
of "patient capital," which was concerned with long-term returns.
The "patience" of capital was the result of the stable company ownership that arose out of the close financial links between large joint
stock companies and their house banks, the high share of family-

owned companies in Germany's Mittelstand—its numerous small and medium-sized enterprises (SMEs)—and the great importance of public enterprises. The emphasis on high-quality production was supported by high investment in R&D, cooperation between engineers and skilled workers thoroughly trained in the dual vocational training system, numerous quality standards in product markets, and German companies' gradual specialization in the high-price, high-quality segments of their product markets. Labor markets were dominated by long-term contractual relationships, which were the result of a high level of dismissal protection, high investment in vocational training for the core workforce, and close cooperation between capital and labor based on industrywide collective agreements and codetermination, implemented through employee participation on supervisory boards and works councils. The high level of job security guaranteed by the regulations governing dismissal protection and codetermination encouraged the development of "productivity coalitions," set up to assist with the modernization of vocational training and corporate reorganization projects. Obligatory social insurance schemes for health care, long-term nursing care (since 1995), accidents, unemployment, and old age created a tightly drawn social security safety net. Stable labor relations and the comprehensive social security safety net gave firms space to innovate in exchange for a high level of employee security. The importance of occupational labor markets and the portability of social security benefits encouraged interfirm mobility, which not only was a precondition for the diffusion of innovation but also helped to boost employability during periods of structural change.

Most analyses of the German model concentrated almost exclusively on the export-oriented segments of the country's manufacturing sector and had little to say about low-skill manufacturing and service jobs, which, even in the German model's heyday, were considerably less well-paid. It was always implicitly assumed that the structures and configurations of actors observed in Germany's export industries could be taken as representative of the system as a whole. For a long time this assumption was to some extent justified. Publicly owned enterprises played a major role in the service sector. The railways, the postal service, local public transport, and the electricity, gas, and water supply industries were all publicly owned, as were many hospitals and child care centers. These industries were highly unionized, and the unions were often granted wide-ranging rights to codetermination similar to those that existed in the coal, iron, and steel industries.[1] Many social services were largely funded by the state but provided by social welfare institutions that adopted public sector pay structures, such as hospitals and child care centers. Thus, governance structures were protected from short-term market pressures, in much the same way as manufacturing firms were sheltered by the availability of patient capital. In these industries too, wages were eliminated as a competitive factor by industrywide collective agreements. In the public sector and in publicly funded social services, the trade unions succeeded in negotiating good wages and social benefits that went beyond the statutory minimum standards, even for low-skill jobs. Some of the collective agreements in private services (such as retailing) were declared generally binding. The collective agreements in the metal and engineering industry also set the pace for the public sector and industries with weaker trade unions, a role that was facilitated by high employment levels and labor shortages. Finally, the dual vocational training system was not confined to craft trades and manufacturing but extended to virtually all service industries as well. In consequence, virtually all industries in Germany had a significantly higher share of skilled workers who were well trained than other OECD countries. Last but not least, labor legislation and social security benefits applied across the board to all employees in a given industry.

It was not until the beginning of the 1990s that the first critical voices began to be heard alongside the occasionally almost euphoric characterizations of the German employment model. It is not surprising that the first such criticism came from a Danish author concerned not only with the core manufacturing industries but also with the welfare state and social services. By this time, women's labor market participation had increased considerably in most of the developed industrialized countries. The Scandinavian countries had reformed their welfare states and been able to open up new areas of employment in social services. Gøsta Esping-Andersen (1990) saw Germany as an exemplar of a conservative welfare state that had failed to implement similar reforms and continued to be tailored to the single male breadwinner. In this model, women in particular derive their social security entitlements from their husband's employment and the state offers strong financial incentives for them either to remain out of the labor market or to accept marginal part-time jobs (so-called mini-jobs). With the increase in female labor market participation, the failure to reform the welfare state proved to be the gateway for the increase in poorly paid, marginal part-time jobs. Initially this attracted little attention in Germany, since well-paid industrial workers—and indeed many women themselves—expected women to have only a second income rather than a living wage.

For a long time the German employment system was admired for its stability in the somewhat too functionally oriented literature. There were good reasons for this. Until the mid-1990s, the German employment system was dominated by the centripetal forces, already described, that kept the share of low-paid workers low despite increasing international competition, a considerable influx of foreign workers, the expansion of the service sector, and rising female participation rates. After the mid-1990s, however, the centrifugal forces clearly became stronger. Since then, both the share of low-paid workers and the pay differentials between the industrial core and the periphery in the German labor market have increased. The link between the still successful and relatively high-paying export-oriented segment of German manufacturing and other industries has obviously become considerably more elastic than it was in the past.

The reasons for the increase in unemployment and low-wage work are hotly debated in Germany, and a number of explanations have been advanced. Herbert Kitschelt and Wolfgang Streeck (2004), for example, see Germany, with its "diversified quality production," as caught in a "high-quality trap" with shrinking markets. Norbert Berthold (1997) points to the decline in the price of low-skill labor as a result of the automation of low-skill jobs (the skill bias of technical progress) and the massive increase in the supply of low-skill labor following the emergence of global markets. Like most German economists, he argues that the only choice available to Germany is that between equality and unemployment and that the country must therefore deregulate its labor market in order to increase employment levels. Other authors, such as Fritz Scharpf (2000), attribute Germany's high unemployment primarily to the underdevelopment of social services and see the country's egalitarian wage structure as a barrier to the expansion of such services. Scharpf bases his argument on William Jack Baumol's (1967) cost-disease theory. According to this theory, social services are resistant to rationalization, which, if these labor-intensive services are expanded in an economy with an egalitarian income distribution, will lead to increasing pressure on wages, particularly when demand for such services is very price-elastic.

These three explanations certainly identify important developments that undoubtedly have the potential to put egalitarian wage systems under pressure. However, other authors argue that these explanations disregard the fact that actual effects can be influenced by political and economic factors as well as institutional changes. Peter Bofinger (2005) and Albrecht Müller (2004), for example, suggest that the high export surpluses of recent years, for which the modernized productive system is largely responsible, undermine the arguments of Kitschelt and Streeck as well as those of Berthold. Both authors identify the consequences of German reunification and a restrictive monetary and fiscal policy as the reasons for high unemployment. One of the arguments advanced in the critique of the notion of a skill bias in technical progress is that a large share of low-paid workers in Germany have good qualifications and there is an antidote on the supply side to this collapse in demand, namely, higher-level training for workers. Richard Freeman and Ronald Schettkat (1999) have shown that German workers' wages, weighted for their skill levels, are not higher than in the United States. Gerhard Bosch and Alexandra Wagner (2005), following Esping-Andersen, argue that rising female participation rates act in the conservative German welfare state as a built-in deregulator of the traditional well-paid standard employment relationship. The cost-disease of social services could be remedied by reforms of the welfare state. They argue that services and not housework should be supported through various measures, including the funding out of taxation, pay-as-you-go financing through the social insurance system, or service vouchers for low earners, as the Scandinavian countries with their large service sectors have shown.

Our objective in this overview is to examine the increase in low-wage work, its effects on working and employment conditions, and the causes of the changes that have taken place. In the course of our efforts, we encountered considerable methodological and theoretical difficulties. So much has changed at the same time in Germany in recent years that it is difficult to judge to which of these factors the increase in low-wage work should be attributed. We are convinced that mono-causal explanations are not sufficient and that the interactions between different factors and the changes they have undergone over time are of crucial importance (Solow 1985). Thus, the key question is why the current mix of institutions and their economic environment has not prevented an increase in low-wage work in Germany, in contrast to the period before 1995. In our view, the answer is twofold: one reason can be found in Germany's economic situation following reunification—which, in combination with a restrictive economic policy, had many and diverse effects on employment as well as on the country's finances and social welfare system—and the other lies in the changes in key institutions in the traditional German employment model under the pressure of high unemployment and also as a result of deliberate political interventions, which have opened up the floodgates for the development of low-wage employment. It should also be remembered that institutions change their character as a result not only of reforms but of a failure to reform in a changed environment. This has been especially true of the German family model, with far-reaching effects on women's pay.

We will begin with data analyses in order to investigate the evolution of low-paid employment, the employment structure, income mobility, and poverty. The wage data analyzed in the following section relate to the hourly and monthly gross earnings of wage and salary workers, which also form the basis for OECD comparisons. However, the suitability of these data for analyzing the evolution of individual living standards and also for international comparisons of earnings is limited, since the same nominal gross wages can be associated with very different additional nonwage costs for employers and net wages and social security contributions for employees. The next section investigates the scale and evolution of these wage-related costs and social benefits, focusing on the low-paid and noting differences between Germany and the United States. In the next part of our analysis, we attempt to explain the increase in low-wage work, the decline in income mobility, and the high concentration of these phenomena in certain categories of workers, industries, firms and jobs. The effects of reunification and macroeconomic policy on employment and unemployment are the subject of the next section. That discussion is followed by an analysis of the institutional remodeling of important pillars of the German employment model. We concentrate on changes in corporate governance structures, in industrial relations, and in the dual vocational training system, as well as in the structure of internal and occupational labor markets and family policy.

We start from the assumption that the increase in low-wage employment in Germany since the mid-1990s can be explained only by the interaction between an extreme external shock (reunification), macroeconomic developments and policies, and the institutionally shaped structures of German product and labor markets. It is not entirely clear whether the old employment system will disintegrate and the low-wage sector will expand further, or whether, under new conditions, it will stabilize and the share of low-paid workers will decrease again. There are good arguments in favor of both scenarios, which we examine by way of conclusion.

THE EXTENT AND STRUCTURE OF LOW-WAGE EMPLOYMENT IN GERMANY

The share of low-paid workers in Germany has been increasing since the mid-1990s. According to a study by the European Commission (2004) based on the European Household Panel, the share of low-paid workers in Germany rose from 14.3 percent to 15.7 percent between 1995 and 2000 (figure 1.1). In 1995 Germany was still under the EU average; by 2000 its share of low-paid workers had exceeded the EU average. Germany and the Netherlands were the only EU member states in which the share of low-wage workers increased between 1995 and 2000. In the other member states, that share declined, in some cases considerably, particularly in Spain, Portugal, Ireland, and the United Kingdom.[2] The share of low-wage work is significantly lower in Denmark (8.6 percent), Italy (9.7 percent), Finland (10.8 percent), and Portugal (10.9 percent). On the other hand, higher shares of low-wage work have been calculated for the United Kingdom (19.4 percent), Ireland (18.7 percent), and the Netherlands (16.6 percent).

To track down the causes of the increase in low-wage work, it is necessary to obtain an up-to-date picture of its structure and distribution among sectors, occupations, and firms of differing sizes. Furthermore, long time series are needed to discern the development dynamic of low-wage work in these various areas.

Existing studies on low-wage employment in Germany neither analyze long time series nor allow a detailed analysis of the structure of the low-wage sector. In attempting to fill this gap with our own analyses, we adopt the OECD definition of the low pay threshold as two-thirds of the median wage. In accordance with the international standard, therefore, we are taking as our starting point a relative definition of low pay. We are well aware that a low wage in Germany—even measured in purchasing power parities—would be a very high wage in less-developed countries. However, by adopting a relative

Figure 1.1 Share of Low Wages in EU Countries, 1995 and 2000

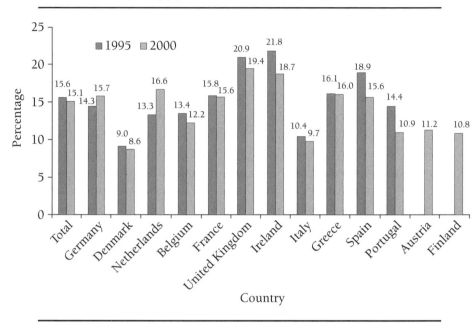

Source: European Commission (2004, 168); authors' calculation.
Note: The low-pay threshold is defined as two-thirds of the country-specific median hourly gross wage. Employees working more than fifteen hours per week are covered, excluding apprentices.

definition of low pay, it becomes possible to measure how equal or unequal the distribution is at the lower end of the income distribution. A standardized indicator of this kind also serves as a basis for international comparisons.

We use two data sources to calculate the share of low-wage workers in Germany. The larger dataset is compiled by the Bundesagentur für Arbeit (BA, Federal Employment Services) and is based on samples of all employees in Germany liable to pay social security contributions. We use three BA datasets that cover different time periods, currently up to the end of 2003. The first is the IAB (Institut für Arbeitsmarkt- und Berufsforschung) employment subsample, a dataset for academic use that contains anonymized data on a percentage of all workers covered by the social insurance system over a twenty-one-year period from 1975 to 1995. Almost 8 million employment reports document the employment biographies of about 560,000 individuals. Some company data taken from social security reports are also included, together with data on periods of benefit claiming (for details, see Bender, Haas, and Klose 2000). The second dataset is the IAB regional sample (IABS-R01), which covers the period from 1975 to 2001. The third is the BA employee panel, which contains data similar to the other two datasets on 1.92 percent of all workers covered by the social insurance system for the period 1998 to 2003, which covers about 80 percent of all employees.[3] As in the other datasets, self-employed workers and civil servants are not included, and we also exclude apprentices. The information contained in these datasets is very comprehensive and makes it possible to differentiate the analyses by sector, individual industry, and occupation, at least for those with a sufficiently large number of employees (such as sales clerks). The data on earnings contained in these datasets relate to gross monthly income.

Because of its size, the BA dataset can also be used for representative analyses by industry of this study's target occupations. However, these analyses can include only full-time workers, since the data on part-time employees do not contain any information on the length of working time. We surmise, however, that there is a higher share of low-wage workers among part-timers than among full-timers (Marlier and Ponthieux 2000; Bollé 1997). For this reason, we also use the German Socio-Economic Panel (GSOEP), a representative annual panel survey of private households that has been carried out, using the same households and persons, since 1984. The following analyses using the SOEP are based on the current U wave from 2004, using samples A through F. The analysis relates to all employees, *including part-time workers*. Categories of workers for whom no meaningful hourly rates could be calculated or to whom special pay rules apply are excluded; these include the self-employed and freelancers, family workers, trainees, interns, people on retraining programs, those undergoing rehabilitation, people on job creation and structural adjustment schemes, employees in workshops for the disabled, conscripts and individuals doing alternative community service, and older workers on partial retirement schemes. Also excluded are high school and university students and pensioners, who typically work only during their spare time. In the analyses using SOEP data, the figures for earned income and working time are obtained primarily from the data on main jobs. Only when there are no data either on working time or on income are the corresponding data on spare-time jobs used. This condition excludes spare-time jobs held in addition to a main job. Thus, every employee is included in the analysis with just one job. Special payments are added to income. The data on special payments applied to the previous year (2003) and are used only when there had been no change of employer in the interim. A mini-job is defined as an employment relationship with monthly earnings of €400 (US$585)[4] or less, irrespective of working time. A full-time job is defined as a job with a working time of thirty-five hours or more per week; accordingly, employment relationships with working times of less than thirty-five hours per week are classified as part-time jobs, unless they fulfill the criterion for classification as mini-jobs.

Because of the small number of cases, detailed analysis of low-paid work in individual occupations in the industries under investigation is not possible. However, the SOEP contains more detailed data on working time and earnings and thus can be used to calculate the hourly wages of part-timers as well. Trainees and individuals on further and advanced training programs are excluded from our analysis of both datasets. Trainees' pay and the allowances paid to those on further training programs cannot be regarded as wages in the strict sense. Individuals on initial or further training programs are generally less productive and contribute to the cost of their training by accepting lower pay. Moreover, Germany, with its dual system of vocational training, has considerably more young people in training than other countries. Around 6 percent of workers in insurable employment are trainees, so that the German figures would be distorted if they were included in an international comparison. Societal investment in training would then appear, quite wrongly, as a social problem.

Initial examination of the evolution over time of the share of low-wage workers among all full-time workers covered by the social insurance system confirms the developments observed by the OECD and the EU. Between 1980 and 1993, the share of low-paid workers among full-timers covered by the social insurance system in West Germany fell from 15.3 percent to 13.8 percent. Since 1995, that share has increased, reaching 17.3 percent in 2003. In post-unification East Germany, the share of low-wage work was initially considerably lower than in West Germany because of the more egalitarian income structure in the former GDR. As the old state-owned enterprises were wound up, the low-wage share in East Germany began to

Figure 1.2 Share of Low-Wage Workers Among Full-Time Workers Covered by the Social Security System (with Separate Low-Wage Thresholds for East and West), 1980 to 2003

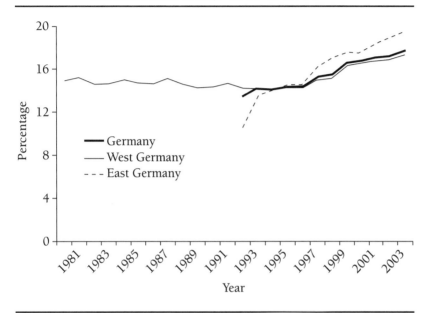

Source: IAB regional sample (IABS-R01) and BA employee panel; authors' calculations.

rise, reaching the West German level by the mid-1990s and overtaking it in 1997 under the pressure of higher unemployment in East Germany. The gap is now considerable and continues to widen (figure 1.2).

Because of the significant wage differences between East and West Germany (Grabka 2000), we have calculated two separate low-wage thresholds—two-thirds of the median wage in East and West Germany, respectively (see table 1.1). Thus, in 2003, 17.3 percent of full-time employees in West Germany and 19.5 percent of full-time employees in East Germany earned less than two-thirds of the relevant median income (less than €1,736 (US$2,540) per month in West Germany; less than €1,309 (US$1,916) per month in East Germany).[5] The mean value for Germany as a whole derived from these figures is 17.7 percent low-wage employment.

If we were to calculate instead a uniform low-wage threshold for

Table 1.1 Low-Wage Thresholds (Gross) and Share of
          Low-Wage Workers Among Full-Time Workers
          Covered by the Social Security System, 2003

	Model 1	Model 2
Median wage		
(euros per month)	€2,492 Germany	€1,963 (East)
		€2,604 (West)
Median wage		
(euros per hour)	€14.94 Germany	€11.77 (East)
		€15.61 (West)
Low-wage threshold		
(euros per month)	€1,661 Germany	€1,309 (East)
		€1,736 (West)
Low-wage threshold		
(euros per hour)	€9.96 Germany	€7.84 (East)
		€10.41 (West)
Share of low-wage workers		
West Germany	15.4%	17.3%
East Germany	36.8	19.5
Germany (East and West)	19.6	17.7

Source: Bundesagentur für Arbeit (BA) employee panel, authors' calculations. Hourly wages are estimated for an average weekly working time of 38.5 hours, as there is no information on working time in the data.

Germany as a whole, this would be €1,661 (US$2,431) per month. Measured against this threshold, the low-wage percentage would be 15.4 percent in West Germany, 36.8 percent in East Germany, and 19.6 percent for Germany as a whole.

Our further analyses are based on model 2 with separate low-wage thresholds for East and West Germany.

Which Workers Are Particularly Affected by Low Wages?

We used three different measured values for the analysis of the structure of low-wage workers:

1. The incidence of low-wage work among all employees or in certain categories (for example, the share of low-wage workers among women)

2. The distribution of low pay (a category's share in the total number of low-wage workers)

3. The concentration—that is, the relationship of the low-wage share within a category to the value for the economy as a whole, or the relationship of that category's share in all low-wage workers to their share of employment in the economy as a whole

Above-average shares of low pay are found among people without a vocational training qualification (30.2 percent), women (30.8 percent), young workers (42.8 percent) and non-nationals (27.0 percent) (see table 1.2). However, the presence of high shares of low pay in individual categories does not mean in every case that these categories make up the bulk of low-paid workers. Examination of the distribution of low-wage workers reveals that 75.5 percent of all low-paid workers have a vocational training qualification, the majority (74.2 percent) are age twenty-five to fifty-four, 89.7 percent are Germans, and 64.1 percent are women.

In East Germany, more than 90 percent of low-wage workers have completed a course of vocational training. The risk of being low-paid is lower for women in East Germany than for women in West Germany. Non-nationals are more likely to be affected by low wages in East Germany than in West Germany.

The incidence of low-wage work and the composition of low-wage workers have changed considerably in the last two decades. Since long time series are available only for West Germany, our observations are restricted to that part of the country. The share of low-paid workers increased between 1980 and 2003 in all skill categories. Measured in percentage points, the increase was greatest among low-skill workers, with a rise of 7.2 percentage points. Among university graduates, the share of low-wage workers more than doubled, making this the largest percentage increase in all the skill categories (table 1.3). Low-wage work is also becoming more of a problem for workers with formally accredited skills. In 1980, 59 percent of all low-wage earners had a vocational training or higher qualification; in 2003 the corresponding figure was 74 percent. (These figures are not included in table 1.3.) Between 1980 and 1995 the share of low-wage workers among women fell considerably, from 36 percent to about 29 percent. Since 1995 there has been a slight increase, to just under 32 percent, although this figure is still significantly lower than that for

Table 1.2 Structural Characteristics of Low-Wage Full-Time Workers Covered by the Social Security System, 2003

	Incidence (in Category)	Distribution (Low-Wage Worker)	Distribution (Total Economy)	Concentration
Educational level[a]				
Unskilled	30.2%	22.2%	13.0%	1.71
Skilled	17.6	75.5	75.6	1.00
College or university	3.6	2.3	11.4	0.20
Sex				
Men	10.0	35.9	63.2	0.57
Women	30.8	64.1	36.8	1.74
Age				
Under twenty-five	42.8	18.0	7.4	2.42
Twenty-five to thirty-four	18.6	25.9	24.6	1.05
Thirty-five to forty-four	14.8	27.8	33.2	0.84
Forty-five to fifty-four	14.5	20.6	25.1	0.82
Fifty-five and older	14.3	7.7	9.6	0.81
Nationality				
German	17.0	89.7	93.3	0.96
Non-national	27.0	10.2	6.7	1.53
Total economy	17.7	100.0	100.0	1.0

Source: BA employee panel; authors' calculations.
[a] In 11.6 percent of all cases, no data on vocational training are available. In the analysis that follows, we have assumed that the cases where this information is missing are equally distributed across all training levels; see Reinberg and Hummel (2002); Riede and Emmerling (1994); Reinberg and Schreyer (2003).

1980. Among men, on the other hand, the low-wage share has virtually doubled, from about 5 percent to more than 9 percent.

The incidence of low-wage work has risen in all age groups. The sharp increase among young people is striking: a 42.3 percent share of low-wage workers means that virtually one in two employees in this category is low-paid (even though we excluded trainees from the calculation). In 1980, in contrast, only one in three was affected by low pay. Nevertheless, because of the rise in low-paid work in all the other age groups, which account for considerably greater numbers of

Table 1.3 Structural Evolution of Low-Wage Work Among West German Full-Time Workers Covered by the Social Security System, 1980 to 2003

	1980	1995	1999	2003
Educational level				
Unskilled	22.6%	23.6%	27.7%	29.8%
Skilled	13.5	13.2	15.5	16.7
College or university	1.8	2.3	3.1	3.7
Sex				
Men	5.1	6.7	8.3	9.3
Women	36.3	29.2	31.3	31.9
Age				
Under twenty-five	33.5	33.7	39.8	42.3
Twenty-five to thirty-four	11.4	13.0	15.6	17.8
Thirty-five to forty-four	10.7	12.3	13.8	14.4
Forty-five to fifty-four	10.4	11.6	13.4	14.0
Fifty-five and older	11.2	11.5	12.8	14.2
Nationality				
German	15.7	13.2	15.5	16.4
Non-national	14.1	23.5	25.6	26.6
Total economy	15.6	14.2	16.3	17.3

Source: BA employee panel and IAB employment subsample; authors' calculations.

workers, young people's share in total low-wage work has actually declined. In 1980, 65 percent of all low-paid workers were twenty-five or older; by 2003 this share had risen to 81 percent. (These figures are not included in table 1.3.)

One particularly striking finding is the change in the share of low-wage workers among non-nationals. In 1980 the share of low-wage workers in this category, at 14.1 percent, was still lower than that among German nationals (15.7 percent). At that time most non-nationals were still employed in the high-wage manufacturing sector. By 2003 the share of low-wage workers in this category had virtually doubled, because the well-paid, low-skill jobs in manufacturing had disappeared by then. Furthermore, increasing numbers of non-national women had taken up paid work and second- and third-generation non-national young people were finding it difficult to gain a foothold in the labor market. The share of low-paid workers among non-nationals began to rise as early as the end of the 1990s, at a time when it was still declining among nationals. The increase in the incidence of low-paid work among non-nationals and in East Germany can possibly be interpreted as an early indicator of the more general development.

For the analysis based on the Socio-Economic Panel, we also calculated separate low-wage thresholds for East and West Germany, defined as two-thirds of the median wage in each region. In West Germany the low-wage threshold was €9.83 (US$14.38) per hour (gross), while for East Germany (including East Berlin) the figure was €7.15 (US$10.46). The thresholds are lower than for the BA dataset, since we now included part-time and marginal part-time workers, two categories with above-average shares of low-paid workers.

According to the SOEP data, the share of low-wage work in Germany as a whole in 2004 was 20.8 percent. With a population of 29 million employees, this means that the earnings of more than 6 million workers are below the low-wage threshold.[6] The SOEP data also show that the incidence of low-wage work in East Germany, at 22.5 percent, is higher than in West Germany, where it stands at 20.5 percent. Since second or side jobs are not included, the values shown have to be regarded as lower limits in any estimate of the real extent of low-wage work in Germany (table 1.4). Compared with all other countries with a minimum wage, which sets a lower limit on pay, what is remarkable about Germany is the considerable downward extension of the wage dispersion. Thus, 9.1 percent of workers in West Germany and 8.6 percent of those in East Germany earn a very low wage (50 percent of the median wage), which is set at €7.38 (US$10.80) per hour in the West and €5.57 (US$8.15) in the East. One and a half million workers in Germany earn less than €5.00

Table 1.4 Low-Wage Thresholds and Shares of Low-Wage Work Among All Workers, Including Part-Time Workers, 2004

	Low-Wage Threshold	Share of Low-Wage Work
West Germany	€9.83	20.5%
East Germany	7.15	22.5
Germany		20.8

Source: German Socio-Economic Panel (GSOEP) 2004; authors' calculations.
Note: Based on 29,044,714 employees.

Table 1.5 Structural Characteristics of All Low-Wage Workers, Including Part-Time Workers, 2004

	Incidence (in Category)	Distribution (Low-Wage Worker)	Distribution (Total Economy)	Concentration
Working time				
Full-time	14.6%	51.5%	72.1%	0.71
Part-time	21.1	22.2	21.6	1.03
Marginal part-time	85.8	26.3	6.3	4.19
Educational level				
Unskilled	42.1	22.4	11.2	2.01
Skilled	21.5	67.2	65.6	1.02
College/university	9.4	10.4	23.2	0.45
Nationality				
German	20.3	92.7	95.2	0.97
Non-national	31.2	7.3	4.8	1.50
Sex				
Men	12.6	30.4	50.7	0.60
Women	29.6	69.6	49.3	1.41
Total economy (based on 29,044,714 employees)	20.8	100	100	1.0

Source: GSOEP (2004); authors' calculations.

(US$7.31) gross per hour, and 876,000 even less than €4.00 (US$5.85).

Part-time and marginal part-time employees are at higher risk of low pay than full-timers (table 1.5). With a share of 48.5 percent, they account for just under half of all low-wage earners, although their share in total employment is only 27.9 percent. This is attributable primarily to the extremely high share of low-wage earners among those employed in mini-jobs—no fewer than 85.8 percent of whom are paid an hourly rate below the low-wage threshold. In stark contrast, the share for part-timers paying full social security contributions is 21.1 percent, just slightly higher than the average of 20.8 percent for the economy as a whole. At 9.4 percent, the share of low-wage workers among graduates is more than twice as high as the figure produced by an analysis based on BA data (3.6 percent).

Presumably these low-paid graduates include many new entrants and university-educated women with children who are only working part-time. The share of women among all low-paid workers is considerably higher compared with the BA data because of the higher part-time rate among women. They account for virtually 70 percent of all low-paid workers.

The Distribution of Low-Wage Workers by Industry, Firm, and Occupation

Above-average shares of low-paid workers are found in agriculture and in some but not all service industries (see table 1.6). Contrary to the general upward trend in low-wage work, the share of such work has actually declined in some core industries, particularly manufacturing and economic transaction services (banking and insurance). This decline is above all a consequence of the outsourcing of certain activities and occupations to other sectors. It should also be noted that the shares of low-wage workers in large and medium-sized firms, which were already below average, have declined still further. In smaller firms (up to ninety-nine employees) and, particularly, very small firms (fewer than twenty employees), on the other hand, the shares of low-wage work have increased considerably from an already high level. One explanation, once again, is the outsourcing of certain occupations from large firms to smaller firms that have no works councils and are not covered by collective agreements. Another major factor is the strong employment growth in new service industries.[7]

Of particular interest for our study are the industries and occupations investigated in chapters 2 to 6. Table 1.7 shows above-average shares of low-wage workers for most of the occupations under study (with the exception of nursing assistants in East Germany). We can also see differences in the share of low pay in an occupation by the industry in which the occupation is located. For example, cleaning staff are better paid in the health sector than in hotels and restaurants.

Examination of the time series from 1980 to 2003 reveals a considerable wage dynamic in the target industries and occupations. Once again, a distinction has to be made between the period from 1980 to 1995, when low-wage work declined in Germany, and the period from 1995 to 2003, when it increased sharply. In the first period, a considerable improvement in the relative earnings position of workers in some of the target occupations (manufacturers of sugar and confectionary goods and hospital and retail workers) can be ob-

Table 1.6 Evolution of Low-Wage Employment Among
West German Full-Time Workers Covered by
the Social Security System, by Characteristics
of the Firm, 1980 to 2003

	1980	1995	1999	2003
Industry[a]				
Agriculture	44.4%	41.6%	38.6%	40.7%
Manufacturing	12.2	8.9	8.9	9.1
Construction	7.9	8.1	10.5	11.4
Infrastructure and transport services	6.2	8.9	12.6	15.3
Business services	28.4	27.5	26.9	27.5
Economic transaction services	23.7	17.1	18.6	18.9
Political transaction services	6.4	6.0	6.7	6.2
Household and personal services	29.0	28.5	31.2	32.1
Size of firm				
One to nineteen	33.6	31.5	34.6	36.4
Twenty to ninety-nine	16.6	14.4	16.5	18.4
100 to 499	11.6	8.4	10.1	10.4
500 and more	4.5	2.3	3.3	3.2
Total economy (share of low pay)	15.6	14.2	16.3	17.3

Source: BA employee panel and IAB employee sample (75–95); authors' calculations.
[a] We aggregated single industries in the following way:
Infrastructure and transport services: electricity, gas and water supply, sewage and refuse disposal, sanitation and similar activities, transport and logistics, post and telecommunications
Business services: research and development, architectural and engineering activities and related technical consultancy, technical testing and analysis, computer and related activities, investigation and security activities, industrial cleaning, services related to management, other business activities
Economic transaction services: commerce, banking and insurance, real estate
Political transaction services: activities of trade unions, business, employers' and professional organizations, activities of other membership organizations, public administration and defense, compulsory social security
Household and personal services: health and social work, education, hotels and restaurants, tourism, recreational, cultural, and sporting activities, other services related to households and persons

served, whereas in the other occupations low-wage work was already beginning to increase during this period. In the second period, the only observable improvement is among cashiers; in all the other target occupations, employees' relative earnings position deteriorated. The most extreme increase is among hospital cleaning staff, who saw

Table 1.7 Share of Low-Wage, Full-Time Workers in the
Case Study Industries and Occupations and
Covered by the Social Security System, 2003

Industry and Occupation	West Germany	East Germany	All of Germany
Food, tobacco (NACE 15, 16)	34.3%	45.9%	36.6%
Producer of meat products and sausage (BKZ 402)	34.8	40.4	36.0
Manufacturer of sugar, confectionary goods, or ice cream (BG2 433)	40.2	(19.7)	35.5
Retail (NACE 52)	33.1	34.9	33.4
Sales assistant or sales clerk (BKZ 682)	41.5	46.8	42.6
Cashier (BKZ 773)	36.8	(27.5)	35.2
Hotels and restaurants (NACE 55)	72.0	65.5	70.5
Other guest attendant (BKZ 913)	82.0	78.4	81.3
Housekeeper (BKZ 923)	88.3	75.9	86.2
Cleaning staff (BKZ 933)	91.7	86.4	90.8
Health (NACE 85)	23.5	19.4	22.6
Nursing assistant (BKZ 854)	25.3	21.3	24.5
Cleaning staff (BKZ 933)	43.3	32.3	41.4
Total economy	17.3	19.5	17.7

Source: BA employee panel; authors' calculations.

their share of low-paid workers virtually doubled within just eight years. Overall, examination of the target occupations shows that, in comparison with the changes in the economy as a whole, the swings here are considerably greater, since this is where low-wage work is concentrated. Thus, low-wage work has increased the most in precisely those occupations in which it was already very high.

Upward Mobility of Low-Wage Earners

From a social policy perspective, short periods in low-wage employment are less problematic than the concentration of low-wage jobs among certain groups and the absence of any prospect that those concerned will move up into more highly paid employment. Never-

Table 1.8 Long-Term Development of the Share of Low-Wage, Full-Time Workers Covered by the Social Security System in the Case Study Industries and Occupations, West Germany, 1980 to 2003

Industry or Occupation	1980	1995	1999	2003
Food	34.3%	33.4%	31.3%	34.3%
Producer of meat products and sausage (BKZ 402)	22.5	31.3	31.8	34.8
Manufacturer of sugar, confectionary goods, or ice cream (BKZ 433)	59.0	39.0	39.0	40.2
Retail	29.9	22.0	32.7	33.1
Sales assistant or sales clerk (BKZ 682)	53.5	36.9	42.0	41.5
Cashier (BKZ 773)	55.4	48.9	37.4	36.8
Hotel and restaurant	62.1	67.9	69.5	72.0
Other guest attendant (BKZ 913)	75.9	81.2	84.2	82.0
Housekeeper (BKZ 923) (for 1980 and 1995 together with BKZ 922: consumer advisers)	84.1	89.2	82.9	88.3
Cleaning staff (BKZ 933)	78.9	91.0	92.6	91.7
Health	20.3	19.7	21.4	23.5
Nursing assistant (BKZ 854)	11.4	9.6	19.3	25.3
Cleaning staff (BKZ 933)	31.0	22.4	37.1	43.3
Total economy	15.6	14.2	16.3	17.3

Source: BA employee panel and IAB-employment subsample; authors' calculations.
Note: Data before 1995 and after 1995 are based on different industry classifications and are not fully comparable.

theless, one of the arguments frequently adduced in Germany in favor of encouraging low-wage jobs is that they offer a low-threshold entry point into better-paid jobs.

Previous studies have revealed that income mobility—movement upward to a better-paid job—was greater in Germany at the beginning of the 1990s than in the United States or the United Kingdom (Keese, Puymoyen, and Swain 1998, 249; OECD 1997, 31). More recent studies have shown that this changed with the increase in low-wage work in Germany. According to a study by the European Commission (2004), upward mobility among low-wage earners between 1995 and 2001 in Germany was below the EU average. Several German studies (Fertig, Kluve, and Scheuer 2004; Kaltenborn and Klös 2002; Rhein, Gartner, and Krug 2005) have also concluded that income mobility in Germany has changed over time. However, the results of these studies are partially contradictory. Consequently, we carried out our own analysis of upward mobility on the basis of the BA data.

To estimate the change in the prospects for upward mobility over time between the 1974 to 1975 period and the 2002 to 2003 period in West Germany, we took a sample of full-time employees who had been low-wage earners on one reference day and then recorded their status on the same reference day the following year. For individuals who were in full-time employment with valid pay data on both reference days, we distinguished between those who had moved up from the low-wage sector and those who had remained in the low-wage sector. Since the results fluctuate with changes in the economic situation, we calculated the trend. The following structural analysis is based on the same procedure, although the period of observation is the five years between 1998 and 2003.

Between 1975 to 1976 and 2000 to 2001, the trend in upward mobility in West Germany was downward, even though there were temporary fluctuations caused by the economic situation (figure 1.3). This downward trend was strongly influenced by the declining growth rates following the reunification boom and could certainly be reversed again by a long period of growth. If the analysis is supplemented by data from the BA employee panel (see the description of the Federal Employment Services datasets in the previous section), it becomes clear that the decline in upward mobility continued in 2002 and 2003.

For the period between 1998 and 2003, the structural analysis shows that, in all, 34.4 percent of low-wage earners managed to hurdle the low-wage threshold (figure 1.4). The probability of upward mobility was considerably higher for men (50.4 percent), university graduates (62.3 percent), and younger people (53.6 percent in the under-twenty-five age group and 40.1 percent in the twenty-five- to thirty-four age group). The overall figure for workers with vocational qualifications was slightly above the average, at 34.7 percent. The chances of being upwardly mobile were greater in West Germany (35.6 percent) than in East Germany (30.5 percent). Women (27.2

Figure 1.3 Share Among West German Full-Time
Workers Covered by the Social Security
System of the Upwardly Mobile from the Low-
Wage Sector, in All Transitions in Each One-
Year Period

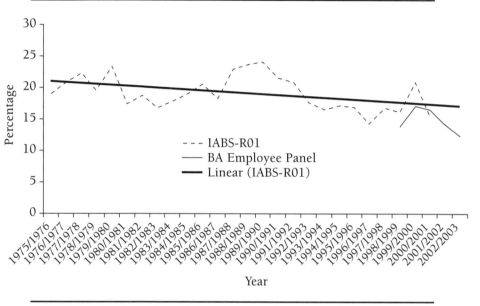

Legend:
- - - IABS-R01
——— BA Employee Panel
——— Linear (IABS-R01)

Year

Source: IAB regional sample and BA employee panel; authors' calculations.

percent), low-skill workers (33.5 percent), and older workers were
the groups with the lowest probability of upward mobility. As far as
older workers are concerned, even those in the relatively young
thirty-five- to forty-four age group, with an upward mobility rate of
just 27.6 percent, had a significantly below-average likelihood of
moving up out of the low-wage sector, while the older age groups,
with an upward mobility rate of considerably less than 20 percent,
had very little chance of improving their income situation.

LOW-WAGE WORK AND POVERTY

Not every low-paid worker is also poor. Poverty is a product of the
household context. Even an individual on a low wage may be living
above the poverty threshold if other family members are well paid or

Figure 1.4 Upward Mobility Out of the Low-Wage Sector
Between 1998 and 2003 for German Full-
Time Workers Covered by the Social Security
System

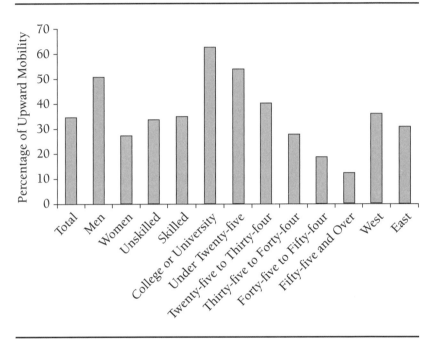

Source: BA employee panel, authors' calculations.

if the household income is topped up by social security benefits.
Conversely, in a large household with just one wage earner, it may
well be that even an income significantly above the low-wage threshold is not sufficient to avoid poverty. Most studies of the link between
gainful employment and poverty—that is, of the working poor—take
a relative definition of poverty as their starting point. All those earning below 60 percent (or 50 percent, or 40 percent, according to the
definition) of the equivalence income, weighted by the number of
household members, are usually regarded as poor.

It should be noted that most poor people in Germany are not economically active. Depending on the definition of poverty, between 21
and 27 percent of poor people are employed (Strengmann-Kuhn
2003, 40). Between 14 and 16 percent are unemployed, and between
57 and 65 percent are not economically active. However, if children

and old people are excluded and the analysis is restricted to the prime working years (age twenty-five to fifty-five), between 39 and 45 percent of poor people are economically active, depending on the statistical base. The rest are either economically inactive or unemployed.

The working poor have been the object of several studies, most of which have not distinguished between low incomes and higher incomes. Only Eric Marlier and Sophie Ponthieux (2000) have investigated the link between low wages and poverty. They define low wages as wages of less than 60 percent of the national monthly median wage[8] and poverty as a household income below the threshold of 60 percent of the national median income, adjusted using the modified OECD equivalence scale. According to their study, 24 percent of low-wage earners in Germany should be classified as poor in their household contexts (For the EU-13, the figure is 20 percent.) Low-wage workers have a considerably greater risk of poverty than the employed population as a whole (10 percent) and the total population (16 percent). In Germany, 41 percent of all poor employees work in the low-wage sector, which is above the EU-13 average of 37 percent. Put another way, 59 percent of all poor workers in Germany and 63 percent in the EU are not employed in the low-wage sector.

Since 1991 the share of poor households in Germany has increased. In that year, 9.3 percent of all households had to get by on an equivalence income of less than 50 percent of the median income; by 2005 that figure had risen to 10.6 percent (Statistisches Bundesamt 2006a, 612). This rise is explained by the Federal Statistical Office as follows: "The increase in inequality that has been observed over many years is attributable primarily to the increasing spread of market incomes" (Statistisches Bundesamt 2006a, 610). As part of its second report on poverty and wealth (Bundesregierung 2005), the German federal government commissioned a special report on the living standards of economically active households; this report makes no distinction, however, between low and higher incomes (Haisken-De New 2004). The report concludes that 8 percent of all economically active households were poor in 2002. The share of poor households among those with one full-time or two part-time wage earners was only 4 percent. In contrast, households with only one part-time wage earner had a poverty rate of 30 percent (Haisken-De New 2004, 31). To escape poverty through paid work, either one must be employed full-time or there must be two part-time wage earners in the family.

Just as the income mobility of low-wage workers has declined, so has that of poor households. The German Council of Economic Experts (Sachverständigenrat 2004) has found that inequality of household incomes (net and market) increased between 1991 and 2002. At the same time, upward mobility among poor households decreased. Although about 55 percent of poor households in West Germany (1990) improved their income position up to 1993, from 1999 to 2002 only 39 percent moved upward. The chances of upward mobility are much better in East Germany (62 percent) than in West Germany (39 percent). Households with at least one dependent employee showed a higher upward mobility (59 percent for Germany) than all households (about 42 percent).

INTERIM CONCLUSION

The aim of the data analysis has been to give a conspectus of the extent, distribution, and dynamic of low-wage work in Germany, that is, to describe the initial empirical situation that is to be analyzed in the following sections. In general terms, we can say that since the mid-1990s the share of low-paid workers in Germany has increased continuously. In contrast to countries with a minimum wage or higher trade union density, the wage spread in Germany extends downward a very long way. Significant numbers of workers earn less than €5 or €4 per hour. Low-skill workers, marginal part-time employees, women, and non-nationals in particular have above-average rates of low or very low pay. The largest increases have been among non-nationals, among whom the low-pay rate was lower than among German nationals in 1980. It should be noted, nevertheless, that around three-quarters of low-paid workers have a vocational training qualification or an academic degree.

Low-wage work is becoming increasingly concentrated in smaller firms and has actually declined in larger ones. The incidence of low-wage work has also declined in industries with a high rate of coverage by collective agreement (for example, manufacturing industries and banking and insurance), whereas it has increased markedly in many service industries. The target industries and occupations have above-average shares of low-wage workers. Between 1980 and 1995 low-wage work declined in individual target occupations, markedly so in some cases, but since 1995 it has risen in virtually all the occupations. Overall, the dynamic of change in the target industries and occupations is considerably stronger than in the economy as a whole. The strongest increases in low-wage work have clearly taken place in those areas where the share of such work was already higher than average.

The share of poor households has also increased since 1991, primarily owing to the spread of market incomes. The share of working poor with a low income in Germany is slightly above the European average. At the same time, the decline in households' income mobility suggests that poverty is becoming more firmly entrenched.

WAGES AND NONWAGE BENEFITS

One characteristic of the Bismarckian German welfare state is the close link between earned income and employment rights and social security entitlements.[9] Wages must be paid not only in respect of work done in the here and now but also for times when employees will not be working (holidays, periods of illness, and so on). Contributions to the statutory social insurance funds must also be paid, as well as collectively agreed and voluntary social security contributions. This "second pay packet," as it is colloquially known, gives rise to entitlements to benefits that are paid at various points of the working life and life course.

Every worker in Germany has a legal entitlement to four weeks of paid annual leave, payment for statutory public holidays (seven to twelve per year, depending on the year and the federal state, or Bundesland),[10] and continued payment of wages in full in the event of sickness (for up to six weeks from the onset of illness).[11] In most collective agreements, the paid annual leave has been increased to six weeks. In 2004, 11.5 percent of annual labor costs per full-time employee was attributable to payments for periods when no work was done (Statistisches Bundesamt 2006b, 44). Payment of the earnings-related social insurance contributions is divided equally between employers and employees. The contributions rate paid by both parties up to a maximum income level[12] in 2007 is as follows: 19.55 percent to the old-age pension fund, an average of 13.31 percent to the health insurance fund, 4.2 percent to the unemployment insurance fund, and 1.7 percent to the long-term nursing care fund. Contributions to the accident insurance fund are paid by employers only. (The rate varies from industry to industry, but in 2005 averaged out at 1.31 percent of the wage bill.) Thus, in addition to the gross wages paid to employees, firms have to pay an additional 20.66 percent in contributions to the statutory social insurance funds.

The level of the subsistence payments made out of the various insurance funds (unemployment benefit, sick pay after the sixth week of illness, pension) is dependent on income. In addition, noncash benefits, such as medical treatment and nursing care, are granted without reference to the level of contributions paid. Additional benefits specified in collective agreements or negotiated at the company level, such as subsidies for private pension funds or further training and compensation in the event of redundancy, may also be paid. In the year 2004 total nonwage costs (that is, all statutory benefits as well as those stipulated in collective agreements and voluntary company agreements as well as expenses for initial and further vocational training) amounted on average to 31.6 percent of total labor costs for full-time employees.[13]

However, there are considerable differences between large and small firms, as well as between high-wage and low-wage industries, particularly when it comes to collectively agreed and voluntary benefits. Thus, nonwage costs in large companies with one thousand or more employees account for 38.1 percent of the average labor cost of €37.19 (US$54.41) per hour, which is considerably higher than in small firms with between ten and forty-nine employees, where they account for 29.1 percent of €21.34 (US$31.24). In retailing the share of nonwage costs per full-time employee is 30.9 percent of total labor costs of €23.88 (US$34.94) per employee per hour, and in hotels and restaurants the figures are 34.3 percent and €15.34 (US$22.44), respectively; in high-wage industries, however, such as energy and water supply, the figure is 48.9 percent of €41.40 (US$60.57) (Statistisches Bundesamt 2006b). The greatest differences in nonwage labor costs between industries and firms of different sizes are to be found in supplementary company pension plans. In the energy supply industry, for example, 20.5 percent of total labor costs are accounted for by supplementary company pension plans; the corresponding figures for retail trade and for restaurants and hotels are just 1.9 percent and 2 percent, respectively.

The differences in total labor costs by industry and company size increased between 1992 and 2004, since in small and medium-sized companies (figure 1.5) and in low-wage sectors many of these additional benefits have been curtailed or abolished altogether. Furthermore, the annual special payments that are part of the direct wage have declined. In the hotel and restaurant sector, for example, their share in gross pay has fallen from 4.5 percent to 4.2 percent, whereas

Figure 1.5 Labor Costs, 2004, and Rate of Change in Labor Costs, 1992 to 2004

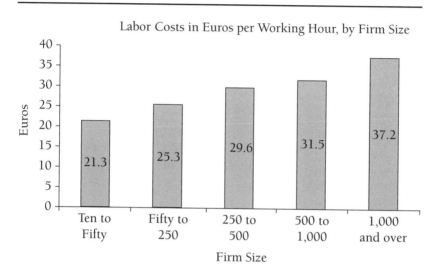

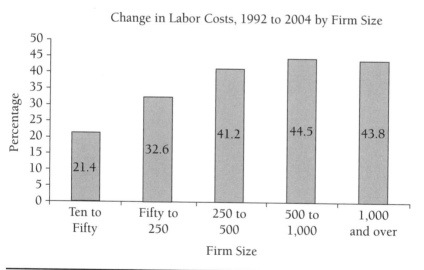

Source: Statistisches Bundesamt (2006b); authors' illustration.

it has increased in the energy and water supply industry, for example, from 11.2 percent to 12.1 percent, and in manufacturing from 9.8 percent to 10.4 percent. Our industry studies and the increasing gap between labor costs in manufacturing and services confirm this trend.

The statutory obligation to respect employment rights and to pay insurance contributions also applies to temporary employees, temporary agency workers, and part-timers. In the past, many part-timers were excluded from collectively agreed or company benefits, but this has been gradually reversed in recent decades by EU directives. Part-timers have a pro-rata entitlement to social insurance benefits and to equal pay. They also acquire full entitlement to the non-cash benefits paid by their health insurance fund, provided they earn more than €400 per month.

Marginal part-time workers (employees earning less than €400 per month [€325 before 2003]) are the only group of employees not covered by the general obligation to pay social insurance contributions. Employers, on the other hand, pay a flat-rate contribution of 30 percent (13 percent for health insurance, 15 percent for old-age pension, and a 2 percent flat-rate tax). They also are required to make payments into an accident insurance fund and an equalization or compensation fund from which sickness benefits are paid. However, this flat-rate employers' contribution does not give marginal part-time employees any entitlement to social insurance benefits. It is intended primarily to ensure that companies do not give preference to mini-jobbers because of the lower nonwage costs. Workers may also hold mini-jobs in addition to their main employment, whether they are employees or self-employed. Mini-jobbers' exemption from tax and social security contributions is a considerable subsidy for the low-wage sector—that is, for jobs that are either low-paid or involve a small number of hours—that is paid completely regardless of other earnings, assets, or household income.

Whereas temporary employees, temporary agency workers, and part-timers in insurable employment generally claim the benefits to which the wage relationship entitles them, this is often not the case with mini-jobs. Mini-jobbers, like all other employees, are legally entitled to holiday and sick pay and other employment rights, but they often are paid only for the hours they work. The surpluses in the equalization fund from which sickness benefits are paid are another indication of illegal practices on the part of employers. Few of the firms that employ marginal part-time workers apply for compensation for the wages they continue to pay to employees who fall sick (Bäcker 2006, 258). The extremely high shares of low pay among mini-jobbers suggest that it is in fact often employers rather than employees who benefit from the subsidy. They pay mini-jobbers lower rates, often in contravention of the relevant collective agreement (Kalina and Weinkopf 2006). Nevertheless, mini-jobs are often also attractive to employees because they derive social security entitlements from their spouses, or because holding a second job exempt from income tax enables them to avoid paying a higher rate of tax, which would not be the case if they worked overtime in their main job. Against this background, the number of mini-jobbers has risen considerably, from 5.53 million in June 2003 to 6.76 million in December 2006 (online database of the Federal Employment Services). Research suggests that this increase does not represent significant positive employment effects but rather a substitution of standard employment relationships with the aim of reducing labor costs (Rudolph 2003, ch. 6).

In 2004 the total tax wedge in Germany (taxes and social contributions) was 38.7 percent of GNP (21.9 percent taxes and 16.8 percent social contributions), which was lower than the EU-15 average of 39.5 percent. Compared with 1999, the tax wedge had fallen by about 3.5 percent, owing largely to tax cuts, particularly in the top rate of income tax and corporation tax (Statistisches Bundesamt 2004, 2006c). Social insurance contributions in particular are the object of lively debate. Because of the social insurance system and the state benefits associated with it, some authors see it as an indicator of a high quality of life and a guarantee of equal opportunities. Others argue, however, that because of the rising costs of the social security system and state bureaucracy, the deductions are an incalculable cause of further wage increases and thus serve to reduce employment, especially of the low-skilled. Although the view that labor costs have been driven too high by tax and social security contributions is not very convincing in the light of the low wage increases since 1995 in Germany, it is this view that underpins policy in Germany.

Governments since 1998 have agreed that the share of nonwage costs in total labor costs should be reduced to below 40 percent. This political target refers to the sum of employers' and employees' social security contributions, excluding accident insurance. Until the mid-1990s, social security contributions rose automatically with increases in gross wages; since then, however, in addition to the usual collective pay bargaining round, there has been a second, political wage round each year in which social security contributions are the object of negotiations. Several pension reforms have led to reductions in pension levels in order to restrict the increases in the contributions made necessary by demographic changes. Cost reduction measures and increases in patient contributions in the health system have made it possible to reduce contributions to health insurance funds slightly since 2005. The contributions to unemployment insurance have been reduced from 6.5 percent to 4.2 percent in 2007. The first coalition between the Sozialdemokratische Partei Deutschland (SPD) and Green parties introduced an environmental tax, some of the revenue from which was paid into the national pension insurance funds, which made it possible to cut contributions. Without these eco-tax receipts, the contribution in 2004 would have been 1.7 percentage points higher (BMF 2004, 11).

Equally controversial is the argument that, particularly in the lower wage sector, there are some unwelcome disincentives to work. The elimination of such low-pay traps is a central feature of both the OECD Job Strategy (OECD 2006, 63) and the European Employment Strategy. This view was also the main driver for key elements of the so-called Hartz reforms.

In 2002 a government commission chaired by the labor director of Volkswagen AG, Peter Hartz, produced a report on the reform of labor market policy. The SDP-Green coalition government, in agreement with most of the Christlich Demokratische Union Deutschlands (CDU) and Christlich-Soziale Union (CSU) opposition in the lower house of the German Parliament, passed a total of four Hartz Acts, which, although they bore the name of the commission chairman, incorporated only some of the commission's proposals. The first Hartz Act—Hartz I—passed in 2003, deregulated agency work and introduced a number of new labor market policy instruments aimed at the unemployed, such as training vouchers. Hartz II introduced new regulations governing mini- and midi-jobs and reorganized job placement services. Hartz III dealt with the restructuring of Federal Employment Services (Bundesgentur für Arbeit). Hartz IV, finally, abolished income-related unemployment assistance and introduced a means-tested basic security benefit, the so-called unemployment benefit II, at the same level as the former social welfare benefit. The unemployment benefit II is a flat-rate allowance unrelated to previous income.[14] It is paid to all the long-term unemployed and to workers whose household income is below the basic security level.

Those who had been in receipt of unemployment assistance and older long-term unemployed people had to accept significant reductions in their previously more generous incomes. Until the end of 2004, the long-term unemployed received—subject to means testing, including spouse's income—unemployment assistance of 53 or 57 percent (with children) of the previous net income; this benefit was funded out of taxation and paid for an unlimited period. Older unemployed people, who are frequently affected by long-term unemployment, could also claim an unemployment benefit at a rate of 63 or 67 percent (with children) of previous net income for up to thirty-two months; for those under fifty-five the maximum period of entitlement was twelve months. This maximum period of entitlement for older workers has been reduced to eighteen months. Furthermore, once their entitlement to the unemployment benefit has expired, all long-term unemployed people can claim only basic security benefits. The objective is to force unemployed people, particularly those who previously earned a good wage, to accept lower-paid jobs. At the same time, the reasonability criteria have been tightened, so that for the long-term unemployed any job paying up to 30 percent below the customary local rate is deemed to be acceptable.

The aim of the Hartz reforms was to cut the costs of the welfare state by reducing unemployment and the benefits paid to the unemployed. Hartz himself predicted a fall in unemployment of more than 2 million. In fact, however, the costs of the basic security benefits introduced in Hartz IV rose significantly in 2005, from an expected €14.6 billion to €25.6 billion (US$21.3 billion to US$37.4 billion). They fell only slightly in 2006, to €24.6 billion (US$36 billion). The most important reason for this cost increase is that in the household groups in receipt of unemployment benefit II all individuals of working age who are able to work for more than three hours per day are now obliged to look for work. By increasing the pressure on all household members to seek jobs, the state has induced many individuals who were previously economically inactive to register as unemployed and claim unemployment benefit II. As a result of this change in the law, the number of registered unemployed has increased by around 380,000 (IMK 2005); this statistical change pushed the unemployed population through the 5 million barrier in 2005. Furthermore, people who are employed and have a household income below the defined subsistence level are increasingly applying to top up their household incomes. The basic security benefits are acting as a negative income tax.

The rise in the income threshold for mini-jobs in April 2003 was accompanied by the simultaneous introduction of a flexible zone for monthly incomes of between €400 and €800 (US$585 and US$1,170) (midi-jobs) within which employees' social insurance contributions gradually rise from 4 percent to the full rate of 21 percent on average. The aim of the Hartz reforms was to reduce the marginal burden of contributions on mini-jobbers while increasing their working times. However, this measure was not particularly effective, since the theoretical models had not taken into account the fact that the marginal tax burden remained high for companies, because of the higher hourly rates for midi-jobs, as well as for mini-jobbers, because of the loss of entitlement to free health insurance derived from their spouses. By the end of 2005, it remained to be ascertained whether this measure had led to any increases in the net wages of 946,000 midi-jobbers (see BA 2007) or whether companies had made corresponding cuts in wages. Of considerably greater significance for the labor market was the Hartz reforms' abolition of income-related unemployment assistance.

Recent research has shown that the reduction in the reservation wage has led to an increase in the labor supply for low-paid jobs, particularly of skilled workers. If household income is below the level of the basic subsistence allowance—the unemployment benefit II—then there is an entitlement to top-up benefits. In October 2006, about 1.1 million workers were in receipt of supplementary benefit in addition to their income (BA 2006). Around half of these were earning an assessable income of less than €400.[15] However, about 440,000 of this number were employed full-time. Others were self-employed and in this way acquired entitlement to health insurance.

Since a basic amount of earnings (€100 [US$146] per month) is disregarded when calculating the subsistence allowance, benefit withdrawal rates rise as incomes rise. This arrangement is often criticized because it means there is little incentive to increase working time (particularly beyond the mini-job level). The introduction of the basic security benefits has given firms in the low-wage segment incentives to reduce their wage rates, since the state makes up the difference. The evidence for this is that, within one year (from 2005 to 2006), the number of full-time employees whose wages were topped up by the basic security benefits doubled from 200,000 to over 400,000. In the political debate, repeated demands are made for labor costs in the lower segment of the labor market to be relieved to an even greater extent of the burden of social security contributions in order to encourage the creation of low-skill jobs. Several regional pilot projects have been carried out, with very disappointing results. Moreover, several econometric studies have shown that such general wage subsidies are extremely costly and have very limited employment effects, since nonsubsidized jobs are squeezed out by subsidized jobs (Jaehrling and Weinkopf 2006).

It is not yet clear what effects the long-term reduction in the level of pensions combined with the increase in low-paid employment will have on the social situation of older people. A worker with an average income has to pay contributions for around 27 years in order to receive a pension above the tax-funded basic subsistence allowance. For a low-wage earner on 75 percent of average income that figure would be 36.3 years, and for someone on half of average income it would take as long as 54 years. As the level of pensions declines further in the decades to come, the time required will increase still further, so that a growing share of low-earners will no longer be in a position to acquire entitlement to a pension above the basic subsistence allowance by making contributions. As a result, they will be reduced to the level of those who have not worked and are also entitled to social assistance, which may reduce the incentive to undertake paid work. However, those in receipt of the basic subsistence allowance have no freedom to choose between working and not working, but have to accept any reasonable offer of employment.

Extensive evaluation of the most wide-ranging welfare reforms in the history of the Federal Republic of Germany has shown that the procedures of Federal Employment Services have become more efficient. To date, however, the new labor market policy has not been shown to have had any more significant autonomous employment effects.

GROWTH AND UNEMPLOYMENT IN GERMANY, 1990 TO 2005

One of the most important reasons for the increase in low-paid employment is the persistently low level of growth in the German economy since the end of the reunification boom in 1992. Between 1993 and 2005 the German economy grew by an average of only 1.5 percent per annum, a rate well below that for most other OECD countries (United States, 3.3 percent; United Kingdom, 2.9 percent; Sweden, 2.9 percent; France, 2.1 percent; EU-15, 2.2 percent; OECD, 2.8 percent). Employment in Germany also grew only 0.27 percent, while it rose much faster in other countries (United States, 1.4 percent; United Kingdom, 1.1 percent; Sweden, 0.6 percent; France, 1.0 percent; EU-15, 1.1 percent; OECD, 1.1 percent) (all calculations based on OECD 2006). Consequently, the German unemployment rate, which in the 1970s and 1980s had always been significantly below the EU and OECD average, rose to a postwar high of 9.2 percent in 2004. Furthermore, Germany's relative income position deteriorated. In 1990 Germany's per capita GNP was still 254 percent of the European average (excluding Germany); by 2002, however, it had fallen to 127 percent (Sachverständigenrat 2002, 309).

The weak growth and the increase in unemployment are to a large extent consequences of the direct and indirect effects of the modalities of German reunification. The direct effects stemmed from the collapse of the East German economy following currency union and the transfer payments from West to East Germany. Currency union, with the one-to-one exchange rate for the East German mark, led to a revaluation of the East German mark of 300 percent in real terms. As a result, the East German economy, with its aging plant and equipment and product portfolio, lost overnight whatever competitiveness it might once have had. Firms now had to pay wages and buy materials in deutschmarks but were unable to sell their products at prices that covered their costs. Moreover, they were burdened by old debts that, at the West German banks' insistence, had been converted at a rate of one-to-two. Consequently, the starting chances for East German companies were considerably worse than those for West German companies after the currency reform of 1949, which freed them from all old debts. At the same time, investment in East Germany was blocked by the stipulation in the unification treaty that the restitution of property should take priority over investment. This triggered a large number of legal disputes, which often dragged on for years (Hankel 1993). To prevent the complete collapse of the East German productive system and provide a welfare safety net for the upheaval taking place—a vital prerequisite if the East German population was to give its assent when called on to vote—massive transfer payments from West Germany became necessary (Bosch and Knuth 1993).

These transfers were funded by increases in taxes and social security contributions and additional borrowing. A solidarity surcharge was levied in addition to income tax, and East German employees were integrated into the social insurance systems. They received benefits without having previously paid any contributions in the West to pension or unemployment funds. The share of social insurance contributions in GDP rose from 15 percent in 1990 to 18.5 percent in 1997 and then declined only slightly (Bofinger 2005, 67). At the same time, public budgets were redistributed in favor of the East German Bundesländer. As a result of this financial equalization, the poorer East German states received a proportion, calculated according to a specified formula, of the tax receipts of the richer West German states. The debt rate (the ratio of state indebtedness to nominal GDP) increased from around 40 percent in 1991 to 60 percent in 2002 (Sachverständigenrat 2002, 320). Since the beginning of the 1990s, the transfers have amounted to around 4 percent of West German GDP. Initially, they were equivalent to 50 percent of East German GDP; they now account for about one-third (Ragnitz 2003).

Without the transfers, Germany would have fulfilled the Maastricht criteria in recent years and in 2006 would already have been recording a budget surplus. The German council of economic experts (Sachverständigenrat) wrote in this regard: "No other country in the European Union has faced comparable economic challenges in the past decade. However, no other European country would have been likely to manage or cope better with burdens of the same magnitude" (Sachverständigenrat 2002, 320).

Following reunification, about 4 million of the 9.8 million jobs in East Germany were lost; these losses were not offset by the growth in jobs resulting from the reunification boom in West Germany. This led to a rise in the unemployment rate in East Germany, which in 2005 was 18.7 percent, almost twice as high as the rate in West Germany; a decline in the employment rate, from 86.7 percent in 1992 to 78.6 percent in 2001; and migration, primarily of younger and well-qualified workers, to the West. In 1989, 16.4 million people lived in the territory of the former GDR; today the population is 15.1 million. In 1990 the majority of Germans, together with their country's economists, still believed that East Germany would quickly catch up with the more developed West. In the light of this expectation, the social partners agreed to a rapid adjustment of wages to the West German level. In fact, GDP per economically active person rose from 41.2 percent of the West German level in 1992 to around 63.1 percent in 1997. Since then the catchup process has stalled: by 2005 GDP per economically active person had risen only slightly, to 67 percent, and in the meantime it has actually declined (Arbeitsgemeinschaft 2006, 260). In the recession of 2001 to 2003, the East German economy even showed itself to be more susceptible to cyclical fluctuations, since the East has a high share of downstream production, while corporate head offices tend to be located in the West.

The indirect effects of reunification are just as important as the direct effects. The redistribution of public funds in favor of the East German states was financed primarily by cuts in investment in infrastructure and in education and training. Between 1991 and 2003 total investment was reduced by 20 percent. As a result, the share of public investment in GDP, which was 4.8 percent in 1970, had fallen by 2004 to 1.7 percent, which is one of the lowest rates in the EU (Mosebach 2005). Furthermore, with the transfer of all West German institutions to East Germany, reforms that had been pending for a long time, particularly in the areas of the family, the labor market, education, and tax policy, sank into oblivion. In the wake of this wholesale transfer of institutions from West to East, the West German system came to be represented as superior; as with colonial powers in the past, the result was a sort of structural conservatism that stifled any attempt to discuss reform. This failure to invest in the future and to engage in continuous institutional reform proved to be an obstacle to growth.

After reunification, domestic demand initially increased because of the high level of investment in East Germany and the high consumption rate of an East German population anxious to catch up with its West German neighbors. The country's domestic capacities were fully stretched, and between 1990 and 1992 Germany's need to import made it the engine of European growth. Once the reunification boom had run its course and the main waves of redundancies in East Germany had subsided, the trade unions managed, against a background of rising unemployment, to obtain only very modest wage increases. Between 1993 and 2005 real wage increases in the private sector were only 0.15 percent per annum, well below the values for other OECD countries (United States, 1.9 percent; United Kingdom, 2.0 percent; France, 0.9 percent; Sweden, 2.5 percent; EU-15, 0.7 percent; OECD, 1.1 percent) (OECD 2006, 22). Since the mid-1990s, domestic demand in Germany has grown only slightly and has acted as a brake

Figure 1.6 Rise in Private Consumer Spending in West Germany in the First Ten Quarters of Each Economic Cycle, up to 1990

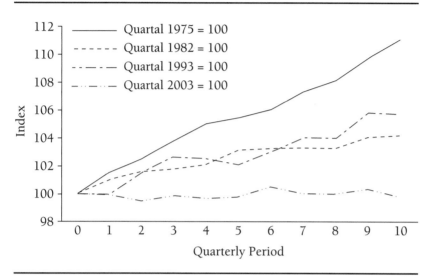

Source: Arbeitsgemeinschaft (2006, 263).

on growth. Figure 1.6 shows that in the 2003 economic cycle, in contrast to earlier cycles, consumer expenditure had not increased even in the tenth quarter following the low point of the cycle.

At the same time, the situation in the export sector of the economy has improved. After 1992, export industries, which at the beginning of the 1990s had forgone market shares abroad because of their concentration on East Germany, became the pioneers of a process of corporate reorganization that is still going on today. This process had several main elements: the globalization of production, concentration on core businesses, the delocation of simple tasks, and the international outsourcing of unskilled jobs (Geishecker 2002); the reorganization of supply chains; attempts to increase transparency through internal controlling systems; and the decentralization of responsibility for production and efforts to make it more flexible through the modernization of work organization. The changes in work organization were facilitated by the German codetermination culture and reforms in vocational training. German firms now have the longest operating hours in the EU (Bauer and Groß 2006) and

Figure 1.7 Germany's Export Surpluses as a Percentage
of GDP

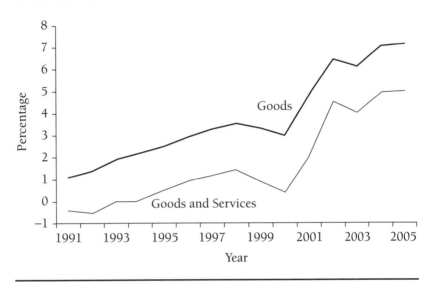

Source: Eurostat, taken from Düthmann et al. (2006, 16).

also make greater use than firms in other countries of internal adjustment instruments, such as flexible working times and functional
flexibility, in order to cope with fluctuations in orders (Schief 2006).
Moreover, German export industries have benefited from the improvement in price competitiveness. Relatively low wage increases
have combined with improvements in productivity to keep German
unit wage costs rising less than in all other OECD countries with the
exception of Japan. As a result, German export surpluses have increased continuously in recent years and are the linchpin of the
country's modest economic growth (figure 1.7).

This particular development path—weak domestic demand and
high export surpluses—has been actively driven forward by economic policy. The strengthening of the competitiveness of Germany's
export industries was and continues to be the focus of national economic debate. The majority of German economists, as well as many
international observers, see excessively high wages, an overly generous welfare state, rigid labor market regulations, and excessively high
company taxation as the main causes of Germany's high unemploy-

ment (Kitschelt and Streeck 2004; OECD 2004b; Siebert 1998; Sinn 2004).

Export companies also dominate the employers' associations. One of the paradoxes of the economic policy debate in Germany is that the most serious weaknesses are perceived to be in precisely those areas in which Germany is particularly strong, while the strengthening of domestic demand and development of the service sector, which remains relatively small owing to the still-dominant conservative family model, has disappeared from the agenda. The tax reforms implemented by the SPD-Green coalition mainly favored large companies and high earners; small business partnerships scarcely benefited at all. The tax reforms were funded by cuts in the education and social security systems and cuts in investment in infrastructure. The tax share of GDP fell from 23.3 percent in 1995 to 20.4 percent in 2004, and the share of taxes and social security contributions combined fell from 38.2 percent to 34.6 percent (BMF 2006). According to recent studies, Germany does indeed have high nominal tax rates for companies, but because of the narrower assessment basis, the actual tax burden is low (Jarass and Obermair 2005). Germany is making tremendous efforts to pursue a policy of devaluation in order to improve its position in export markets. Since variations in exchange rates are no longer possible within the euro zone, real devaluations can be achieved only by restricting rises in real wages. The German Council of Economic Advisers (Sachverständigenrat 2004) puts this devaluation in the euro zone at 5 percent just for the period between 2001 and 2004.

This German development path has had visible effects on the wage structure. Because of weak domestic demand and low trade union density and coverage by collective agreements in private services, wage increases in services have lagged behind those in manufacturing. As a result, the gap between labor costs in the two sectors, already greater than the European average, is widening further (figure 1.8).

Closer scrutiny of individual subsectors reveals this divergence in labor costs even more clearly, since individual service industries are expanding and are closely linked to the export industry. Thus, between 1997 and 2006 labor costs per hour worked rose in manufacturing by 22 percent and in banking and insurance by 24.9 percent; in hotels and restaurants, however, the rise was only 1 percent. The already very marked pay differentiation between strong and weak in-

Figure 1.8 Evolution of Labor Costs in the Private Service
Sector Relative to Manufacturing

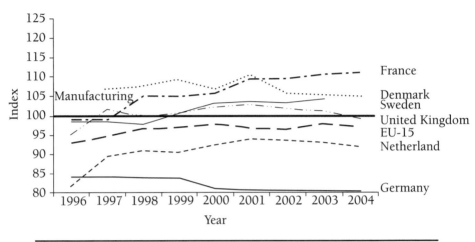

Source: Eurostat, taken from Düthmann et al. (2006, 13).
Note: Index, manufacturing = 100.

dustries has therefore increased still further in the last decade, contributing to the increase in the share of low-wage work. We will see that this divergence in pay is also attributable to the shifting of many activities from high-wage to low-wage industries by means of outsourcing and to the fact that the agreements of the metal and engineering workers' union, the IG Metall, are no longer the pacesetter for other industries.

CORPORATE GOVERNANCE: CAPITAL BECOMES IMPATIENT

In contrast to companies in the English-speaking world, German companies historically were not subject to frequent changes of ownership. The majority shareholders were usually other joint stock companies or the house banks. Companies were protected from takeovers because only 25 percent of shares were held by diverse shareholders (Höpner 2003). In their multiple roles as owners, financiers, and controllers of companies through the supervisory board, the banks concentrated on maximizing long-term returns.[16] This also applies to the Mittelstand, which have been described by several authors (for example, Simon 1996) as the "hidden champions," or the innovative backbone of the German economy. Just as the major private banks financed larger companies, the local savings banks made "patient capital" available to these SMEs. In addition, there was an extensive publicly owned sector made up of companies providing basic public services (post office, railways, water and energy providers, hospitals, and so on).

However, the old Germany plc (public limited company) is now breaking up as a result of changes in the regulatory system and the new strategies adopted by shareholders. The first SPD-Green coalition government introduced a reform exempting from taxation the capital gains accruing from the sale of shares. This capital gains tax had previously acted as a barrier to the disposal of hidden reserves on corporate balance sheets. The so-called affiliation privilege, or participation exemption—whereby dividends on shareholdings of more than 25 percent were exempt from taxation—had previously been abolished (Hanke 2006, 24). In the wake of globalization, the large German joint stock companies have now been concentrating on their core businesses. They have sold many of their financial holdings in other companies in order to stock up their war chests for future acquisitions in their core areas of activity. The banks have withdrawn from the business of providing long-term financing for manufacturing and are concentrating increasingly on the more profitable area of investment banking. All this has happened with astonishing speed. At the beginning of 2000, 20 percent of Deutsche Bank's capital was still tied up in industrial holdings; by 2004 this share had fallen to just 3.9 percent (Hanke 2006, 23). The place of the banks and companies has been taken primarily by institutional investors, many of whom have very short-term expectations of the returns they want to make and a greater willingness to offload their equity stakes after a short time.

Of equal significance were the various privatizations of publicly owned companies in areas such as postal and telecommunications services, railways, energy and water supply, and local transport, which were forced largely by EU regulations. As a result, areas that had been the recipients of long-term state investment and from which competition had been excluded in favor of public monopolies were forced to adopt private-sector profitability criteria and prove themselves in a competitive market. The adoption of private-sector budget controls in the public sector, particularly in elder care and hospitals, is the functional equivalent of financialization in the private sector (Kädtler 2003). Between the reductions in the receipts from social security contributions and the increase in demand caused by demographic changes, this whole sector is under considerable financial pressure. Thus, in the past, hospitals had their actual costs reimbursed; today, following the introduction of case-based lump sums, the pressure to reduce costs is being passed on to hospitals. A new form of competitive pressure is also emerging for firms bidding for large public contracts, which now have to be put out to tender across Europe.

There is some debate as to whether the changes in corporate governance have led to companies giving greater priority to short-term concerns. Peter Fiss and Edward Zajac suggest that, in the larger joint stock companies at least, there has in fact been greater continuity than some suspect: "We also find evidence that German firms engage in decoupling by espousing but not implementing a shareholder value orientation (. . .)"(2004,501). Sigurt Vitols (2003) talks of a form of shareholder value negotiated with various stakeholders, including employees and trade unions, that fits more easily into the tradition of the German employment system. This culture of negotiation and the modernizing alliances between capital and labor that lie behind it have been evident primarily in joint stock companies, which in recent years have significantly reduced their core workforces. The increasing cost pressures on companies have been alleviated to some extent by the outsourcing of many jobs to industries with lower pay rates. Because of the considerable wage differences between industries and the small number of generally binding collective agreements, which limited wage competition between firms bound by collective agreements and those not so bound, the German model was very vulnerable to the increased cost pressures ensuing from changes in governance structures, unlike the Scandinavian countries, where wage differences between industries are small, and France and the Netherlands, where virtually all collective agreements are declared generally binding.

Industrial Relations: Increasingly Ineffective Collective Agreements

Germany's relatively low level of wage inequality in the past was attributable primarily to the area-wide collective agreements and the high rate of coverage by collective agreement. Area-wide collective agreements are concluded between trade unions and employers' associations. Because they cover all establishments in the industry in question, homogenous pay structures have developed within individual industries.

The right of trade unions and employers' associations to conclude legally binding collective agreements regulating wages and workplace conditions free from the intervention of third parties is a fundamental characteristic of the German industrial relations system. Following the disastrous experiences of state intervention in industrial disputes in the Weimar Republic, the state plays no part in collective bargaining. The 1949 Collective Agreement Act enshrined in law the privileged role of employers' associations and trade unions in collective bargaining. The collective agreements apply to all members of the representative organizations on both sides. However, firms bound by a collective agreement pay the collectively agreed rate to employees who are not members of the relevant trade union, because otherwise such employees would have an incentive to join a union.

Collectively agreed standards are legally protected in several ways. They cannot be undercut by negotiations at the establishment level but only improved (the so-called favorableness, or "to the workers' advantage," principle). If a company leaves the employers' association, the collective agreement remains in force until a new collective agreement or a new individual contract is concluded. This makes it difficult for companies with strong unions and works councils to escape being bound by collective agreements. To prevent companies from concluding new collective agreements with company or other employer-friendly unions, trade unions must have a certain degree of power (membership, ability to take industrial action) in order to be able to conclude collective agreements. However, the courts now no longer scrutinize these conditions, so that, for instance, the Christian Trade Union Federation has concluded many new agreements for firms in which it has no representation. Finally, workers in firms with weak trade union representation and no works councils are often successfully pressured to accept less favorable individual agreements.

On the employees' side, the dominant unions are those belonging to the German Trade Union Federation (DGB), which negotiate most collective agreements individually. The DGB is not allowed by its members to take part in collective bargaining. The DGB unions represent more than 85 percent of all trade union members. In addition, there is a large trade union representing Beamte (administrative-grade civil servants); the small and extremely employer-friendly Christian Trade Union Federation, which cannot take industrial action because of its very small membership; and several professional associations (representing doctors, pilots, engine drivers, and so on).

After several mergers, the DGB is now made up of eight individual unions. The largest are IG Metall and Ver.di, each of which has more than two million members. The employers are also organized at the industry level. Their organizational structure, however, is smaller in scale than that of the trade unions. The employers' collective bargaining policy is coordinated centrally by the Confederation of German Employers' Associations (BDA). In the past, the metal and engineering workers' union, IG Metall, usually played the role of pacesetter in each collective bargaining round. Roughly every six to seven years, there was a major industrial dispute in the metal and engineering industry about one controversial object of negotiation or another (for example, continued payment of wages for manual workers in the event of sickness in 1956, or the reduction of working time below forty hours in 1984). The other industries generally followed the agreements concluded in the metal and engineering industry. Unlike in France, Italy, Spain, and the Benelux countries, in Germany only a few collective agreements were declared as generally binding on the recommendation of the joint collective bargaining committee, mainly in industries with many SMEs and weak trade unions, like the retail trade. Because the agreements concluded in the metal and engineering industry functioned as benchmarks for other industries, negotiations between the social partners in this industry were geared increasingly to the general economic situation rather than to the situation in individual industries. However, it should be noted that there were already considerable differences in pay between the various industries and that pay levels in the metal and engineering industry were significantly above average. Additionally, in the past, the tendency of real wages to rise more quickly than the collectively agreed rates in economically healthy firms gave rise to considerable wage drift, particularly in the 1960s and 1970s.

This wage drift was generally negotiated between works councils and company management in a "second wage round" at the establishment level. According to the Works Constitution Act, works councils can be elected in all establishments with more than five employees. They are obliged to work for the good of the company, and they have no power to call strikes, which is a right reserved for trade unions. Because of this division of powers, reference is often made to the dual system of interest representation in Germany. According to the Works Constitution Act, it is the duty of works councils to ensure compliance with legislation and collective agreements. In matters of staffing in particular, they have strong rights of codetermination (for example, approval of overtime). Works councilors are entitled to attend regular further training courses related to their activities at the employer's expense, and they have the right to unpaid leave for additional training. Works councils must be provided with appropriate equipment and personnel. From a certain size of firm upward, works councilors are released from work in order to perform their duties.[17] These provisions of the Works Constitution Act have led to works councils becoming highly professionalized, particularly in large companies. In certain establishments that serve political, religious, charitable, educational, scientific, or artistic aims or engage in news reporting and the expression of opinion, the Works Constitution Act applies only partially or not at all. Since many publicly funded social services (child care centers, nursing homes, hospitals) are delivered by churches, many employees are affected by this provision.

In medium-sized and larger establishments in particular, works councils are effective in ensuring compliance with collective agreements. Of the approximately 220,000 elected works councilors, between 60 and 80 percent, depending on the particular industry, belong to a DGB trade union. Most of the remaining works councilors are not union members (Rudolph and Wassermann 2003). Representation by works councils varies considerably with the size of the firm. For example, in West Germany 11 percent of employees in establishments with between five and fifty employees, but 94 percent of those in large establishments, are represented by a works council (Ellguth and Kohaut 2004, 452). To increase works council density and improve the effectiveness of interest representation in small and medium-sized firms, the former SPD-Green coalition government amended the Works Constitution Act in 2001. At least a works councilor now has to be released from work in establishments with upward of two hundred employees, rather than three hundred, as previously. Furthermore, the voting procedures have been simplified. Thus, in SMEs the election must take place within a week of being proposed, and employers now have less opportunity to prevent it (Bosch 2004b). These amendments to the legislation have led to an increase in the number of works council members and also to the election of many new works councils (Rudolph and Wassermann 2003, 8f).

Until the beginning of the 1990s, the collective agreements negotiated between trade unions and employers' associations laid down minimum conditions in the labor market. In 1990 over 80 percent of employees were covered by a collective agreement (OECD 2004a, 145). Most firms not bound by a collective agreement followed the agreement for their particular industry. Structural change in the economy did not jeopardize coverage by collective agreement because new firms soon joined the employers' association and expanding companies were not trying to shift jobs to industries not covered by collective agreements. All the actors were agreed that, under these circumstances, a legal minimum wage was unnecessary. The 1952 legislation on the fixing of minimum employment conditions, which gives the government the power to introduce a minimum wage, has remained unused to date. In other areas, such as working time, the legal standards lagged a long way behind the collectively agreed norms, since the state did not see any need to take action itself in view of the right to autonomous collective bargaining the social partners enjoyed. Thus, the statutory maximum working time is forty-eight hours per week, whereas the collectively agreed weekly working time is usually between thirty-five and forty hours.

Since the beginning of the 1990s, however, the collective bargaining system has become increasingly full of holes. Coverage by collective agreement has declined considerably; the decline is greater in East Germany than in the West (figure 1.9). Moreover, those firms not covered by a collective agreement are increasingly unlikely to use a collective agreement as a benchmark in setting pay and working conditions. As the segments of the labor market no longer regulated by collective agreements have increased in size, so pay levels have once again became a factor in competition.

There are several reasons for this. First, competition in the labor market has intensified as a result of rising unemployment. This has given many firms outsider opportunities to recruit workers at below collectively agreed rates in order to obtain a competitive advantage. Second, the new governance structures have given many companies an opportunity to undercut wage rates. The privatization of publicly owned companies and the new budget regulations (in the hospital industry, for example) have led to increasing wage competition be-

Figure 1.9 Coverage of Employees by Collective
            Agreements in West and East Germany

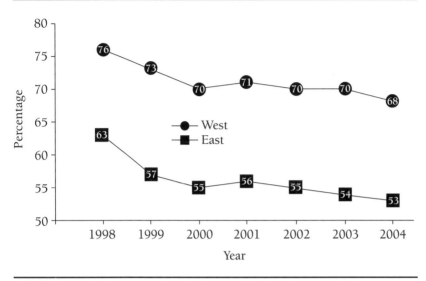

Source: IAB establishment panel, DGB (2004); Ellguth and Kohaut (2005); authors'
illustration.

tween the former public sector companies, with their high levels of
union membership, and new competitors not bound by collective
agreements, whose rates of pay are often 30 to 40 percent lower.
Third, the freedom to provide services within the European Union
means that contracts can be awarded to foreign firms operating in
Germany with workers employed on the basis of the employment
conditions prevailing in their home country (the "country of origin"
principle); this has the effect of undermining the territorial principle
of industrywide collective agreements. The construction industry is
the main destination industry for these so-called posted or seconded
workers, who now account for up to 17 percent of the industry's
workforce (Bosch and Zühlke-Robinet 2003). Since the EU's eastward expansion, the meat-processing industry has increasingly become another destination industry for posted workers. Fourth, firms
in industries with strong trade unions and a high rate of coverage by
collective agreement are increasingly exploiting the high inter-indus-
trial pay differentials in order to outsource certain activities, such as
cleaning, catering, and logistics, to other collective bargaining areas

or areas in which there are no collective agreements. Fifth, the employers' associations have revoked the traditional consensus on limiting wage competition. Under pressure from its members that benefit from outsourcing, the Confederation of German Employers' Associations is blocking any attempt by the joint collective bargaining committee to declare collectively agreed wage rates generally binding. Consequently, wage competition between firms covered by collective agreements and those not so covered is no longer restricted by declaring collective agreements generally binding.

This abandonment of consensus reflects the increasing weakness of the associations involved. The number of trade union members fell from 11.8 million in 1991 to 6.8 million in 2005, and trade union density declined from 31.2 percent in 1990 to 22.6 percent in 2003 (Visser 2006). Employers are thus under increasingly less pressure to join a representative association; this can be illustrated by the example of the metal and engineering employers' associations, which between 1993 and 2003 in West Germany alone suffered a decline in membership from 46 to 25 percent of establishments (and in terms of employees from 70 to 58 percent) (Haipeter and Schilling 2006). This decline in the membership rate on the employers' side is attributable to some extent to resignations from employers' associations; the main reason, however, is the failure of newly established firms to join an association. Many new firms, primarily but not only in service industries, are no longer members of an employers' association. Some firms bound by collective agreements are setting up separate establishments not bound by collective agreements for new activities (call centers, for example). In some industries, the trade unions have become so weak that they are no longer able to renegotiate collective agreements (for example, the meat-processing industry). Nevertheless, to win new members, many employers' associations are now even offering a category of membership that does not require members to be bound by a collective agreement (Haipeter and Schilling 2005).

The key role played by the outsourcing of jobs from the core industries of the German economy and from well-organized firms and the trend toward locating start-ups in industries with lower standards are reflected in the gradual relocation of low-wage work to unregulated or only weakly regulated segments of the labor market. These segments are mainly located in small and medium-sized firms with low levels of coverage by collective agreements and no works councils. In recent years, because hourly labor costs have risen considerably less in these segments than in larger firms, they have found it increasingly attractive to outsource certain activities. One indicator of this is the decline between 1980 and 1995 in the share of low-paid workers in manufacturing and in banking and insurance, as well as in large firms; however, in the service sector and in small firms, which often have no works council, the share of low-paid work increased or at least remained the same (see table 1.6).

Thus, the peculiarly German "negotiated shareholder value" has not prevented the increase in low-wage work as a result of outsourcing. Nor has it been able to avert a decline in standards in the core industries of the economy. In virtually all industries, the social partners have now agreed to derogation or hardship clauses that permit firms bound by collective agreements to cut wages and extend working time without wage compensation if they are experiencing economic difficulties. In many cases, however, works councils have extracted promises of increased investment and job guarantees in exchange. These economic "difficulties" are not infrequently the result of the financialization of companies. Thus, investment funds are increasingly buying companies with the aim of selling them after a short time for a profit. The costs of the takeover are shouldered by the companies, and concessions are then often successfully demanded of the workforce in order to restore profitability.

In the core industries of manufacturing, however, the trade unions are still so strong that the employers continue to be interested in joint projects to reform collective bargaining. Thus, in 2003, the social partners in the metal and engineering industry concluded a new collective agreement that abolishes the old distinction between manual and white collar workers throughout the industry and provides for a remuneration system geared more to a modern, less hierarchical corporate organizational structure, with premium payments for group work, and so on. This collective agreement covers an industry with 2.3 million employees and saves employers the high transaction costs that would have been incurred if the reform had been negotiated at the individual firm level. The same industry has also seen the negotiation of training agreements that give every employee a right to an annual training interview and provide for the introduction of necessary training programs.

In many other industries, however, this classic corporatism no longer functions. Although both sides regard the collective bargaining procedure as in need of overhaul, new agreements are not being concluded. The trade unions' weakness has so disrupted the balance of power that the employers are no longer willing to compromise. Their very weakness is causing the unions to cling to the past, since they fear that they otherwise stand to lose too much (as in the retail trade and confectionary industries). In cases where the DGB unions are unwilling to make the compromises demanded of them, employers' associations are increasingly entering into agreements with employer-friendly unions (such as the Christian Trade Union Federation in the temporary work agency industry). The DGB unions have taken legal action, with no success, in order to establish that these organizations cannot be regarded as bona-fide trade unions, on the grounds that they lack the power to enter into industrial disputes. The widening gap between industries in terms of working and employment conditions is also reflected in the evolution of wages. The weaker industries are no longer implementing the pay increases negotiated in the metal and engineering industry.

The trade unions try to extend the area over which collective agreements are applied by having them declared generally binding. However, the previous consensus with the employers no longer exists. Some of the employers' associations—mainly those in the Federation of German Industries (BDI), which represent large manufacturers—are arguing that establishment-level bargaining should take precedence and that the "favorableness" or "to the workers' advantage" principle should be abolished in order to support bargaining at that level. The conservative and liberal parties—the CDU/CSU and the Freie Demokratische Partei (FDP)—are in favor of this. The Confederation of German Employers' Associations, which coordinates collective bargaining policy, is still defending the German collective bargaining system publicly but wants only outline agreements to be concluded, with the regulation of working time and pay being devolved to the establishment level. The minimum rates of pay negotiated by the social partners in the construction industry against the background of the increase in the number of posted workers were declared generally binding by a decree issued by the Ministry of Labor. This possibility of declaring minimum wages for posted workers generally binding by decree was created in 1998 because the BDA refused to declare minimum wage agreements concluded at the industry level generally binding. In many industries (hospitals and utility companies, for example) the trade unions are being forced to accept wage cuts and the addition of low-wage grades to existing collective agreements in order to ensure the survival of companies facing competition from firms not bound by collective agreements and to limit outsourcing. Since the trade unions are no longer able to set minimum standards through the collective bargaining system, those in the weaker industries in particular are now demanding not only that collective agreements be declared generally binding but that a legal minimum wage be established. The unions in the stronger industries were initially dismissive, since they saw these demands as a threat to their higher standards. However, they now support the introduction of a minimum wage as a means of limiting the increase in low pay (Bosch and Weinkopf 2006).

Vocational Training and Occupational Labor Markets

Germany's skill structure is not typical of an OECD country. In 2003 the share of university graduates of typical graduate age was 19.5 percent, a long way below the OECD average of 32.2 percent (OECD 2005). Furthermore, this percentage hardly rose between 1991 and 2001, whereas in most other OECD countries it increased considerably. The reason for this singularity, which Germany shares with Austria, Switzerland, and Denmark, is the highly developed vocational training system. Around two-thirds of young people acquire a qualification in the German "skills machine" (Culpepper and Finegold 1999), most of them after a course lasting three years. Thus, the majority of young people obtain their skills and qualifications in the vocational training system. Apprentices enter into an apprenticeship contract with a firm and are trained in the firm and in state-run vocational schools. In social and health-related occupations in particular, school-based training programs are supplemented by placements in relevant establishments. Training is provided in nationally recognized occupations. In the dual system, standards for some 340 occupations are drawn up jointly by employers and trade unions; standards for the school-based programs are based on state regulations. The dual system developed in the craft sector and in the last century was gradually extended to manufacturing and the service sector. Anyone completing a vocational training program can extend his or her training by taking an advanced course that leads to recognized qualifications as a technician or master craftsman, or its equivalent in the service sector (Fachwirt, or business administrator). The curricula for advanced courses are also drawn up by employers and unions.

Probably the most important difference between the German system and the purely school-based vocational training systems in other countries is the close link with occupational labor markets. In 2004, 83 percent of all employees with a vocational qualification stated that they were working in the kind of job for which their training had prepared them. This figure is actually slightly higher even than that for university graduates (80 percent), and it has remained stable over the last two decades (Konsortium Bildungsberichterstattung 2006, 185). The close links between training and the labor market would be inconceivable without the direct involvement of the social partners in the development of vocational training. The same organizations that jointly draw up the standards for vocational training programs also negotiate on pay. Consequently, the pay grades in German collective agreements largely parallel the training system. In contrast to the English-speaking or Latin countries,[18] therefore, formal qualifications play a greater role in determining pay than seniority (Blöndal, Filed, and Girouard 2002). The same applies to the school-based training programs, since here too pay differentials are most easily legitimated if the dominant structuring principle of the German labor market—namely, occupation—is followed. Furthermore, because of the high share of public provision in both social and health services, the principal actor in school-based vocational training—the state—is responsible for both training and pay negotiations. In public services, however, seniority does play a greater role in determining pay. Middle management and specialist staff are recruited less among university graduates, as in many other countries, than from those who have completed a course of advanced further training. Around 10 percent of those who complete their initial vocational training go on to acquire a recognized advanced qualification (Krewerth 2004, 10f). The state offers means-tested grants and loans for these advanced training programs, as well as grants for apprentices who are no longer living with their parents and are being paid only a small training wage. Essentially, the grant arrangements for students in higher education have been extended to vocational training.

Comparative studies of German, American, and British firms in manufacturing as well as in services have shown that the practice of recruiting managers from the shop floor has its advantages. With their operational knowledge, middle managers are the conduits who ensure a good flow of communication between senior management and the shop floor. The broad base of operational skills on the shop floor facilitates the diffusion of new knowledge. Comparative studies have shown that, in ideal cases, this gives German firms productivity advantages of up to 30 percent over comparable firms in other countries with more polarized skill structures (Finegold and Wagner 1998; Prais and Wagner 1983; Wagner and Finegold 1999). The good supply of highly skilled workers is the basis for specialization in high-value products. These interactions between the training system, on the one hand, and productive efficiency and product portfolio, on the other, are the preconditions for Germany's high-skill equilibrium (Finegold and Soskice 1988).

In some segments of the labor market, the occupational principle is maintained by product market regulations. Until 2004, there were ninety-four craft occupations in which a master craftsman's diploma was an essential prerequisite for operating a company. Furthermore, firms from other trades were barred from engaging in these trades' activities. Consequently, the craft sector in Germany has a different company structure from that in many other countries. In the construction industry, for example, the share of self-employed workers is substantially lower than in most other European countries; at the same time, firms are somewhat larger and more stable (Bosch and Philips 2003). There is no doubt that these regulations were a quality assurance instrument. They had their cost, it is true, but they also contributed to the good reputation of German craft workers, and with the public support available for those seeking to train as master craftsmen, there were no shortages in the product market. Nevertheless, in 2004 the craft ordinance was largely deregulated in order to cut prices in the craft sector. The number of craft occupations for which accreditation is compulsory was reduced to forty-one. These are mainly occupations that carry a certain degree of risk, such as gas fitter. Furthermore, qualified workers without the master craftsman's certificate can now set up their own companies after six years' experience in their trade. In some of the fifty-three completely deregulated occupations, such as industrial or commercial cleaner and tiler, this has led to a substantial decrease of training and a massive increase in start-ups, many of them very small companies with little chance of survival.

The vocational training system has considerable effects on wages. First, the high average productivity has allowed wages to remain relatively high by international standards, despite the pay moderation of recent years. This is particularly true for manufacturing, where, in contrast to the United States, France, and the United Kingdom, the workforce is made up largely of skilled workers, with just a few unskilled or semiskilled workers. Second, a flat skills hierarchy has led to a more egalitarian income distribution than in countries with a more polarized skill structure. Richard Freeman and Ronald Schettkat (1999) estimate that around 40 percent of the difference in income distribution between the United States and Germany is attributable to the differences in skills between the two countries. Third, Germany's occupational labor markets and the opportunities for promotion open to those with a vocational qualification make the incentives to invest in training in the lower-intermediate and intermediate areas of the skill hierarchy considerably greater than in the United States (Freeman and Schettkat 2001). Figure 1.10 shows that the earnings distribution for workers with a vocational qualification has a second peak at around €5,000 to €5,099 (US$7,315 to US$7,460) per month, which suggests high upward mobility to middle management.[19] In addition, there are self-employed company proprietors with a master craftsman's diploma who are not recorded in these statistics.

Fourth, however, it is also evident from figure 1.10 that a vocational qualification does not protect workers from low wages. Incidentally, the strong attachment to a job in the occupation for which one has trained often gives workers a strong motivation not to give up their jobs, despite poor pay. This was observed at least in the retail trade, while skilled workers in the hotel sector, where wages are even lower than in retailing, frequently move to other industries because of the low pay. Because of the dominance of occupational labor markets, even firms in industries with high shares of low-paid workers recruit their new staff from apprentices in the dual system (as in retail trade; see Hieming et al. 2005); the small pool of unskilled labor in Germany makes this the only way they can obtain new staff with the required capabilities. This is the main reason why more than three-quarters of all low-wage workers have a higher-level qualification (vocational qualification or university degree). In contrast, around 70 percent of low-wage workers in the United States have no qualifications or at best graduated only from high school; their level of education and training is thus below that of someone who has completed a vocational training program in Germany (CBO 2006, 18).

Figure 1.10 Earnings Distribution for West German Full-
Time Employees Covered by the Social
Security System, by Educational Level, 2003

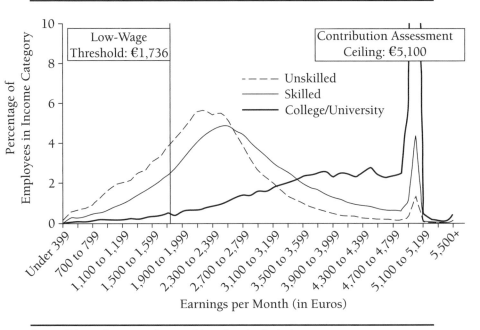

Source: BA employee panel, wave 24, authors' calculations.

With the introduction of new forms of work organization in the
1990s, vocational training in Germany began to attract criticism.
Continuing the American debate on the demarcation between different trades or occupations, Charles Sabel (1995) saw the specialization of skilled workers in Germany as a barrier to the introduction of
teamwork. Although there was no institutionalized demarcation between trades in Germany, except in the craft sector, the modernization of occupational profiles had in fact not kept pace with the
changes in the demands being made of workers. They were too technical and overly concerned with behavior in hierarchical management structures. In the mid-1990s, therefore, the social partners
reached agreement on the development of new occupations and the
rapid modernization of existing ones. Between 1996 and July 2006,
68 new occupations were created—virtually all for the service sector—and 209 of the 340 existing occupations were modernized. The

most successful new occupations included the 8 IT or media occupations, which extended the dual system into new areas of activity. In modernizing the existing occupations, account was taken of the requirements of modern forms of work organization and flexible careers (Bosch 2005). In the latest reform of the metal and engineering occupations, for example, the 16 existing occupations were reduced to five basic occupations with a broad skill base. (Prior to 1987, there were 45 occupations.) Training in all industries is increasingly being delivered through practical projects in order to ensure that young people become accustomed at an early stage to dealing with customers and working in teams made up of people from various occupational backgrounds.

As a result of the modernization of both the content and delivery of vocational training, it has been transformed from an obstacle into a driver of corporate reorganization, particularly in firms that have retained traditional organizational structures (Schumann 2002). As a consequence, it has regained its role as a pillar of the high-skill equilibrium. Of course, this general statement conceals divergent trends in individual industries. In the banking and insurance industry, for example, the training rate is declining. For some time now banks and insurance companies have been recruiting graduates instead. In the meat-processing industry the classic craft training has declined in importance, but increasing automation will expand the need in the future for specialists in food technology. There are also strong indications that apprentices in some industries are being used as cheap labor. This is true of the hotel and restaurant industry, for example, in which only 30 percent of apprentices after the completion of their training are offered jobs by the firms responsible for their training; this compares with a figure of 70 percent in the producer goods industry (Konsortium Bildungsberichterstattung 2006, 266).

Despite this general overhaul, the vocational training system still faces considerable problems, most of which arise out of an inadequate supply of training places. Since the 1990s, demand for training places has exceeded supply and the supply has not increased commensurately. One explanation is to be found in the demand for training places, which was increasing until 2007 because large birth cohorts have been entering the labor market. A second reason is to be found in the long-term decline in firms' willingness to provide training. Thus, the share of firms providing training declined from 34.3 percent in 1985[20] to 24.3 percent in 2002; in the East German states, the rate was only 19.5 percent (BMBF 2004). The reasons adduced for this decline include the structural collapse of the East German economy and new corporate governance structures that give greater priority to short-term considerations than to long-term investment in human capital. Legislation introducing an apprenticeship levy, which would have obliged companies not offering training to contribute to the costs of vocational training, was passed in 2004 but not implemented because of strong opposition from employers' associations (Bosch 2004a).

The massive surpluses in the demand for apprenticeship places have changed school-to-work transitions in recent years. Employers are able to select the best young people. Since the modernization of occupational profiles has increased the demands on young people, employers are increasingly recruiting school-leavers with a certificate from an intermediate or upper secondary school. In 1970, 80 percent of apprentices had only a lower secondary school-leaving certificate; by 2004 this share had fallen to just 37 percent. Most apprentices now have a higher-level school certificate. As recently as 1993, two-thirds of all young people concluded an apprenticeship contract in the dual system; in 2004 that share had declined to 59.5 percent (65 percent among men, 45 percent among women),[21] of whom a not inconsiderable proportion are also subsidized by the state, particularly in East Germany. A growing share, particularly among women, are going into school-based training, which is expanding because of the growing importance of social services; as a result, the share of young people without vocational training has remained constant for years at about 11 percent (Troltsch 2006). Increasingly, young people are not entering training until they have completed a state-funded vocational preparation course (Konsortium Bildungsberichterstattung 2006, 80).

The evident deterioration in the training opportunities open to young people leaving lower secondary school (Hauptschule) has had negative effects on the motivation of students in these schools. This is particularly true of students from non-German family backgrounds, a high share of whom attend Hauptschulen and of whom only 25 percent obtained an apprenticeship place in the dual system in 2004, compared with a figure of 59 percent for German students (Uhly and Granato 2006, 52). In large urban areas in particular, Hauptschulen are becoming "sink schools" for the children of immigrant families living in difficult circumstances. The German school system scored badly in the Program for International Student Assessment (PISA) study because it is less successful than education systems in other countries in compensating for the disadvantages associated with class affiliation. For this reason, the report on Germany's technological capability (BMBF 2006) rightly talks of "cracks in the foundations" of an economy that depends above all on skill.

At the same time, the dual system may well lose the best young people because of the planned expansion of higher education. To sustain the attractiveness of vocational training, a master craftsman's diploma now gives access to higher education. The Fachhochschulen (polytechnics or universities of applied sciences) are increasingly offering courses that combine vocational training and degree-level studies. It may therefore be that the dual training principle is moving one rung higher up the educational ladder.

Internal Labor Markets and Employment Stability

In contrast to Japan and the Latin countries, closed internal labor markets, in which internal career ladders and remuneration by age and seniority restrict interfirm mobility, have developed in only a few areas in Germany, such as in the public services. The tendency in Germany is more toward hybrid forms of both occupational and internal labor markets. The high share of employees with a recognized occupation and the organization of workplace hierarchies on the basis of vocational qualifications have facilitated interfirm mobility without loss of income or status. At the same time, however, a high level of dismissal protection and the strong system of workplace interest representation based on the works councils have helped to maintain wages at a good level and to stabilize employment. Because of these structural characteristics, employment stability is higher than in the English-speaking countries, with their highly developed external labor markets, but lower than in Japan or the Latin countries, with their strong internal labor markets. In 1998 average job tenure in Germany was 10.4 years, in the United Kingdom 8.2 years, in the United States 6.6 years, in Italy 12.1 years, and in Japan 11.6 years (Auer and Cazes 2000).

The decisive factor in the development of internal labor markets is the dismissal protection for workers on standard employment contracts, which can be divided into individual and collective protection.

The regulations on individual dismissal protection specify the rights of the individual employee. In essence, dismissals must be justified—that is, there must be verifiable grounds for dismissal, which may be related to operational requirements (such as rationalization or the order book situation) or to the employee's behavior (for example, theft). The notice periods for dismissal increase from one month after the end of the probationary period, which may last up to six months, to seven months at the end of the calendar year after twenty years in a job. In many collective agreements, the statutory notice periods are increased, either generally or for individual groups (for older employees in particular). In some cases, however, they are reduced in order to take account of the specific conditions in a particular industry (such as construction). Collective dismissal protection includes the rights of works councils to veto dismissals or redundancies when employees could instead be redeployed within the company or to negotiate so-called social plans (redundancy programs) in the event of mass redundancies. The main element of these social plans is the negotiated redundancy payments. The level of these payments depends on the company's economic situation. The formula used to calculate the level of the payments is generally half a month's pay for each year of service, although no payments at all may be made if the company is insolvent or otherwise in a weak financial position. Dismissal protection is not affected by changes in company ownership. If a company is sold, in whole or in part, the new owner is bound by the existing contractual relationships.

The extent of both individual and collective dismissal protection varies by size of firm. Social plans cannot be negotiated unless there are more than twenty employees in the establishment. In establishments with fewer than ten employees (before 2004, twenty employees), the employers no longer have to demonstrate that the dismissal is justified but merely have to give the correct periods of notice. Low-wage work has migrated in recent years to small and medium-sized firms, which is precisely where dismissal protection is weaker.

In its international comparisons, the OECD has classified the German provisions on dismissal protection for regular employees as relatively strict. In 2003 these provisions earned the country a score of 2.7 on a scale of 1 to 6, compared with 0.2 for the United States, 1.1 for the United Kingdom, 1.5 for Denmark, 2.5 for France, and 3.1 for the Netherlands. Germany also has a high score—3.8—on the indicator for mass redundancies (compared with 3.9 for Denmark, 2.1 for

France, 3.0 for the Netherlands, 2.9 for the United Kingdom, and 2.9 for the United States) (OECD 2004a, 117). However, this indicator does not take account of the considerable differences in dismissal protection in Germany depending on seniority, size of establishment, and the company's economic situation. These differences have facilitated the development of very different labor market segments. In industries with considerable fluctuations in workloads and low average establishment size, such as hotels and catering, average job tenure is significantly lower than in industries with larger establishments and more stable workloads, such as banking and insurance.

The regulations on dismissal protection and the long job tenures are seen by some authors as preconditions for high investment in training and further training for employees and the development of internal functional and numerical (working time) flexibility—and thus as pillars of "diversified quality production." Others see dismissal protection as a restriction on employment because of the high severance costs associated with it. To make recruitment easier for small firms, the regulations on dismissal protection have been amended several times in recent years. Thus, in 1998 the threshold for dismissal protection was lifted from five to ten employees, then reduced again, and finally, in 2004, raised once more to ten. Several empirical studies of this "real-life experiment" have concluded that small firms' recruiting behavior has not changed as a result of changes in dismissal protection, probably because of the relatively undisputed nature of dismissals (a low rate of objections against dismissals) and the low costs (virtually no redundancy payments in SMEs) (Pfarr et al. 2004).

There have been considerably more changes on the margins of the labor market. In the mid-1980s, restrictions on the use of fixed-term employment contracts were eased. Fixed-term contracts that run for several years were legalized, subject to justification on commercial or operational grounds (temporary need, cover for another employee). To encourage the spread of part-time work, legislation was passed stipulating equal treatment for part-timers with regard to pay and all social benefits. In addition, full-timers were granted the right to reduce their working time temporarily. The earnings threshold for non-insurable, marginal part-time jobs was also raised. It is true that those who hold these mini-jobs are formally covered by the same regulations on dismissal protection as workers on standard employment contracts; in practice, however, they are treated as workers who can be dismissed at any time.

The greatest changes were in the area of temporary agency work, which was prohibited until 1972. After it was legalized, it was initially strictly regulated. Agencies had to apply for authorization to provide temporary agency workers, and that authorization could be rescinded in the event of noncompliance with regulations. Temporary agency workers basically had to be given a permanent employment contract. It was not permitted to synchronize the duration of an employment contract with that of a contract for the supply of a temporary agency worker. To prevent permanent workers from being replaced by temporary staff, the maximum period a temporary agency worker could work for any one firm was limited initially to three months. This period was extended on several occasions to up to two years. Because of these regulations, temporary agency work in Germany was regarded as highly regulated (Storrie 2002). However, the Hartz Acts of 2003 largely removed the regulations governing temporary agency work. The ban on the synchronization of contracts was lifted, as were the restrictions on the maximum period of engagement by any one company. In exchange, temporary agency workers were given a right to equal pay, unless a collective agreement for temporary agency workers stipulated to the contrary.

Temporary agency workers can now be deployed in a firm without time limit. Collective agreements that infringe the equal treatment principle have become the rule. Several smaller employers' associations and companies have concluded collective agreements with the employer-friendly Christian Trade Union Federation that stipulate starting rates of between €4.83 and €6.80 (US$7.07 and US$9.95) per hour, which equate to only 31 to 43 percent of the full-time-median wage in West Germany. The DGB unions have concluded collective agreements with two larger employers' associations that stipulate somewhat higher starting rates (currently €7 to €7.20 [US$10.24 to US$10.54] per hour in West Germany and €6.06 to €6.26 [US$8.87 to US$9.16] in East Germany). Works councils in establishments that hire temporary agency workers have recently been given the right to represent such workers. Temporary agency workers themselves have a double vote in works council elections, in both the agency that employs them and the firm in which they are deployed. In practice, however, only a very few temporary work agencies actually have a works council.

Finally, mention should be made of the freedom to provide services throughout Europe. German companies can contract with com-

panies from other EU member states to carry out certain activities using their own workers. These workers are not paid German rates but
are subject to the standards prevailing in their country of origin. To
restrict wage dumping, the EU directive concerning the posting of
workers stipulates that member states may establish minimum
wages.[22] In Germany, such minimum wages for foreign posted workers have existed since the beginning of 1997 in the construction industry, but not in other industries. Before these wage rates can be declared generally binding by the Ministry of Labor, an industry-level
collective agreement must be in place, which is not the case in many
industries with contractors from other EU member states. Posted
contract workers from abroad have mainly squeezed out non-national workers, who had hitherto received domestic rates of pay. This
can be clearly observed in the meat-processing industry and the construction industry, where the majority of posted workers are concentrated. In the German construction industry, the proportion of non-
national employees fell from 20 percent in 1970 to 9 percent in 2002,
while at the same time the share of posted contract workers had increased to 16.4 percent of all blue collar construction workers by
2002 (Bosch and Zühlke-Robinet 2003).

As a result not only of these changes in the law but also, and more
particularly, of new company strategies, labor market structures in
Germany have changed over the last twenty years. First, peripheral
employment forms have become more important (figure 1.11). Individual employment forms have not evolved independently of each
other. In general, the more poorly regulated forms are driving out the
better-regulated ones. The greatest increases have been in the number of temporary agency workers and marginal part-timers not liable
for social insurance contributions; on the other hand, the number of
workers on fixed-term contracts has scarcely risen at all (figure 1.11).

Because of the regulations on equal treatment, part-timers in insurable jobs do not account for a disproportionate share of low-paid
workers, and so for the most part do not count as part of the peripheral segment of the labor market. The main reason for the increase in
the number of such part-timers is the rising female employment rate.
To some extent, insurable part-time jobs have been squeezed out by
mini-jobs. Surveys of working-time preferences show that many
women in short-hours part-time work would be happy to work between twenty and thirty hours per week (Bielenski, Bosch, and Wagner 2002) but are trapped in mini-jobs because of the legislative

Figure 1.11 Number of Employees, by Employment Form, up to 1990 in West Germany and After 1991 in Germany Including East Germany

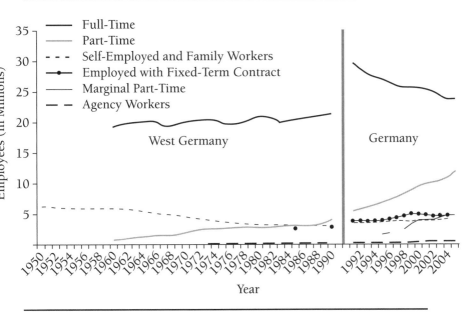

Source: Federal Employment Services; Federal Statistical Office, Eurostat; authors' illustration.

framework. Mini-jobs are concentrated in service activities and in particular in retailing, cleaning services, and catering. While the share of women in mini-jobs is high (64.4 percent), temporary agency work is a male domain in which women have only a 27 percent share. Temporary agency work is concentrated in manufacturing. In 2002 temporary agency workers earned 42 percent less than regular employees (Jahn 2004, 225). Furthermore, the chances of temporary agency workers being offered regular employment have decreased because of the lifting of the prohibition on contract synchronization and the large wage gap (particularly for unskilled workers). There are indications that companies are increasingly resorting to temporary agency workers on a permanent basis for certain tasks (Weinkopf 2006).

For workers on fixed-term contracts, the employment opportunities are significantly more favorable. As a company's direct employees, they are not only paid the same wages but also have a good chance of being offered a permanent contract. Around two-thirds of them move into permanent employment (Giesecke and Gross 2006). The number of posted workers from EU member states has also risen. Figures are available only for the construction industry (since it was made compulsory to register posted workers when a minimum wage was introduced): in 2002 around 120,000 posted workers were employed in the construction industry (Bosch and Worthmann 2006). The number of self-employed workers has also increased. They increasingly include "one-man bands" that work for only one client for low rates of pay, frequently earning less than employees in a similar position but above all without any social protection (Betzelt and Fachinger 2004).

Analyses of internal labor markets reveal the changes that have taken place over the last twenty years even more clearly. In many cases, internal labor markets that used to be vertically structured, with internal mobility and training chains and high job security, have been restructured with a new emphasis on performance. Companies no longer promise permanent employment; rather, employees must repeatedly "earn" their positions on the basis of success indicators. What is surprising is that, despite greater turbulence in product markets and new internal governance mechanisms, average job tenure has scarcely changed (Erlinghagen 2006). One explanation is that today's more demanding skill requirements make hiring more costly. Consequently, German companies have focused on developing their internal flexibility. The new occupational profiles and the introduction of teamwork have helped to increase functional flexibility, while the flexible working times negotiated with the trade unions have increased numerical flexibility. European comparisons show that German firms are now the leaders when it comes to working time flexibility (Schief 2006).

At the same time, internal labor markets have shrunk as a result of the shifting of functions to the margins of companies or outsourcing to other companies. In particular, hitherto well-paid but low-skill activities, such as simple assembly-line work, security, canteen services, cleaning, and transport, have been transferred to industries less regulated by labor law and collective agreements (Köhler et al. 2008). External labor markets with low levels of regulation have expanded; mutual commitment between employers and employees is low in these markets because of low pay and readily substitutable skills, and there are few legal impediments to dismissal. This picture is confirmed by the decline we have observed in low wages in core industries of the German economy and the increasing concentration of low-paid work in small and medium-sized firms with a low level of legal protection against dismissal and virtually no works councils and in industries with low levels of coverage by collective agreement. The disproportionate increase in low-paid non-national workers suggests that they are increasingly concentrated in the new peripheral labor markets.

The Welfare State and Family Policy

Between 1949 and 1990, East and West Germany developed completely different family policies. One of the GDR's policy objectives was a high female employment rate, and this was made possible by a highly developed system of child care centers and schools that stayed open all day. The female employment rate was almost as high as that for men, and the part-time rate was low. As a result of their labor force participation, women acquired their own entitlement to social security benefits. In West Germany, on the other hand, in reaction to the Nazi regime but also to developments in the GDR, raising children was considered a matter purely for the family, and any state intervention was rejected as an unwarranted intrusion into the private sphere. For children under three years of age, there were virtually no public child care facilities. Centers for children between the ages of three and six usually closed at midday, schools were open only in the mornings, there were no guaranteed school times (for example, if a teacher was ill, the children were sent home), and after-school care was available only for the socially disadvantaged children—regarded as pitiable—whose mothers had to work. The social insurance system was geared to the single male breadwinner. Married women and children obtained their health insurance at no extra cost through the family breadwinner, and a woman's most important source of old-age insurance was her husband's pension or, if he died, the widow's pension. Men were obliged to pay maintenance for their economically inactive former wives if they divorced, whereas divorced women in East Germany had to fend for themselves. In 1958 the so-called splitting system of assessing married couples' income tax—both partners' pretax income is divided in two and then taxed—was introduced in West Germany. In a strongly progressive taxation regime like that in

Germany, this system favors households with one earner or those with two earners whose incomes diverge sharply. In particular, it reduces the tax burden for high earners, which is why the splitting system is vigorously defended by this group. It is also supported by firms that take advantage of the protection given to women by the welfare state in order to fragment employment relationships. This is particularly evident in the retail trade.

The West German family model differed little from those in other Western countries in the postwar period. The only unusual thing about it is that, despite completely changed family structures and patterns of labor market behavior, it has survived until the present day. When firms set up so-called housewife shifts in the 1960s because of labor shortages, marginal part-time work was introduced. Workers employed for up to fifteen hours per week were not liable for social security contributions and paid only a modest flat-rate tax. These mini-jobs are attractive to housewives, since the income advantage is preserved by the splitting system and the derived entitlement to social protection. These jobs are equally attractive to high school and university students and pensioners, who obtain their social protection in other ways. The marginal deduction rates for an increase in working time above the mini-job threshold is extremely high; depending on the family's tax rate, they can easily be in excess of 100 percent, and thus they act as a very effective brake on any increase in the female labor supply in particular, as the sharp increase in marginal part-time work shows. It is astonishing that German economists, who otherwise produce very detailed calculations of low-wage gaps, have been complicit in making the German family model a political taboo and to date have shunned any analysis of the effects of the splitting system and mini-jobs on the labor market and the funding of the welfare state.

With reunification, the West German family model was transferred to East Germany. In the wake of the massive deindustrialization, far more women than men were made redundant. The employment rate for East German women fell, while that for West German women increased. Although, owing to high unemployment in East Germany, the employment rates for women age nineteen to fifty-nine in East and West Germany are now more in line with each other, attitudes to paid work continue to differ. In the year 2000 the activity rate for East German women in this age group—which includes the registered unemployed—was 83 percent, which was considerably higher than the 70 percent recorded for West Germany (Holst and Schupp 2001). The relatively comparable employment rates also conceal considerable differences in the volume of work actually done. In 2003 the part-time rate for East German women was 26.6 percent, compared with 44.7 percent for their West German counterparts (Sachverständigenrat 2004, 173). Sixty-five percent of West German women gave family commitments as the reason for working part-time, while 52 percent of East German women stated that they had been unable to find a full-time job (Statistisches Bundesamt 2001, 28). The employment rate for women with children in East Germany is actually higher than the employment rate for all women, whereas the converse is the case in West Germany (Statistisches Bundesamt 2001, 36). One of the reasons for these different patterns of labor market behavior among women is the greater provision of public child care facilities in East Germany (figure 1.12).

Despite swinging cuts in child care provision after reunification, there were facilities for 36.6 percent of children under three years of age in East Germany in 2004, compared with 28.8 percent in the West German city-states of Hamburg, Bremen, and Berlin—and only 2.4 percent in the other states (Konsortium Bildungsberichterstattung 2006, 34). At first sight, the supply of places for older children (age three to six years) seems to be virtually identical. Eighty percent of West German and 85 percent of East German children age three to six attend a child care center; in West Germany, however, 80 percent go only in the mornings, whereas 71 percent of children in East Germany attend for the whole day (Spiess, Büchel, and Frick 2002). All-day care for school-age children (either all-day school or after-school care facilities) is available in the East German states for 50 to 70 percent of children, but for fewer than 20 percent in West Germany (Konsortium Bildungsberichterstattung 2006, 59).

Austria and Germany are the only EU-15 member states in which, despite an increase in the number of people working, the employment rate of women expressed in full-time equivalents actually declined—as a result of the severe fragmentation resulting from part-time work and mini-jobs (see table 1.9).

The low level of economic activity among women is one of the reasons why employment rates in social and personal services are lower in Germany than in countries with higher female employment rates. Several studies of the "service gap" in Germany have shown that the outsourcing of services from private households is one of the most

Figure 1.12 Evolution of the Provision of Day Care for
Children Age Zero to Three, by Region, 1965
to 2004

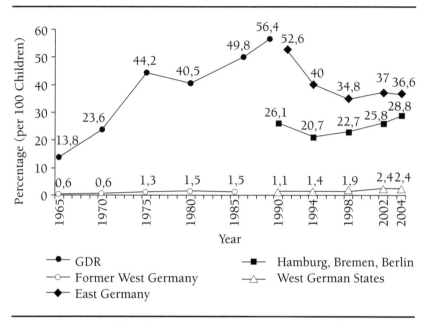

Source: Konsortium Bildungsberichterstattung (2006, 34); authors' illustration.

important forces driving the growth of such services (Bosch and
Wagner 2005; Freeman and Schettkat 1998).

It is only in recent years that the ideological foundations of the
German family model have begun to crumble. Attitudes to the family
have changed considerably in West Germany since German unification. Thus, in 1991, 74 percent of East Germans (77 percent of
women) but only 43 percent of West Germans (49 percent of
women) regarded paid work as having no negative consequences for
child raising. In 2004 the figures were 88 percent (92 percent of
women) in East Germany and 59 percent in West Germany (67 percent of women) (Statistisches Bundesamt 2006a, 518). In addition,
the decline in the birthrate and the poor results in the international
PISA benchmarking study, combined with the considerable expenditure required by German family policy and—since reunification—the
influence of East German institutions and preferences, have raised
questions about the efficacy of that policy. Germany spends around

Table 1.9 Employment Rate for Women Age Fifteen to Sixty-four, 1993 to 2005

	Germany		Netherlands		United Kingdom		Denmark		France	
	1993	2005	1993	2005	1993	2005	1993	2005	1993	2005
Employment rate	55.1	59.6	52.2	66.4	60.8	65.9	68.2	71.9	51.5	57.6
Employment rate in full-time equivalents	46.4	45.2	33.6	41.7	46.4	51.5	58	61.1	46.3	50.8

Source: European Commission (2006).

1.9 percent of GNP on family policy. Of this, the greatest share goes to cash benefits (the splitting system and child benefits), and only 0.8 percent goes to services, such as child care facilities. In France and Denmark, the share spent on such services is considerably higher: 2.3 percent in Denmark and 1.3 percent in France (BMFSFJ 2006, 67).[23] In no other European country do families receive as much in child benefits as in Germany.[24]

The slow change in attitudes is reflected in the fact that the development of child care facilities is no longer regarded as interference in the rights of parents. Indeed, compulsory preschool attendance for non-German children is now being discussed, in order to improve their chances of receiving a good education by giving them an opportunity to acquire an adequate command of German.

At the beginning of its time in office, the former SPD-Green coalition government followed the West German tradition and significantly increased cash benefits to households by raising child benefits. Toward the end of its time in office, it introduced two important measures aimed at extending services for families. Against the wishes of several CDU-governed states that still clung to the old family model, €4 billion (US$5.85 billion) was made available to the states for the development of all-day schools. The funds were to remain available until 2007. The 2005 Day Care Development Act provides for a rise in the number of child care places, from 60,000 to 120,000 in 2006 and 230,000 in 2010. In conjunction with these measures, however, the government raised the earnings threshold for mini-jobs, thereby providing an additional subsidy for the old family model. The new "grand coalition" government has now introduced a parental allowance along Swedish lines. From the beginning of 2007, working mothers and fathers who take a break from work following the birth of a child receive a parental allowance equivalent to two-thirds of their previous income, up to a limit of €1,800 (US$2,634) per month. The aim is to reduce the loss of income associated with the birth of a child. If the other partner also takes a break from work, the allowance is paid for a further two months. At the beginning of 2007, the "grand coalition" government agreed to increase the number of child care places to 750,000 by 2013, thereby making places available for one-third of all children. Additionally, the German Council of Economic Advisers for the first time called into question the fiscal and social insurance arrangements that underpin mini-jobs. However, the council was concerned less with changing the family model than with increasing the incentives (or pressure) to work in the low-wage segment.[25]

Despite the initial reform measures, the old German family model remains intact; at the same time, politicians are taking the first steps toward reforming the conservative German welfare state. However, as long as the old model, with its high costs, continues to be funded, the new reforms will remain underfunded. It is not yet clear how the additional child care places will be funded. The incentives for women to enter into fragmented employment relationships cannot be ended until the regulations on marginal part-time employment have been reformed, along with the income-splitting tax system and the derived entitlements for spouses in the welfare system. On the demand side, this must be supported by adequate financing of the new occupations in the social services (child care, care of the elderly, and so on)—that is, by the development of a sustainable service economy.

IS THE GERMAN EMPLOYMENT SYSTEM DISINTEGRATING?

The German employment system is undoubtedly going through a period of upheaval. One important indicator of this is the constant increase in low-paid workers and the decline in their income mobility since 1995. In the past, a network of institutions ensured that the share of low-paid workers was kept low. A decisive role in this regard was played by corporate governance structures in product markets, which protected companies from short-term profitability expectations, together with the high level of coverage by collective agreement. The vocational training system and the development of internal labor markets with strong works councils and a high level of dismissal protection provided further support for the system, while a family policy geared to the single male breadwinner led to the fragmentation of women's employment relationships. The German employment system always had low-paid jobs. However, a dominant role was played by those mechanisms that ensured that wage increases in the core areas of "diversified quality production" were followed by wage increases in the industries with lower wages. Until the beginning of the 1990s, unemployment was certainly low by international standards, so a certain shortage of labor was one of the main reasons for the more or less uniform wage increases in all industries.

This common bond between better-paid and more poorly paid activities and industries has to some extent been broken. It is virtually impossible to judge whether German reunification, with the ensuing weak growth and increased unemployment, or the restructuring of key institutions is the main cause of this. It is probable that the inter- action between these factors explains the expansion of the low-wage sector, all the more so since the important political decisions on in- stitutional restructuring were justified on the grounds of high unem- ployment and weak growth.

The high level of coverage by collective agreement was decisively breached by the change in corporate governance structures following the breakup of the close ties between companies and banks with regard to ownership and the privatization of many publicly owned compa- nies. In view of a level of union density that was only moderate com- pared to countries like Denmark and Sweden, and without the cover provided by the state and its power to declare collective agreements and minimum wages generally binding, as happens in France and the Netherlands, the power of the social partners to establish labor stan- dards autonomously proved too weak to absorb the new competition between firms bound by collective agreements and those not so bound. Coverage by collective agreement has declined significantly, especially in SMEs. As a result of outsourcing into SMEs with less coverage, no unions and work councils, and less legal employment protection, jobs have migrated into areas less regulated. Similar effects can be attributed to the significant increase in new, less regulated, and deregulated em- ployment forms, such as temporary agency work, mini-jobs, and con- tract work performed by posted workers who are typically paid lower wages. As a result of this migration, the share of low-wage earners in the core industries of the economy has actually declined in recent years, while it has increased sharply on the periphery of the labor mar- ket. With its high unemployment, East Germany was the precursor in this regard, with West Germany following close on its heels.

At the same time, the old employment system has been revitalized to some extent. The trade unions in the core industries are still strong enough to be able to push through new reform projects, such as col- lective agreements on training, although these cover a smaller num- ber of core workers than in the past. The social partners have also worked together to overhaul the vocational training system by intro- ducing new occupations and modernizing existing ones. This was one of the preconditions for strengthening the skill base so essential to Germany's export industries.

The state has acted in contradictory ways. On the one hand, it has deregulated new employment forms, such as temporary agency work and mini-jobs; on the other hand, it has strengthened workplace codetermination and taken the first hesitant steps toward restructuring the conservative family model. The comprehensive German welfare system and labor legislation have not, it is true, been able to prevent the increase in low-paid work. However, they have been able to prevent poverty from growing at the same rate. Unlike in the United States, all low-paid workers are entitled to paid vacations and public holidays and, with the exception of those in mini-jobs,[26] to health, long-term nursing care, and old-age insurance. For this reason, international comparisons, particularly those between European welfare states and the United States, must take account not only of hourly wage rates but also of income over the year and indeed the life course. Since the welfare state and labor law apply nearly universally, employees in both the primary and secondary segments have a common interest in retaining both, and they express that interest clearly in elections. The traditional German social model still has enough support that it can at least influence several important political decisions.

Thus, our analysis has shown that Germany's high unemployment is above all a consequence of reunification, a restrictive fiscal policy, the relative uncompetitiveness of the country's export industries in the early 1990s, and the political difficulties inherent in restructuring the traditional welfare state and developing social services. The competitive weakness has been more than offset by the modernizing of Germany's manufacturing sector and a policy of wage restraint. The collapse in demand for low-skill work as a result of international outsourcing has been countered—albeit inadequately—by improved vocational training. The lopsided focus on competitiveness—a political consequence of the dominance of exporting industries in Germany—has diverted attention away from the need to reform the welfare state, develop social services, and strengthen domestic demand through increases in wages. Thus, to return to the earlier theoretical debate on the weakness of Germany's economic growth, we see no evidence of the "high-quality trap" in which Germany's export industries, which continue to be successful, are said to be caught. Nor are rigid labor markets and excessively high wages a cogent explanation for the weak growth. Wages have risen less than in other countries, and labor markets have been made so flexible that the wage spread has widened to a greater extent than in other countries. The upshot of this ten-year "real-world experiment" is that employment levels have not been increased and the employment situation of low-skill workers has not been improved. The German low-wage segment primarily employs skilled workers who, because of the oversupply of labor, have squeezed low-skill workers out of low-skill jobs as well. Further widening of the wage spread and wage restraint would merely exacerbate the current economic problems, which are also linked to weak domestic demand.

There are two conceivable scenarios for the future. In the first, unemployment will remain high because of the stalling of the catching-up process in the East German economy and the weakness of domestic demand. The political advocates of a breakup of the German social welfare system will gain a majority, ease the regulations on dismissal protection, and legalize company agreements that diverge from the industry-level agreement. As a result, the trade unions will be marginalized and wages will become the decisive factor in inter-firm competition, leading to a further polarization of wage structures. Because of the restrictive economic policy, low wage increases, and the underfunding of social services, unemployment will remain high. In the second scenario, the German economy will recover by virtue of its increased international competitiveness and will pull the East German economy along with it. After years of wage restraint, real wages will rise in line with the productivity increases, and the state will increase its investment. As unemployment declines, the internal erosion of collective agreements will be halted, and firms will begin to seek consensus with the trade unions again. As a result, traditional corporatism will regain its importance. At the same time, in view of the improved economic environment, there will be no political support at the central level for radical deregulation; rather, there are likely to be powerful forces pushing for the introduction of a minimum wage, the declaration of industry-level collective agreements as generally binding, and a family policy along Scandinavian lines.

The economic upturn of 2006 and 2007 suggests that the second scenario might be possible. After years of declining domestic demand, private investment is increasing again, since firms have a great deal of lost time to make up and are also expanding their capacities because of the high demand for exports. As it once again meets the Maastricht criteria, the government can also start investing again as a result of higher tax revenues, and a new social security benefit, the parental allowance, has even been introduced. With their entry into the "grand coalition," the conservative CDU/CSU parties have had to abandon their radical deregulation strategy. The "grand coalition" offers an opportunity to reform family policy further, since the two major parties no longer need to be afraid that the still strong bastions of the old model in their electorates will be mobilized against such reforms. Which road the country will go down depends not only on political and economic developments at home but also, and not least, on developments in other EU member states and the joint effort of the European states to develop a European social model in a market with open frontiers.

APPENDIX

Table 1A.1 Share of Low-Wage, Full-Time Workers, Covered by the Social Security System, in the Case Study Industries, 2003

NACE	Industry	Low-Wage Share
15.11	Production and preserving of meat	25.07%
15.12	Production and preserving of poultry meat	57.66
15.13	Production of meat and poultry-meat products	49.41
15.81	Manufacture of bread, fresh pastry goods, and cakes	62.41
15.82	Manufacture of rusks and biscuits, preserved pastry goods, and cakes	30.77
15.84	Manufacture of cocoa, chocolate, and sugar confectionary	28.84
52.11	Retail sale in nonspecialized stores with food, beverages, or tobacco predominating	28.65
52.12	Other retail sale in nonspecialized stores	22.71
52.2	Retail sale of food, beverages, and tobacco in specialized stores	62.49
52.45	Retail sale of electrical household appliances and radio and television goods	26.46
55.1	Hotels	61.09
74.5	Labor recruitment and provision of personnel	71.50
74.7	Industrial cleaning	56.19
74.86	Call center activities	52.63
85.11	Hospital activities	5.66

Source: BA employee panel, weakly anonymized version, teleprocessing.

Table 1A.2 Share of Low-Wage, Full-Time Workers, Covered by the Social Security System, in the Case Study Industries and Occupations, 2003

	Industry	Occupation	Low-Wage Share
15.11	Production and preserving of meat	Case study occupations[a]	25.32%
15.12	Production and preserving of poultry meat	Case study occupations	63.89
15.13	Production of meat and poultry-meat products	Case study occupations	40.97
15.81	Manufacture of bread; fresh pastry goods, and cakes	Case study occupations[b]	44.32
15.82	Manufacture of rusks and biscuits, preserved pastry goods, and cakes	Case study occupations	36.99
15.84	Manufacture of cocoa, chocolate, and sugar confectionary	Case study occupations	39.78
52.11	Retail sale in nonspecialized stores with food, beverages, or tobacco predominating	Sales assistant or sales clerk (BKZ 682)	41.12
52.11	Retail sale in nonspecialized stores with food, beverages, or tobacco predominating	Cashier (BKZ 773)	26.42
52.12	Other retail sale in nonspecialized stores	Sales assistant or sales clerk (BKZ 682)	28.30
52.12	Other retail sale in nonspecialized stores	Cashier (BKZ 773)	27.08[c]
52.2	Retail sale of food, beverages, and tobacco in specialized stores	Sales assistant or sales clerk (BKZ 682)	74.61
52.2	Retail sale of food, beverages, and tobacco in specialized stores	Cashier (BKZ 773)	100.00[c]
52.45	Retail sale of electrical household appliances and radio and television goods	Sales assistant or sales clerk (BKZ 682)	23.74
52.45	Retail sale of electrical household appliances and radio and television goods	Cashier (BKZ 773)	48.84
55.1	Hotels	Other guest attendant (BKZ 913)	72.78
55.1	Hotels	Housekeeper (BKZ 923)	89.74
55.1	Hotels	Cleaning staff (BKZ 933)	93.86
85.11	Hospital activities	Nursing assistant (BKZ 854)	8.78
85.11	Hospital activities	Cleaning staff (BKZ 933)	19.64

Source: BA employee panel, weakly anonymized version, teleprocessing.
[a] In meat and poultry production the relevant occupations are: BKZ 402, BKZ 522, BKZ 531, and BKZ 744.
[b] In the manufacture of bread, pastry goods, cakes, and biscuits the relevant occupations are: BKZ 391, BKZ 433, BKZ 522, BKZ 531, and

Table 1A.3 All Employees Covered by the Social Security System by Full-Time, Part-Time, Mini-Job, and Industry and Occupation, 2003

Industry and Occupation	Full-Time	Part-Time	Mini-Job
Food, tobacco (NACE 15, 16)	75.6%	7.4%	17.0%
Producer of meat products and sausage			
(BKZ 402)	89.0	3.7	7.3
Manufacturer of sugar, confectionary goods,			
or ice cream (BKZ 433)	93.3	4.0	2.8
Retail (NACE 52)	49.8	24.8	25.4
Sales assistant or sales clerk (BKZ 682)	38.7	33.1	28.2
Cashier (BKZ 773)	22.8	66.9	10.3
Hotel and restaurant (NACE 55)	51.3	12.5	36.2
Other guest attendant (BKZ 913)	41.5	17.2	41.3
Housekeeper (BKZ 923)	56.0	12.9	31.1
Cleaning staff (BKZ 933)	26.7	17.2	56.1
Health (NACE 85)	61.6	26.3	12.2
Nursing assistant (BKZ 854)	54.0	33.1	12.9
Cleaning staff (BKZ 933)	17.1	29.0	53.9
Total economy	71.8	13.7	14.5

Source: BA employee panel; authors' calculations.

Note: Based on a dataset from the Federal Employment Services. Contrary to all other tables based on this dataset, this table includes part-time workers. This is possible because the information provided does not refer to the low-wage sector but to total employment in the industry and occupation.

Table 1A.4 All Employees Covered by the Social Security
         System, by Educational Level and Industry and
         Occupation, 2003

Industry and Occupation	Unskilled	Skilled	College or University
Food, tobacco (NACE 15, 16)	22.6%	74.6%	2.8%
Producer of meat products and sausage (BKZ 402)	50.2	49.4	0.4
Manufacturer of sugar, confectionary goods, or ice cream (BKZ 433)	59.5	40.5	0.0
Retail (NACE 52)	16.6	80.6	2.8
Sales assistant or sales clerk (BKZ 682)	17.4	82.2	0.4
Cashier (BKZ 773)	22.2	77.4	0.3
Hotel and restaurant (NACE 55)	33.9	64.7	1.5
Other guest attendant (BKZ 913)	40.3	58.9	0.8
Housekeeper (BKZ 923)	57.2	42.5	0.3
Cleaning staff (BKZ 933)	64.4	34.4	1.2
Health (NACE 85)	12.1	77.7	10.1
Nursing assistant (BKZ 854)	29.1	70.4	0.6
Cleaning staff (BKZ 933)	61.9	37.7	0.4
Total economy	16.3	73.3	10.4

Source: BA employee panel, authors' calculations.
Note: Based on a dataset from the Federal Employment Services. Contrary to all other tables based on this dataset, this table includes part-time workers. This is possible because the information provided does not refer to the low-wage sector but to total employment in the industry and occupation.

Table 1A.5 All Employees' Covered by the Social Security System, by Sex and Industry and Occupation, 2003

Industry and Occupation	Men	Women
Food, tobacco (NACE 15,16)	45.8%	54.2%
Producer of meat products and sausage (BKZ 402)	59.3	40.7
Manufacturer of sugar, confectionary goods, or ice cream (BKZ 433)	36.8	63.2
Retail (NACE 52)	27.3	72.7
Sales assistant or sales clerk (BKZ 682)	17.1	82.9
Cashier (BKZ 773)	4.6	95.4
Hotel and restaurant (NACE 55)	37.9	62.1
Other guest attendant (BKZ 913)	34.9	65.1
Housekeeper (BKZ 923)	4.5	95.5
Cleaning staff (BKZ 933)	20.3	79.7
Health (NACE 85)	19.2	80.8
Nursing assistant (BKZ 854)	23.6	76.4
Cleaning staff (BKZ 933)	4.2	95.8
Total economy	51.3	48.7

Source: BA employee panel, authors' calculations.
Note: Based on a dataset from the Federal Employment Services. Contrary to all other tables based on this dataset, this table includes part-time workers. This is possible because the information provided does not refer to the low-wage sector but to total employment in the industry and occupation.

Table 1A.6 Logistic Regression for the Probability of Full-Time Employees Covered by the Social Security System Being Low-Paid, 2003 (Odds-Ratios)

Independent Variable	Without Establishment Characteristics	With Establishment Characteristics
Sex (ref.: men)		
Women	4.20**	4.19**
Age (ref.: forty-five to fifty-four)		
Under twenty-five	4.10**	3.94**
Twenty-five to thirty-four	1.30**	1.21**
Thirty-five to forty-four	1.09**	1.06**
Fifty-five and over	1.02	0.99
Nationality (ref.: German)		
Non-national	1.48**	1.68**
Educational level (ref.: skilled)		
Unskilled	2.16**	2.61**
College or university	0.21**	0.31**
Industry (ref.: manufacturing)		
Agriculture		2.54**
Construction		0.56**
Infrastructure and transport services		1.23**
Business services		2.62**
Economic transaction services		1.12**
Political transaction services		0.50**
Household and personal services		3.22**
Occupational group (ref.: production-oriented activities)		
Primary services		0.84**
Secondary services		0.29**
Establishment size (ref.: one to nineteen)		
Twenty to ninety-nine		0.41**
100 to 499		0.22**
500 and over		0.06**
East/West (ref.: West Germany)		
East Germany		1.09**
Pseudo R^2	0.1615	0.2845

Source: BA employee panel, authors' calculations.
**$p \leq 0.01$ (other values are not significant)

NOTES

1. In the coal, iron, and steel industries, capital and labor had equal representation on supervisory boards and the trade unions had the right to appoint the labor director, the member of the executive board with responsibility for staff and welfare matters.
2. Comparable data for 1995 are not available for Austria and Finland.
3. The BA employee panel (BA-Beschäftigtenpanel) is drawn from anonymized quartile statistics from the employee statistics of the Federal Employment Services. This dataset is provided by the Zentralarchiv für Empirische Sozialforschung (in Cologne). The federal employment agency has no responsibility for the use of this data in the following analysis.
4. All U.S. dollar equivalents calculated in November 2007.
5. The data relate to gross income, including annual bonuses and other special payments.
6. If high school and university students and pensioners are included in the analysis, 22.1 percent of a total population of 31 million employees are low-paid, which in absolute terms equates to some 6.9 million low-wage workers.
7. The high incidence of low pay in certain industries and for certain groups of employees is also confirmed by a logistic regression analysis (see table 1A.5).
8. These monthly wages do not include social insurance contributions and taxes. Only employees working at least fifteen hours per week are included in the analysis.
9. In the literature on varieties of capitalism, the term "Bismarckian German welfare state" denotes those welfare state regimes in which entitlement to benefits is strongly linked to economic activity through social insurance contributions. We are not happy with the term, since the social insurance funds put in place by Bismarck were intended to support only a modest level of subsistence. The significant improvements in welfare benefits in the century following Bismarck were the result of sometimes violent labor disputes.
10. Provided they fall on a normal working day.
11. In addition, employees in most German states are entitled to one week's paid training leave per year, although only 1 percent of employees actually take up this entitlement.
12. For old-age and unemployment insurance, the contribution assessment ceiling in 2007 is €5,250 (US$7.683) per month in West Germany and €4,550 (US$6,658) in East Germany; the figure for health and nursing care insurance is €3,562.50 (US$5,213.25).
13. If payments for days not worked are included, the nonwage labor costs

amount to 43.3 percent. Only establishments with more than nine employees are included in the labor cost survey.

14. The monthly payment was €347 (US$508) in 2007 for single people.
Housing costs and heating costs are paid on top of that.

15. This is frequently described as "abuse." However, such a view completely ignores the fact that employers frequently prefer mini-jobs and
that unemployed individuals are not necessarily choosing not to work
longer hours (Jaehrling and Weinkopf 2006).

16. "That is how the same managers kept on meeting each other on the supervisory boards of German joint stock companies—Germany plc was
regulating itself, which certainly did not meet with the approval of
Anglo-Saxon investors in particular" ("Die Entflechtung der Deutschland AG" ["The Unbundling of the Germany plc"], Handelsblatt, August 31, 2005, 30).

17. Thus, in firms with ten thousand employees, twelve works councilors
must be released from work.

18. "Latin countries" refers to nations with languages that derive from
Latin—France, Spain, Portugal, etc.

19. The peak for university graduates at €5,000 to €5,099 per month is explained by the contribution assessment threshold. About 34.2 percent
of university graduates are in this income group. Up to the threshold
of €5,100, contributions have to be paid to the pension insurance
fund. The employee data compiled by the Federal Employment Services record incomes up to this threshold only. The recorded incomes
may exceed the contribution assessment threshold in individual
months but not over the year as a whole.

20. This figure was itself a historic high that followed Helmut Kohl's training place campaign, which took place in a favorable economic climate.

21. Young women account for a higher share of participants in school-
based vocational training in health and social occupations.

22. Directive 96/71/EC of the European Parliament and of the Council of
December 16, 1996, concerning the posting of workers in the framework of the provision of services, article 3.

23. These shares do not include family-related elements in other parts of
the social system, such as free social insurance for children and wives
or the surviving dependents' pension. In Germany to date there has
been no reliable itemization of all family-related state benefits.

24. Families with two children age six to eighteen receive €308 (US$450)
per month in Germany, €206 (US$301) in Denmark, €111 (US$162)
in France, and €140 (US$205) in the Netherlands. See http://de
.wikipedia.org/wiki/Kindergeld.

25. The basic subsistence allowance known as unemployment benefit II is
to be cut by 30 percent and the pay threshold for mini-jobs is to be re-

duced to €200 (US$293) per month. At the same time, the marginal deduction rates are to be changed: earnings up to €200 are to be disregarded completely in calculating unemployment benefit II, while the disregard rate for earnings between €200 and €800 (US$1,170) is to be raised from 20 percent to 50 percent (Sachverständigenrat 2006, 26ff).

26. However, mini-jobbers generally have derived rights through their partners, which give them entitlement to these welfare benefits.

REFERENCES

Arbeitsgemeinschaft deutscher wirtschaftswissenschaftlicher Forschunginstitute e.V. (Arbeitsgemeinschaft). 2006. "Die Lage der Weltwirtschaft und der deutschen Wirtschaft im Frühjahr 2006" ["The Global Economic Situation and the German Economy in the Spring of 2006"]. *DIW-Wochenbericht* 06(18): 225–87.

Auer, Peter, and Sandrine Cazes. 2000. "The Resilience of the Long-term Employment Relationship: Evidence from the Industrialized Countries." *International Labour Review* 139(4): 379–409.

Bäcker, Gerhard. 2006. "Was heißt hier „geringfügig"? Minijobs als wachsendes Segment prekärer Beschäftigung" ["What Does 'Marginal Part-Time' Mean Here? Mini–Jobs as an Expanding Area of Precarious Employment"]. *WSI-Mitteilungen* 2006(5): 255–61.

Bauer, Frank, and Hermann Groß. 2006. "Betriebszeiten in Europa—Wo stehen die deutschen Betriebe" ["Operating Hours in Europe—What's the Situation in German Firms?"]. *WSI-Mitteilungen* 2006(6): 314–9.

Baumol, William Jack. 1967. "Macroeconomics of Unbalanced Growth: The Anatomy of Urban Crisis." *American Economic Review* 57(3): 416–26.

Bender, Stefan, Anette Haas, and Christoph Klose. 2000. "IAB Employment Subsample 1975–1995. Opportunities for Analysis Provided by the Anonymised Subsample." IZA Discussion Paper No. 117. Bonn, Germany.

Berthold, Norbert. 1997. "Arbeitslosigkeit oder Einkommensungleichheit— Fluch globaler Märkte?" ["Unemployment or Income Inequality—The Curse of Global Markets?"] *Politische Studien* 48(352): 36–57.

Betzelt, Sigrid, and Uwe Fachinger. 2004. "Jenseits des „Normalunternehmers"—Selbständige Erwerbsformen und ihre soziale Absicherung" ["Beyond the Standard Entrepreneur—Self-Employment and Social Protection"]. *Zeitschrift für Sozialreform* 50: 312–43.

Bielenski, Harald, Gerhard Bosch, and Alexandra Wagner. 2002. *Working Time Preferences in Sixteen European Countries.* Dublin: European Foundation for the Improvement of Living and Working Conditions.

Blöndal, Sveinbjörn, Simon Filed, and Nathalie Girouard. 2002. "Investment in Human Capital through Upper-Secondary and Tertiary Education." *OECD Economic Studies* Nr. 34: 41–89.

Bofinger, Peter. 2005. *Wir sind besser als wir glauben* [*We're Better than We Think*]. München, Germany: Pearson Studium.

Bollé, Patrick. 1997. "Perspectives. Part-Time Work: Solution or Trap?" *International Labour Review* 136(4): 557–79.

Bosch, Gerhard. 2004a. "Die Krise der Selbstverpflichtung" ["The Crisis of Commitment"]. *ifo Schnelldienst* 2004(6): 16–20.

———. 2004b. "The Changing Nature of Collective Bargaining in Germany: Coordinated Decentralization." In *The New Structure of Labor Relations: Tripartism and Decentralization*, edited by Harry Charles Katz, Wonduck Lee, and Joohee Lee. Ithaca, N.Y.: ILR Press.

———. 2005. "Vocational Training in Germany." Paper presented at 2nd int. conference of the project "A Comparative Perspective on Vocational Training in Ten Countries: Systems, Innovations, and Results". November 28–29, 2005, Gelsenkirchen, Germany.

Bosch, Gerhard, and Matthias Knuth. 1993. "The Labour Market in East Germany." *Cambridge Journal of Economics* 17(3): 295–308.

Bosch, Gerhard, and Peter Philips, editors. 2003. *Building Chaos: An International Comparison of Deregulation in the Construction Industry*. London: Routledge.

Bosch, Gerhard, and Alexandra Wagner. 2005. "Measuring Economic Tertiarisation: A Map of Various European Service Societies." In *Working in the Service Sector. A Tale from Different Worlds*, edited by Gerhard Bosch and Steffen Lehndorff. London: Routledge.

Bosch, Gerhard, and Claudia Weinkopf, with Thorsten Kalina. 2006. *Gesetzliche Mindestlöhne auch in Deutschland?* [*Statutory Minimum Wage in Germany Too?*]. Expertise im Auftrag der Friedrich-Ebert-Stiftung, Gesprächskreis Arbeit und Qualifizierung. Bonn, Gemany: Friedrich Ebert Foundation.

Bosch, Gerhard, and Georg Worthmann. 2006. *Arbeitsmobilität in der EU. Bisherige Erfahrungen und künftige Herausforderungen* [*Labor Mobility in the EU. Experiences to Date and Future Challenges*]. *Arbeit* 15(4): 292–7.

Bosch, Gerhard, and Klaus Zühlke-Robinet. 2003. "Germany: The Labor Market in the German Construction Industry." In *Building Chaos: An International Comparison of Deregulation in the Construction Industry*, edited by Gerhard Bosch and Peter Philips. London: Routledge.

Bundesagentur für Arbeit (BA). 2006. *Beschäftigung von erwerbsfähigen Hilfebedürftigen* [*The Employment of People Capable of Work but in Need of Assistance*]. October 2006. Nürnberg, Germany: Bundesagentur für Arbeit.

———. 2007. *Mini- und Midijobs in Deutschland* [*Mini- and Midi-Jobs in Germany*]. May 2007. Nürnberg, Germany: Bundesagentur für Arbeit.

Bundesministerium der Finanzen (BMF). 2004. *Bilanz der Ökologischen*

Steuerreform [*Review of the Environmental Tax Reform*]. Berlin: Bundesministerium der Finanzen.

————. 2006. *Die wichtigsten Steuern im internationalen Vergleich 2005* [*The Most Important Taxes in International Perspective*]. Berlin: Bundesministerium der Finanzen.

Bundesministerium für Bildung und Forschung (BMBF). 2004. *Berufsbildungsbericht 2004* [*Vocational Training Report 2004*]. Berlin: Bundesministerium für Bildung und Forschung.

————. 2006. *Bericht zur technologischen Leistungsfähigkeit Deutschlands 2006* [*Report on Germany's Technological Capability 2006*]. Berlin: Bundesministerium für Bildung und Forschung.

Bundesministerium für Jugend, Senioren, Frauen und Jugend (BMFSFJ). 2006. *Siebter Familienbericht, Familie zwischen Flexibilität und Verlässlichkeit* [*Seventh Report on the Family: The Family between Flexibility and Reliability*]. Berlin: Bundesministerium für Jugend, Senioren, Frauen und Jugend.

Bundesregierung. 2005. *Lebenslagen in Deutschland. Der 2. Armuts- und Reichtumsbericht der Bundesregierung* [*Living Circumstances in Germany. The Federal Government's 2nd Report on Poverty and Wealth*]. Bonn, Germany: Bundesministerium für Gesundheit und Soziale Sicherung, Information, Publikation, Redaktion.

Congressional Budget Office (CBO). 2006. *Changes in the Low-Wage Labor Markets Between 1979 and 2005*. Congress of the United States. Washington: Congressional Budget Office.

Culpepper, Pepper D., and David Finegold. 1999. *The German Skills Machine. Sustaining Comparative Advantage in a Global Economy*. New York/Oxford: Berghahn Books.

Deutscher Gewerkschaftsbund (DGB). 2004. *Tarifbindung: Flucht aus Tarifverträgen gestoppt* [*Coverage by Collective Agreement: The flight from Collective Agreements Halted*]. DGB-Einblick 17.

Düthmann, Anja, Peter Hohlfeld, Gustav Horn, Camille Logeay, Katja Rietzler, Sabine Stephan, and Rudolf Zwiener. 2006. *Arbeitskosten in Deutschland bisher überschätzt. Auswertung der neuen Eurostat-Statistik* [*Labor Costs in Germany Overestimated. Analysis of the New Eurostat Statistics*]. IMK-Report Nr. 11. Institut für Makroökonomie und Konjunkturforschung (IMK) in der Hans-Böckler-Stiftung, Düsseldorf, Germany.

Ellguth, Peter, and Susanne Kohaut. 2004. "Tarifbindung und betriebliche Interessenvertretung: Ergebnisse des IAB-Betriebspanels 2003" ["Collective Agreement Coverage and Workplace Representation of Interests: Results of the 2003 IAB Establishment Panel"]. *WSI-Mitteilungen* 2004(8): 450–4. Accessed at http://www.boeckler.de/cps/rde/xchg/SID-3D0AB75D-B1965313/hbs/hs.xsl/169_30905.html.

————. 2005. "Tarifbindung und betriebliche Interessenvertretung Ergebnisse aus dem IAB-Betriebspanel" ["Collective Agreement Coverage and Workplace Representation of Interests: Results of the IAB Establishment Panel"]. *WSI-Mitteilungen* 2005(7): 398–403.

Erlinghagen, Marcel. 2006. "The Case of West Germany—Flexibility and Continuity in the German Labour Market." In *Trends in Employment Stability and Labour Market Segmentation. Current Debates and Findings in Eastern and Western Europe*, edited by Christoph Köhler, Kyra Junge, Tim Schröder, and Olaf Struck. Sonderforschungsbereich (SFB) 580 Mitteilungen 2006, Nr. 16 Jena.

Esping-Andersen, Gøsta. 1990. *The Three Worlds of Welfare Capitalism.* Cambridge: Polity Press.

European Commission. 2004. *Employment in Europe 2004.* Luxembourg: Office for Official Publications of the European Communities.

———. 2006. *Employment in Europe 2006.* Luxembourg: Office for Official Publications of the European Communities.

Fertig, Michael, Jochen Kluve, and Markus Scheuer. 2004. *Aspekte der Entwicklung von Minijobs* [*Aspects of the Development of Mini-Jobs*]. Essen, Germany: Abschlussbericht. Rheinisch-Westfälisches Institut für Wirtschaftsforschung.

Finegold, David, and David Soskice. 1988. "The Failure of Training in Britain: Analysis and Prescription." *Oxford Review of Economic Policy* 4(3): 21–51.

Finegold, David, and Karin Wagner. 1998. "The Search for Flexibility: Workplace Innovation in the German Pump Industry." *British Journal of Industrial Relations* 36(3): 469–87.

Fiss, Peer C., and Edward J. Zajac. 2004. "The Diffusion of Ideas over Contested Terrain: The (Non)adaptation of a Shareholder Value Orientation Among German Firms." *Administrative Science Quarterly* 49(4): 501–34.

Freeman, Richard, and Ronald Schettkat. 1998. "Low Wages Services: Interpreting the US-German Difference" Paper to the LOWER Conference, November 19–21, 1998, Groningen, The Netherlands.

———. 1999. "The Role of Wage and Skill Differences in US-German Employment Differences." *Jahrbücher für Nationalökonomie und Statistik* 219(1–2): 49–66.

———. 2001. "Skill Compression, Wage Differentials and Employment: Germany vs. the US." *Oxford Economic Papers* 53(3): 582–603.

Geishecker Ingo. 2002. "Outsourcing and the Demand for Low-Skilled Labour in German Manufacturing: New evidence." DIW Discussion papers 313. Berlin

Giesecke, Johannes, and Martin Gross. 2006. "Befristete Beschäftigung" ["Temporary Employment"]. *WSI-Mitteilungen* 2006(5): 247–54.

Grabka, Markus M. 2000. "Einkommensverteilung in Deutschland— Stärkere Umverteilungseffekte in Ostdeutschland" ["Income Distribution in Germany—Stronger Redistribution Effects in East Germany"]. *DIW-Wochenbericht* 00(19): 291–7.

Haipeter, Thomas, and Gabi Schilling. 2005. "Tarifbindung und Organisationsentwicklung: OT-Verbände als Organisationsstrategie der metallindustriellen Arbeitgeberverbände" ["Coverage by Collective Agreement and Organisational Development: Affiliated Associations Not Bound by Collective Agreements as an Organisational Strategy Among Employers' Asociations in the Metal and Engineering Industry"]. *Institut Arbeit und Technik: Jahrbuch 2005*: 169–84.

———. 2006. *Arbeitgeberverbände in der Metall- und Elektroindustrie: Tarifbindung, Organisationsentwicklung und Strategiebildung* [*Employers' Associations in the Metal, Engineering and Electrical Industry: Coverage by Collective Agreement, Organizational Development and Strategy Development*]. Hamburg, Germany: VSA.

Haisken-De New, John. 2004. *Lebensstandarddefizite bei Erwerbstätigenhaushalten* [*Inadequate Living Standards Among Economically Active Households*]. Forschungsprojekt des Bundesministeriums für Gesundheit und Soziale Sicherung. Edited by Rheinisch-Westfälisches Institut für Wirtschaftsforschung. Essen, Germany.

Hanke, Thomas. 2006. *Der neue deutsche Kapitalismus. Republik im Wandel* [*The New German Capitalism. A Republic in Flux*]. Frankfurt / New York: Campus.

Hankel, Wilhelm. 1993. *Die sieben Todsünden der Vereinigung. Wege aus dem Wirtschaftsdesaster* [*The Seven Deadly Sins of Unification. Ways Out of the Economic Disaster*]. Berlin: Siedler.

Hieming, Bettina, Karen Jaehrling, Thorsten Kalina, Achim Vanselow, and Claudia Weinkopf. 2005. *Stellenbesetzung im Bereich „einfacher" Dienstleistungen* [*Recruitment Processes in "Low-Skill" Services*]. Abschlussbericht einer Studie im Auftrag des Bundesministeriums für Wirtschaft und Arbeit. BMWA-Dokumentation Nr. 550. Berlin.

Holst, Elke, and Jürgen Schupp. 2001. "Erwerbsverhalten von Frauen: Trotz Annäherung immer noch deutliche Unterschiede zwischen Ost und West" ["Women's Labor Market Behavior: Despite a Closing of the Gap, Considerable Differences Remain Between East and West"]. *DIW-Wochenbericht* 01(42): 648–58.

Höpner, Martin. 2003. *Wer beherrscht die Unternehmen? Shareholder Value, Managerherrschaft und Mitbestimmung in Deutschland* [*Who Controls the Corporations? Shareholder Value, Management Prerogative and Codetermination in Germany*]. Frankfurt/New York: Campus.

Institut für Makroökonomie und Konjunkturforschung (IMK) 2005. "Wirtschaftliche Entwicklung 2006: Vor schwierigen Weichenstellungen" ["Economic Development 2006: The Difficulties of Setting a Course for the Future"]. IMK Report 3/2005. Düsseldorf, Germany: Institut für Makroökonomie und Konjunkturforschung.

Jaehrling, Karen, and Claudia Weinkopf, with Bettina Hieming and Bruno Kaltenborn. 2006. "Kombilöhne—neue Wege, alte Pfade, Irrweg?" ["Wage Subsidies—New Ways, Old Paths, Wrong Track?"]. Expertise im Auftrag der Friedrich-Ebert-Stiftung, Gesprächskreis Arbeit und Qualifizierung. Bonn, Germany: Friedrich-Ebert-Siftung.

Jahn, Elke. 2004. "Leiharbeit—für Arbeitslose (k)eine Perspektive?" ["Temporary Agency Work—A Prospect for the Unemployed?"]. In *Ungleichheit und Umverteilung [Inequality and Rearrangement]*, edited by Van Anne Aaken and Gerd Grözinger. Marburg, Germany: Metropolis.

Jarass, Lorenz, and Gustav M. Obermair. 2005. *Geheimnisse der Unternehmenssteuern. Steigende Dividenden, sinkendes Steueraufkommen. Eine Analyse der DAX30-Geschäftsberichte 1996–2002 unter Berücksichtigung der Volkswirtschaftlichen Gesamtrechnung [Corporation Tax Secrets. Rising Dividends, Declining Tax Receipts. An Analysis of DAX 30 Company Reports 1996–2002 in the Light of National Income Accounting]*. 2nd edition. Marburg, Germany: Metropolis.

Kädtler, Jürgen. 2003. "Globalisierung und Finanzialisierung. Zur Entstehung eines neuen Begründungskontextes für ökonomisches Handeln" ["Globalization and Financialization. On the Emergence of a New Context for Economic Activity"]. In *Das neue Marktregime [The New Market Regime]*, edited by Klaus Dörre and Bernd Röttger. Hamburg, Germany: VSA.

Kalina, Thorsten, and Claudia Weinkopf. 2006. "Mindestens sechs Millionen Niedriglohnbeschäftigte in Deutschland: welche Rolle spielen Teilzeitbeschäftigung und Minijobs?" ["At Least Six Million Low-Wage Jobs in Germany: What Role is Played by Part-Time work and Mini-Jobs?"]. IAT-Report Nr. 2006–03. Gelsenkirchen, Germany: IAT.

Kaltenborn, Bruno, and Hans-Peter Klös. 2002. "Niedriglöhne und Kombi-Einkommen—Sackgasse oder Ausgangspunkt einer Karriere? Eine Mobilitätsuntersuchung für Westdeutschland 1984/96" ["Low Wages and Wage Subsidies—Cul-de-sac or Starting Point for a Career? An Investigation of Mobility in West Germany 1984/96"]. In *Kombi-Einkommen - Ein Weg aus der Sozialhilfe? [Combination Income: A Way Out of Social Welfare Assistance?]*, edited by Sabine Dann, Andrea Kirchmann, and Alexander Spermann. Baden-Baden, Germany: Nomos.

Keese, Mark, Agnès Puymoyen, and Paul Swain. 1998. "The Incidence and Dynamics of Low-Paid Employment in OECD Countries." In *Low Pay and Earnings Mobility in Europe*, edited by Rita Asplund, Peter J. Sloane, and Ioannis Theodossiou. Cheltenham/ Northampton, England: Edward Elgar.

Kitschelt, Herbert, and Wolfgang Streeck. 2004. "From Stability to Stagnation: Germany at the Beginning of the Twenty-first Century." In *Germany: Beyond the Stable State*, edited by Herbert Kitschelt and Wolfgang Streeck. London: Frank Cass.

Köhler, Christoph, Michael Grotheer, Alexandra Krause, Ina Krause, Tim

Schröder, and Olaf Struck. 2008. *Offene und geschlossene Beschäfti-gungssysteme—Risiken und Nebenwirkungen [Open and Closed Occupation Systems—Risks and Side Effects]*. Wiesbaden, Germany: VS-Verlag.

Konsortium Bildungsberichterstattung. 2006. *Bildung in Deutschland. Ein indikatorengestützter Bericht mit einer Analyse zu Bildung und Migration, Bundesministerium für Bildung und Forschung, Berlin [Education and Training in Germany. An Indicator-Based Report with an Analysis of Education and Migration, Federal Ministry for Education and Training, Berlin]*. Accessed at http://www.bildungsbericht.de/daten/gesamtbericht.pdf.

Krewerth, Andreas. 2004. "Aspekte des lebenslangen Lernens: Absolvierung von Aufstiegsfortbildungen und nachträglicher Erwerb von Studien-berechtigungen. Ein Vergleich von Bildungsverläufen in unterschied-lichen Alterskohorten" ["Aspects of Lifelong Learning: The Completion of Promotional Training Courses and the Subsequent Acquisition of Enti-tlements to Higher Education"]. Wissenschaftliche Diskussionspapiere Heft 70. Bundesinstitut für Berufsbildung. Bonn, Germany.

Marlier, Eric, and Sophie Ponthieux. 2000. *Low-Wage Employees in EU Countries*. European Commission, Statistical Office: Statistics in focus / Population and social conditions 11/2000. Luxembourg: Eurostat.

Mosebach, Kai. 2005. "Erosion of the Tax Basis. Fiscal Policy and Interna-tional Tax Competition." In *Surviving Globalization? Perspectives for the German Economic Model*, edited by Stefan Beck, Frank Klobes, and Christoph Scherrer. Berlin: Springer.

Müller, Albrecht. 2004. *Die Reformlüge [The Reform Lie]*. München: Droe-mer Knaur.

OECD. 1996. *Employment Outlook*. Paris: OECD.

———. 1997. *Employment Outlook*. Paris: OECD.

———. 2004a. *Employment Outlook*. Paris: OECD.

———. 2004b. *Economic Surveys 2004: Germany*. Volume 2004/12. Paris: OECD.

———. 2005. *Education at a Glance*. Paris: OECD.

———. 2006. *Employment Outlook*. Paris: OECD.

Pfarr, Heide, Julia Scheider, Silke Bothfeld, Karen Ullmann, Martin Kim-mich, and Markus Bradtke. 2004. "Personalpolitik und Arbeitsrecht—Differenzierung nach Betriebsgröße" ["Personnel Policy and Labor Law—Differentiation by Size of Firm"]. *Recht der Arbeit* 57(4): 193–200.

Prais, Sig J., and Karin Wagner. 1983. "Some Practical Aspects of Human Capital Investment: Training Standards in Five Occupations in Britain and Germany." *National Institute Economic Review* 105(1): 46–65.

Ragnitz, Joachim. 2003. *Wie hoch sind die Transferleistungen für die neuen Länder? [How High are the Transfer Payments to the New Länder?]*. IWH Pressemitteilung 21/2003. Halle, Germany: Institut für Wirtschafts-forschung.

Reinberg, Alexander, and Markus Hummel. 2002. *Qualifikationsspezifische Arbeitslosenquoten - reale Entwicklung oder statistisches Artefakt? [Qualification–Specific Unemployment Rates—Real Development or Statistical Ertefact?]*. IAB-Werkstattbericht 4. Nürnberg, Germany: Institut für Arbeitsmarkt- und Berufsforschung.

Reinberg, Alexander, and Franziska Schreyer. 2003. *Studieren lohnt sich auch in Zukunft [A Degree Will Pay Off in the Future as Well]*. University IAB-Kurzbericht 20. Nürnberg, Gemany: Institut für Arbeitsmarkt- und Berufsforschung.

Rhein, Thomas, Hermann Gartner, and Gerhard Krug 2005. *Niedriglohnsektor. Aufstiegschancen für Geringverdiener verschlechtert [Low-Wage Sector. Opportunities for Advancement for Low Earners Have Deteriorated]*. IAB-Kurzbericht 3/2005. Nürnberg, Germany: Institut für Arbeitsmarkt- und Berufsforschung.

Riede, Thomas, and Dieter Emmerling. 1994. "Analysen zur Freiwilligkeit der Auskunfterteilung im Mikrozensus. Sind Stichprobenergebnisse bei freiwilliger Auskunfterteilung verzerrt?" ["Analyses of Voluntary Information Disclosure in the Microcensus. Are Sample Results Distorted When Disclosure is Voluntary?"]. *Wirtschaft und Statistik* 46(9): 733–42.

Rudolph, Helmut. 2003. *Mini- und Midijobs. Geringfügige Beschäftigung in neuem Outfit [Mini and Midi-Jobs. Marginal Part-Time Employment in New Clothes]*. IAB-Kurzbericht 6. Nürnberg, Germany.

Rudolph, Wolfgang, and Wolfram Wassermann. 2003. *Trendwende zu mehr Stabilität und Repräsentanz des Betriebsrätewesens. Ergebnisse aus den Betriebsrätewahlen 2002 [Change of Trend Towards Greater Stability and Representation in the Works Council System. Results from the 2002 Works Council Elections]*. Kassel, Germany: Büro für Sozialforschung.

Sabel, Charles F. 1995. "Regionale Basis globaler Wettbewerbsfähigkeit" ["The Regional Basis of Global Competitiveness"]. In *Regiovision - Neue Strategien für alte Industrieregionen [Regiovision: New Strategies for Old Industrial Regions]*, edited by Franz Lehner, Friederich Schmidt-Bleek, and Heiderose Kilper. München/Mering, Germany: Hampp.

Sachverständigenrat. 2002. *Zwanzig Punkte für Beschäftigung und Wachstum. Jahresgutachten des Sachverständigenrats 2002/3. [Twenty Proposals for Employment and Growth. Annual Report of the German Council of Economic Experts]*. Wiesbaden, Germany. Accessed at http://www.sachverstaendigenrat-wirtschaft.de/gutacht/02_ii.pdf.

———. 2004. *External Sucesses—Internal Challenges, Annual Report 2004/5*. Summary in English. Accessed at http://www.sachverstaendigenrat-wirtschaft.de/englisch/gutachten/eng_04.pdf

———. 2006. *Wiederstreitende Interessen—Ungenutzte Chancen, Jahresgutachten des Sachverständigenrats 2006/7 [Conflicting Interests—Missed Opportunities, Annual Report of the German Council of Economic Experts]*.

Wiesbaden, Germany. Accessed at http://www.sachverstaendigenrat-wirts chaft.de.

Scharpf, Fritz W. 2000. "Economic Changes, Vulnerabilities, and Institutional Capabilities." In *Welfare and Work in the Open Economy, Vol. I: From Vulnerability to Competiveness,* edited by Fritz W. Scharpf and Vivien Ann Schmidt. Oxford: Oxford University Press.

Schief, Sebastian. 2006. "Nationale oder unternehmensspezifische Muster der Flexibilität? Eine empirische Untersuchung von Flexibilitätsmustern aus- und inländischer Unternehmen in fünf europäischen Ländern" ["National or Company-Specific Flexibility Models? An Empirical Investigation of Flexibility Models in Foreign and Domestic Companies in Five European Countries"]. In *Das Politische in der Arbeitspolitik: Ansatzpunkte für eine nachhaltige Arbeits- und Arbeitszeitgestaltung [The Political Aspects of Work and Employment Policy: Towards a Sustainable Mode of Work and Working Time Organization],* edited by Steffen Lehndorff. Berlin: Edition Sigma.

Schumann, Michael. 2002. *Struktureller Wandel und Entwicklung der Qualifikationsanforderungen [Structural Change and Changing Skill Requirements].* Vortrag auf dem 4. BiBB-Fachkongress 2002. Berlin, 23.–25.10.2002.

Siebert, Horst. 1998. *Arbeitslos ohne Ende? Strategien für mehr Beschäftigung [Unemployed Forever? Strategies for a Higher Employment Rate].* Wiesbaden, Germany: Gabler.

Simon, Hermann. 1996. *Die heimlichen Gewinner. Erfolgsstrategien unbekannter Weltmarktführer [The Secret Winners. Unknown World Market Leaders and their Strategies for Success].* Frankfurt/New York: Campus.

Sinn, Hans-Werner. 2004. *Ist Deutschland noch zu retten? [Can Germany Be Saved?].* München, Germany: Econ Verlag.

Solow, Robert M. 1985. "Economic History and Economics." *American Economic Review* 75(2): 328–31.

Spiess, Katharina C., Felix Büchel, and Joachim R. Frick. 2002. "Kinderbetreuung in West- und Ostdeutschland: Sozioökonomischer Hintergrund entscheidend" ["Childcare in West and East Germany: Socioeconomic Background Decisive"]. *DIW-Wochenbericht* 02(31): 518–24.

Statistisches Bundesamt. 2001. *Leben und Arbeiten in Deutschland. Ergebnisse des Mikrozensus 2000 [Living and Working in Germany. Results of the 2000 Microcensus].* Wiesbaden, Germany: Statistisches Bundesamt.

———. 2004. *Statistisches Jahrbuch für die Bundesrepublik Deutschland 2004 [Statistical Year Book for the Federal Republic of Germany 2004].* Wiesbaden, Germany: Statistisches Bundesamt.

———. 2006a. *Datenreport 2006. Zahlen und Fakten über die Bundesrepublik Deutschland, Teil II [Data Report 2006. Facts and Figures on the Federal Republic of Germany].* Wiesbaden, Germany: Statistisches Bundesamt. Accessed at http://www.destatis.de/datenreport/d_datend.htm.

————. 2006b. *Was kostet Arbeit in Deutschland. Ergebnisse der Arbeit-skostenerhebung 2004, Wiesbaden* [*What Does Labor Cost in Germany. Results of the 2004 Labor Costs Survey*]. Accessed at https://www-ec.desta tis.de/csp/shop/sfg/bpm.html.cms.cBroker.cls?cmspath=struktur,vollan zeige.csp&ID=1019156.

————. 2006c. *Statistisches Jahrbuch 2006* [*Statistical Year Book for 2006*]. Wiesbaden, Germany: Statistisches Bundesamt.

Storrie, Donald. 2002. *Temporary Agency Work in the European Union*. Dublin: European Foundation for the Improvement of Living and Working Conditions.

Streeck, Wolfgang. 1991. "On the Institutional Conditions of Diversified Quality Production." In *Beyond Keynesianism: The Socio-Economics of Production and Employment*, edited by Egon Matzner, and Wolfgang Streeck.. London: Edward Elgar.

Strengmann-Kuhn, Wolfgang. 2003. *Armut trotz Erwerbstätigkeit* [*Poverty Despite Gainful Employment*]. Frankfurt/Main: Campus.

Troltsch, Klaus. 2006. "1,6 Millionen Jugendliche im Abseits? Strukturelle Arbeitslosigkeit in Deutschland" ["1.6 Million Young People Excluded from the Labor Market? Structural Unemployment in Germany"]. *Berufsbildung in Wissenschaft und Praxis* 2006(3): 44–46.

Uhly, Alexandra, and Mona Granato. 2006. "Werden ausländische Jugendliche aus dem dualen System der Berufsausbildung verdrängt?" ["Are Non-German Young People Being Squeezed Out of the Dual System of Vocational Training?"]. *Berufsbildung in Wissenschaft und Praxis* 2006(3): 51–55.

Visser Jelle. 2006. "Union Membership Statistics in 24 Countries." *Monthly Labour Review* 129(1): 38–49.

Vitols, Sigurt. 2003. "Negotiated Shareholder Value: The German Version of an Anglo-American Practice." Discussion Paper SP II 2003–25. Wissenschaftszentrum Berlin.

Wagner, Karin, and David Finegold. 1999. "The German Skill-Creation System and Team-Based Production: Competitive Asset or Liability?" In *The German Skills Machine: Sustaining Comparative Advantage in a Global Economy*, edited by Pepper D. Culpepper and David Finegold. New York/Oxford: Berghahn Books.

Weinkopf, Claudia. 2006. "A Changing Role of Temporary Agency Work in the German Employment Model?" *International Employment Relations Review* 12(1): 77–94.

CHAPTER 2

Pay in Customer Services Under Pressure: Call Center Agents

Claudia Weinkopf

Call centers have certain features that set them apart from the other industries under study. They do not in fact constitute an industry as such, but a specific form of work organization. Telephone customer inquiries, which formerly used to be scattered among the various departments of companies, are centralized in a call center. Very frequently the goals behind this decision are to intensify the company's customer orientation, on the one hand, and to handle customer communication more cost-effectively and efficiently, on the other hand. Call centers may be either units within existing companies in various industries or new independent service providers that work for one or several principals. Only in the case of the latter organizational form can we speak of a new (emerging) "industry." Moreover, the tasks performed in call centers are by no means all simple and standardized: they can range from very simple processing to more complex clerical work or even highly skilled (academic) consulting.

The division of the call center market between independent service providers and in-house call centers, the dual objectives, and the broad range of activities, which may also include skilled tasks, explain why the range of wage levels and working conditions among call center agents appears to be extremely broad. According to the findings of a nationwide survey of call center managers, gross hourly wages of "typical" call center agents in Germany were between €6.00 (US$8.77) and (exceptionally) €40.00 (US$58.46) in 2004 (Holtgrewe 2005, 29). The average hourly wage was €11.30 (US$16.52), which is equivalent to just under 76 percent of the median for full-time employees and thus above the low-wage threshold in Germany.[1]

The broad variation in pay seems to be closely related to the fact that some (mainly in-house) call centers are firmly anchored in the German model, whereas others—namely, the large majority of independent service providers—operate more or less apart from the traditional institutions that typically frame pay levels and working conditions in Germany, such as collective agreements and works councils. This feature could well also be an important causal factor in the fast growth of the segment of independent service providers: many companies have set up call centers partly or mainly with the objective of cutting costs, and that is most simply achieved by outsourcing jobs to companies not bound by collective wage agreements. However, call centers are set up not only for cost-cutting reasons but often also with the aim of improving customer service and loyalty.

Wages in the call centers in the utilities and financial services sectors included in our study are frequently (and in some cases considerably) higher than this average figure. There are two reasons for the relatively high wages in these subsectors. First, call center agents' tasks in these industries are mainly carried out on a medium level of complexity or above. Second, the in-house call centers at least are subject to the same collective wage agreements as their parent companies, which also have typically strong works councils. Both factors help directly and indirectly to prevent or hinder purely cost-oriented strategies and instead favor the adoption of more quality-oriented strategies, such as restrictions on rigid monitoring methods, higher job security, and a preference for functional rather than numerical flexibility.

To date, practices in in-house call centers have even had (at least to some extent) repercussions on the external service provider segment. However, wage levels in the latter are on average 20 percent below those in in-house call centers, and costs in other areas (stemming, for instance, from lower company social expenditure, fewer days' leave, or longer working hours) are lower as well. In combination with intensified competition and attempts to reduce costs in the industries under study, this appears to create strong incentives for increased outsourcing, simultaneously placing considerable and increasing pressure on wage levels in in-house call centers. Our company case studies indicate how different companies react to these factors.

This chapter starts by presenting a brief overview of the call center "industry" and the case study sample. Taking as a starting point the different influence of industrial relations on in-house call centers and external service providers, I go on to focus on pay and working conditions in German call centers, paying particular attention to the im-

pact of collective agreements and works councils and the consequences of the intensified competition and cost pressures. The following section analyzes where commonalities and differences exist in
corporate strategies with regard to employee structure, the use of various options for increasing staff flexibility, and work organization and
seeks to explain these differences. Finally, I summarize the findings
and assess the prospects for job quality in German call centers.

THE CALL CENTER "INDUSTRY" AND THE COMPANY CASE STUDIES

With regard to the history of the German call center market, the public directory assistance of the former Deutsche Bundespost is often
cited as an early prototype of today's call centers. The first private call
centers in Germany were founded at the end of the 1970s to provide
mainly telemarketing services, followed in the 1980s by the call centers of the large mail-order companies. In the 1990s the German call
center market surged in various industries in response to both technological developments and commercial pressures. Around 80 percent of all call centers in Germany are assumed to have been established since 1992 (Kolinko 2002). In the second half of the 1990s,
call centers were one of the employment fields in Germany that
showed highly dynamic job growth. However, some people have
questioned whether the increasing number of call center jobs in Germany is really equivalent to a comparable increase in total employment. Critical voices have argued that a substantial proportion of the
new jobs may have replaced other jobs within the client companies
for which the call centers provide services. Positive effects on the labor market only emerge if the services provided really increased or if
a redistribution of labor took place (Michalke 1999, 26).

   The fact that call centers take so many different forms makes it almost impossible to trace their quantitative development by means of
existing statistics. Thus, for several reasons, all information on the
development of the "industry" generally has a high uncertainty factor. First, there is no precise definition of the term "call center." Katrin Arnold and Mariusz Ptaszek (2003, 40) point out, for example,
that about half of the companies referring to themselves as call centers do not use the standard technical systems such as automatic call
distribution (ACD) or computer telephony integration (CTI) (see the
glossary in the appendix). In-house call centers as parts of companies

operating in a number of different industries are difficult to identify. Thus, the available data usually rely on estimates, which differ considerably from one another in some respects. For instance, the figures for the number of call centers in Germany for the year 2000 vary between 2,450 and 4,000, and the number of employees in call centers between 148,000 and 357,000 (Weinkopf 2002).

Table 2.1 presents recent estimates by one of the leading call center associations (Deutscher Direktmarketing Verband 2006) on the development of German call centers between 1995 and 2006, including the number of employees and workplaces (typically called "seats"). In 2006, 380,000 employees were working in 5,700 call centers. It should be noted, however, that the sources of these data are not specified. Furthermore, the numbers take little if any account of the crisis in the market that has been reported recently, particularly in 2001–2002 (for example, dismissals by large providers such as Comdirect and Citibank and the insolvencies of several smaller firms; Kolinko 2002).

The lack of reliable statistical data on call center employment also makes it impossible to calculate the share of low wages in this particular "industry."[2] Against this background, this chapter frequently refers to the findings of a nationwide telephone survey of call center managers that was carried out in 2004 as part of the international Global Call Center Project (referred to here as the GCC survey).[3] Although the survey findings do not provide data on the current number of call centers in Germany, they do give an interesting insight into important structural characteristics of the companies and employees.

However, one factor must be borne in mind: the share of in-house call centers in this survey was only around one-third (Holtgrewe 2005, 5); that is a significantly lower estimate than other estimates, which put their market share at between 62 and 80 percent at the end of the 1990s (Bittner et al. 2000, 46). In another, more recent study, the authors report a share of some 44 percent for purely in-house call centers (ProfiTel 2006).[4] There are several possible explanations for these differences: an increasing trend toward the outsourcing of call center activities in recent years; the underrepresentation of in-house call centers in the GCC survey because, as parts of existing companies in various industries, they are difficult to identify; or diverging differentiation criteria between the call center types. For instance, making a clear distinction between outsourced subsidiaries and independent service providers (Scholten and Holtgrewe 2006, 6) appears sometimes to be rather difficult. Accordingly, the call center benchmark

Table 2.1 The Call Center Industry in Germany

Year	Number of Call Centers	Number of Employees	Number of Seats
1995		44,800	31,000
1996		85,100	44,800
1997		116,100	61,100
1998	1,600	150,500	79,200
1999	2,300	187,300	98,600
2000	2,750	224,800	108,300
2001	3,350	261,800	137,800
2002	3,750	280,000	150,000
2003	4,300	320,000	162,000
2004	4,900	330,000	170,000
2005	5,550	350,000	175,000
2006	5,700	380,000	190,000

Source: Author's compilation, from Deutscher Direktmarketing Verband (2006).

study (ProfiTel 2006) differentiates between in-house centers, independent service providers (15.8 percent), and "mixed centers" (40.6 percent), this last group being former in-house centers that have been outsourced and now also provide services for other companies. In this chapter, we differentiate only between in-house call centers, on the one hand, and external service providers that are financially independent and work for several client companies, on the other.

Regardless of these diverging definitions and distinctions, it is obvious that the share of in-house call centers in Germany is lower than in several other countries where the average proportion of this call center type is around 75 percent and as high as 86 percent in the United States. The higher proportion of outsourced or independent call centers in Germany could be put down to the fact that the incentives to engage external service companies are particularly high, since this offers the opportunity to undermine existing collective agreements in order to reduce costs. This assumption is backed up by the fact that—as shown later in the chapter—the impact of the typical institutions that shape employment relationships on external service providers is significantly weaker and wages are frequently considerably lower than in in-house call centers.

There are a number of interesting differences between the German call center market and that in the United States. For example, there is not yet a recognizable trend toward relocating and centralizing call centers in "remote areas" (Batt 2001, 428). In Germany physical proximity to the parent or customer companies is still a key criterion in the choice of location—even if such a location entails higher costs (Arnold and Ptaszek 2003, 45f). Specialization in specific customer segments also seems to be less advanced in Germany than in the United States, where less than one-fifth of call centers serve both business and private customers (Batt, Doellgast, and Kwon 2004, 2). In Germany, in comparison, this type constitutes a significant majority, accounting for 59.2 percent of the total (Holtgrewe 2005, 9). Employees' level of specialization in specific tasks or subject areas is different in the two countries: in contrast to the United States, German call centers still tend to prefer employees to have a broad range of possible tasks. Last not least, the transfer of call centers to other (low-wage) countries (offshoring) has not been an important issue so far in Germany, perhaps because only a few people in India, for example, are fluent in German. However, other regions such as Turkey, Eastern Europe, South Africa, and the Canary Islands are regarded as potentially appropriate locations for the offshoring of German call center activities (Pause 2005).

The call center case studies carried out in the course of our project focused on both in-house call centers and external service providers in two subsectors: financial services and utilities. The main reason for selecting financial services was that, according to numerous previous studies (Bittner, Schietinger, and Weinkopf 2002, 54; Holtgrewe 2005, 6), a considerable part of the overall call center market is concentrated in this area. Call centers in utilities are less significant quantitatively, but interesting for other reasons. For instance, there has been very little research on call centers in this area to date. The utilities industry, formerly part of the public sector, has been significantly affected by the restructuring measures put in place with the rise of privatization and deregulation in recent years. In the light of these factors, we were particularly interested in the effects of this development on the organization of call center services and their employees. In both subsectors, the focus was on inbound activities.[5]

THE SAMPLE AND THE METHODOLOGY

The focus of the study was on call center agents—those employees responsible for communication with customers. Six case studies in call centers, all in West Germany, were carried out over the course of the study—four in the utilities sector and two in the financial services sector.[6] The utilities case studies involved two in-house call centers and two external service providers; the two case studies in the financial services sector were of in-house call centers. The size of the call center units in our sample ranged from under twenty up to almost seven hundred employees.

Interviews were conducted with individuals at various levels within the companies (management, supervisors, team leaders, training officers, employees, works councils). The total number of interviewees in the case study companies was thirty-eight—ranging between one and up to ten per case. Most of the interviews lasted between one and two hours. With one exception, all case studies were carried out by two researchers.[7] In most cases, the companies also provided additional written material such as annual reports, presentations, and training guidelines. Further information came from context interviews with trade unions, temporary work agencies, and employees and works councils in other call centers, as well as from press and Internet research.

THE IMPACT OF INSTITUTIONS ON INDUSTRIAL RELATIONS

Although all call centers in Germany are subject to central statutory labor market regulations, there are considerable differences between in-house call centers and independent external service providers in the extent of trade union presence and worker representation. In-house call centers share an institutional framework with the companies to which they belong and thus are subject to the same collective agreements and have their workplace interests represented in similar ways. It should be borne in mind, however, that the scope and frequency of these agreements and representatives differ according to industry and company size: collective agreements and works councils in Germany are more widespread and tend to have a greater influence in the manufacturing sector than in some service industries, and firm size makes a difference as well. The utilities and financial services industries involved in our study traditionally have a high level of collective agreement obligations in Germany and are also regarded as sectors with above-average pay.

At the heart of the call center "industry," however, are the external service providers, which thus far have largely avoided being directly affected by the typical features of the German industrial relations system. One reason is that the industry is relatively new and the corresponding structures are developing slowly. Another reason, however, is that a central business concept of many external service providers is to operate outside of collectively agreed standards so as to provide services at lower cost. This is undoubtedly also one of the driving forces behind the growth of this market segment in Germany.

At the end of the 1990s, trade unions estimated the share of call centers with collective agreements at 50 to 60 percent (Meier 1999). In the German GCC survey, the share of call centers with collective agreements was even far smaller, at 25.7 percent; that low share is likely to be related to the relatively low proportion of in-house call centers in the sample. Of these, some 45.8 percent had collective agreements, whereas the large majority of the external service providers (over four-fifths) were not subject to collective agreements (Holtgrewe 2005, 13f). In those cases where a collective agreement did exist, the majority of in-house call centers had an agreement for the industry as a whole, whereas company-specific agreements predominated among external service providers (Scholten and Holtgrewe 2006, 29). In our case studies, in contrast, the proportion of call centers with collective agreements was significantly higher than this figure, at four out of six companies. Unsurprisingly, however, in light of the tendencies outlined here, the companies without collectively agreed wages were the two external service providers.

According to the findings of the GCC survey, works councils or other forms of employee interest representation exist in 45 percent of German call centers and are thus considerably more common than collective agreements. Here too, however, there are clear differences between the two basic types of call centers. Whereas works councils exist in 82 percent of in-house call centers, this is the case for only 22.2 percent of external service providers. The outsourced subsidiaries fall between these two figures, at 45 percent (Scholten and Holtgrewe 2006, 29), which could be due to the fact that they have in part retained the traditions of the parent company. In this respect, our sample deviated significantly: all call centers in the study had a works council. However, these bodies appeared to have less influence within the external service providers.

Thus, the German call center market comprises two separate segments. Whereas in-house call centers do not differ markedly from other industries because they are part of a company within their industry, many external service providers operate without direct trade union influence. The relatively minor significance of collective agreements in this market segment is also due to the fact that the actors required to promote them are either not represented or have little effect. German trade unions are typically industrial unions. Consequently, a number of different unions claim responsibility for call centers, and there has been some dispute over which of them should represent call center workers. There have been only a few individual cases of company agreements being set up for external service providers that work in several different industries to date. The conditions for concluding industrywide collective agreements—which have been achieved, for instance, in the Netherlands (de Grip, Sieben, and van Jaarsveld 2005) and Sweden (EIROnline 2001)—are rather unfavorable in Germany, partly because of the lack of suitable actors on the employers' side. The existing call center associations do not define themselves as employer associations responsible for collective bargaining procedures and are largely pursuing different objectives.[8]

In the late 1990, the trade unions launched numerous initiatives, workshops, and projects with the aim of focusing attention on working conditions in call centers and improving them. Most of these activities, however, have since been wound down, partly on the grounds that it is particularly difficult to raise the level of organization among call center employees and partly because the need for savings due to decreasing membership has forced the unions to concentrate on more promising areas.

As our company case studies illustrate in more detail, the existence of collective agreements and works councils is a key influence on pay, working conditions, and work organization in call centers. In addition to wages and special company payments, many collective agreements establish whether and to what extent employees are entitled to extra pay for working at certain unsocial hours. In the subsectors on which our study focuses, collective agreements also often contain agreements protecting existing employees in the event of internal relocations to other jobs or wage reductions when new pay systems are introduced (Bestandsschutz, right of continuance).[9] Additionally, on the basis of the Works Constitution Act (Betriebsverfassungsgesetz), works councils have relatively broad options for influencing important working conditions, such as individual workplace monitoring (Michalke 1999).

General industrial legislation, such as protection against wrongful dismissal, restrictions on the use of fixed-term employment contracts, nondiscrimination against part-time employees, and statutory annual leave, applies to all call centers. In some cases, however, the actual effectiveness of these regulations is influenced by whether works councils monitor their observance or whether additional collective agreements are in place. In cases where there is no collective agreement, for example, there is often no extra pay for night or weekend shifts.

One former potential restriction on call centers that operate for long hours was the Sunday work permit requirement. However, most Bundesländer passed general exceptions for all call centers several years ago (Bittner et al. 2000, 21). There are additional specific restrictions on call centers in Germany (as in several other countries) covering "cold calls"—unsolicited outbound calls to private households. Cold calling is not permitted without customers' written consent. However, it appears that it is not unusual for companies to violate this rule—and that such practices have substantially increased recently—because it is very difficult to effectively monitor such practices, which are also subject to rather low fines (Koch 2006).

The question of whether and to what extent the German institutional system of dual vocational training is relevant for call centers is contested. Ursula Holtgrewe and Jessica Scholten (2005, 10), for example, assume that "qualification in call centres . . . is de-institutionalised and turned into portfolios of firm-specific, short-term skills and ascribed personality traits." According to our assessment, however, blanket conclusions should be avoided in this area. Although specific vocational training courses for call center occupations were not introduced until 2005 and it is still impossible to predict to what extent call centers will make use of them in the future, existing studies do unanimously indicate that the vast majority of call center agents in Germany possess a completed vocational qualification in other areas. In fact, in most companies in our sample, such a qualification was an important selection criterion and the vocational skills learned on these training courses were often put to good use.

WAGES AND WORKING CONDITIONS

The establishment of call centers entails a new intra- or interdepartmental division of labor, which is frequently characterized by standardized and fragmented work tasks. This is the characteristic that often leads observers to describe call centers as prototypes of "neo-Taylorist" work organization in the service sector, and indeed, job quality in call centers (in terms of remuneration and working conditions) is often considered to be rather low. However, previous research has already underlined that it is inappropriate to lump all call centers together (see, for instance, Batt, Hunter, and Wilk 2002; Frenkel et al. 1999; Weinkopf 2006). An important question in this regard is the extent to which differences in the influence of the industrial relations system affect job quality. In Germany, recent surveys for the industry as a whole and the findings of our company case studies indicate that, in many cases, wages are above the low-wage threshold but are currently under considerable pressure. In relation to working conditions, this chapter goes into several selected aspects in detail, such as physical workplace conditions and technical equipment. Later I discuss other important elements, such as the use of different work forms, that we regard as key features of the companies' strategies.

Wages: Relatively High, but Under Pressure

The findings of the GCC survey showed that the range of gross hourly wages for "typical" agents in German call centers was between €6.00 and (exceptional) €40.00 in 2004 (Holtgrewe 2005, 29). The average hourly wage of €11.30 is equivalent to 75.6 percent of the German full-time median and is thus above the low-wage threshold. Comparing pay by type of call centers indicates that collective agreements have a positive impact on wage levels. The average hourly wage in in-house call centers of €13.19 (US$19.28) (88.3 percent of the median) is significantly higher than the average hourly wage at external service providers (€10.47 (US$15.31), or 70 percent of the median), which are considerably less likely to have collective agreements. A comparison between call centers with and without collectively agreed wages shows similar differences: mean hourly wages are €13.72 and €10.55 (US$20.06 and US$15.42), respectively (Holtgrewe 2005, 31).

The call centers in the utilities and financial services subsectors in which we carried out company case studies mainly offered jobs that were not at the lower end of the wage range. Most starting wages (not including extra payments) ranged between just under €11 (US$16) and more than €16 (US$23) gross per hour (approximately 73 to 107 percent of the median). The most striking exception was one of the two external service providers in our sample, which offered entry-level wages of only just over €6 (US$8.77) (40 percent of the median) and paid a maximum of slightly above €10 (US$14.62) gross (for agents who had been with the company for a long time and taken on additional responsibilities), which is roughly equivalent to the level of the low-wage threshold in Germany.[10] In contrast, the highest collectively agreed hourly wages in our sample that experienced agents could achieve after a certain length of employment amounted to more than €20 (US$29.24) (around 134 percent of the median). According to the available information, particularly low wages tend to be found in other subsectors with comparatively simple tasks, such as the mail-order industry, and are more frequently found in call centers located in East Germany.[11] From press reports and other sources, we know that gross hourly wages in these areas can be considerably lower, in some cases between €3 and €5 (US$4.39 and US$7.31) (20 to 33.5 percent of the German median wage).

On an annual basis and including extra payments such as Christmas bonuses, vacation pay, and performance bonuses—which differ from one company to the next but were paid in all cases but one—the pay of full-time agents in our sample ranged between €12,688 and €45,242 per year (US$18,549 and US$66,152).[12] The wage differences were thus considerable—in relation to the median wage for Germany as a whole, they varied between around 42 percent and just above 151 percent. As expected, the highest wages were paid by in-house call centers covered by collective wage agreements, and the lowest by the two external service providers that had no collective agreement covering pay rates.

One factor worth noting, however, is that with the exception of two call centers whose pay structures were transparent and relatively undifferentiated, there were some large wage differences between employees within the individual call centers that were not based on differences in responsibilities, experience, or job tenure. In the in-house call centers, these wage variations were primarily the result of the aforementioned legal protection of the status quo (Bestandsschutz), which ensures that employees will maintain their highest wage level even if they take on work that would actually be lower-paid due to a relocation within the company or the introduction of a new wage structure. In one company with low labor turnover and high employment stability, this law had led to employees being paid according to four different wage systems. This was also the only case study company that provided individual performance-based bonuses for completed sales (at a maximum level of one monthly wage per year).

In-company wage differences can also have entirely different causes. Until recently, the smaller external service provider in our sample that had no collective agreement had negotiated wages individually, so that the specific wage agreed on depended on the manager's "goodwill" and the employee's bargaining skills. This practice had led to considerable wage differences, and the works council regarded it as one of its most important tasks to increase transparency and fairness in wage setting.

In contrast, one of the in-house call centers set a positive example. After buying out some other companies, this company had considerable wage differences at its several locations, and managers saw that as a problem. Management therefore took the initiative and negotiated a collective agreement with the trade union providing for hourly wages of between 75 and 90 percent of the median for the agents, plus a relatively high annual bonus (up to two months' salary). All interviewees agreed that, because of the new agreement, employees were now better off—in some cases even by €250 to €300 per month (US$365 and US$439).

The collectively agreed wages in the other in-house call centers, however, were under considerable pressure. This pressure affected not only the call center employees but also the entire staffs of the companies that operated them. As a result of intensified competition (and for the utility companies, privatization as well), the relatively high pay that was traditional in both industries—which to some extent used public sector pay scales and pay awards as benchmarks—was being increasingly called into question. New collective agreements had since been made in all three companies, establishing less favorable conditions in many respects, including both wages and other working conditions (for example, bonuses, extra payments, and working hours). Initially, these new agreements often affected only new employees, because of the legal regulations protecting existing employees. In many cases, however, the claims of existing employees would be offset against future wage increases, reducing the differences between old and new employees over time.

The new collective agreements had also introduced additional pay grades at the lower end of the wage range. This change was generally justified on the grounds that the company would otherwise not be competitive, especially in the area of low-skill services. The trade union and works councils emphasized that they had agreed to this new development in order to reduce the huge incentives for more outsourcing of certain activities (including the call centers): "Otherwise we can't keep the jobs." The typical argument was that keeping the jobs under the roof of the parent company, even at the price of lower wages, at least had the advantage of retaining the additional benefits not offered by external service providers—in particular higher job security and more favorable working time standards.

Working Conditions

Working conditions in call centers are frequently thought to be rather unfavorable, owing, for instance, to the long operating hours, the high workloads, and the physical and mental stress of working on the telephone. Our case studies reveal, however, considerable differences between the companies and several attempts to provide better working conditions.

Call center operating hours do in fact tend to be long, but they varied greatly within our sample, ranging from normal or only slightly extended office hours (predominantly in utilities) to twenty-four hours a day, seven days a week (financial services). The latter, however, was only an option, and one that was very rarely used. In addition, staffing levels on night and weekend shifts were always very low—because customers tend to make very little use of services at these times, but also because some of the companies consciously set lower service targets (with regard to availability and quality) for these times. We identified clear differences in companies' approaches to staffing these shifts. Whereas some call centers expected all employees to take on night and weekend shifts, others made exceptions for specific groups of employees (such as single parents). In some cases, these times were covered solely by special teams or on a fundamentally voluntary basis, which appeared to work well—particularly if attractive bonuses were offered. There were also considerable differences in the provision of the legally mandated five-minute hourly breaks from the computer screen. Whereas this break was explicitly part of the shift planning in one company, all of the other call centers in our sample dealt with it "more flexibly."

In comparison to other call centers we know about from an earlier study, the design of the working spaces and workstations in our sample was mainly good. Most of the desks were large, with modern technical equipment. Only in two cases were the workplaces comparatively cramped or the technology not entirely up to date. In four out of six call centers, the employees had their own workstations that they could set up as they liked. In addition, all call centers in the sample had quite decent canteens and rooms for staff breaks. In some companies, employees were also offered free hot and cold drinks in these areas (and even fresh fruit in one case).

All the companies had advanced technical systems, which not only control the distribution of incoming calls but also generate a large amount of data and codes—for example, on the current service level, the average length of calls, or the number of available agents. These systems make it possible to evaluate employees' individual performance. In the majority of cases, however, these data were not used for individual performance assessment or disciplinary purposes but only for evaluations and communications on the team level. The average number of calls taken per hour was between 7.5 and 11.5 per agent, with an average length per call including follow-up processing of between three and eight minutes. The processing stage in the utility call centers tended to take slightly longer on average than in financial services.

In all call centers in the sample, working on the telephone and computer took up a large part of the total working hours. Only one company arranged for a systematic mix with other tasks: its call center employees now mainly worked as the back office for two external service providers. In the other cases, such work either hardly existed or was carried out by other employees. Surprisingly, the employees we interviewed hardly criticized the low share of nontelephone work.[13] Most of them appeared to assume that this was unavoidable in call centers.

Typically, the Achilles' heel of call center work is seen in the lack of opportunities for internal promotion—partly due to the usually flat hierarchies. In the companies in our sample, there were particularly few opportunities: in four out of the six cases, staffing levels were stable or even declining, and management did not always wish to recruit team leaders from among the agents. The possibilities for moving to other parts of the companies were also limited—at the external service providers because there were very few other areas, and at the in-house call centers because of job cuts across the companies.

And partly because of Germany's high unemployment rates, even the external labor market offered very few attractive alternatives in most cases.

HUMAN RESOURCE MANAGEMENT AND CORPORATE STRATEGIES

Our analysis of human resource management strategies in the sample call centers illustrates that despite similar market conditions, the companies operated very differently—for example, on the issue of outsourcing. What they had in common in several other areas, however, deviated from the typical patterns in other countries (particularly the United States) and also in part from other service industries in Germany. In the following section, we detail the employee structure, the use of various work and flexibility forms, the content of the work and employee discretion, and, finally, the dominant corporate strategies.

THE EMPLOYEES: WELL QUALIFIED AND NOT ALWAYS YOUNG

The public image of the typical call center agent is a young female with rather low qualifications. Although this profile does actually seem to fit the average call center employee in some countries, previous studies and our own company case studies indicate that the employee structure in Germany is, to varying degrees, rather different—particularly with regard to qualification levels, but also when it comes to the age structure.

It is correct, however, that women make up the majority of call center agents. According to the GCC survey, women constitute just under 72 percent of agents in Germany (Scholten and Holtgrewe 2006, 16), which is even slightly above the figure for the United States. In our case studies, women also made up the majority of agents in the companies, with two exceptions (both in utilities). The highest percentage by far (85.3 percent) was in an in-house call center in the financial services sector to which many female employees who previously made bookings manually had been transferred.

The qualification level of employees in German call centers, by contrast, is by no means low. More than three-quarters of call center agents in Germany have a vocational qualification, and 10.4 percent even have a university degree. A further 9.5 percent are university students (Scholten and Holtgrewe 2006, 16). Other studies have also found that few employees with low formal qualification levels are employed in German call centers (Bittner, Schietinger, and Weinkopf 2002; ProfiTel 2006). It is clear from our case studies that a vocational qualification was an important recruitment criterion for most companies. This did not necessarily have to be a relevant qualification within the industry in question; however, employees with a business qualification were often preferred in both subsectors. Thus, call centers make considerable use of the German vocational training system as a selection criterion. This could also be one reason why the initial training phase is relatively short in comparison to the United States and particularly the United Kingdom (Holman, Batt, and Holtgrewe 2007). Later we examine in greater depth our assessment that the comparatively high qualification level of employees in German call centers has direct and indirect effects on work organization and therefore also on job quality.

According to the findings of the U.S. GCC survey, the typical agent in the United States is thirty years old (Batt et al. 2004, 9), and findings for other countries also indicate that the large majority of call center employees are very young. One survey in Germany found that just under half of call center agents are under the age of thirty-one (soCa 2004, 9f). In the call centers in our sample, however, the picture was different. The percentage of over-thirties was between 56 percent and more than 92 percent. Although this did not apply in all the case studies, there is some evidence that there are significant differences between in-house call centers and external service providers with regard to the typical age of agents. The in-house call centers frequently recruit their staff among the companies' existing employees, and thus the average age tends to be higher. The generally low turnover levels at call centers also give us reason to assume that employees often "grow old" along with their call center.

External service providers and, particularly, call centers with a high level of student employees tend to have a high percentage of young employees. According to the German GCC survey, the average proportion of students, at 9.5 percent, is lower than generally assumed (Holtgrewe 2005, 36). This could well be due to the fact that many call centers employ no students at all. In our sample, this was the case for two companies. In the other companies, the percentage of students was between 7.8 and 19.6 percent.

According to our assessment, the comparatively high levels of formally qualified and older employees in in-house call centers are fostered by collective agreements and company regulations that, in protecting employees' existing rights and protecting them from dismissal, prevent a human resources policy designed along "purely market economy lines." Because in-house call centers in companies with highly effective representation of employee interests often have to accept employees from other areas of the company, external recruitment is possible only to a limited extent, if at all. Ultimately, this is not such a disadvantage, as one of our case studies illustrates. Although the financial services call center in question had never recruited externally and many of the agents originated from entirely different areas of the company, the company's customer service quality ranked very high in comparative studies.

SHIFT WORK, PART-TIME WORK, AND OUTSOURCING AS KEY STRATEGIES FOR INCREASED FLEXIBILITY

What instruments do call centers use most frequently to adjust staffing as flexibly and precisely as possible to variations in call volumes during the course of the day and the week? Our interviewees stated that these variations are generally relatively easy to anticipate on the basis of long-term experience, with the exception of unforeseeable events (for example, major power failures or press reports on security gaps in online banking). Especially in the larger call centers with long operating hours, staffing levels are controlled by more or less complicated shift systems. Additional flexibility is usually ensured by the use of both annual working time accounts and part-time employees.

The information on the percentage of part-time employees in German call centers varies. Whereas one study (ProfiTel 2006) concludes that part-timers constitute almost one-half of the workforce, the GCC survey puts the average part-time rate substantially lower, at 42.8 percent (Holtgrewe 2005, 20). In our case studies, we found a very broad range. Whereas the part-time rate was around 40 percent in four of the companies, the smallest in-house call center with operating hours similar to typical office hours had only 25 percent part-timers. In contrast, the large external service provider had by far the highest part-time level (78 percent) and used a special strategy of flexible working hours rather than working time accounts, which shifts the workload risk to the employees for the most part. The company mainly offered employment contracts with relatively low working-time volumes (for example, ten hours per week), but it could call on significantly more working hours as required, with the employee's consent.

It is noteworthy that German call centers—in contrast to companies in other service industries, such as retail and commercial cleaning—rarely make use of marginal part-time work with a low hourly volume (the so-called mini-jobs with monthly earnings of up to €400 (US$585)). According to one recent study, the level of mini-jobs in call centers is only 2.6 percent (ProfiTel 2006). In the GCC survey, some 10.5 percent of all positions were mini-jobs; however, more than 75 percent of call centers made no use whatsoever of this type of employment (Holtgrewe 2005, 19f). In our sample, only two companies used mini-jobs at all, and even then only occasionally. Moreover, without exception, the managers emphasized that this type of employment was not suitable for call centers, as it is not worth investing the relatively high training input for such low work volumes.

The second cornerstone of the call centers' flexibility strategies is undoubtedly outsourcing. This is indicated by the comparatively high level of external service providers among German call centers in comparison to other countries and by the findings of our case studies. However, we found considerable differences in this respect between the companies. The two external service providers benefited from their clients' outsourcing strategies, in both cases to a considerable degree, although they did emphasize that most commissions were for outbound calls, since many of their client companies still preferred to deal with their inbound business themselves.

Three of the four companies in our sample with in-house call centers cooperated with external service providers, although for very different purposes. The company with the highest wages among the in-house call centers had been outsourcing for several years and was doing so to an increasing extent. The two service providers it used, which paid significantly lower wages, had now taken over the major part of the company's total call volume. At the same time, the number of employees in the client's internal call center had been significantly reduced. The remaining staff now mainly carried out back-office tasks (for example, handling more complex and nonstandard customer inquiries and doing follow-up processing). Aside from a small team of students who were employed solely on the telephones, the vast majority of employees worked in the call center only a few days a month. In the event of an unexpectedly high call volume that the two service providers could not deal with, however, the company could react quickly by calling on the back-office employees. Thus, in this case, it was the client's employees who functioned as a buffer for fluctuations in call volumes rather than the external service providers, as is usually the case.

In the other two cases, only a small part of the call volume was processed by external service providers. One company used its external service provider only for one specific task; the other used its external services provider only at certain times in the evening and on the weekend in order to cut costs (mainly by not paying collectively agreed bonuses for these times). The management at this latter company gave a further argument, namely, that this arrangement was designed to reduce pressure on the company's own staff. The employees themselves, however, took a more ambivalent view. Some were glad that they no longer had to work until 11:00 PM; others had been able to integrate these hours into their private life well and regretted the loss of bonuses. The works council assumed that the initially strictly limited use of outsourcing was a test run for management, which may have intended to increase its use of outsourcing significantly in the future.

Regardless of the actual use of outsourcing in the companies, this option did have further far-reaching effects: as already mentioned, the new collective agreements in three of the four in-house call centers contained lower pay grades, to which the trade union and works councils had consented in order to reduce the companies' financial incentives for outsourcing. In some cases, it was argued that it would be possible to retain the companies' own call centers only by establishing a balanced mix of internal and external services. The outsourcing option thus exerted direct pressure on wages in in-house call centers, but could also contribute to maintaining at least some in-house capacities and improving the working conditions of the employees concerned (see also Doellgast 2005, 115).

The most significant of the other instruments for flexible staffing in call centers is the use of fixed-term employment contracts; according to the GCC survey, such contracts account for 20.1 percent of total employment on average (Scholten and Holtgrewe 2006, 15). All the call centers in our sample had fixed-term employment contracts, although the percentages were usually lower, at between 7.5 percent and just over 20 percent. Almost 60 percent of all employment contracts at the large external service provider, however, were fixed-term contracts, and the company always used every possible legal opportunity to extend temporary contracts for further terms before granting employees permanent contracts. This was intended to achieve the highest possible flexibility: the company would be able to cut excess personnel quickly in the event of the loss of major client commissions, which are typically offered for limited periods.

According to the findings of the German GCC survey, freelance workers without employment contracts (12.6 percent) and, to a lesser extent, temporary workers (4.9 percent) play a certain role in some call centers, although their use is concentrated in a relatively small number of call centers (Scholten and Holtgrewe 2006, 15). Freelancers were not used at all in our sample.[14] Temporary agency workers also played a quantitatively minor role—in contrast to the United Kingdom and the Netherlands (de Grip, Sieben, and Jaarsveld 2005). Although about half of the companies in our sample did use temps, they did so to a comparatively minor extent. In one case, temporary agency workers were mainly used as an additional instrument for recruiting and testing out new staff, whereas the other in-house call centers used temps to cover for staff shortages, which could not be covered by hiring new regular employees because management had imposed a general ban on recruitment.

Work Content and Employee Discretion

The tasks carried out by call centers range from simple information services (such as directory assistance) to very specialized consulting (for example, medical assistance provided by doctors). In our sample, the work mainly covered intermediate-level activities (clerical work): some inquiries were very simple to deal with (for example, address changes or direct debits), whereas others required specialized knowledge and experience (for example, being able to handle a wide range of different and sometimes very particular nonstandard customer inquiries). In both subsectors, the call center agents typically worked with company-specific software programs (SAP-based) for which standard computer skills were not sufficient. Although there was a certain level of specialization among the staff in a few cases, all the companies emphasized that they expected the agents to be capable of processing a broad range of different customer inquiries. The employees were expected to avoid passing on inquiries as far as possible and to process a high percentage of calls to their conclusion. In combination, these statements indicate that the activities were at least of moderate complexity, with a particular emphasis on employees' functional flexibility. In the United States, in contrast, there appears to be a strong tendency toward segmenting call center activities according to customer groups and different types of tasks. Batt (2001, 428f) remarks that this creates scope for greater differentiation of wages and demands on agents ("sorting mechanism for the demand of skill") and increases efficiency. In contrast, one advantage of the dominant strategy in Germany of making greater use of employees' functional flexibility is that such employees can cope better than highly specialized agents with variations in the volume of work and in the type of customer inquiry.

Further indicators of the complexity level of activities are the length of the initial training period and the time required until employees become proficient on the job. Most companies in our sample stated that it took at least six months until new employees reached full proficiency. In one case, it was pointed out that it actually took four to five years for agents to have full command of the entire range of possible tasks. These findings partially contradict the results of the international GCC surveys, according to which the average length of these periods is shorter in Germany than in several other countries. The differences between Germany and the United Kingdom are particularly marked, and slightly less so in the case of the United States (Holman, Batt, and Holtgrewe 2007). For instance, the average period until agents can work fully independently in the United States, at twenty weeks, is almost double the length in Germany (11.1 weeks). In the United Kingdom, more than 50 percent of call centers give a figure of more than twenty-four weeks for this initial period, whereas the same statistic is considerably lower in Germany, at less than 16 percent. It must also be taken into account, however, that the initial training input also depends on the educational level of new employees (see Batt 2002, 588). If this level is relatively high, as in Germany, shorter training periods may be sufficient to prepare agents for complex tasks.

This correlation is best illustrated by the example of an in-house call center that traditionally only recruited internally. In recent years new recruits had mainly been young employees who had just completed a three-year specialized vocational training program within the company (as bank clerks or office clerks). Moving to the call center was currently the only option for remaining employed at the company. For the employees in question, this option frequently failed to meet their wishes and expectations, particularly because the pay was relatively low. From the point of view of the call center management, however, this recruiting method had the advantage that new staff required very little specific initial training because they already possessed all the necessary specialized and company-related knowledge and skills and had already spent several months in the call center during their vocational training programs.

In an international comparison, the GCC findings indicate that employees have above-average scope for independent action and decisionmaking (discretion) in Germany; only Denmark has an approximately comparable level. Whereas 38 percent of call centers in Germany grant "considerable discretion," this level is considerably lower in the United Kingdom (11 percent) and especially in the Netherlands (8 percent) (Holman, Batt, and Holtgrewe 2007).[15] Almost the same applies to the United States: "We found that call center workers had very low levels of discretion at work" (Batt, Doellgast, and Kwon 2004, 18).

The findings of Virginia Doellgast (2005) point in a similar direction. Her research on the basis of German-American comparisons found that "innovative work practices" (fewer binding scripts and less-rigid monitoring, for instance) are significantly more widespread in Germany than in the United States. In our opinion, this could be due to several mutually conducive influences. The majority of call center employees in Germany are well qualified and turnover is frequently low, partly owing to corporate strategies and partly owing to the influence of works councils and collective agreements (particularly in in-house call centers). Longer job tenure and experience provide good conditions for granting employees greater discretion and successfully implementing "innovative work practices."

The situation among the external service providers, however, is less clear-cut. Those independent call centers that work on a mainly quality-oriented basis tend to follow the strategies of the in-house call centers, whereas a second segment focuses predominantly on cutting costs, frequently taking higher labor turnover rates into account. According to the German GCC survey, turnover is considerably higher in external service providers than in in-house call centers, particularly with respect to dismissals: accounting for 21 percent of turnover, dismissals are more than ten times more frequent in external service providers than in in-house call centers (Holtgrewe 2005, 42).

THE DOMINANT HUMAN RESOURCE STRATEGY: HIGH INVOLVEMENT, BUT WITH VARYING LEVELS OF CONCESSIONS

As mentioned earlier, call centers pursue differing objectives, which tend to be contradictory: on the one hand, reducing costs, and on the other hand, increasing service quality and customer loyalty. In general, both objectives play a role, but the focus differs from one company to the next. This corresponds with the usual ideal-typical distinction in the literature between the two poles of "mass production and high-involvement (or high-performance) work systems" (Appelbaum and Batt 1994).

Typical characteristics of strategies based on mass production or a strong cost orientation are a high level of standardization, low demands on agents, little agent discretion, a high level of control and monitoring, and low investment in training (Batt 2001). None of our cases can be placed in this category without reservation, but the clearest emphasis on cost-cutting was observed in the large external service provider, which had a competitive strategy characterized by the motto "highest possible quality at low cost." In this company, low wage levels were accompanied by comprehensive use of various instruments for increasing staff flexibility—particularly high rates of fixed-term employment contracts and part-time work, which was also very flexibly structured in favor of the company. This was alleviated only by the fact that the contracts with client companies also contained binding minimum quality requirements (see also Doellgast forthcoming).

The other call centers in our sample described their strategies as mainly "quality-oriented," which tended to be in line with their human resource management strategies: they relied on qualified staff and their high functional flexibility, high employment stability, and relatively good working conditions. These companies can be categorized as the "high-involvement" type: "Firms pursuing this approach are likely to retain higher-skilled employees, design jobs giving employees greater discretion, and provide commitment-enhancing incentives such as investment in training and employee development, performance-based pay, and employment security" (Batt 2001, 431).

However, as we have already pointed out, there were some significant differences within this group in pay and working conditions as well as in the extent of their use of flexible work forms. The differences in work organization and the extent of employee discretion, in contrast, were minor. In some cases, agents could decide independently when to take their breaks, and they had some influence over the scheduling of their working hours. Furthermore, they had a relatively high level of discretion in their communication with customers. However, the point at which tasks were carried out was mainly determined by the incoming customer calls, which were diverted to the agents via the ACD system. The findings of an earlier survey of German call center agents emphasize this assessment: only 27 percent of interviewees agreed with the statement that they could influence the distribution of work, and only 22 percent stated that they were able to influence the form of their direct working environment (John and Schmitz 2002, 15).

With the exception of the in-house call center that now carried out mainly back-office tasks, the strategy of creating a broader mix of activities, which was widely discussed in Germany a few years ago and called for by the trade unions in particular in order to improve working conditions (Mola and Zimmermann 2001), did not play a role in the case study companies. We found problem-solving groups, quality circles, or self-organized teams in a few companies only, and in rather underdeveloped forms, although more than one-third of the managers interviewed for the German GCC survey reported adopting innovative approaches of this kind (Scholten and Holtgrewe 2006, 27ff). In our view, this might be due to the fact that managers tend to exaggerate when responding to questions on the use of innovative human resource instruments.

SUMMARY AND CONCLUSIONS

In contrast to the other industries and target occupations under investigation, it is impossible to assess the incidence of low wages among call center employees because of the different types of call centers and the lack of reliable data. Among the external providers of call center services registered as call centers in the statistics of the Federal Employment Services, around one-half of the employees have hourly earnings below the low pay threshold (see table 1A.1). This is at least a slight indicator that low pay is relatively widespread in that market segment.

Our analysis drawing on company case studies in financial services and utilities has shown that the quality of call center jobs in these subsectors is frequently relatively good and that low pay is not very widespread, for a number of reasons. Depending on the tasks required, the demands are by no means low, which is also reflected in the employees' relatively high level of vocational training. In-house call centers, in which collective agreements and works councils are relatively widespread, are especially likely to offer decent working conditions and relatively high pay. The presence of unions and employee representative bodies helps in various ways to prevent companies from adopting cost-oriented strategies and encourages them to implement more quality-oriented strategies. Even among the external service providers, whose market success is frequently based on providing call center services at lower cost, there is evidence of at least the beginnings of a stronger process of institutionalization. An increasing number of companies are members of regional or national associations, which serve as platforms for dialogue or carry out joint public relations work. In some cases, there are also internal interest representation bodies, which may improve the chances for improving working conditions or even for concluding company-specific collective agreements.

Our case studies have also shown, however, that quality-oriented high-involvement strategies with comparatively high wages are currently coming under increasing pressure, owing mainly to increased competition and a predominance of cost-cutting strategies. The possibility of saving costs by means of outsourcing has a dual effect in this respect. Either companies actually use this option and outsource at least part of their total call volume to external service providers, or they achieve wage cuts in in-house call centers (and often across the whole company) simply through the threat of outsourcing. In some cases, both options are even combined. The trade unions and works councils, at least in the subsectors involved in our study, appear to be less and less capable of preventing this. Virginia Doellgast and Ian Greer (2007, 70) describe this as "an increasingly complex mix of firm, sectoral and occupational bargaining structures"—with some companies also using "the threat of vertical disintegration to win concessions in-house." The results of a recent benchmark indicate that, on average, the wages of call center agents decreased by 5 percent between 2004 and 2006, and among team leaders even by 10 percent (ProfiTel 2006).

Whether and to what extent attempts to obtain such concessions will become more widespread is also partly determined by the demands that client companies make of their external service providers. In our sample, some of the companies hoped that external call centers would provide comparatively good service quality at lower cost. This could lead to external service providers paying greater attention to the quality of their services and tending to follow the human resource strategies of the in-house call centers—for example, by also emphasizing a high vocational training level for employees and low turnover. Other companies, however, deliberately exchanged a loss of quality through outsourcing for lower costs. Under these conditions, external service providers can maintain their strong cost orientation, accompanied by low wage levels, comparatively high labor turnover, and extensive use of various strategies for increased flexibility. Or they may even be forced by their clients' demands to seek further opportunities for savings, which further intensifies the pressure on wages.

From our point of view, it is still open as to which combination of these differing strategies will be used in the future and how this will affect the quality of jobs in German call centers. As far as wages are concerned, we expect a trend toward a more compressed wage structure, that is, a decline in very low and very high wages. A prominent example of a substantial wage-cutting strategy was the conflict in the spring of 2007 at Deutsche Telekom, where no fewer than fifty thousand customer service employees will be shifted to a new service unit not subject to the usual collectively agreed pay levels. The reason emphasized by management was that the current pay level was substantially higher than that of competitors. The compromise found after several weeks of strikes organized by the trade union Vereinigte Dienstleistungsgewerkschaft (Ver.di) and the works council includes slightly reduced wage cuttings for current employees (6.5 percent less instead of 9 percent less), but an extension of weekly working time (without wage compensation) from thirty-four hours up to thirty-eight hours, as originally intended by management. Additionally, the job quality for new entrants will be downgraded substantially: Entry wage levels will be reduced considerably—from €30,000 (US$43,862) or even more to between €21,400 and €23,200 per annum (US$31,288 and

US$33,920) (see Frankfurter Rundschau 2007; Mitteldeutscher Rund-funk 2007), which is only slightly above the low-wage threshold. It remains to be seen whether this strategy will in fact be compatible with management's second goal: increasing the quality of services in order to stop the ongoing loss of customers. It seems more likely that after Deutsche Telekom, one of the better-off companies in Germany, has been successful in pushing through substantial deteriorations of employment standards, other call centers with comparatively high wage levels will try to reach similar concessions.

With regard to work organization, one of the questions that arise concerns the extent to which German call centers will follow the American trend toward stronger segmentation by task and customer group or continue to make use of employees' high functional flexibility. The latter strategy has had the advantage of enabling German call centers to react more flexibly to variations in customer frequency, and it has efficiency benefits in other areas. If German call centers continue to take this approach, high-involvement strategies would continue to be of great significance to them, and such strategies might be further encouraged by increasing customer demands for high service quality, which could lead to greater competition for qualified staff in the future.

Beyond this uncertainty over future developments, it remains noteworthy from a gender perspective that call center work seems to be relatively attractive for women in Germany, in comparison with the other occupations and industries under study, many of which also have high percentages of female employees. The relatively higher attractiveness of call center work is due first to the type of working contracts on offer: whereas in several other service industries (for example, retail, commercial cleaning, and hotels) mini-jobs with short working hours and maximum monthly wages of €400 (US$585) are becoming increasingly widespread, call centers tend to offer far better opportunities for part-time or even full-time work subject to social insurance. Second, wages in call centers are frequently higher than in other typically female industries, and higher wages, in combination with longer working hours, increases the opportunities to earn an independent living. In this context, it is worth noting that female median wages (even in full-time employment) in Germany are still at least 20 percent lower than those of men. This is by far one of the largest gender pay gaps in the EU-15 (Bundesministerium für Familie, Senioren, Frauen, und Jugend 2005). Whereas the average hourly wage in call centers only marginally exceeds the low-wage threshold for men, call center work frequently offers women, in contrast, still comparatively high wages.

APPENDIX: GLOSSARY OF CALL CENTER TERMS

In-house call center: A call center that is part of a larger company in various industries

External or independent service provider: A specialized subcontractor that provides call center services for several client companies

Inbound calls: Incoming calls initiated by customers

Outbound calls: Outgoing calls initiated by call center agents

Automatic call distribution (ACD): A telephone facility that manages incoming calls and distributes them to agents according to certain rules

Computer telephony integration (CTI): An advanced technical system to manage and handle incoming calls—that is, to connect them with the customer database

NOTES

1. See the overview on the median wages of full-time employees in Germany in chapter 1. Here I refer to the figures for Germany as a whole— that is, median wages of €14.94 per hour (US$21.84), €2,492 per month (US$3,643), and €29,904 per annum and the respective low-wage thresholds of €9.96 per hour and €1,661 per month (US$43,716) (see table 1.1).

2. This is also the reason why the calculations presented in chapter 1 do not include call center activities. The only exception is table 1A.1, which contains the share of low-paid full-time employees in call centers who are registered in this statistical category—mainly the segment of external service providers. Thus, the reported rate of 52.63 percent earning low wages should not be regarded as applicable to all call centers but only as a rough estimation indicating that low wages are relatively widespread in the more or less unregulated subsector of independent providers.

3. The network behind this project—directed by Rosemary Batt—carried out comparable surveys in many different countries. For an internationally comparative analysis of the findings, see Holman, Batt, and Holtgrewe (2007).

4. The German GCC survey distinguishes between in-house call centers, "outsourced subsidiaries," and "service contractors," which make up the majority at 53.6 percent (Holtgrewe 2005, 5).

5. It is often assumed that the majority of companies in Germany, about two-thirds, are (mainly) inbound and that only one-third are (mainly) outbound. The GCC survey puts this ratio at 70 to 30 percent (Holtgrewe 2005, 12).

6. However, the reference values used to assess wage levels relate to the median wages for Germany as a whole, since the GCC survey used for purposes of comparison makes no distinction between East and West Germany.

7. Special thanks to my colleague Bettina Hieming for her very efficient support in this regard.

8. Their activities include—among other things—organizing annual conferences, developing guidelines for training courses, issuing benchmarks, and publishing websites, newsletters, and several industry-specific magazines.

9. In one collective agreement, this was formulated as follows: "More favorable working conditions to which an employee is entitled through a company agreement or on the basis of a specific employment contract shall remain in place."

10. This is an estimate, since the management of this company did not allow any precise statements on wage levels. When we tried to get access to this information from another external call center, our request was denied because the wage level was to remain a "company secret." This experience highlights the fact that wage costs are frequently a key competitive factor in the external service provider segment.

11. The complexity of the tasks is not decisive, however, in every case. For example, we know of a subcontractor in the field of market and opinion research who pays very low hourly starting wages (€5 gross), although the requirements are by no means low. The company appears to be exploiting the fact that a large number of students and high unemployment rates have given the region an abundant labor supply.

12. Notably, these amounts did not include extra pay related to individual circumstances (for example, pay on the basis of the number of an employee's children was available in four cases) or premiums for working "unsocial hours," which was particularly common at the two call centers in financial services.

13. For a broader view of employees' individual evaluations of the quality

and constraints of call center work based on a written survey among call center agents in Germany, see Weinkopf (2006).

14. However, we know from context interviews that "bottom feeders" sometimes use freelancers as a further cost-cutting option if the regional labor market allows them to do so.

15. According to managers, German call center agents mainly have high levels of discretion in "interaction with customers" (56.5 percent have "considerable" or "very considerable" discretion), taking breaks (48.4 percent), and handling "unexpected customer requests" (39.2 percent), "daily work tasks" (35.3 percent), and "the pace of work" (34.2 percent) (Holtgrewe 2005, 22).

REFERENCES

Appelbaum, Eileen, and Rosemary Batt. 1994. *The New American Workplace: Transforming Work Systems in the United States.* Ithaca, N.Y.: ILR Press.

Arnold, Katrin, and Mariusz Ptaszek. 2003. "Die deutsche Call Center-Landschaft: Regionale Disparitäten und Arbeitsmarktstrukturen" ["The German Call Center Landscape; Regional Disparities and Labor Market Structures"]. In *Immer Anschluss unter dieser Nummer: Rationalisierte Dienstleistung und subjektivierte Arbeit in Call Centern [Always Connected Under this Number. Rationalised Service and Subjectified Work in Call Centers],* edited by Frank Kleemann and Ingo Matuschek. Berlin: edition sigma.

Batt, Rosemary. 2001. "Explaining Wage Inequality in Telecommunications Services: Customer Segmentation, Human Resource Practices, and Union Decline." *Industrial and Labor Relations Review* 34(2A): 425–49.

———. 2002. "Managing Customer Services: Human Resource Practices, Quit Rates, and Sales Growth." *Academy of Management Journal* 45(3): 587–97.

Batt, Rosemary, Virginia Doellgast, and Hyunji Kwon. 2004. *The U.S. Call Center Industry 2004: National Benchmarking Report: Strategy, HR Practices, and Performance.* Ithaca, N.Y.: Cornell University Press.

Batt, Rosemary, Larry W. Hunter, and Steffanie Wilk. 2002. "How and When Does Management Matter? Job Quality and Career Opportunities for Call Center Workers." In *Low-Wage America: How Employers Are Reshaping Opportunity in the Workplace,* edited by Eileen Appelbaum, Annette Bernhardt, and Richard J. Murnane. New York: Russell Sage Foundation.

Bittner, Susanne, Marc Schietinger, and Claudia Weinkopf. 2002. *Zwischen Kosteneffizienz und Servicequalität—Personalmanagement in Call Centern und im Handel [Between Cost Efficiency and Service Quality—HR Management in Call Centers and Retail Trade].* Instituts Arbeit und Technik series, volume 22. München/Mering, Germany: Hampp.

Bittner, Susanne, Marc Schietinger, Jochen Schroth, and Claudia Weinkopf. 2000. *Call Center—Entwicklungsstand und Perspektiven: Eine Literaturanalyse [Call Centers—State of Development and Perspectives. A Literature Review]*. Gelsenkirchen, Germany: Institut Arbeit und Technik.

Bundesministerium für Familie, Senioren, Frauen, und Jugend. 2005. "Gender-Datenreport: 1. Kommentierter Datenreport zur Gleichstellung von Frauen und Männern in der Bundesrepublik Deutschland" ["Gender Data Report. Commented Data Report on the Equality of Women and Men in Germany"]. Provided by the Deutsche Jugendinstitut, in cooperation with the Statistischen Bundesamt, under the direction of Waltraud Cornelißen. November 2, 2005, München, Germany. Accessed at http://www.bmfsfj.de/Publikationen/genderreport/root.html.

De Grip, Andries, Inge Sieben, and Danielle van Jaarsveld. 2005. "Employment and Industrial Relations in the Dutch Call Center Sector." Maastricht, Germany: Research Center for Education and the Labor Market.

Deutscher Direktmarketing Verband. 2006. *Wirtschaftszahlen im Bereich Direktmarketing/Telefonmarketing [Economic Data for Direct Marketing/Telephone Marketing]*. Wiesbaden, Germany: Deutscher Direktmarketing Verband. Accessed at http://www.ddv.de/downloads/WirtschaftsfaktorCall Center.pdf.

Doellgast, Virginia. 2005. "Regulating the Flexible Workplace: Union Strategies Toward Call Center Outsourcing in the United States and Germany." In *Neue Medien im Alltag: Befunde aus den Bereichen: Arbeit, Lernen, und Freizeit [New Media in Everyday Life: Findings from the Ranges: Work, Learning, and Spare Time]*, edited by Astrid Schütz, Stephan Habscheid, Werner Holly, Josef Krems, and G. Günter Voss. Berlin: Pabst.

———. Forthcoming. "Collective Bargaining and High Involvement Management in Comparative Perspective: Evidence from U.S. and German Call Centers." *Industrial Relations*.

Doellgast, Virginia, and Ian Greer. 2007. "Vertical Disintegration and the Disorganization of German Industrial Relations." *British Journal of Industrial Relations* 45(1): 55–76.

EIROnline. 2001. "First Collective Agreement Signed for Call Centers and Telemarketing." Accessed at http://www.eurofound.europa.eu/eiro/2001/02/inbrief/se0102183n.htm.

Frankfurter Rundschau. 2007. "Telekom will Gehalt kürzen: Einschnitte bei Berufsanfängern" ["Telekom Wants to Cut Wages. Reductions for New Entrants"]. FR-Ausgabe, April 3, 2007. Accessed at http://www.axeltroost.de/article/953.telekom_will_gehalt_kuerzen.html.

Frenkel, Stephen J., Marek Korczynski, Karen Shire, and May Tam. 1999. *On the Front Line: Organization of Work in the Information Society*. Ithaca, N.Y.: ILR Press.

Holman, David, Rosemary Batt, and Ursula Holtgrewe. 2007. *The Global*

Call Center Report: International Perspectives on Management and Employment. Ithaca, N.Y.: ILR Press.

Holtgrewe, Ursula. 2005. "Call Centers in Germany: Preliminary Findings from the Global Call Center Project—Germany." Report for the Russell Sage Foundation (April). Duisburg, Germany.

Holtgrewe, Ursula, and Jessica Scholten. 2005. "Call Centers in a Coordinated Economy: Flexible Skill, Skilled Flexibility." Contribution to workshop 1, "ICT and Skill Change" at the NOW/SISWO conference "ICT, the Knowledge Society, and Changes in Work." June 9–10, 2005, The Hague, Netherlands.

John, Hester, and Eva Schmitz. 2002. "Mitarbeitermotivation im Call Center. Ergebnisse der Mitarbeiterbefragung 2001" ["Employees' Motivation in Call Centers. Results of an Employee Survey 2001"]. Ergebnisse Forschungsprojekt FREQUENZ. Personalmanagement—Call Center und Handel. Band 2. Bonn.

Koch, Moritz. 2006. "Zwielichtige Geschäfte am Telefon: Werbeanrufe sind verboten, dennoch nutzen viele Unternehmen die umstrittene Marketingmethode: Verbraucherschützer ratlos" ["Shady Deals on the Phone. Cold Calls are Prohibited but Many Companies Use the Disputed Marketing Instrument. Consumer Protections Helpless"]. *Süddeutsche Zeitung* June 22-23, 2006, 29.

Kolinko. 2002. "Hotlines: Call Center Untersuchung" ["Hotlines. Call Center Study"]. Accessed at http://www.nadir.org/nadir/initiativ/kolinko/lebuk/d_lebuk.htm.

Meier, Christine. 1999. "Strategien zur Verbesserung der Arbeitsbedingungen in Call Centern aus gewerkschaftlicher Sicht" ["Strategies to Improve the working Conditions in Call Centers from a Union Perspective"]. Lecture on the occasion of the press conference, "Arbeit im Call Center: Arbeitsplatz der Zukunft mit Schattenseiten" der Redaktion „Computer-Fachwissen für Betriebs- und Personalräte", June 15, 1999, Frankfurt, Germany.

Michalke, Friedhelm. 1999. "Handlungsanleitung für Betriebs- und Personalräte" ["Guidelines for Works Councils"]. *Gewerkschaftliche Praxis* 1(2): 22–46.

Mitteldeutscher Rundfunk. 2007. "Tarifkonflikt: Ver.di und Telekom geben Einigung bekannt" ["Collective Bargaining Conflict. Ver.di and telekom Announce Agreement"]. Press release of June 20, 2007. Accessed at http://www.mdr.de/mdr-info/4608457.html.

Mola, Eva, and Eberhard Zimmermann. 2001. "Arbeitsorganisation im Call Center: Chancen einer menschenzentrierten Arbeitsgestaltung" ["Work Organization in Call Centers—Opportunities of a Human-Oriented Work Design"]. In *Arbeitsorganisation im Call Center: Teamarbeit mit qualifizierten Beschäftigten [Work Organization in Call Centers: Team Work with*

Qualified Employees]. Meeting documentation from Hans-Böckler-Stiftung, Kooperationsbüro Multimedia und Arbeitswelt, and TBS beim DGB NRW e.V.

Pause, Christoph. 2005. "Standorte im fernen Ausland können das Unternehmen stärken" ["Subsidiaries Abroad May Strengthen the Company"]. *Teletalk* 2: 22ff.

ProfiTel. 2006. *Die Call Center Benchmarkstudie 2006 [The Call Center Benchmark Study 2006]*. Hamburg, Germany: ProfiTel.

Scholten, Jessica, and Ursula Holtgrewe. 2006. "The Global Call Center Industry Project: Deutschland: Erste Ergebnisse der Telefonumfrage für Deutschland" ["The Global Call Center Industry Project—Germany. First Results of the German Survey"]. Duisburger Beiträge zur soziologischen Forschung 2/2006: Duisburg. Accessed at http://soziologie.uni-duisburg .de/forschung/DuBei_2_2006.pdf.

soCa. 2004. *Die soCa-Beschäftigtenbefragung: Ausgewählte Daten [The soCa Employee Survey—Selected Data]*. Bremen, Germany: soCa.

Weinkopf, Claudia. 2002. "Call Center Work: Specific Characteristics and the Challenges of Work Organization." *Transfer* 8(3): 456–66.

———. 2006. "German Call Centers Between Service Orientation and Efficiency: 'The Polyphony of Telephony.'" In *Developments in the Call Center Industry: Analysis, Changes, and Challenges*, edited by John Burgess and Julia Connell. London: Routledge.

CHAPTER 3

Wild West Conditions in Germany?!
Low-Skill Jobs in Food Processing

Lars Czommer

Wild West Conditions in Germany" ran the headline of a January 2005 article in the German weekly *STERN* on the German meat processing industry. The quotation came from Danish trade union boss Peter Bostrup, who had said, referring to Tulip and Danish Crown, the two Danish meat processing companies that had transferred many jobs to Germany in order to cut costs: "It's like the Wild West in Germany and they're paying starvation wages there." On the same subject, the largest Danish daily newspaper, *Jyllands-Posten*, wrote: "German abattoir workers cost a third as much as Danish workers." The background to these stories is that, since 2004, Eastern European contract workers have been recruited in increasing numbers on "dumping" wages to work in the German meat processing industry. From a purely legal point of view, the same thing could also happen in Denmark, but, according to a statement by a spokeswoman for Danish Crown, such a recruitment strategy is out of the question: "We have collective agreements, and we're sticking to them" (Borchert 2005). In Germany, on the other hand, press reports suggest that some Eastern European contract workers in abattoirs are now being paid just €1.90 (US$2.78) per hour and that these wage levels have led to the loss of many jobs (Lorscheid 2005; Meichsner 2007).

Although such practices have not yet spread to the food industry as a whole, the situation in many abattoirs highlights the fact that it is much more difficult to implement minimum pay standards in Germany than in many other countries. Against this background, voices are increasingly being raised (even in the center-right Christian democratic parties, which tend to have a critical stance on minimum wages) in favor of generally binding minimum standards for the meat processing industry that could be applied even to foreign contractors and their workers by incorporating the industry into the Posted

Workers Act (*Ad-Hoc-News* 2007). However, the meat processing industry fails to meet one important precondition for such legislation: there is no national collective agreement that could be declared generally binding; there is not even an employers' association with which the food and restaurant workers' union, NGG (Gewerkschaft Nahrung-Genuss-Gaststätten), could negotiate such a collective agreement. The meat processing industry is a glaring illustration of the fact that, in low-wage sectors in particular, Germany's collective agreement system has become full of holes. Indeed, in many industries that system has never been able to ensure universal compliance with minimum standards. In other parts of the German food industry, such as the confectionary sector, the situation is somewhat more favorable. It is true that low wages are not exactly a rarity there either, but at least there are still industrywide collective agreements that help to prevent abuses such as those in the meat processing industry, and particularly in abattoirs. However, low-skill jobs in both these subsectors of the food industry are exposed to very considerable competitive and cost pressures, which of course have consequences for employees' pay and working conditions.

This chapter begins with a brief survey of the industry and the case studies. I go on to focus on the effects of the strong competitive pressures to which producers in the meat processing and confectionary industries are exposed. The next section builds on this analysis and looks at the institutional environment and pay in the two industries and how they have developed over time. That is followed by a section in which the companies investigated are assigned to various strategy types and the internal and external strategies they adopt to meet their competitive challenges are revealed. The focus here is on the working and employment conditions of production workers in the lower wage brackets. Finally, the results of the investigation are summarized with a view to assessing the future significance of low-skill occupations in the industries under investigation.

THE INDUSTRY AND THE CASE STUDIES

The German food industry has a sales volume of over €130 billion (US$190 billion) and an export ratio of 14.8 percent (NGG 2006a), making it one of the most important sectors in Germany in terms of economic and employment policy. Within the manufacturing industries, the food-processing industry comes in fourth, behind the chemistry, machine tool, and metal industries. The German food-processing industry is currently in the process of far-reaching structural change. Like other industries, the food-processing industry, with its focus on small and medium-sized enterprises (SMEs), is increasingly feeling the effects of the weak economy. It has been apparent for a while that the German food market is stagnating, with surplus capacity accumulating in a number of subsectors. Future markets are expected to emerge primarily in trade with the new European Union member states. The need to open up new markets and, at the same time, hold out against foreign competition heightens the importance of the content of future EU directives in the areas of food safety and issues of foreign trade and customs legislation. Areas that are expected to see rising growth rates are those involved with producing and selling convenience foods, health foods, and organic products.

Although the concentration process in Germany is not nearly as far advanced as it is in Denmark, the Netherlands, and the United States, the pressure toward concentration is constantly growing, largely because more and more financially strong multinational companies (MNCs) are pushing their way onto the German market. Takeovers and mergers have so far been concentrated primarily in the abattoir and meat processing subsectors and in the dairy and bakery industries. The German food-processing industry continues to have a large proportion of SMEs. In 2005 its subsectors comprised 5,925 companies employing a total of 521,727 people (average size: 88 employees).[1] Around 61 percent of employees worked in SMEs with fewer than 250 employees. By contrast, only 21 percent of employees were employed in businesses with more than 500 employees, which is a much lower share than in the economy as a whole (around 40 percent) (Statistisches Bundesamt 2005). Of the industry's total sales in 2004, almost one-third were generated by two key sectors: meat processing (20 percent) and confectionary (10.9 percent). The level of concentration within the industry is very low. In 2004 the ten largest producers had a share of just 15 percent of the industry. By contrast, the ten largest suppliers in the food retail sector accounted for 85 percent of total sales (see Dresdner Bank 2005).

Market saturation, price dictation from the retail sector, and stiffer competition for submarkets are making more and more companies optimize their product ranges and cut costs. There has also been an increase in the number of collaborative ventures and takeovers. Company restructuring is always closely linked to staff restructuring processes, with the low-skill occupations suffering particularly from cost and competitive pressure. This issue is especially apparent in the area of employee pay conditions. Traditionally, the food industry makes considerable use of low-skill labor, particularly in production and packing occupations. At the same time, entry-level wages are particularly low compared with other manufacturing industries (such as metal and chemistry). Our calculations using BA (Bundesagentur für Arbeit) employee panel data show that in 2003 around 23 percent of employees in the food industry as a whole (including tobacco) had not completed any vocational training courses (total economy 16.3 percent).

The meat processing and confectionary subsectors have above-average levels of low-skill industrial workers. In the target occupations of the meat processing industry, around 50 percent of all employees have no vocational qualification. In confectionary, the figure is even higher, at just under 60 percent (see table 1A.4). A large proportion of these positions are low-wage jobs. Whereas, in 2003, 36.6 percent of full-time employees in the food industry as a whole received an hourly wage below the low-wage threshold (total economy 17.7 percent), the figures for the meat processing and confectionary production subsectors were 49.4 percent and 28.8 percent, respectively. High levels of low-wage employment are also found in the target occupations. In 2003, 36 percent of full-time employees in the occupational category "production of meat and sausages" and 35.5 percent of employees working as "manufacturers of sugar, confectionary goods, or ice cream" were low-paid (that is, they earned gross hourly rates below €10.41 (US$15.25) in West Germany and €7.84 (US$11.48) in East Germany). One of the reasons for the relatively high incidence of low pay is that the collective bargaining system in the food industry is fragmented; in some places, in fact, it is even collapsing, as can be seen in the meat processing industry. Unlike France, the Netherlands, and the United Kingdom, Germany has no statutory minimum wage (see chapters 1 and 7); as a result, companies' cost-cutting strategies are not restricted by any generally binding lower limit.

In the following, we discuss the strategies and measures that companies in the food industry are using to deal with the unrelenting structural change and their impact on employees' pay and working conditions. The focus is on the results of company case studies carried out in the confectionary and meat processing industries (excluding abattoirs). These subsectors were selected because they differ from each other in concentration level, use of technological innovations, impact of the general institutional framework, and pay and working conditions.

THE SAMPLE AND THE METHODOLOGY

The focus of our research was on low-skill occupations in two subsectors of food processing. Finding companies to take part in our study was difficult in the food industry because at the time of our investigation the meat processing industry in particular was on the receiving end of considerable criticism because of various rotten meat scandals and press reports on the use of Eastern European contract workers.

The sample comprises seven companies: four from the meat processing industry and three from the confectionary industry. Among these seven are two niche suppliers and five bulk producers. Four of the companies are global players with branches in several countries. All case study companies are located in West Germany, owing in part to the low concentration of food-processing companies in East Germany, but also to difficulties in getting access to East German subsidiaries. Compared to the average size of food-processing establishments in Germany, larger companies are overrepresented in our sample. With the exception of one company that had 60 employees, the number of employees ranged from 270 up to more than 1,000.

In five of the seven case study companies, interviews were conducted at various levels: for example, general management, human resource management, production leaders, works councils, and—where possible—employees in target occupations. In two cases, for internal reasons, we were able to conduct interviews only with the responsible works councils. The case study interviews were accompanied by context discussions and expert interviews with trade unionists, representatives of employers' associations, training bodies, and so on.

PRICE PRESSURE AND COMPETITION

The meat processing and confectionary subsectors are undergoing significant structural changes. Because concentration is proceeding much faster in the food retail sector (see chapter 6) than in the food-processing industry, the supply-and-demand relationship between the retail sector and the food industry has shifted over recent years, with the terms of business largely determined by the growing buying power of the discounters and other large retail corporate groups. To counter the downward pressure on prices from the food retail sector and to keep up with the increased competition demands, some companies based in Germany have introduced advanced production technologies and complex safety and certification processes. In addition, the EU's eastward enlargement in May 2004 and the associated partial lifting of customs regulations created an opportunity to import low-cost raw and finished products from the new member states. Moreover, it is now easier to establish subsidiaries and to transfer some production divisions abroad or to employ workers from Eastern Europe in Germany quite legally. Only financially strong companies, however, can afford to invest in new technologies and enter new markets. Most of the SMEs in the subsectors under investigation do not have enough equity capital to undertake these kinds of investment. In this context, more mergers and business transfers can be expected, in line with similar developments in the United States (Lane et al. 2003, 251). With the MNCs' increasing market dominance, the development of fully automatic cutting and wrapping machines is likely to keep spreading, leading probably to a decline in low-skill occupations within the production areas of the meat processing and confectionary industries.

Existing overcapacity and the arrival in the market of large MNCs have placed particularly intense competitive and price pressures on companies in the confectionary industry. The manufacturers' product ranges can be divided into a budget segment and a premium segment. In no other branch of the food industry is the innovation pressure on companies as high as it is in this subsector, particularly on makers of branded products in the premium segment. In 2004 high growth rates were recorded in sales of high-quality premium products like chocolates and chocolate bars, while attainable earnings in the budget segment are stagnating (NGG 2006b). Attempts by manufacturers to pass on the increasing costs of raw materials (cocoa, sugar, and so on) and packaging (crude oil prices) directly to the end user backfired. Customers had become too accustomed to low-price discount products. In this context, increasing numbers of distributors of dealers' brands are attempting to increase the price pressure on manufacturers.

Alongside the broad product range offered by large MNCs, some smaller suppliers have succeeded in identifying niches and establishing their own manufacturer's or dealer's brands in the market. Niche segments are largely concentrated in chocolate production, with products being made in some cases by smaller businesses with a semimanual setup. There are particular market opportunities in high-quality branded products that use selected organic or "fair trade" ingredients, for instance. Whether this subsector can continue to hold its own successfully in international competition will depend on the future development of the legal, political, and economic framework. Discussions are currently under way at the EU level on draft legislation that would restrict the advertising of nutritional and health information related to fortified foods (for example, products with added vitamins) that could lead to substantial restrictions on the German market. By contrast, German companies are welcoming the European Commission's draft legislation to reform the European Community (EC) sugar regime, since a relaxation of EU sugar prices may lead to higher export ratios (BDSI 2004).

Within the German meat industry too, there is considerable downward pressure on prices and cutthroat competition. In recent years consumers have increasingly been buying self-service products. A large proportion of self-service products (40 percent of prepacked sausage and meat products) are sold by discounters. The discounters use their sales to extend their market power, driving the traditional specialist meat trade further and further into retreat. The pressure exerted by discounters on SMEs in the meat industry is enormous. Producers who want to keep pace in the unrelenting price war have to keep finding new ways of reducing costs. The global battle for market shares within the meat industry has led to whole production areas being outsourced and to the recruitment of Eastern European labor at "dumping" prices. Because of the intense competition for submarkets, international groups in particular are pushing their way onto the market and trying to secure their market power by means of takeovers. For instance, the Dutch company Bestmeat Company BV (part of the Vion group since 2005) has bought a majority share in the German companies Moksel and Nordfleisch. Similar trends can also be observed in Danish Crown, a major Danish company, with its purchase of the Oldenburger Fleischwarenfabrik. One consulting firm is predicting that the European meat processing industry will become increasingly concentrated and that by 2008 the market will be dominated by no more than five global players (NGG 2006c). In this context, there is reason to suppose that meat processing companies will adapt to current developments and either enter into collaborative ventures and mergers or attempt to identify and occupy niche segments. A similar picture is emerging in the confectionary industry.

In both subsectors, SMEs in particular are not equal to the challenges of the unrelenting competition. Although SMEs can respond flexibly to changes in consumer demands, they do not usually have sufficient financial resources to market their products and brands internationally and to invest at the same time in new production technologies. The food and restaurant workers' union, NGG, expects that the majority of SMEs will disappear from the market in the long term, since it will primarily be the large international companies that become established. SMEs have a chance to survive in the future only if they succeed in occupying niche segments that are unattractive to major suppliers because of the relatively low profit margins that can be expected. SMEs that continue to attempt to keep step in the price war between discounters will be left behind sooner or later. With food scandals happening so frequently, niches can be found in the production and marketing of regional and organic products, which are now stocked by all major discounters. In addition, the poultry sector continues to be a production niche in which good sales revenues can be generated from the production of convenience products.

INDUSTRIAL RELATIONS

According to the NGG, collective bargaining in the food industry is more fragmented than in any other German industry. In 2001, in the trade union's collective bargaining sphere (food industry and hotel and hospitality industry), there were 2,426 collective agreements, 65 percent of which were concluded at the company or local level. In contrast, only 704 collective agreements were signed at the federal state level and 140 at the national level (Deutscher Bundestag 2005, 53). Very few collective agreements in this industry are extended to employers and employees not previously bound by them. In 2002 only 19 collective agreements were declared to be generally binding in this way.[2] The parties to collective bargaining include the NGG and the member associations of the food industry employers' federation, the Arbeitgebervereinigung Nahrung und Genuss (ANG). The

ANG's task is to discuss and coordinate central social and wage policy issues with the NGG. Unlike its regional and subsector-specific member associations, the ANG itself does not bargain directly with the union. According to the NGG, collective wage bargaining is particularly complicated in some subsectors because there are often no employers' associations at the federal level with which, for example, industrywide collective agreements could be negotiated (NGG 2003). The inconsistent wage structure in the industry becomes particularly apparent when the wage framework in the confectionary industry is compared with that in the meat industry.

WAGE BARGAINING POLICY IN THE CONFECTIONARY INDUSTRY: A REFLECTION OF THE GERMAN MODEL

In the case of the German confectionary industry, an industrywide collective pay structure, which is largely comparable with that of the manufacturing sector as a whole (see chapter 1), has been in place for some time.[3] As far back as the start of the twentieth century, the chocolate industry had by far the largest average company size in the food industry, with an average of almost one hundred employees. As the sales market for cocoa products flourished, the first pioneers in the industrial production of confectionary began investing determinedly in new technology, with the result that the sector quickly became a technologically advanced one. With the mechanization of the confectionary companies, manual occupations in the production of cocoa mass were replaced by machines, while at the same time the need for low-skill occupations in the sorting and packing of the mass-produced products increased (see the detailed description in Ellerbrock 1993, 315f). The unions realized very early on that the industrial mass production of chocolate would lead inevitably to workforce restructuring and that henceforth there would be a small number of craft workers (confectioners, patissiers, and so on), on the one hand, and a large number of less-skilled industrial workers, on the other. The NGG's aim was, and still is, to represent the interests of both the craft workers and the industrial workers vis-à-vis the employers' associations, although unionizing the craft workers proved difficult.

Nevertheless, over the years the union has succeeded in combining the different interests and negotiating industrywide collective agreements with the industry's employers' association, the Bundesverband der deutschen Süsswarenindustrie (BDSI). An industrywide collective agreement exists for the German confectionary industry that regulates working conditions through a framework agreement on employment conditions (covering both East and West Germany), and there are various regional collective pay agreements (at the NGG district organization level) that were concluded between the NGG and the BDSI. There are also agreements on issues such as partial retirement or employment benefits to encourage capital formation. The collectively agreed rate for the lowest pay grades for semiskilled and unskilled workers in production and final packing is between €8.40 and €8.90 (US$12.30 and US$13.04) gross per hour, depending on region and age. This corresponds to between 54 and 57 percent of the West German full-time median wage—that is, it is a rate well below the low-wage threshold.

In addition, the framework agreement on industrywide employment conditions in West Germany lays down the weekly full-time working time (thirty-eight hours), premiums for overtime (25 to 40 percent) and for work on Sundays (60 percent) and public holidays (125 to 150 percent), alternating shift allowances (5 percent), and other benefits such as a Christmas bonus (100 percent of the relevant collectively agreed monthly gross pay) and holiday pay (€13.80 [US$20.21] for each collectively agreed leave day).

With regard to the effective gross pay for full-time employees in the confectionary branch, our calculations for West Germany[4] show that the proportion of low-wage earners in the target occupations of production and packing fell from 59 percent to 39 percent between 1980 and 1995—probably for the most part because increasing use of new technologies led to the loss of low-skill jobs. This figure remained largely constant until 1999, but then rose slightly to 40.2 percent by 2003 (see table 1.8). The proportion of low-wage earners is reduced only slightly if the values for East Germany are included. The incidence of low pay for Germany as a whole was 35.5 percent in 2003 (see table 7.1). In the NACE 15.82 (manufacture of rusks, biscuits, pastry goods, and cakes) and 15.84 (manufacture of cocoa, chocolate, and sugar confectionary) sectors, 37 percent and 40 percent of employees, respectively, in the case study occupations were below the low-wage threshold. This shows clearly that a significant proportion of employees in the target occupations within production and packing are on a low wage. However, if the bargaining parties had not succeeded in establishing industrywide pay structures, the proportion of employees on a low wage would probably have been much higher.

Overall, the collective bargaining situation in the confectionary sector can be regarded as relatively stable, largely because the majority of the employers continue to belong to the trade association, BDSI, which takes part in collective bargaining and represents their interests. With a unionization level of around 30 percent, the NGG—in cooperation with the works councils—has a considerable say within the companies. Nevertheless, pressure is increasing to accept pay freezes and pay cuts. Collective bargaining rounds have become increasingly tough in recent years. In the 2005 bargaining round, the NGG did succeed in pushing through pay rises of 1.8 percent across the board for the confectionary sector and in resisting demands from employers for multi-year wage agreements with one-off payments and a reduction of entry pay levels for new recruits to 80 percent. However, the employers' side continues to demand an extension of working time without pay compensation, reductions in vacation and Christmas bonuses, and so on. Some employers are even threatening to leave the employers' association if their demands are not met. Whether they will stick to that threat in the future remains to be seen. The fact is that the number of members not bound by collective agreements for the whole of the food industry has increased in recent years.

To be able to give more room for maneuver for the companies' demands concerning the arrangement of company-specific working time regulations, the NGG and the ANG have agreed on joint recommendations for greater "flexibility." Since April 2004, for instance, the bargaining parties have altered collectively agreed working time regulations by means of company-level agreements. In addition, companies in financial difficulties can use "hardship provisions" to reduce collectively agreed payments if by doing so they can safeguard jobs and increase the company's competitiveness (ANG/NGG 2004). In practice, however, little use has been made of these recommendations so far, as is also confirmed by the three case studies carried out in the confectionary industry. They can be regarded as the "stable core" within our sample, and in this respect they differ completely from the meat processing case studies.

THE MEAT INDUSTRY: A GRAY AREA FOR COLLECTIVE BARGAINING

The collective bargaining structures in the meat industry present a totally different picture. This can generally be described as a gray area for collective bargaining within the German industrial relations system. According to the NGG, it has so far not managed to push through industrywide collective agreements for the meat processing industry or abattoirs. Regional collective agreements exist only in Bavaria and Hesse (Deutscher Bundestag 2005, 53). But even these collective agreements must be scrutinized with a critical eye in terms of their scope, because some of the labor-intensive larger companies are bound not by an industrywide wage agreement but by company-specific agreements.[5] In the other Bundesländer, there are either no collective agreements at all or only company agreements. The reason lies in the fragmentation and lack of concentration in the meat industry.

Compared with the confectionary industry, the industrial production of meat products began relatively late. Around 1900, industrial meat production was virtually unknown and processing was largely carried out by hand— thus the occupational image of the butcher. Industrial processing of meat did not take hold until after the end of the Second World War, when it served primarily to supply the population with basic foods. With the economic recovery of the 1950s, the eating habits of a large part of the population changed. Whereas meat had until then been a specialty, eaten no more than once a week, increased spending power led to an increased demand to eat sausage and meat almost every day.

This demand initially led a small number of SMEs in the meat industry to discover a gap in the market for assembly-line production of meat products and switch to developing plants for the mass production of cooked and raw meat products. Unlike the "older" confectionary industry, the market was still largely unstructured, but competition between companies with identical or similar products was soon intense. In this context, producers began to mistrust each other. Several companies were interested only in maximizing their own profit margin, to the exclusion of all else, which ran counter to the grouping of common interests in trade associations concerned with wage policy. As a result, on the employers' side there was comparatively little interest in collective bargaining on standard wage agreements. The aim was rather to create pay conditions in a flexible manner tailored to the economic situation of the particular company concerned. Because of the employers' adverse reaction to concluding collective wage agreements, the union always had trouble developing industrywide pay structures and recruiting members in the meat processing industry. Although it did succeed over the following years in negotiating a few industrywide agreements (for example, in North Rhine-Westphalia), the mutual mistrust between the producers became more intense, until there was no longer a grouping of common interests. Since the end of the 1970s, most trade associations in the meat industry have no longer felt responsible for negotiating collective agreements.[6]

Today, the collective agreements concluded within the meat processing industry are typically between the regionally based unions and the employers concerned, and they take the form of company-related or group agreements. According to information provided by the trade union, there are 136 different collective agreements in the food industry (Endling 2007), most of them (almost 90 percent) company-related. A recent study has shown that the average hourly wage in 2005 was €13.40 (Beile, Klein, and Maack 2007; Maack 2007), which was substantially below the median wage for 2003 of €14.94 (see table 1.1). Our case studies indicate that collectively agreed wages in the lower wage bracket were between €6.98 and €9.83 (US$10.23 and US$14.40) per hour (44.7 to 63 percent of the West German median), and thus all below the low pay threshold. In some cases—depending on the agreement in question—they may also include entitlements to bonus payments and further special annual payments such as Christmas and vacation bonuses.[7]

A case study in a niche segment showed clearly how great the scope for individual creativity is when it comes to company wage scales. In this case, in order to avoid company redundancies, the trade union signed an agreement providing for hourly rates for all new recruits that were approximately €1 lower than the hourly rates of the existing workforce in the lower pay grades. A provision was included to safeguard existing rates for the existing workforce. In another case, the applicable regional wage scale was relaxed in favor of increasing wages for higher-skilled employees, and additional intermediate-wage groups were introduced to facilitate internal promotion for employees in multitask jobs.

Hardly any reliable information is available about the pay and working conditions of employees in meat processing companies that are not covered by company or group wage agreements, since they represent a gray area that is inaccessible to trade unions. Our sample included only one niche supplier not bound by any collective agreement. However, hourly pay rates there started at €8.60 (US$12.60), which appeared to be typical for the region. From this point of view, this company's pay conditions must be considered an example of best practice. According to NGG union representatives, it can be assumed that in companies not bound by collective agreements, the lowest hourly gross rate is no more than between €6.00 and €8.00 (US$8.79 and US$11.72) (between 38.4 and 51.2 percent of the West German full-time median, and thus far below the low-wage threshold), and that additional payments are very much the exception. According to our own long-term calculations, the proportion of low-wage workers in the West German meat processing industry increased steadily between 1980 and 2003. Whereas in 1980 around 22.5 percent of employees in the target occupations were low-paid, by 2003 the figure had risen to almost 35 percent (see table 1.8). This figure remains largely stable even when the figures available for East Germany for 2003 are included. According to these figures, 36 percent of workers in Germany as a whole in the target occupation "producer of meat products and sausage" received a wage below the low-wage threshold in 2003 (see table 7.1). In the particular subsector under study (NACE 15.13), the figure was as high as 41 percent. The figures clearly show that low wages are widespread within the industry and that the proportion of employees on low wages is considerably higher than is found in many other industries.

This situation is exacerbated by the fact that some companies' practices are often on the fringes of legality (and thus not included in the data on low-wage shares presented here). The tip of the iceberg is visible in the massive recruitment of Polish workers at "dumping wages" of between €1.90 and €5.00 (US$2.78 and US$7.33) in German abattoirs. To prevent wage dumping, the union is calling for an extension of the Arbeitnehmer-Entsendegesetz (the German law on the posting of workers) and the introduction of a general statutory minimum wage—a move reminiscent of the situation in the construction industry. The rate of €7.50 (US$10.99) gross per hour currently demanded by the German trade unions (see chapter 7) would probably lead to some considerable wage increases, particularly among employees in companies not bound by collective agreements.

FIRM STRATEGIES

As already mentioned, the meat processing and confectionary industries in Germany have traditionally been dominated by SMEs, unlike in neighboring countries like Denmark and the Netherlands, and are therefore facing more intense competition because of the current competitive situation. With over 1,300 companies in the abattoir and meat processing sector and 250 companies in the area of confectionary and preserved bakery products production, both subsectors are still highly fragmented. However, trends can be observed indicating that these subsectors will become much more highly concentrated in the foreseeable future as a result of further collaborative ventures and mergers among global players. Until a high level of concentration is reached, however, the companies remain exposed to more intense competitive pressures, which will inevitably lead to company restructuring. The emphasis in the interviews was therefore on the responses of the companies in our sample to the unrelenting competitive pressure, the strategies they were developing, and the impact of their implementation of these strategies on pay and working conditions.

The companies can be roughly divided into two types: those that were concerned primarily with cutting costs and those that focused on innovation and higher quality. The first type was typically represented by traditional, family-run firms where semiautomatic production methods were used and necessary investments in new technology and staff training were the exception rather than the rule. Companies in the second group, in contrast, tended to be larger companies; some had been taken over by financially strong international players that were endeavoring to meet the challenges of the unrelenting competition with maximum product quality. In most cases, such efforts involved investing in new technology, restructuring work processes, and providing more basic and advanced training for the workforce.

CUTTING COSTS AS A SURVIVAL STRATEGY

Companies of the first type—those primarily concerned with cost-cutting—represent the majority of SMEs in the meat and confectionary industries. Typically, these companies were run in the past by just one person (usually the owner of the business). Consequently, the internal organizational structure tends to be a classic hierarchical one. Changes to company leadership usually occur when the owner is replaced by a family member or by an employed business manager with a manager's profile, or when the business is taken over by a large corporation.

In particular, SMEs that do not merge with a financially strong MNC find it hard to remain competitive in the more intense competitive environment, since they have only limited opportunities to sell their brands internationally. Some suppliers have therefore started giving up their own brands and switched to producing for other large suppliers or for the retail trade. In both markets, the product prices tend to be low and sales revenue is mainly determined by quantity, which for some companies is severely limited because of production capacity. Their ability to compete in these markets is compromised by their antiquated production equipment, but the majority of them are not in a financial position to make significant investments in new technology; production in most of these traditional businesses remains semiautomatic. A large number of them are fighting to survive and need to respond flexibly to, for example, seasonal fluctuations. What are the consequences of this competitive situation for pay and working conditions?

The results of the case studies clearly show that wages in this type of company are under considerable pressure, particularly in SMEs in the meat processing industry owing to the general lack of an industrywide, collectively agreed wage structure. When wage agreements are negotiated at the company level, pressure is frequently exerted on the union to accept wage cuts—as happened in the example mentioned earlier of a company in a niche segment where a reduction of €1 in the hourly wage for new recruits was accepted by the union in order to prevent redundancies. The reduction of supplementary wage components like bonuses and piece rates is often on the agenda as well. Cuts like these have been made in all the case study companies of this cost-cutting type in recent years, leading to wage cuts of up to 12 percent. Companies that still pay bonuses are regarded by the union as rare exceptions—"oases of happiness" indeed. In general, many companies are not only cutting bonuses but demanding that working time be increased without pay compensation. Moreover, several companies are also contracting out parts of production and packing, a strategy that in most cases gradually reduces the core workforce to a minimum.

Seeking Competitive Advantages Through Quality Assurance

Companies of the second type present a different picture. These are companies that have been bought up by larger companies or groups and have seen increased investment as a result. The interviews showed clearly that the takeovers were sometimes seen by both management and employee representatives as an opportunity to break down traditional inflexible structures and to reorganize the internal organizational structure. The aim was to meet the unrelenting competitive pressure by increasing quality and safety standards while at the same time increasing productivity on the lines. Work organization systems had been developed that centered on extended employee responsibility and provided incentives for higher productivity. The focus was on the introduction of group work and multitask jobs (as it was at one of the American cases; see Lane et al. 2003, 248). At the implementation stage, classic hierarchies consisting of plant management, production management, foremen, and line workers were replaced by leaner hierarchies. In most cases, individual production lines were grouped into teams, and the classic foreman role was replaced by team leaders or spokespersons. The new group philosophy was explained to all staff by external consultants during workshops. The employees who would be working in multitask jobs also received in-house training offers. With the restructuring of the work flow, even employees in the lower pay grades now enjoyed the prospect of internal promotion if they were prepared to extend their range of duties.

In one of the companies under study, the existing regional pay scale was even broadened and intermediate pay grades were introduced alongside the collectively agreed pay structure, making it easier for employees to move up to the next pay grade. The company also introduced a new bonus and premium system that increased the average remuneration quite significantly—up to a level above the actual agreed local wage. In another company in our sample, it became clear that internal mobility was severely restricted when upward mobility opportunities were exclusively linked to job descriptions in existing collective agreements that were themselves so out of date that they provided no scope for promotion to group work or multitask jobs. To be able to create more incentives for employees in the lower pay grades, the works council and management were discussing the introduction of a simplified monetary bonus system.

It has been shown that work processes can usually be reorganized easily if plant management is given sufficient decisionmaking authority by group management and can manage the reorganization in a decentralized manner. The more the sales revenue is in line with the specifications of group management, the greater the scope for decentralized decisionmaking accorded to the site in question. On the other hand, revenue fluctuations can lead to the discontinuation or even abandonment of work processes, such as group work, that have already been implemented. The implementation of new work processes can be speeded up if the company has a powerful works council that is convinced of the advantages of the reorganization because it expects financial advantages for the employees and a reduction in the typically high physical workload. From the case study companies it became clear, however, that it takes a long time for employees to get used to the reorganization of work processes, largely because the majority of them have spent their working lives in classic organizational structures and are used to working only to the instructions of the foreman. The opportunity to have a say in team meetings, which are frequently attended by company and production managers as well, is new to most employees and takes some getting used to. From the managers' perspective, restructuring the hierarchy usually brings considerable benefits. Among other things, productivity on the lines increases because machine running times are extended. At the same time, employees notice faults on the lines faster and can usually remedy the problems themselves immediately.

FORMS OF FLEXIBILITY

The company typology has already shown that some of the companies studied chose to increase their competitiveness by cutting staff costs. With pay rates and special payments constantly on the agenda for renegotiation, we can say that in the majority of these SMEs components of the employees' income had worsened over recent years. Even where basic pay had not been cut, employees had often had to accept reductions in the traditional bonus payments or had seen them disappear altogether. In addition, a large number of the companies combined internal and external forms of flexibility—with companies exposed to high seasonal fluctuations being especially likely to use external forms of flexibility. In most companies, the workforce structure was based on three pillars: (1) a permanent, usually full-time, core workforce; (2) temporary seasonal workers, some of them in mini-jobs; and (3) temporary agency workers deployed to cope with peaks in orders. How and to what degree the various types of employment were used varied from company to company.

Internal Flexibility   Most of the companies under investigation had a strategy of dealing with peaks in demand primarily by internal means through flexible working time models. Only when it could be foreseen that high seasonal fluctuations were likely to lead to production bottlenecks did the companies fall back on external instruments to increase their flexibility.

Companies can be grouped according to subsector in their internal flexibility arrangements. It emerges that companies in the confectionary industry faced much longer-term seasonal fluctuations than companies in the meat processing industry because of the typical production peaks between June and February. Because of the extremely high capacity utilization during the peak season, three-shift systems were much more common in the mass production of confectionary. All the companies under study ran these shift systems, some with an alternating shift pattern, some with a permanent night shift. By contrast, our sample in the meat processing subsector included only one large company that ran a three-shift system for certain product types. Generally, it was possible to add Saturday and Sunday shifts when bottlenecks occurred. Most companies had flexible working time accounts. It became clear that working time rules were adapted flexibly to meet the requirements of the company. For instance, one company—in cooperation with the works council and the union—had increased the collectively agreed working time of thirty-eight hours per week to forty hours between June and February. To keep the lines running to capacity even on Saturdays during peak times, there was also an agreement that all employees would work extra shifts (usually cleaning shifts) on ten Saturdays per year. The overtime hours amassed in the working time accounts had to be used up in the quiet months. This led to a large number of the permanent staff being on leave for up to seven weeks.

One company in the meat processing industry used a totally different strategy. Despite an existing two-shift arrangement, this company had started introducing additional part-time jobs. It expected these workers to be very flexible, however, and to increase their part-time employment status to full-time at short notice, with full pay compensation during peak order times. The case studies show that companies generally made use of working time models that enabled flexible management of working time for the permanent staff without paying bonuses. Overall, however, part-time work did not seem to play a major role in this context. In contrast to the food and tobacco industry as a whole, in which just under one-quarter of all employees are part-timers (including mini-jobs), the part-time rates in the two subsectors under study are considerably lower—11 percent for producers of meat products and sausage and as low as 6.8 percent for manufacturers of sugar, confectionary goods, or ice cream (see table 1A.3).

External Flexibility   To achieve maximum flexibility, several companies had also begun contracting out parts of production and packing to external providers within the plant. Some large companies dealt with peaks in orders by using temporary agency workers, since these workers—depending on the order status—could be employed by the day. This strategy is illustrated by one case study company in the confectionary industry where seasonal business was no longer managed by using classic seasonal employment but by increasing temporary agency work.[8] To cut costs still further, the company had also begun outsourcing parts of its production to Eastern Europe, and this move in turn had led to job reductions among the permanent staff in Germany. From the context discussions with the responsible union it became apparent, however, that this form of outsourcing cannot be viewed as a general trend in the confectionary sector. The union officials were aware of only one other company that had acted in a similar way, but it had since admitted to having made a mistake, since the outsourcing of whole spheres of activity is generally accompanied by a significant loss of quality. In one region, criticism by the food retail industry of the quality of the final packaging led to the outsourced packing division being brought back in-house.

On the other hand, it is apparent that other companies deliberately avoid using temporary agency workers—particularly those companies whose competitive strategy is focused on high product quality and product safety. One company we studied avoided using temporary agency workers altogether, since it had had bad experiences with them. It also became apparent that companies whose production was focused on group work and multitask jobs rarely managed seasonal fluctuations by employing greater numbers of temporary agency workers. The reasons for this are self-evident. The employees who worked on the team had mostly been trained in-house and were used to working as a team. Group productivity was therefore linked to close collaboration. The use of external, constantly changing staff would have necessitated an enormous amount of induction work, and team productivity would have suffered.

To balance out seasonal fluctuations, some companies were endeavoring to extend their product range to cover all-season products. In one company this effort had reduced the number of temporary agency workers it used from approximately four hundred per year to just fifteen.

The Use of Eastern European Contract Workers   There is one form of "external flexibility" that we did not find in our company case studies: the above-mentioned use of Eastern European posted workers, or contract workers. Their absence from these companies might be due to the fact that the practice so far is mainly apparent in abattoirs, which were not involved in our study. But because the whole range of company strategies to achieve a flexible and cheap usage of labor would be incomplete without dealing with this issue, we look here at the background to this practice and its impact on the food industry in Germany.

Since the enlargement of the European Union in May 2004, companies from the ten "accession countries" have been able to provide services in Germany. As a result, German companies can now enter into agreements with Eastern European subcontractors to hand over whole areas of production to foreign contract workers. Such contracts are awarded in accordance with the legislated "freedom to provide services," under which the services in question are subject to the labor legislation prevailing in the subcontractor's country of origin.[9] Thus, companies from EU member states can send their employees to Germany to carry out contract work at the rates of pay that prevail in their country of origin. To date, minimum wages in accordance with the Posted Workers Act have been negotiated and declared generally binding in only a small number of sectors, such as the construction industry and the craft segment of the roofing trade.

Since May 2004, many German abattoirs have been taking advantage of this situation and handing over large parts of the slaughtering and butchering process to cheap work gangs from Eastern Europe, while reducing their own core workforces to a bare minimum (Czommer and Worthmann 2005). Many of these workers earn only €2 to €5 (US$2.93 to US$7.33) per hour, and the trend is downward (Meichsner 2007). The NGG union has spoken of the emergence of a "new form of slave labor." According to figures published by customs authorities who carried out inspections in 385 companies in the meat processing industry in the winter of 2006–2007, irregularities concerning the status of the workers as well as their working conditions were found in around 25 percent of the firms. "Besides clandestine workers, officials are said to have come across many bogus self-employed workers or illegally provided workers" (Sirleschtov 2007).

WORKING CONDITIONS AND JOB SATISFACTION

Low-paid occupations in the meat processing industry are typically found in the wet and cold preliminary production areas (laying the raw meat mixture on the conveyor belts, filling casings, and so on), and especially in final packing. These occupations generally involve heavy physical, semiautomatic, monotonous work. In addition, employees are exposed to a continuously high noise level because of the use of machines. Equivalent to the cold and wet areas in meat processing are the confectionary industry's boiling and baking areas, where workers are exposed to the heat and dust associated with the use of flour, baking powder, cocoa, and nut mixtures. The level of mechanization in the confectionary industry is much higher than in the meat processing industry. Low-skill occupations here usually involve just the few monotonous hand movements used to adjust and sort on the lines and to do the final packing. All the companies we studied endeavored to maintain high quality and safety standards. Violations of hygiene rules were immediately punished by management, and a sufficient number of changing facilities, toilets, and washrooms were available for the staff. All the companies had canteens and staff rooms, some of them lavishly equipped. It is self-evident, however, that working conditions in the companies under study should be viewed as examples of best practice. There is every reason to assume that working conditions are likely to be much worse in companies that have neither collective wage agreements nor works councils.

In our interviews with employees, it became apparent that the level of physical and psychological stress was perceived differently among the employees. All those questioned said they were happy to have a job at all in view of the high unemployment level. In view of the difficult labor market situation, it is not surprising that a large number of those questioned seemed perfectly willing to accept a reduction in pay if this meant that their job would be safeguarded. The companies too were aware of the difficult employment situation, which was why collective wage negotiations always included their demands for special payments to be scrapped, hourly wages to be reduced, working times to be increased without compensation, and so on. The extent to which the companies can exert pressure at this level depends largely on the commitment and willingness of the works councils and union officials to stand up for employees' interests in the face of employer demands. The case studies show that it is easier for employees in large companies who are freed from work duties to serve as full-time works councilors to enforce employees' interests than it is for works councils in typical SMEs. In both the confectionary industry and the meat processing industry, the degree of unionization in SMEs is usually between 10 and 20 percent, whereas in companies with more than five hundred employees it is often between 40 and 50 percent. In one of our case study confectionary companies, the level of unionization was extraordinarily high at around 60 percent. We did not obtain precise information about the wage pressures to which employees in companies without works councils are exposed, since in our sample there was only one company without a works council. It can be assumed, however, that without a works council, a company can make employees redundant, cut wages, remove special payments, and so on, more easily.

As far as the basic and advanced training of employees in the lower pay grades is concerned, it became apparent that in SMEs training generally means on-the-job training. Exceptions occur when packing facilities, for example, are controlled by new computer-based logistical processes. In these cases, suitable employees are given the chance to attend the necessary computer training courses. Only in the large companies we studied, which focused on group work, multiskilling, and job rotation, was basic and advanced training provided on a larger scale that created internal promotion opportunities for staff in the lower pay grades, regardless of their level of vocational qualification. It also became apparent that increasing concentration in the industry will lead to advanced mechanization. It can be assumed that the introduction of more technical innovations will result in a large number of simple manual occupations being replaced by a few highly skilled food technicians. In mechanized production, the skilled food and confectionary technicians operate, regulate, and monitor nearly all the tasks, from receiving the raw materials to packing. Simple occupations in these subsectors will be exposed to rationalization processes similar to those already introduced in breweries and dairies.

In terms of job satisfaction, it appears that staff who have already worked for several years in a company generally identify with that company and the daily work. Identification problems occur when there are changes in company management, for example, and the old "company patriarch" is replaced by an external successor with a manager profile, or when the company is taken over by an MNC. The results of the case studies show that productivity and job satisfaction in shift-work companies is much higher when the production lines are manned by a stable core of workers—in other words, when social contact and communication between employees is ensured. This was particularly evident in companies that relied increasingly on the flexible use of external workers.

Personnel changes on the lines put permanent employees under continuous pressure. They have to train and introduce the temporary agency workers, who are usually new to production, while maintaining the planned production levels on the lines. It is obvious that this extra workload leads to a considerable intensification of work for the permanent staff—for which they are not paid extra. Add to their stress the fact that increasing mechanization of production processes, the transfer of divisions to other countries, and the increased use of temporary agency staff is leading to jobs being lost, and the remaining permanent staff are worrying as well about keeping their jobs.

SUMMARY AND CONCLUSIONS

The "Wild West" conditions mentioned at the beginning of this chapter are not found throughout the food industry as a whole or in all parts of the meat processing sector. Rather, they have been concentrated to date in abattoirs, probably because it is easier to hand over to subcontractors the easily definable tasks in these workplaces than it is the manufacture of meat products. However, since "Wild West" conditions are already appearing in some workplaces besides abattoirs and other dubious practices are rampant (such as setting up letterbox companies in order to fulfill the requirement to have business premises in the country of origin, or using forged passports and papers for contract workers), the possibility that such machinations will spread further within the meat processing industry cannot be excluded. This is all the more likely since the free mobility of labor comes into force no later than May 2011, and it will no longer be necessary then to declare the use of low-paid Eastern European workers as contract labor. In the absence of effective policy measures to ensure that minimum standards can be enforced for all workers deployed in Germany, this will lead to further abuses, more wage dumping, and more job losses.

With a view primarily to restricting the wage dumping associated with the use of cheap Eastern European labor, there is currently much discussion about establishing industry-specific minimum standards by extending the Posted Workers Act to include the food industry. Such an extension would have no effect, however, because of the absence of the necessary preconditions, in particular industrywide collective agreements. In the meat processing industry, there is not yet even a negotiating partner on the employers' side. Attempts by the federal government in May 2007 to urge employers in the meat processing industry to put in place the arrangements required to prevent wage dumping by negotiating industrywide collective agreements have so far proved to be fruitless (von Riegen 2007).

Our study focused on the confectionary industry and on those parts of the meat processing industry that have not yet been affected to any great extent by such practices. The results of the case studies and background interviews, however, make it clear that these two subsectors of the food industry are also going through a dramatic upheaval with far-reaching consequences for employees, particularly in the lower wage brackets. The collective bargaining situations in the two subsectors are very different. The confectionary industry still has reasonably stable collective bargaining arrangements, with uniform working and employment conditions and pay scales that apply across the industry. In the meat processing industry, on the other hand, the interests of employers and trade unions are so far apart that industrywide collective agreements can be concluded only in exceptional cases. Because the employers' associations are so fragmented, it frequently proves impossible even to get employers and trade unions to sit around the same table. If any agreements at all are concluded, they are mainly company or group agreements that are not suitable vehicles for standardizing wages and working conditions throughout the industry and enforcing minimum standards.

Both the meat processing and confectionary industries are going through a streamlining process—in other words, concentration is set to intensify. Typical SMEs that do not find a niche segment for their brands will find themselves left behind in the future. In addition, there will be increasing numbers of redundancies among low-skill and low-wage employees as the level of technological innovation continues to rise. This will be particularly true for employees in the confectionary industry, where it is much easier to design machines to take in chocolate hardware than to suck in, say, slippery pieces of raw meat. Until the market is streamlined and the situation resembles Denmark, where Danish Crown controls 80 percent of the Danish meat market, most of the German SMEs fighting for survival will attempt to save on labor costs. Some of these companies are using methods that defy regulation by any collective agreements and are sometimes on the fringes of legality, as can be seen in the employment practices involving Eastern European contract workers. If governments do not succeed in regulating the obvious weaknesses of the EU enlargement through national and international legislation, the floodgates will be opened to practices that circumvent the existing collective bargaining system.

The NGG union has only limited room for maneuver when it comes to improvements in pay and working conditions. Compared with the metal industry, the food industry's union must be regarded as weak, with an average unionization level of approximately 30 percent and a collective bargaining landscape that is fragmented among the various subsectors. Many union activists hope that, besides bringing job losses, the concentration process will improve the opportunities for concluding collective agreements. Some of them take the view that the streamlining of the market will leave only a handful of MNCs, with which standard collective group agreements can then be negotiated. Whether things turn out as they predict remains to be seen. What is known, however, is that the NGG has so far found it easier to recruit members in large companies than in SMEs. It seems unlikely that it will be able to achieve Denmark's unionization rates of over 90 percent.

Finally, the question arises as to what the future holds for low-skill and low-paid workers in the subsectors under study. We cannot paint a rosy picture here. As already mentioned, the financially strong companies that remain in the market will invest in new technology, which will make work easier for a small proportion of employees and bring opportunities for training linked to improvements in internal promotion. For the majority of those employed in packing, however, such investments will probably lead to job losses. It can be expected that, in the transitional period, the financially weaker SMEs will continue to try to keep pace with the unrelenting price war and to achieve competitive advantages through savings in wage costs. To safeguard their own existence, these companies will use any means at their disposal. Sooner or later, there will be no place for low-skill occupations, particularly in confectionary companies, since they can increasingly be replaced by new technologies. Robots are already being tried out in some companies.

NOTES

1. This is slightly above the average size of enterprises in the American food manufacturing industry—73 employees (see Lane et al. 2003, 238). It should be noted, however, that the German figures relate exclusively to businesses with more than twenty employees.
2. The reason for the low level of generally binding collective agreements in the food industry is that a significant number of companies, such as meat processing companies, do not belong to an employers' association that concludes wage agreements; as a result, the basic requirement for extension (that at least 50 percent of employees must work for employers bound by collective agreements) cannot be met (see chapter 1). The nineteen collective agreements with extensions are concentrated in three subsectors: pastry goods and cakes, the bread industry, and hotels and catering.
3. The pay structure in the confectionary industry is followed by companies that produce chocolate, sugar confectionary, preserved bakery products, ice cream, snacks, and raw materials.
4. Long-term calculations for the years 1980 to 2003 can be carried out only for West Germany because no comparable figures were recorded for East Germany before 1992.
5. The binding effect of collective agreements within a company agreement can be established in a number of different ways, "either in the form of a recognition agreement in which the collectively agreed conditions of an industry-wide collective agreement are adopted unchanged or with modifications. Or in the form of a separate wage agreement, where all the terms and conditions of employment normally regulated in an industry-wide agreement are agreed specifically for the contracting company" (IG Metall 2006, 4).
6. The exceptions are Bavaria and Hesse, where there are framework and pay agreements negotiated by the NGG at the level of the state. In addition, in North Rhine-Westphalia some of the provisions of a 1994 framework agreement on employment conditions still apply, since it was never officially rescinded by the parties.
7. In addition to bonuses and piecework rates, performance- or profit-

related pay elements also include group bonuses and other forms of commission.

8.   "Classic seasonal employment" refers to the housewives who used to be employed for up to six months at regular, collectively agreed pay rates and who were subject to social insurance contributions.

9.   The legal provisions governing the "freedom to provide services" are laid down in the treaty establishing the European Community, articles 49–55.

REFERENCES

Ad-Hoc-News. 2007. "Blickpunkt Fleischindustrie" ["Focus on Meat Processing"]. *Ad-Hoc-News,* June 7, 2007. Accessed at http://www.ad-hoc-news .de/Marktberichte/12022808.

Arbeitgebervereinigung Nahrung und Genuss (ANG) and Gewerkschaft Nahrung-Genuss-Gaststätten (NGG). 2004. "Ernährungswirtschaft: Tarifverträge werden flexibler" ["Food Processing Industry: More Flexible Collective Agreements"]. Joint press release of ANG and NGG. Hamburg, Germany: ANG/NGG.

Beile, Judith, Max Klein, and Klaus Maack. 2007. *Zukunft der Fleischwirtschaft* [*The Future of Meat Processing*]. Düsseldorf, Germany: Edition der Hans-Böckler-Stiftung (no. 186).

Borchert, Thomas. 2005. "Wildwestzustände in Deutschland" ["Wild West Conditions in Germany"]. *STERN,* January 26 2005. Accessed at http:// www.stern.de/politik/ausland/535778.html.

Bundesverband der Deutschen Süsswarenindustrie e.V. (BDSI). 2004. Pressemitteilung EU-Zuckermarktordnung [Press release on EU regulation of the sugar market]. Bonn, Germany: BDSI.

Czommer, Lars, and Georg Worthmann. 2005. "Von der Baustelle auf den Schlachthof: Zur Übertragbarkeit des Arbeitnehmer-Entsendegesetzes auf die deutsche Fleischbranche" ["From Construction Site to Abattoirs: About the Transferability of the Posting of Workers Directive to the German Meat Processing Industry"]. Report 2005-03. Gelsenkirchen, Germany: IAT.

Deutscher Bundestag. 2005. "Materialien zur öffentlichen Anhörung von Sachverständigen in Berlin am 27. Juni 2005 zum Entwurf eines Gesetzes zur Änderung des Arbeitnehmer-Entsendegesetzes—Drucksache 15/ 5445—Zusammenstellung der schriftlichen Stellungnahmen" ["Materials of the public hearing of experts according to a revision of the posting of workers directive in Berlin on June, 27 2005"]. Berlin: Deutscher Bundestag.

Dresdner Bank. 2005. "Branchen-Report Ernährungsgewerbe (15): Markenpflege immer teurer und schwieriger" ["Industry Report Food Processing (15). Brand Management Becomes More Expensive and More Difficult"]. Frankfurt, Germany: Dresdner Bank.

Ellerbrock, Karl-Peter. 1993. *Geschichte der deutschen Nahrungs- und Genussmittelindustrie 1750–1914* [*History of the German Food Industry, 1750-1914*]. Stuttgart, Germany: Franz Steiner.

Endling, Wolfgang. 2007. *Arbeitsbedingungen in Deutschland* [*Working Conditions in Germany*]. Powerpoint presentation to a conference. Foliensatz, Bildungszentrum Oberjosbach, February 7–8, 2007.

Gewerkschaft Nahrung-Genuss-Gaststätten (NGG). 2003. *Geschäftsbericht 1998 bis 2002* [*Business Report 1998 to 2002*]. Hannover, Germany: NGG.

————. 2006a. *Branchenbericht 2005 einschl: 1. Halbjahr 2006 des Ernährungsgewerbes* [*Industry Report 2005 Including First Term of 2006, Food Processing*]. Hamburg, Germany: NGG.

————. 2006b. *Branchenbericht 2005 einschl: 1. Halbjahr 2006 der Süsswarenindustrie* [*Industry Report 2005 Including First Term of 2006, Confectionary*]. Hamburg, Germany: NGG.

————. 2006c. *Branchenbericht 2005 einschl: 1. Halbjahr 2006 der Schlacht- und Verarbeitungsbranche* [Industry Report 2005 Including First Term of 2006, Abattoirs and Meat Processing]. Hamburg, Germany: NGG.

IG Metall Verwaltungsstelle. 2006. "Tarifbindung" ["Collective Bargaining Coverage"]. Accessed at http://www2.igmetall.de/homepages/bielefeld/file_uploads/050909_fragenundantwortenzutarifvertrag-tarifflucht-ta.pdf.

Lane, Julia, Philip Moss, Harold Salzman, and Chris Tilly. 2003. "Too Many Cooks? Tracking Internal Labor Market Dynamics in Food Service with Case Studies and Quantitative Data." In *Low-Wage America: How Employers Are Reshaping Opportunities in the Workplace*, edited by Eileen Appelbaum, Annette Bernhardt, and Richard J. Murnane. New York: Russell Sage Foundation.

Lorscheid, Helmut. 2005. "Billiglohn im Schlachtgewerbe: Auch ohne Dienstleistungsrichtlinie funktioniert die Ausbeutung" ["Low Pay in Abattoirs. Exploitation Works Even Without Services Directive"]. March 11, 2005. Accessed at http://www.heise.de/tp/r4/artikel/19/19629/1.html.

Maack, Klaus. 2007. "Zukunft der Fleischwirtschaft" ["The Future of Meat Processing"]. Studie und Konferenz der Hans-Böckler-Stiftung kofinanziert durch die Gewerkschaft NGG, Bildungszentrum Oberjosbach, February 7–8. Wilke, Maack und Partner, wmp consult, Foliensatz.

Meichsner, Julia. 2007. "Hängepartie im Schlachthof" ["Adjourned Game in Abbatoirs"]. *Financial Times Deutschland*, May 24, 2007.

Sirleschtov, Antje. 2007. "Regierung geht gegen die Fleischindustrie vor" ["Government Intervenes in Meat Processing"]. *Tagesspiegel*, May 4, 2007. Accessed at http://www.tagesspiegel.de/wirtschaft/;art271,1938722.

Statistisches Bundesamt. 2005. "Fachserie 4 / Reihe 4.1.2. Produzierendes Gewerbe" ["Manufacturing"]. Wiesbaden, Germany: Statistisches Bundesamt.

von Riegen, Marc-Oliver. 2007. "Osterweiterung: Lohndumping in der Fleischbranche" ["Eastward Enlargement: Wage Dumping in Meat Processing"]. *STERN*, May 3, 2007. Accessed at http://www.stern.de/wirtschaft/arbeit-karriere/arbeit/588375.html.

CHAPTER 4

The Polarization of Working Conditions: Cleaners and Nursing Assistants in Hospitals

Karen Jaehrling

The hospital sector is not one of the typical low-wage sectors, but it is traditionally characterized by low wage differentiation, a core feature of "German capitalism" (Streeck 1997). For a long period, even the two groups of employees who are the focus of this chapter, nursing assistants and cleaning staff, generally received collectively agreed wages, which after a certain length of employment were only a little below the entry-level wages for qualified nurses; sometimes they even exceeded this level. These wage levels prevailed at both for-profit and nonprofit private hospitals, since they regularly adopted the agreed wage levels for the public sector.

Since the early 1990s, however, changes to financing regulations have placed hospitals under high cost pressure and weakened this informal wage coordination. Additionally, the trend of evading the relatively high wage level in the public sector by outsourcing ancillary services (such as cleaning, catering, and laundry) has accelerated. Unlike in the United States or France, however, the number of nursing assistants in German hospitals has not been increased for the purpose of reducing costs. In fact, quite the opposite has happened: already a minor percentage of nursing staffs, their numbers are continuing to decrease. This applies to both types of nursing assistants working in German hospitals: unqualified nursing assistants without formal training of any kind and Krankenpflegehelfer, qualified nursing assistants who have one year's training and have passed a state exam. Instead, basic nursing tasks are being increasingly integrated into the job profile of qualified nurses with three years' training.

The effects of the increasing cost pressure and further sector-specific changes on wage differentiation and division of labor differ according to occupation: the increase in low-paid work among cleaners contrasts with the increased use of higher-paid qualified employees among nursing staffs. This chapter investigates the backgrounds to these disparities as well as the differences with other countries, the role of the institutions of the industrial relations system and the vocational training system, and the development of pay, division of labor, and further aspects of job quality in the two areas.

THE SAMPLE AND THE METHODOLOGY

The focus of the study is on cleaners and nursing assistants. The analysis is empirically based on case studies in six hospitals. We were careful to select hospitals run by different types of providers: public hospitals (two), private for-profit hospitals (two), and private non-profit hospitals (two). The second selection criterion was the regional labor market situation, measured on the basis of the local unemployment rate, which ranged from 6 to 19 percent in the selected regions. The hospitals are medium- to large-sized, with the number of beds ranging from 320 to 750 and the number of employees ranging from 460 to 1,350 (full-time equivalents).

We carried out interviews at each hospital—as far as possible—with employees, employee representation bodies, frontline managers, and hospital management for each of the two areas (cleaning and nursing). In most cases, both managers and employees provided additional information through questionnaires. In three hospitals, interviews with cleaning staff were not permitted; to compensate we established contact with two additional hospitals through the trade union, which at least made it possible for us to interview employee representatives for the cleaning staff. We conducted a total of fifty-one interviews, out of which twenty-five were with managers, nineteen were with employees, and eight were with employee representatives.

In addition to the case studies, we carried out fourteen interviews with representatives of trade unions, professional associations, and employers' associations on the regional and national levels.

We begin by describing the employment conditions in the hospital sector as they had evolved before the wide-reaching financing reforms that began in the early 1990s. The following sections detail the more recent developments in both areas regarding pay, work organization, and, finally, further aspects of job quality, including the issue of mobility.

THE GERMAN MODEL IN THE HOSPITAL SECTOR: A "WAGE PARADISE" FOR LOW-SKILL WORK

In the past, the employment conditions of the public sector applied in almost all hospitals in Germany, although a large proportion of hospitals have always been run by private providers, in contrast to other countries. The public authorities can influence employment conditions in hospitals not only in their role as an employer but also through the public demand monopoly: even services in private hospitals are primarily financed by the public system.[1] Thus, the price for hospital services is not set by the market but to a large extent is fixed by statutory and administrative regulations. Up to the early 1990s, these financing rules were designed according to the principle of cost coverage, which allowed hospitals to pass increasing personnel costs on to the statutory health insurance schemes for the most part. On this basis, the nonprofit private hospitals generally took over the collectively agreed wage structures and increases from the public hospitals. The financing rules thus had a strongly standardizing effect on wages and ensured that the public employment conditions were extended across the entire hospital sector.

Key features of public sector employment are high employment stability, high seniority-based wage increases, and the dominance of internal recruitment for promotion; these are all core characteristics of internal labor markets (Keller 1985). With regard to the employment groups examined in this chapter, three characteristics are particularly significant: whereas the wage differences between the public and private sectors are not great for the medium- and higher-qualification groups, low-skill employees are comparatively well paid in the public sector (Keller 1993, 119). This is particularly true for female-dominated occupations, since the public sector has also taken on a pioneering role in the reduction of gender-specific wage differences. For this reason, the greatest difference between the public and private sectors is for female blue collar workers (Keller 1993, 166). A second characteristic is that wage differences between skilled and low-skilled work are comparatively low. A third is that a large variety of benefits are added to the basic wage—for example, the occupational pension scheme and increments depending on the size of the employee's family.

The comparatively high pay in lower wage groups is not simply the result of a targeted trade union wage policy in the 1960s and 1970s (Keller 1993, 159). The success of this "leveling policy" is mainly due to the fact that the unionization level among blue collar workers in the public sector used to be significantly higher than that of white collar employees; in addition, the organizational decision-making process within the trade unions as well as the collective bargaining process in the public sector have always been highly centralized. Even before the merger of several service-sector trade unions to form the Vereinigte Dienstleistungsgewerkschaft (Ver.di) in 2001, the organizational structures of the trade unions were characterized by a low level of fragmentation. The trade union with the largest membership, Öffentliche Dienste, Transporte, Verkehr (ÖTV), was organized on the industrial trade union principle: to represent all employees in a particular industry without differentiating according to occupation or employer. One distinctive feature of the public sector is that it includes many different branches of the economy (transport, health, utilities). Alongside the ÖTV, there were several more status group–specific or occupational trade unions, such as the white collar Deutsche Angestellten-Gewerkschaft (DAG) and the doctors' trade union, Marburger Bund. The ÖTV, however, functioned as a de facto "wage-leader" union, since the outcome of its negotiations strongly determined the course of negotiations with other trade unions (Keller 1993, 157). Within the ÖTV, there was originally an occupation-based organization in the nursing field that separated unqualified and qualified nursing staff; that approach was abandoned in the late 1960s (Hassel 1999, 179).[2] The collective negotiations for public hospitals are strongly centralized: wage level, wage groups, working hours, annual leave, and other core aspects of the employment contract are agreed on at the national level.

The structures of collective wage negotiations on the private hospital side are more strongly differentiated by region and individual hospital. Additionally, the church employers enjoy a greater degree of autonomy in determining working conditions. Wages and employment conditions are traditionally set within a process that the churches refer to as the "third way"—a middle path between unilateral prescription of wages and collective wage negotiations. Instead of independent, full-time trade union representatives, this process involves employee representatives from company-level staff representation bodies (Mitarbeitervertretungen, or MAV), the church equivalent of the works councils in secular businesses. As part of the Arbeitsrechtliche Kommissionen (labor law commissions), these staff representatives participate in the formulation of Arbeitsvertrags-Richtlinien (AVR; employment contract guidelines), which are similar in content to collective agreements. In the event of conflict, however, these guidelines can also be amended unilaterally by the employers. At the establishment level, too, the negotiation parties on the employee side are weaker than in secular hospitals because church-owned hospitals are not subject to the Works Constitution Act but instead are governed by their own church laws, which grant the MAV fewer codetermination rights (Baumann-Czichon and Gathmann 2006).

These restrictions in church workplaces can be regarded as one of the key causes for the low trade union density in the health sector (22 percent in 1990), because they also restrict the trade unions' ability to recruit and mobilize members in the nonprofit private hospitals (Hassel 1999, 174f). In the past, however, these institutional differences and low levels of unionization were of minor significance. For the most part, negotiations between church employers and employee representatives were free of conflict, since the AVRs were oriented along the lines of the public agreements or almost identical to them.

Thus, a high overall level of collective agreements was achieved in hospitals and was maintained until the recent past. Particularly for low-skill employees, the hospital sector can be referred to as a "wage paradise," because pay is significantly higher than that of other subsectors of the health sector and other branches of the economy. An important caveat, however, is that these high wage differences prompted evasion of collective agreements at an early point. There was only a brief temporal delay between wage increases for the lower pay groups in the nonprofit and public hospitals in the 1970s and 1980s and full or partial outsourcing of cleaning services to the private cleaning industry, where working conditions were significantly poorer (Mayer-Ahuja 2003). Alongside the features of church labor legislation just described and the associated rather low trade union density, this early evasion of collective agreements in the field of cleaning work is another aspect of the hospital sector that keeps it from being a typical example of the German employment model.

PAY: FROM ONE TO MANY WORLDS OF EMPLOYMENT

Whereas the hospital sector could be described in the past as "quasi-public," despite the fragmented employer structure, since the early

1990s it has developed into a "quasi-market," as in other countries (LeGrand and Bartlett 1993). In the German hospital sector, the aim of quasi-market policies—namely, to restrict public expenses and increase cost efficiency—was mainly achieved by a reform of hospital financing. The reform weakened the previous informal wage coordination, putting pressure on pay. This section starts by detailing the altered conditions, then goes on to analyze their effects on wage development. I focus first on the hospitals' decentralized strategies for undercutting collective agreements, particularly outsourcing. Then I set out the wage cuts and more significant wage differentiations undertaken on the collective agreement level.

INDUSTRIAL RESTRUCTURING: FROM QUASI-PUBLIC TO QUASI-MARKET STRUCTURES

In the 1990s, the modifications of the financing rules gradually reduced hospitals' scope for passing cost increases on to their main customers, the statutory health insurance schemes. First, the settlement of deficits by the health insurance schemes was gradually restricted. Deficits now have to be settled by the hospital owners. Since 1997, cost increases resulting from collectively agreed wage rises have no longer been exempted from budget capping and statutory insurance schemes have paid these extra costs only up to the extent of their own earnings growth. Finally, flat rates have been introduced step by step in place of daily rates, following the example of the American diagnosis-related groups (DRGs). Since 2005, the hospitals' accounts with the health insurance schemes have been switched entirely to DRGs; the level of case flat rates will continue to vary between hospitals during a transitional phase lasting until 2009. This change puts pressure on costs, particularly for those hospitals—primarily larger ones, most of which are publicly run—that previously had case costs above the now-binding flat rates. The hospitals are experiencing additional financial restrictions on investment costs, which are funded by the Bundesländer in the German financing system. Over the past fifteen years, tight local authority budgets have resulted in major cuts in investment in public hospitals, below hospitals' actual requirements. Hospitals therefore now generate a considerable part of their investment funding through operative business (20.5 percent), funding from the owner (5.5 percent), or loans (3.6 percent) (Blum and Schilz 2005, 25).

One consequence of this increasing financial pressure is a change in the provider mix: public hospitals in particular have been sold to private owners over the past fifteen years. In 2004 only 37 percent of hospitals dealing with acute cases were still publicly run (down from 47 percent in 1990), and the number of private for-profit hospitals had risen from 15 percent to 25 percent; the percentage of nonprofit private hospitals remained more or less constant at 38 percent (39 percent in 1990) (Federal Statistical Office, hospital statistics). Compared to other European countries, for-profit hospitals in Germany not only make up a much more important share of the acute care hospital segment but also, owing to strong concentration processes, stand out in company size: the majority of private for-profit hospitals are run as chains, and each of the three largest companies employed a total of more than 25,000 employees in 2006 (Stumpfögger 2007).[3] Concentration is also taking place among the remaining public hospitals. To achieve synergy effects—and in some cases also to defend a local monopoly position against private competitors—some economically healthy public hospitals are buying up or merging with other hospitals in their area.

WAGE POLICY BEYOND COLLECTIVE NEGOTIATIONS: OUTSOURCING

Before the recent cuts in collectively agreed wages, outsourcing was the only possible way for hospitals to save costs through wage reductions. There are no precise statistics available on the extent of outsourcing. The employment development in the ancillary services, including cleaning staff and employees in kitchens, laundries, and transport, can be used as a rough indicator: between 1991 and 2004, employees were reduced by 41 percent to 57,000 (full-time equivalent) (Federal Statistical Office, hospital statistics). The hospitals in our sample also indicated that they had made broad use of outsourcing: in six out of eight hospitals, the cleaning staff were no longer employed by the hospital itself, but by external service providers or Service-GmbHs owned by the hospitals. In a seventh hospital, cleaning services were in the process of being outsourced. In the three church-owned hospitals, outsourcing took place prior to the 1990s.

Outsourcing does not actually shift cleaning work to a zone without collective agreements: the private cleaning sector is one of the very few industries with a generally binding collective wage agreement. Even companies not organized in the employers' association therefore currently (2005) have to pay hourly wages of €7.87 (US$11.54) (West Germany) or €6.36 (US$9.32) (East Germany), corresponding to 53 percent (West) and 59 percent (East) of the median wage.[4] However, since they do not grant any further benefits (such as a Christmas bonus or pension schemes), the private cleaning industry pays wages that are up to 40 percent below those in public hospitals (see table 4.2) and certainly below the low-wage threshold (€9.83 [US$14.41] per hour in West Germany and €7.15 [US$10.48] in East Germany). In addition, companies appear to undercut the collective agreement fairly often, despite it being generally binding (Gather et al. 2005, 145).

Because outsourcing is a decentralized strategy, it could be assumed that the institutional differences between church-run and public hospitals with regard to the existence and codetermination rights of establishment-level employee representation bodies are significant. The case studies confirmed this assumption only to a limited extent. In fact, the influence of the regional economic situation appears to be more important. In economically prosperous regions with many well-paid, privately insured employees, earnings from this group of patients can create important additional income for hospitals, which in turn gives them the financial freedom to pay cleaning staff on the basis of the public sector wage scale.[5] One of the for-profit hospitals in the sample, for instance, is located in such a region and was the only one in our sample in which cleaning services were provided solely by its own employees, who were paid according to the public sector wage scale. According to local trade union representatives, this was also true of most of the hospitals in the city.

The fact that hospitals' ownership plays a more minor role than we might assume is also related to the limited recourse to legal objections and appeals concerning the outsourcing of parts of companies granted to works councils by the Works Constitution Act or to employees themselves by the Dismissal Protection Act. The most significant factor is probably the additional protection from dismissal anchored in the public sector collective agreement (and thus in the church guidelines), which protects employees from being terminated after fifteen years of employment. A comparison of two cases in the sample illustrates the importance of the additional dismissal protection. In one of the public hospitals located in West Germany, despite initiating codetermination proceedings and a public mobilization campaign, the personnel council was not successful in its attempts to prevent a transfer of the cleaning work to an external service provider.[6] However, the case is an example of a successive and so-cially cushioned outsourcing: employees were not dismissed but were only replaced by employees of the service provider after having left voluntarily (to retire, move away, and so on). This approach was at least partly due to employees' long employment periods with the hospital: in 2005 well over 50 percent of the remaining in-house em-ployees had been at the hospital for more than twenty years and thus could not be dismissed under the public collective agreement. By contrast, in one local authority-run hospital (in East Germany), cleaning services were outsourced in the late 1990s. Hospital man-agement used incentive payments to persuade employees to hand in their notice voluntarily and accept the offer of a new employment contract with the external service provider, at the significantly lower wage level of the private cleaning sector. The hospital thus evaded even the minimal statutory regulations in the event of a transfer of undertakings. These stipulate that employees should receive the wages to which they were previously entitled for at least one year. Ac-cording to the chairman of the personnel council, he had few options at the time, since the employees accepted management's offer (a lump-sum payment and a new contract). They did so because they were afraid they would not otherwise be offered employment by the new company in the light of the high regional unemployment rate and because they simultaneously saw little chance of resisting dis-missal by the hospital. Thus, in this case having less protection from dismissal played a role: unlike in the West German hospital, the East German hospital cleaning staff had not yet gained sufficient em-ployment years since reunification to receive the special protection accorded by the collective agreement. Other possible factors were the employees' lesser willingness to take risks due to the region's extremely high unemployment rate, a less-developed trust in the protection of institutions, and the personnel council's relative un-familiarity with the legal options, as it had existed for only a limited period.

The main differences in the current outsourcing processes are thus related to the dynamics of these processes. The result, however, is al-most identical: wages in all outsourced cleaning services are at the level of the commercial cleaning wage scale. This is also true of the Service-GmbHs—the subsidiary companies in which the hospitals hold the major interest. Using this method, hospitals can legally save the 19 percent sales tax they would have to pay to external companies. For this reason, an increasing number of hospitals are beginning to contract their long-outsourced cleaning services back to their subsidiaries. In our sample, two hospitals had done so several years before, and one other hospital was planning such a move in the near future. For the employees, however, this did not entail improved pay. In both Service-GmbHs in our samples, wages were not above the cleaning-sector collective agreement.

This section has focused on the cleaning industry. Both the case studies and further reports from employee representation bodies, however, indicate that some church-run and private hospitals are beginning to set up subsidiaries for nursing assistants or even for a broader range of employees, including qualified staff. New employees in these subsidiaries are hired at significantly lower wages (Gutt 2006). Overall, however, outsourcing nursing assistant services does not appear to be a widespread cost-cutting strategy in hospitals, probably because of their comparatively low numbers and their further reduced employment in hospitals.

STRONGER WAGE DIFFERENTIATION UNDER COLLECTIVE AGREEMENTS

Wage cuts and a stronger wage differentiation have also been included in collective agreements in the past ten years. At first glance, the wage structures appear relatively stable: an analysis of the effectively paid wages in hospitals indicates that the hospital sector still occupies a leading position concerning wages. The rise of low-paid employment is primarily concentrated in the other subsectors of the health sector. Whereas 22.6 percent of full-time employees in the health sector as a whole earned less than the low-wage threshold in 2003 (up from 20.3 percent in 1999), the equivalent figure for hospital workers is only 5.7 percent (see tables 1A.1 and 7.1). The low-wage rate among full-time nursing assistants in the health sector as a whole is almost three times as high (24.5 percent) as in hospitals (8.8 percent), and cleaning staff in the total health sector are more than twice as likely to earn low pay (41.4 percent) than their colleagues employed in hospitals (19.6 percent) (see tables 1A.2 and 7.1).

However, essential aspects of the more recent dynamic, and thus a good part of low-wage employment, are not reflected in these figures—especially cleaning jobs that have switched to a different sector of the economy with lower wage levels through outsourcing, even if the workplace is still a hospital. Second, the figures relate to full-time employees only; low-wage work is more widespread, however, among part-time employees and mini-jobbers in particular (see table 1.5). Because the part-time rates in both target occupations are far above average and still on the rise, the low-wage rate in both groups can be assumed to be much higher than the figures cited here. This also mainly concerns cleaners, since mini-jobs are the dominant employment form in this group. In 2004, 88 percent of cleaners with a mini-job earned an hourly wage below the low-wage threshold (Jaehrling et al. 2006, 117). And finally, the numerous wage cuts negotiated in collective agreements since the mid-1990s are only gradually taking effect in the form of lower wages. The reason for this is Besitzstand regulations, which fully or partly exempt existing employees from wage cuts. Thus, it will not be possible to measure empirically the full effects of the collectively agreed cuts detailed here until the point in the future when increasing numbers of new recruits have become subject to the new regulations.

The agreed wage cuts have different impacts on the various groups of hospital employees. Since the mid-1990s, basic wages for the lower wage groups in the ancillary services have been significantly reduced. A second wave of wage cuts that is currently taking place affects all employees, including the more highly qualified core employees. The main focus is on cutting additional benefits and increasing weekly working hours; basic wages are also being reduced, but to a lesser extent than for the ancillary services. The speed and extent of these developments vary according to the type of ownership. The institutional differences detailed in the previous section are developing their full effect under the new financing rules by opening up differing reaction options for hospital managements and associations.

In the wage agreements of the church-run hospitals, wages for ancillary services such as cleaning were already cut to up to 25 percent below the level of the public sector agreement in the late 1990s (see table 4.2). The church-run hospitals also took the lead in cutting wages for the other employee groups by means of delegation clauses in the second half of the 1990s.[7] These relatively early cuts reflect, among other factors, the church employers' greater autonomy in the matter of setting employment conditions. For example, the delegation clauses in the regional wage agreements were in some cases unilaterally established, against the resistance of the employee representatives (see Ver.di 2004a, 9ff, 14–15).

However, even the higher unionization levels in privatized, formerly local authority–run hospitals and the Works Constitution Act offer only limited permanent protection against a deterioration of working conditions in the lower wage segment. The trade union frequently negotiates transition contracts in the event of privatization; these are intended to contractually prevent staff cuts and deterioration of working conditions. A study commissioned by the trade union Ver.di comes to the conclusion, however, that the common feature of the privatization cases in the study is a stronger wage differentiation, with doctors and qualified nurses tending to earn more and service staff and assistants less (PLS Ramboll 2003, 5). In one of the private for-profit hospitals in the sample, the new wage agreement included wage reductions for most employees' groups; the new wages for nurses were also 6 percent below the level of the previously valid public wage scale. The situation in the other private for-profit hospital, in contrast, appeared surprising at first glance: the in-house collective agreement in this formerly church-run hospital was still based on the public sector agreement—unlike in other hospitals belonging to the same private chain. The former owner, a Protestant institution that still held 25 percent of the shares, had made this a condition of the sale. Again, the regional economy presumably also played a significant role in explaining this anomaly. The second hospital was in a prosperous region, whereas the first hospital was in a region of East Germany with high unemployment and generally low wage levels.

As already indicated, the collective negotiations in private for-profit hospitals are strongly decentralized; in-house agreements remain the dominant form. However, this began to change in 2005, when the trade union Ver.di finally succeeded in entering into negotiations with a number of hospital chains for company-level wage agreements.[8] This move toward a recentralization of collective bargaining was at least partly stimulated by new legislation implementing recent European jurisdiction over working time in the health sector.[9]

In the remaining publicly run hospitals, the continued commitment to the public sector wage scheme does not offer lasting protection against wage cuts. Initially, there were no reductions in collectively agreed wages, partly because hospital wages are not negotiated separately but jointly with other parts of the public sector. Even after the government's 1997 decision to have health insurers compensate for cost increases caused by wage increases only to a minor extent, wage agreements were signed at higher levels than the hospital budget increase rates defined in the legislation (Rocke 2003). This prompted the hospital associations to call for a separate industry-level collective agreement for hospitals (DKG/VKA/VKD 2002), although these demands were unsuccessful. Because hospital operators are generally unable to withdraw from the public sector wage scale, they also fell back on increased outsourcing of parts of their operations, which has had a significant impact on cleaning staff in particular[10] The comprehensive reform of the public sector wage scale in 2005 therefore presumably affects only a minority of hospital cleaning staff.

The public sector wage scale reform was prompted not least by the low wages paid by for-profit and nonprofit private providers of formerly public services, although the reform is not restricted to wage reductions but constitutes a fundamental modernization of the wage structures that was also actively supported by the trade union. The main objective of the reform was to make pay more strongly influenced by the type of activity and less by seniority, family status, or formal qualifications. However, the union also signaled its willingness to accept wage reductions in the lower income band at an early point in order to counteract the continuing flight from collective agreements through privatization and outsourcing in the service areas and to obtain a sector-level wage scale (Ver.di 2004b).

As a result, family-based increments were axed for all occupational groups in the new public sector collective agreement (Tarifvertrag für den öffentlichen Dienst, TVöD); in return, performance-oriented bonuses were introduced in 2007, to be raised successively to 8 percent of each hospital's total annual wage payments. At the time of writing, however, these bonuses had not been put into practice because the modus operandi remained to be negotiated. Additionally, the national agreement allows scope for extending working hours without extra pay. Finally, the basic wage level has also been reduced in many employee groups, including nursing staff (see table 4.1). In contrast, the wage differences between unqualified and qualified nurses have been only slightly increased. Owing to Besitzstand regulations, the changes apply to existing employees only partially, and with a temporal delay.

The cuts for cleaning staff are greater. The new wage scale intro-

Table 4.1 Collectively Agreed Wages for Nursing Staff in Public Hospitals, 2005

Occupation/Pay	BAT (Until January 31, 2005)[a]		TVöD (Since October 1, 2005)[b]	
	East	West	East	West
Unqualified nursing assistant				
Monthly	€1,746 to €2,074	€1,923 to €2,283	€1,570 to €2,073	€1,693 to €2,237
Hourly[c]	€10.07 to €11.97	€11.53 to €13.68	€9.06 to €11.96	€10.15 to €13.41
Nursing assistant with state exam				
Monthly	€1,817 to €2,337	€2,000 to €2,555	€1,626 to €2,332	€1,776 to €2,516
Hourly[c]	€10.48 to €13.48	€11.99 to €15.31	€9.38 to €13.45	€10.65 to €15.08
Nurse (entry-level)				
Monthly	€1,992 to €2,540	€2,175 to €2,778	€1,993 to €2,523	€2,150 to €2,723
Hourly[c]	€11.49 to €14.65	€13.04 to €16.65	€11.50 to €14.56	€12.89 to €16.32
Low-wage threshold (2004)				
Hourly[c]	€7.15 (East); €9.83 (West)			

Source: Author's compilation.

[a] Bundesangestellten Tarifvertrag; eight to nine seniority-based increments, the last received after a maximum of sixteen years; wages (gross) for married employees, including Christmas and holiday pay, excluding children allowance.

[b] Tarifvertrag für den Öffentlichen Dienst Kommunen: four to five seniority-based increments, the last received after fifteen years; wages (gross), including Christmas and holiday pay, excluding performance-related payments.

[c] Hourly wages are calculated for the collectively agreed weekly working time, which is forty hours in East Germany and thirty-eight and a half hours in West Germany. However, in some West German regions, weekly hours have been extended without pay compensation; accordingly, hourly wages are lower in these regions.

duced a new low-wage group, with a monthly entry-level basic wage in 2005 of €1,286 (US$1,885) in West Germany and €1,209 (US $1,773) in East Germany; in West Germany at least, this is below the standard wage in the private cleaning sector. In contrast to the private cleaning industry, however, employees in this wage group continue to receive seniority-based wage increases, as well as benefits such as Christmas bonuses, and are insured under the additional public sector pension scheme, elevating the wages slightly above the wage level in the private cleaning industry (see table 4.2). The new wage group also applies only to new employees. Newly recruited cleaning staff, however, do not automatically fall into the new wage group. In the national wage negotiations, only a limited number of activities were categorized in this group, not including interior cleaning. But the national agreement contains a number of delegation clauses for decentralized negotiations on the state level, and this opens up the possibility that additions might be made to this activity catalog. Additionally, low-skill employees "in danger of outsourcing" might be paid the wage level of the new low wage group. In the future, therefore, we can expect the pay of cleaning staff and other ancillary services employees in public hospitals to show significantly stronger variation by region and individual hospital and to be significantly below the previous wage level, at least in part.

Our case studies give little ground for the trade union's hope that individual hospitals would "in-source" their external cleaning staff again after the reform: because of bonuses and seniority-based increases, pay under the new wage scale is still higher than the wage level in the private cleaning industry. Several hospitals in our sample gave this as a reason why "in-sourcing" was not a viable option for them.

A further consequence of the wage reform is the stronger fragmentation of collective negotiations, both on a regional level and according to occupational groups. The doctors' trade union, Marburger Bund, terminated its collaboration with Ver.di because it was dissatisfied with the outcome of the negotiations, and it has since been carrying out its own negotiations with the hospitals. There has also been fragmentation on the part of the employers: During the negotiations for the TVöD, the Bundesländer left the wage coordination system; as a result, working conditions for employees in the university hospitals, operated by the Bundesländer, and employees in the local-authority-run hospitals have since been negotiated separately. Finally, the TVöD contains, as described earlier, various delegation clauses

Table 4.2 Collectively Agreed Wages for Hospital Cleaning Staff, 2005

Pay	Public Hospitals (BMT-G, Until January 31, 2005)[a]	Public Hospitals (TVöD, Since October 1, 2005)[b]		Church-Owned Hospitals (AVR-DW-EKD, Since June 1, 2004)[a]	Private Cleaning Industry (Since January 1, 2005)
		New Low-Wage Group	Highest-Wage Group for Cleaners		
West					
Monthly	€1,733 to €1,976	€1,386 to €1,548	€1,558 to €1,957	€1,386 to €1,468	€1,330
Hourly[c]	€10.39 to €11.84	€8.28 to €9.28	€9.34 to €11.73	€8.31 to €8.80	€7.87
East					
Monthly	€1,573 to €1,794	€1,281 to €1,435	€1,444 to €1,813	€1,257 to €1,332	€1,075
Hourly[c]	€9.08 to €10.35	€7.39 to €8.28	€8.33 to €10.46	€7.25 to €7.68	€6.36
Low-wage threshold (2004)		€7.15 (East); €9.83 (West)			

Source: Author's compilation.

[a] Wages (gross) for married employees, including Christmas and holiday pay, excluding children allowance.

[b] Wages (gross), including Christmas and holiday pay, excluding performance-related payments.

[c] Hourly wages are calculated for the collectively agreed weekly working time (see table 4.1 notes for more details on public hospitals). In the private cleaning industry, weekly working time is thirty-nine hours in both East and West Germany.

on central issues (working time, pay), making the regional and company-level negotiations more significant.

To summarize, most of the changes in the wage structure affect the employee group of cleaners and more generally the employee group of housekeeping staff. The institutional differences between hospitals with different types of owners have prompted a diverging dynamic rather than different outcomes, at least where wage levels are concerned. Initially, hospital owners responded to the changes to the financing rules with strategies that diverged because of the differences in institutional options. However, these responses set in motion a downward spiral that has at last reached the public sector and is now leading to a realignment of wages—on a much lower level. The new public wage scheme still provides for a better remuneration of cleaners than the collective agreements for private and church-owned hospitals, but the differences are less pronounced. Even within the group of public hospitals, the collective agreement's unifying effect on wages has weakened owing to the various delegation clauses. Therefore, even if the trade union succeeds in making the new public wage scale a benchmark for collective agreements with the privately run hospital chains, this benchmark, at least in some regions, will be only a little higher than the collectively agreed wages in the private cleaning industry. Hence, if pay differences among hospitals persist at all, it can be assumed that regional factors will play a more determining role than differences with regard to ownership. As we have seen, the regional labor market situation has already played out as a differentiating factor in the past: a high unemployment rate facilitates the enforcement of unilateral wage cuts (through either outsourcing or "negotiated" wage cuts), and an overall high unemployment rate also limits hospitals' financial resources and therefore increases the pressure on wages in general.

WORK ORGANIZATION: THE REDUCTION OF INTERMEDIATE OCCUPATIONS

Like outsourcing, changing the organization of work is another decentralized strategy pursued by hospitals that affects the quality and quantity of the target occupations in our study. In both housekeeping and nursing, "intermediate" occupations, which bridge the gaps in status, pay, and qualifications between occupations requiring three years' vocational training and activities with no formal qualification requirements, are on the decline. Unlike in countries such as France and the United Kingdom, there has been greater vertical integration of unskilled nursing activities into the profile of qualified nurses with three years' vocational training in Germany. In the area of non-patient-related housekeeping tasks, in contrast, Germany is characterized by a strong division of labor between employee groups with rather narrow task profiles. There have been very few attempts to combine housekeeping tasks—in contrast to the United States, where recruitment problems in the 1990s prompted hospitals to at least partly aim for improvements in job quality in housekeeping services (Appelbaum et al. 2003).

One of the obvious reasons for this difference between the United States and Germany is that there have not been any recruitment problems in Germany for the two occupations under study for a very long time, regardless of whether the respective local unemployment rate is (relatively) low or high (Hieming et al. 2005). In West Germany, this oversupply of labor is due to the high unemployment rate among the low-skilled in general, but particularly among both skilled and low-skilled female migrant workers, who often make up the majority of the cleaning staff in the hospitals. In East Germany, hospitals have no problems recruiting among German nationals owing to the very high overall unemployment rate.

NURSING ASSISTANTS: WHO IS WASHING THE PATIENTS?

Compared to hospitals in other countries, German hospitals employ a conspicuously low and still-declining number of nursing assistants. Currently, there is approximately one nursing assistant for every twelve qualified nurses (see table 4.3), whereas the ratio in other countries is around one to two and a half (United Kingdom) or even one to one (France) (Carroll et al. 2006).

These differences in the composition of nursing staffs have not always been so stark; the development in postwar Germany was initially similar to that in other countries. In 1963 recruitment problems for qualified and unqualified nursing staff paved the way for the introduction of a state examination for nursing assistants, which is taken after one year's training. As in France and the United Kingdom, a formal status for a "second type of nurse" was thus created in Germany (Kreutzer 2005, 260), despite initial resistance on the part of

Table 4.3 Employee Groups in Hospitals That Assumed Assisting Tasks in Nursing, 1991 to 2004

Year	Full-time Equivalents (Annual Average)		Number of Employees (as of December 31)				
	Nurses[a]	Nursing Assistants[a]	Nurses[b]	Nursing Assistants[b]	Nurses in Training	Nursing Assistants in Training	Community Service Conscripts
1991	n.a.	n.a.	322,655	66,856	n.a	n.a	n.a.
1997	376,000	44,000	364,911	55,395	n.a.	n.a.	n.a.
2000	383,000	39,000	367,076	47,402	70,578	1,876	n.a.
2002	376,000	37,000	372,723	44,559	68,287	1,850	16,728
2004	371,000	33,000	357,843	38,848	64,701	1,527	14,070
2006	363,000	30,000	354,967	37,744	62,557	1,678	13,081
Changes	1997 to 2006: −3%	1997 to 2006: −32%	1991 to 2006: +10%	1991 to 2006: −44%	2000 to 2006: −11%	2000 to 2006: −11%	2000 to 2006: −22%

Source: Federal Statistical Office, hospital statistics, vol. 2000 to 2004; DKG (2004, 38, 41); author's calculations.
[a] Including nurses and nursing assistants not based on the wards and nurses and nursing assistants in training.
[b] Only nurses and nursing assistants based on the wards; not including nurses and nursing assistants in training.

trade unions and nursing associations. This new type was differentiated from the group of unqualified nursing assistants by an institutionalized training program and correspondingly higher pay.[11] By 1974 the number of qualified and unqualified nursing assistants amounted to about one-third of all nursing staffs (Simon 2000, 56). Since then, however, their numbers have continually declined. Thus, we may ask: who takes over tasks such as washing patients in their place? And what are the reasons for this obviously altered work organization?

Somewhat surprisingly, demographic change and changes in medical technology and practices seem to be of minor importance for the division of labor between nurses and nursing assistants: the decreases in the length of stay and the altered patient population (older and sicker) in acute care hospitals have not been mentioned by care managers as reasons to refrain from employing nursing assistants. Instead, three key combinations of causes for this development can be made out from the case studies: first, the traditionally low staffing levels in the nursing staff group, which demand high temporal and functional flexibility; second, the small wage difference between nursing assistants and qualified nurses; and third, the existence of a number of cheaper "assistants."

The first cause, low staffing levels in care, is a characteristic feature that has distinguished the employment structure in German hospitals from that in other countries for some time. As Heinz Rothgang (1994, 371f) shows in his comparison of the United Kingdom and Germany, the comparatively low number of nursing staff per bed is the consequence of cost-containment efforts that have frozen the traditionally low ratio of nursing staff to doctors in Germany.[12] The strategy of cost reduction via a restrictive staffing policy (rather than wage cuts) is also a typical reaction to the financial restrictions across the entire public sector since the mid-1970s; according to Bernd Keller (1993, 194), the public sector was a trendsetter in this regard.

The hospitals involved in our research can be used to show why this strategy influences the use of qualified nursing assistants. New employees from this group are no longer recruited in any of the hospitals. The main reason given for this development is the need for temporal and functional flexibility in nursing staff: "Because the staffing levels in the individual wards and departments is getting lower and lower," said the works council chairwoman in a public hospital, "you have to make sure that the few jobs there are go to staff who can do everything—who can work all the shifts." Many nurse managers, head nurses, and employee representatives made similar statements. Our interviewees were in fact broadly unanimous in testifying to a strong overlapping of tasks between the qualified nurses and the qualified nursing assistants who had long-term tenure in their jobs (Bachstein 2004, 223)—meaning that the latter have been functionally flexible. But this appears to be mainly the result of the repeated shortages of qualified staff, which have led to more highly skilled tasks being entrusted to experienced nursing assistants—for example, according to one nurse manager, nursing assistants were allowed to take over night shifts on the ward. However, such flexible uses of nursing assistants have become less common recently. Although there are no statutory regulations preventing the previously accepted transfer of tasks, increasing restrictions are arising from liability law. As an apparent result of legislation, and certainly also in the light of the altered patient structure (due to the demographic change and shorter periods of stay in hospitals), a standard for staffing night shifts has now developed, and the majority of nursing managers in our study observed it: at least one qualified nurse is scheduled per ward, and a second nurse is scheduled if the ward includes more than about thirty-five patients. Under these circumstances, hospitals decide against recruiting nursing assistants with the one-year qualification.

A second cause also plays an important role, namely, the low wage differences. This nursing director at a public hospital spoke for many of the nurse managers we interviewed in presenting the following argument: "If they hardly cost me any less than a qualified nurse, I don't need them. . . . Then I'd rather take a twenty-one- or twenty-two-year-old nurse. She's still quite cheap, but she has the full competence." The use of the "second type of nurse" under the old model—that is, with a higher overlap of tasks between nursing assistants and nurses—thus appears to be on its way out, since the low wage differences are no longer balanced out against the increasing differences in temporal and functional flexibility from the perspective of nursing management.

The situation in the case of unqualified nursing assistants—who are, to a certain extent, a "third type of nurse"—is slightly different. Although their percentages are also declining, our case study hospitals were still recruiting staff in this group, albeit to a relatively limited extent: one to two new unqualified nursing assistants had been recruited in each of only two hospitals over the past few years. The reasons for deciding in favor of unqualified nursing assistants were lower wage costs and simultaneously an altered model of division of labor, which appeared to make formal qualifications redundant for nursing assistants. The new nursing assistants were responsible for a very limited area of tasks; mainly, they washed patients on the early shift. In both hospitals, it was no coincidence that this task was delegated to nursing assistants on large wards with forty to fifty beds. In these larger organizational units, the hours needed for the limited task area added up to at least a part-time job, and the restricted flexibility of nursing assistants was not of major concern.

Another alternative to nursing assistants is the use of interns, community service conscripts (Zivildienstleistende, ZDLs), student assistants, and nurses in training—what we could refer to as a "fourth type of nurse." Trainee nurses are the largest such group—in one case in our sample, the head nurse stated that up to six nurses in training sometimes worked alongside eleven and a half qualified nurses. The common feature of all the aforementioned groups is that their pay is significantly below that of regular nursing assistants; they are also— with the exception of the ZDLs and some interns—in training for a nursing or medical occupation and therefore already possess vocational skills, depending on the phase of their training. However, only a few hospitals stated that they recruited additional employees from these groups, and only two hospitals planned to recruit more ZDLs in the future (or their female equivalents—that is, young women taking part in a "voluntary social year" program). One of the hospitals intended to do so as a reaction, not to a reduction in nursing assistants, but to recent changes in the vocational training regulations, which have increased the amount of classroom time for nurses in training and thus reduced their hours on the wards.[13] The available statistics (see table 4.3) indicate that the number of members of these groups who are employed is declining. Thus, although the use of these groups of employees may partly explain the lower numbers of nursing assistants in German hospitals that has been observable for some time, there is no indication that the use of these groups is *currently* increasing.

Overall, despite occasional new recruitments of unqualified nursing assistants or ZDLs, we can thus observe a decline in the employee groups that take over basic care tasks—in particular, from nurses. Activities such as washing patients are increasingly becoming the responsibility of qualified nurses with three years' training. In contrast to the cleaning subsector, a stronger vertical integration of tasks is therefore taking place in patient care. The general wish for stronger vertical differentiation that many nurse managers expressed in the interviews can, however, be interpreted as an indication that the current concentration on nurses with three years' training is not a stable and standard model that will permanently replace the old model of work organization and wage differentiation. Should further reforms adapt vocational training for nurses to that of other countries, such as the United Kingdom, in the future—nursing associations and academic institutions have been calling for this step for several years, partly prompted by corresponding political initiatives on the European level (the "Bologna process")—this may provide hospitals with an incentive to increase their use of nursing assistants once again. In the absence of such a centrally negotiated reform of the vocational training system, however, it is also possible that hospitals might start employing increasing numbers of unqualified nursing assistants on a decentralized basis—perhaps also, as is already the case with a few hospitals, outside of the previously valid public sector wage structures.

CLEANING: WHO IS MOPPING THE FLOOR?

Housekeeping services in German hospitals, including cleaning, are divided between a large number of occupations with rather narrow ranges of tasks. Those employees who clean the patients' rooms are not generally responsible for other tasks that are more closely patient-related. Distributing meals and cleaning bedside tables are partly the tasks of other housekeeping staff or the nursing staff themselves.

This is another area in which opposite approaches were originally taken. In the 1950s, the concept of a "senior ward assistant" endorsed greater relief to nurses from patient-related housekeeping tasks (Kreutzer 2005, 255ff). The transfer of activities such as food portioning, meal distribution, and cleaning of bedside tables to the existing housekeeping staff was intended to be accompanied by improved pay. Further-reaching demands called for this work to be transferred to a new occupational group, which was conceived as an advanced position for unskilled janitorial staff (such as cleaning staff) and distinguished by formal qualifications. In practice, a distinction between ward assistants and cleaning staff appears to have been established in many hospitals for several decades at least, whereas a formal qualification for ward assistants has remained an exception.

The current work organization in hospitals is not standardized: in some of our case studies, nursing staff were responsible for many housekeeping tasks. In nearly all of the hospitals, for instance, it was the nursing staff and trainees who distributed meals, and in some cases they were also responsible for making up empty beds and cleaning bedside tables (see also Blum 2003). Other tasks, such as cleaning up vomit, were carried out by nursing staff when no house-keeping staff were present on the wards—as was frequently the case in the afternoons, at night, and on weekends, since the cleaning staff's working hours were restricted to mornings and in some cases ended as early as 10:00 or 11:00 A.M. Some hospitals had stand-in services to work afternoons and weekends, but they did not seem to be sufficiently staffed to cover all the work that arose: both ward managers and the nursing staff stated in our interviews that they carried out cleaning tasks themselves several times a week. Another reason was that a number of activities (food portioning, bed cleaning, running errands) have been outsourced from the wards over the course of the centralizations that began in the 1970s and divided between several employee groups; in some cases, the activity in question was subsequently outsourced entirely to external service providers. Most hospitals therefore no longer employed ward assistants, who had carried out a broad range of tasks on the ward, spending correspondingly longer hours there.

The housekeeping activities previously combined in the job profile of the nursing staff and ward assistants is thus now carried out by various employee groups: cleaning of the patients' direct surroundings (bedside tables) is generally the task of the cleaning staff, usually employed externally; meals are prepared and portioned in a central kitchen, which is frequently run by external service providers; and beds are often cleaned centrally. This division of activities has almost certainly made outsourcing easier; in addition, transferring tasks to various external service providers has raised the barriers for reintegrating these tasks. On the other hand, the transfer of several tasks to a single service provider (as in one of the hospitals) or the reintegration of outsourced ancillary services into hospital-owned services companies (as in two hospitals) opens up the theoretical possibility of more strongly combining the various tasks once again. However, only one hospital, primarily motivated by financial reasons, has done this. Combining activities is connected to a leveling of wage differences at the lower level of the cleaning staff. According to the project manager, another reason in favor of this stronger integration is greater flexibility and simpler staff planning, since all employees can now stand in for each other in the event of absences.[14] In the other hospitals, in which the activities are not combined, other housekeepers on the wards are also paid on the same wage scale as the cleaning staff.

As with nursing assistants, ward assistants have been a temporary "intermediate" employee group who are intended to take the pressure off qualified nurses to do housekeeping tasks and who are between cleaning staff and nursing staff in status, pay, and qualifications. However, this approach has been in decline for some time.

CHANGES IN JOB QUALITY AND MOBILITY

Further hospital strategies for dealing with the altered basic conditions have affected other aspects of the employment relationship in both employee groups; in part, the developments observed there are also a direct consequence of the changes in pay structures and work organization described here.

INCREASING WORKLOADS

Cleaning staff in particular are affected by increasing workloads. The most common form is raising the required cleaning area per person and working hour. This strategy is closely linked with outsourcing activities; it has been practiced in particular by private cleaning companies since the 1970s and has led to a huge increase in cleaning area guidelines (Mayer-Ahuja 2003, 181ff). As various studies show (Gather et al. 2005, 146ff; Hieming et al. 2005, 106), this strategy is particularly used to compensate for wage increases or when contracts are renegotiated: in the event of increases in collectively agreed wages, this method is used to sidestep wage rises in a (semi-) legal manner, since the total wages for the area to be cleaned are kept constant by simultaneously reducing the paid working hours. When new contracts are signed or extended with clients, the scheduled working hours and thus the total price are reduced, to avoid being underbid by the competition. Clients are generally willing to award contracts to the cheapest company—taking into account the consequences for the quality of cleaning services and demands on cleaning staff. This is even the case when a company has previously provided inferior cleaning services. One of the public hospitals, for instance, had received frequent complaints about the quality of the cleaning provided by the previous company, but it awarded the next contract to an even cheaper service provider. The profit margins for cleaning services are correspondingly low; even the high market concentration in hospital cleaning does not appear to allow the large cleaning companies to set higher prices.[15]

In those case study hospitals that provided information on the subject, the guidelines for cleaning patients' rooms were between 170 and 260 square meters per hour. However, these figures alone are not particularly informative, since the time required for cleaning depends on the cleaning intensity. Comparison with another statistic makes this clear: in one hospital, each cleaning employee had a target area rate of 190 square meters per hour, equivalent to around two and a half hours for cleaning a ward with thirty-seven beds (in patient rooms, ancillary rooms, and corridors). In another hospital, a cleaning employee had an only slightly lower target area rate of 170 square meters per hour for the same tasks on a ward of similar size (thirty-six beds) and around 50 percent more time (three hours and fifty minutes). The differences may have been at least partially due to different equipment and fittings and different cleaning method requirements (cleaning floors once or twice). In general, however, requirements at the sample hospitals were significantly above the recommendation made by REFA-Bundesverband.[16] The organization's 2002 recommendation for hospital rooms varied between 112 and 150 square meters per hour, depending on the fittings and cleaning intensity (REFA-Bundesverband 2002). The extremely high fluctuation levels in the private cleaning sector (Hieming et al. 2005, 74) are caused not least by these ever-increasing workloads; it is not unusual for staff to be dismissed—or even to resign of their own accord—because they cannot meet the high performance demands over the long term (Jaehrling and Weinkopf 2005).

Increasing workloads were also reported for the nursing staff; for sheer numerical reasons, this mainly concerns qualified nurses. The statements of nursing staff in our case studies are confirmed by a recent survey among nurse managers: more than 90 percent of them declared that workloads for nursing staff are continuously increasing and that this factor—apart from the additional time and effort needed for coordination, administration, and documentation tasks—was a major reason for higher patient turnover and an increased need of care per patient (Isforth and Weidner 2007).[17]

WORKING TIME

As in the economy as a whole, there has been a rise in part-time employment in the two target occupations over the past few years. In 2003, 46 percent of nursing assistants and 83 percent of cleaners in the health sector worked part-time—above the already high overall part-time rate in hospitals of 36.5 percent (see table 1A.3). Mini-jobs are particularly widespread among cleaners (54 percent), whereas for nursing assistants the share of mini-jobs is below average (13 percent). These figures do not reveal whether part-time work in these occupations is voluntary or involuntary. On the basis of the low number of employees we were able to interview, I cannot make any statement about the voluntary or involuntary status of their part-time work. Our case studies, however, do clearly indicate that it is increasingly rare for employees to have a choice about working full-time or part-time. In part, dividing the work volume between several part-time jobs rather than maintaining full-time jobs results from the changes already described here and is a conscious employer strategy, in the case of both nursing assistants and cleaning staff.

With cleaning staff, the practice referred to here as a "part-time strategy" is also a complementary strategy to increasing workloads. A Service-GmbH in one of the public hospitals, for instance, recruited new staff only with part-time contracts—"simply because we assume that someone who works fifty, sixty-five, or seventy-five percent of the day can achieve the workload far better than someone who has to work one hundred percent," said the manager. In fact, this is a "best case" example, because all employees in the company were offered at least part-time contracts for over nineteen hours per week. In the other hospitals, in contrast, up to 60 percent of the external service providers' staff were employed on a mini-job basis.

Another barrier for employment contracts with longer hours is the rather narrow range of tasks, for which the work per day adds up to only a few (consecutive) hours. This is particularly the case for unqualified nursing assistants, only very few of whom are employed in hospitals: those few hospitals that do still recruit them explicitly ad-vertise part-time jobs (up to 50 percent), whereas the qualified nurs-ing assistants with a broader range of tasks in these hospitals tend to have full-time jobs. In the case of cleaning staff, in contrast, there seems to be scope for employment contracts with more hours despite the narrow range of tasks. This becomes clear through the example of one of the public hospitals in our sample, which still employed some cleaning staff directly, almost two-thirds of whom actually worked full-time; the rest worked part-time (more than 50 percent). The strong concentration of cleaning activities in the early morning—which was standard in the other hospitals and rendered employment contracts with longer hours impossible, with only a few exceptions—thus does not appear to be strictly necessary.

The already low earning possibilities due to low hourly wages are thus reduced by this part-time strategy. Although the hourly wages for nursing assistants are above the low-wage threshold, the high part-time rate makes it difficult to earn a living income in this occupation.

INTERNAL LABOR MARKETS AND MOBILITY BETWEEN COMPANIES

Both outsourcing and the developments in the field of work organi-zation have direct consequences for employees' upward mobility. Outsourcing in many ancillary services makes it more difficult for cleaning staff to switch to better-paid jobs within the hospital. In the past, such transfers were made easier by the fact that jobs were often initially advertised internally. In one of the public hospitals, for ex-ample, it was not unusual for the hospital-employed cleaning staff to make internal applications for higher-paid jobs in the kitchens or laundry. The ward assistants (still employed in this hospital) were also primarily recruited from among the cleaning staff. The more ac-tivities are outsourced, however, the higher the mobility barriers be-come. First, there are hardly any jobs remaining within the hospital for which employees can apply internally. If various external service providers are contracted, an employee can no longer change occupa-tions within the same company but must change employers. Fur-thermore, changing jobs is hardly financially attractive any longer, because the previously existing wage differences—for example, be-tween cleaning staff and ward assistants—have been extensively lev-eled out in parallel with the outsourcing process.

Another barrier for advancement arises from the fact that the intermediate positions that can bridge the gap between unqualified and qualified activities no longer exist to any significant extent. For example, unlike nursing assistants with one year's training, unqualified nursing assistants cannot register for a reduced two-year nursing training program. A further hurdle is that the nursing training program cannot be pursued part-time alongside work: it is offered almost exclusively on a full-time basis. Unlike in other occupations, it is also impossible to take an external examination after six years' vocational experience. Nursing assistants therefore have to be prepared to live on a comparatively low training grant (€695 [US$1,019] in East Germany, €729 [US$1,069] in West Germany) during the three-year nurses' training program. This illustrates that the vocational training system is particularly designed for young school-leavers who still live with their parents and less for older employees who have to gain their living on their own.

Particularly in comparison to British hospitals (Grimshaw and Carroll, forthcoming), unqualified nursing assistants have low promotion and advancement chances in German hospitals. This example thus also highlights the negative side of the German vocational training system, which results in poorer employment and advancement possibilities for those who do not complete vocational training early in life than for those pursuing this training in countries with less relevant, less standardized vocational training systems, such as the United Kingdom and the United States (Mason, Finegold, and Wagner 2000). The decreasing percentage of nursing assistants in hospitals, however, also enables an increasing percentage of nursing staff to profit from the vocational training system—in that they acquire broadly applicable skills and qualifications that bring them relatively early promotion possibilities, among other effects (Mason, Finegold, and Wagner 2000). To this extent, we can speak of a polarization of advancement possibilities among nursing staff, whereby the pole with the deteriorating advancement possibilities (nursing assistants) is of declining significance.

SUMMARY AND CONCLUSIONS

Earning possibilities for nursing and cleaning work are currently developing in two different directions: wage cuts, cuts in working hours, and worsened possibilities for promotion and advancement mainly affect cleaning staff. In nursing, by contrast, the percentage of low-skill and low-paid employees (nursing assistants) is decreasing.

What role has been played in this development by the institutional infrastructure of the German model, particularly the system of industrial relations and the vocational training system? From a purely descriptive standpoint, we can first establish that the changes for cleaning staff are to a great extent the result of *bypassing* the previously relevant institutions—particularly by means of outsourcing—and that ultimately has a reciprocal effect on these institutions: the wage decreases in the outsourced areas have also made their way into the public sector wage scale by means of the recent reforms. On the other hand, the declining percentages of nursing assistants equate to an *increase* in the significance of the vocational training system, since almost all nursing staff now pass through the three-year vocational training program. The developments in nursing and cleaning are thus diverging not only with regard to pay but also with regard to institutional stability.

Nevertheless, we may be able to use one single explanation to understand these differing developments: "Employer interest, not just union strength, accounts for the stability of the system," Kathleen Thelen and Ikuo Kume (1999, 490) conclude in their analysis of the German system of industrial relations. In other words, the stability of traditional institutions is not necessarily a result of institutional "inertia" or successful trade union defense activities and thus a relic of times past. Instead, it is at least also due to the active support of employers, who are committed to these institutions for economic reasons. Thelen and Kume's explanation is primarily based on the metalworking industry; however, it can also claim significant plausibility in the hospital sector. From the employer perspective, the advantage of an increased percentage of qualified nurses consists of cost savings that can be made through the functional and temporal flexibility of the qualified employees. Thus, employers, partly in their own interests, continue using a strategy that is based on the institutional infrastructure of the vocational training system. This strategy simultaneously creates greater relevance for the system. The (as yet few) examples of hospitals that pursue a different strategy—namely, making more extensive use of inexpensive nursing assistants—show that "union strength" at least also confirms hospitals in their choice, since it is no coincidence that public hospitals, with their traditionally stronger representation of employee interests, appear to have refrained from this step to date—even though they have the same statutory possibilities.

In the reverse form, the thesis can also contribute to an understanding of the institutional *erosion* process: "Employer *dis*interest, not just union *weakness*," is a decisive reason for the dissolution of the informal wage coordination and wage cuts in the hospital sector. Union weakness was already a characteristic of broad sections of the hospital sector in the past. Previously, however, informal wage coordination was very much in the interest of the nonprofit private hospitals, which thereby reduced recruitment problems in the face of perennially low supplies of qualified staff. In the case of cleaning staff, this thesis applies only in a milder form, since employers' interest in exploiting wages differences was already great during the heyday of the German model, as the early use of outsourcing illustrates. However, these possibilities are exploited even more today. Thus, the change is not primarily in the institutions, which have always harbored gaps in the regulations, but in employers' willingness to make use of these gaps to cut costs. High unemployment rates also contribute to existing institutions' loss of relevance: employees do not call on their support for fear of losing their jobs. In this sense, trade unions' and works councils' relative inability to effectively close the gaps in the regulations also plays a role.

The importance of the employers' self-interest also focuses attention on the factors influencing them—namely, the financing rules. Up to the early 1990s, the financing rules were "neutral" to such an extent that they set few limits on the collective negotiations between employers and trade unions and informal wage coordination, since wage-led cost increases could be passed on to the statutory health insurance schemes. Yet the modifications of these financing rules since then have given employers reason to develop a strong interest in avoiding comparatively high wages and informal wage coordination in order to comply with the budget restrictions. Policy decisions that set the financial conditions into the form of a "quasi-market" have thereby gained significance. Thus, a second arena has emerged to a certain extent alongside collective negotiations, one in which important decisions are made concerning wages in hospitals. As a result, trade unions must devote energy not only to the strategies of corporatist negotiations but also even greater energy to the strategies of political lobbying.

NOTES

1. In 2004, 84 percent of hospitals' operating costs were paid by the public sector—the lion's share (81 percent) by the statutory health insurance schemes (Federal Statistical Office, health expenditure statistics).

2. This constitutes a significant difference from the United Kingdom, where the most influential interest organization for nursing staff, the Royal College of Nursing (RCN), represents only the specific interests of the occupational group of qualified nurses (Hassel 1999, 179f). Unlike the RCN, the German professional organizations in nursing, the most influential of which is the Deutsche Berufsverband für Pflege (DBfK), have no direct influence on wage negotiations but concentrate on coregulating and codeveloping vocational training.

3. The privatization and concentration processes in the hospital sector have also attracted investors from abroad. In August 2006, for the first time, a European health care company (Capio AB) took over a German hospital chain. (A global private equity group, Apax Partners, took over Capio only three months later.)

4. The figures refer to the median wages in 2004, calculated separately for East and West Germany. The median wages relate to all employees (full-time as well as part-time). For further details, see chapter 1, table 1.4.

5. From a certain monthly income level—currently €3,938 (US$5,774)—employees can take out private insurance rather than remain in the statutory health insurance schemes. Such a patient is lucrative for hospitals because they can invoice special services to the private insurer—such as accommodation in a better-equipped room or treatment by senior consultants. In 2004, 10 percent of the expenses for hospitals were financed by private insurance (Federal Statistical Office, health expenditure statistics).

6. In-house employee representation bodies in public companies and administration are referred to as personnel councils. Their codetermination rights are broadly identical with those of works councils on most issues.

7. The Protestant Church's social outreach ministries (Diakonische Werke) in parts of Northrhine-Westphalia, for example, concluded a "job-securing regulation" (Beschäftigungssicherungsordnung) in 1999 that provided hospitals with the option of either cutting the Christmas bonus (as of 2004, by half) or extending weekly working hours without extra pay (as of 2004, to up to forty hours per week) in exchange for a one-year dismissal stop. According to their own information, nearly 20 percent of employees in Protestant hospitals and other social institutions in Germany were affected by this and similar emergency agreements in 2004 (see Die Welt, April 22, 2005, 12).

8. The first company-level agreement was concluded in January 2007 with the second-largest chain (Helios Kliniken GmbH).

9. The new law on working time to some extent supports unions in their efforts to get employers back to the bargaining table, because the law makes exemptions from maximum limits for daily and weekly working hours conditional on the conclusion of a collective agreement. Because hospitals are strongly interested in an extension of working time for some of their employee groups (primarily doctors), Ver.di is trying to use this as a lever to conclude package deals, that is, to negotiate not only working time for some employee groups but working conditions in general for all employee groups. However, the breakup of Marburger Bund and Ver.di and the fact that Marburger Bund has also begun to conclude separate agreements with private hospital chains has made this lever less powerful.

10. At the very least, local-authority hospitals governed by public law are unable to withdraw from the public sector wage scale. In this case, it is the local authorities, not hospital management, who are members of the employers' association, Vereinigung der kommunalen Arbeitgeberverbände (VKA), so it would be possible only for the whole local authority to leave the association. Public hospitals under private law can withdraw, however, and a number of them have indeed done so, particularly in East Germany during the latest negotiations on the reform of collective bargaining law in the public service.

11. As is the case with the three-year nurses' training program, the one-year training course takes place in specific vocational schools that are usually affiliated with hospitals; as in the dual vocational training system, however, the phases of practical learning on the job outweigh the theoretical elements.

12. A central control mechanism here can be found in the "staff reference figures" (Personalanhaltszahlen), that is, the standard values for the number of employees per bed day. These were used as early as the beginning of the 1970s by the statutory health insurance schemes in budget negotiations with the hospitals as a means of containing job expansion and therefore cost expansion. Staffing increases as a result of service expansion therefore occurred only belatedly and remained significantly below the increase in British nursing staff per bed day (Rothgang 1994, 358ff).

13. Although nurses' training is nominally classroom-based, the practical aspects occupy a broad part of it: until recently, it was standard for nurses in training to spend four days in the hospital and one day in the classroom.

14. Improvement of job quality was cited as another reason: "Because you also raise the image of the normal cleaner . . . [they have to] not just

plow through the square meters, but by making coffee or handing out and collecting trays they also get a bit more contact with the nurses and patients," said one manager of a Service-GmbH in a public hospital. This extension of tasks was therefore positively evaluated by most cleaning staff, according to the management, even if it did not entail wage rises. With regard to the extremely high physical demands in room cleaning ("plow[ing] through the square meters"), this seems understandable. However, we were not able to interview the employees themselves.

15. The example of ISS Facility Services—an internationally operating cleaning company with headquarters in Denmark—proves this point. It was the market leader in Germany for a certain period but withdrew from the segment in 2005. Alongside the loss of contracts as a consequence of the increasingly common Service-GmbHs, the company's general manager for human resources also put this decision down to the high price pressure and the very low profit margins compared to other countries (less than 5 percent).

16. REFA-Bundesverband, a national organization, has a long tradition in the field of measuring labor productivity, and representatives of employers' associations and trade unions sit on its industry committees.

17. Moreover, more than 40 percent of the nurse managers expected the situation to be aggravated by the collectively agreed wage increases for doctors, which it was assumed would lead to staff cuts among nursing staff.

REFERENCES

Appelbaum, Eileen, Peter Berg, Ann Frost, and Gil Preuss. 2003. "The Effects of Work Restructuring on Low-Wage, Low-Skilled Workers in U.S. Hospitals." In *Low-Wage America: How Employers Are Reshaping Opportunities in the Workplace*, edited by Eileen Appelbaum, Annette Bernhardt, and Richard J. Murnane. New York: Russell Sage Foundation.

Bachstein, Elke. 2004. "Pflegefremde Mitarbeiter im Krankenhaus" ["Hospital Workers Not Involved in Patient Care"]. *Pflege Aktuell* (April): 222–6.

Baumann-Czichon, Bernhard, and Mira Gathmann. 2006. "Kirchliche Mitbestimmung im Vergleich: BetrVG–MVG/EKD–MAVO" ["Codetermination in Churches Compared"]. Berlin: Ver.di (Vereinigte Dienstleistungsgewerkschaft).

Blum, Karl. 2003. *Pflegefremde und patientenferne Tätigkeiten im Pflegedienst der Krankenhäuser: Bestandsaufnahme und Verbesserungsvorschläge [Activities Unrelated to Patient Care in Hospital Nursing Departments—A Review of the Situation and Proposals for Improvement]*. Düsseldorf: Deutsches Krankenhaus-Institut.

Blum, Karl, and Patricia Schilz. 2005. *Krankenhaus-Barometer: Umfrage 2005 [Hospital Barometer: Survey 2005]*. Düsseldorf: Deutsches Kranken-haus-Institut.

Carroll, Marilyn, Damian Grimshaw, Karen Jaehrling, and Philippe Méhaut. 2006. "Shaping and Reshaping the Work Organization: Including or Excluding Low-Skilled Labor? The Case of the Nurse Assistant in Germany, France, and the United Kingdom." Paper prepared for the SASE conference. Trier, Germany, July 2006.

DKG/VKA/VKD. 2002. "Krankenhausverbände fordern einen Spartentar-ifvertrag," Gemeinsame Presseerklärung der Deutschen Krankenhausge-sellschaft (DKG), der Vereinigung der kommunalen Arbeitgeberverbände (VKA), und des Verbands der Krankenhausdirektoren Deutschlands (VKD) ["Hospital Associations Demand a Sectoral Collective Agree-ment." Joint Press Statement by the German Hospital Organisation, the Union of Local Authority Employers' Associations and the Association of Hospital Directors]. Berlin, September 16, 2002.

Gather, Claudia, Ute Gerhard, Heidi Schroth, and Lena Schürmann. 2005. *Vergeben und vergessen? Gebäudereinigung im Spannungsfeld zwis-chen kommunalen Diensten und Privatisierung [Farmed Out and Forgotten? Cleaning Services Between Municipal Provision of Services and Privatiza-tion]*. Hamburg, Germany: VSA.

Grimshaw, Damian, and Marilyn Carroll. Forthcoming. "Improving the Po-sition of Low-Wage Workers Through New Coordinating Institutions: The Case of Public Hospitals." In *Low-Wage Work in the United Kingdom*, edited by Caroline Lloyd, Geoff Mason, and Ken Mayhew. New York: Rus-sell Sage Foundation.

Gutt, Helga. 2006. "Erklärung der Arbeitnehmerseite der Arbeitsrechtlichen Kommission des Diakonischen Werks der EKD (ARK-DW-EKD)" ["State-ment by the Employees' Side of the Labor Law Committee of the German Protestant Church Social Outreach Ministry"]. May 22, 2006.

Hassel, Anke. 1999. *Gewerkschaften und sozialer Wandel: Mitgliederrekru-tierung und Arbeitsbeziehungen in Deutschland und Grossbritannien [Trade Unions and Social Change. Union Recruitment and Working and Employ-ment Conditions in Germany and the United Kingdom]*. Baden-Baden, Ger-many: Nomos.

Hieming, Bettina, Karen Jaehrling, Thorsten Kalina, Achim Vanselow, and Claudia Weinkopf. 2005. "Stellenbesetzungsprozesse im Bereich 'ein-facher' Dienstleistungen" ["Recruitment Processes in 'Low-Skill' Ser-vices"]. Report 550. Berlin: Bundesministerium für Wirtschaft und Ar-beit.

Isforth, Michael, and Frank Weidner. 2007. *Pflege-Thermometer 2007. Eine bundesweite repräsentative Befragung zur Situation und zum Leistungsspek-trum des Pflegepersonals sowie zur Patientensicherheit im Krankenhaus*

[*Care Thermometer 2007. A Survey on the Situation and Activities of Nursing Staff and on Patient's Security in Hospitals*]. Köln, Germany: Deutsches Institut für angewandte Pflegeforschung e.V. Accessed at http://www.dip.de/material/downloads/Pflege-Thermometer2007.pdf.

Jaehrling, Karen, and Claudia Weinkopf. 2005. "Low-Skill Work in Flux." *Management Review* 16(3): 389–403.

Jaehrling, Karen, Thorsten Kalina, Achim Vanselow, and Dorothea Voss-Dahm. 2006. "Niedriglohnarbeit in der Praxis - Arbeit in Häppchen für wenig Geld" ["Low-Wage Work in Practice: Small Chunks of Work for Little Reward"]. In *Mindestlöhne gegen Lohndumping: Rahmenbedingungen, Erfahrungen, Strategien* [*Minimum Wages Against Wage Dumping: General Conditions, Experiences and Strategies*], edited by Gabriele Sterkel, Thorsten Schulten, and Jörg Wiedemuth. Hamburg, Germany: VSA.

Keller, Bernd. 1985. "Zur Soziologie von Arbeitsmärkten: Segmentationstheorien und die Arbeitsmärkte des öffentlichen Dienstes" ["On the Sociology of Labor Markets: Segmentation Theories and Public Service Labor Markets"]. *Kölner Zeitschrift für Soziologie und Sozialpsychologie* 37: 649–76.

———. 1993. *Arbeitspolitik des öffentlichen Sektors* [*Work and Employment Policy in the Public sector*]. Baden-Baden, Germany: Nomos.

Kreutzer, Susanne. 2005. *Vom "Liebesdienst" zum modernen Frauenberuf: Die Reform der Krankenpflege nach 1945* [*From "Labor of Love" to a Modern Female Occupation. The Reform of Nursing After 1945*]. Frankfurt am Main, Germany: Campus.

LeGrand, Julien, and Will Bartlett. 1993. *Quasi-Markets and Social Policy*. Houndmills, U.K.: Macmillan.

Mason, Geoff, David Finegold, and Karin Wagner. 2000. "National Skill-Creation Systems and Career Paths for Service Workers: Hotels in the United States, Germany, and the United Kingdom." *International Journal of Human Resource Management* 11(3): 497–516.

Mayer-Ahuja, Nicole. 2003. *Wieder dienen lernen? Vom westdeutschen "Normalarbeitsverhältnis" zu prekärer Beschäftigung seit 1973* [*Learning to Serve Again? From the West German "Standard Employment Relationship" to Precarious Employment Since 1973*]. Berlin: edition sigma.

PLS Ramboll Management. 2003. *Fallstudie: Privatisierung von Krankenhäusern* [*Case Study: Privatization of Hospitals*]. Study commissioned by Vereinigen Dienstleistungsgewerkschaft (Ver.di).

REFA-Bundesverband. 2002. *Handbuch Objektbezogene Leistungskennzahlen für den Reinigungsdienst im Krankenhaus*. Darmstadt: REFA-Bundesverband e.V.

Rocke, Burghard. 2003. "Flucht aus dem BAT und aus der Zusatzversorgung?" ["Exodus from the National Collective Agreement for Public

Sector White Collar Workers and from the Supplementary Pension Scheme?"]. *Das Krankenhaus* 6: 449–53.

Rothgang, Heinz. 1994. "Der Einfluss der Finanzierungssysteme und Entscheidungsregeln auf Beschäftigungsstrukturen und -volumina englischer und deutscher Krankenhäuser" ["The Influence of Funding Systems and Decision-Making Rules on the Structure and Volume of Employment in English and German Hospitals"]. PhD dissertation, University of Chicago.

Simon, Michael. 2000. *Krankenhauspolitik in der Bundesrepublik Deutschland: Historische Entwicklung und Probleme der politischen Steuerung stationärer Krankenversorgung* [*Hospital Policy in the Federal Republic of Germany. Historical Development and Problems with the Political Control of In-Patient Care*]. Opladen, Geramany: Westdeutscher Verlag.

Streeck, Wolfgang. 1997. "German Capitalism: Does It Exist? Can It Survive?" In *Political Economy of Modern Capitalism: Mapping Convergence and Diversity*, edited by Colin Crouch and Wolfgang Streeck. London: Sage Publications.

Stumpfögger, Niko. 2007. *Krankenhausfusionen und Wettbewerbsrecht: Unternehmenskonzentration im deutschen Krankenhausmarkt 2003 bis 2007* [*Hospital Mergers and Competition Law. Concentration in the German Hospital Market*]. Excerpts from a study commissioned by Ver.di (Vereinigte Dienstleistungsgewerkschaft). Accessed at http://gesundheit-soziales .verdi.de/branchenpolitik/krankenhaeuser/data/krankenhausmarkt-2007.pdf.

Thelen, Kathleen, and Ikuo Kume. 1999. "The Effects of Globalization on Labor Revisited: Lessons from Germany and Japan." *Politics and Society* 27(4): 477–505.

Vereinigte Dienstleistungsgewerkschaft (Ver.di). (2004a) Ver.di-Uirchen-lafo No. 1/2004.

———— 2004b. "Beschluss 1/2004 der Verhandlungskommission zur Neugestaltung des Tarifrechts im öffentlichen Dienst" ["Decision no. 1/2004 by the Negotiating Committee on the Reform of Collective Bargaining Law in the Public Sector"]. Reprinted in *ver.di TS berichtet* 61.

CHAPTER 5

Still Lost and Forgotten? The Work of Hotel Room Attendants in Germany

Achim Vanselow

In Franz Kafka's novel *The Castle*, written in the early 1920s, Pepi the chambermaid wrestles with her fate: "As a chambermaid one did in time come to feel one was quite lost and forgotten; it was like working down a mine" (Kafka 1988, 379). Pepi feels that she is "invisible," working hard without much recognition and little hope to make a better life. This example illustrates that room-cleaning work in German hospitality has always been associated with low social status.[1] In the early days of the labor movement in this business, the trade union had to fight simply to ensure that employers paid chambermaids regularly for their work. Their compensation was made up of tips, board, and lodgings and sometimes a small cash wage. Such workers had to work many hours in order to earn enough money to survive in this way. The positive economic development starting with the German Wirtschaftswunder (West German economic boom of the 1950s) obstructs our view of the wage gap between the core industries of the German model and many private sector services. In the early 1960s, the average wages of employees in the hotel and restaurant industry represented only 75 percent of the average of the total economy. Moreover, working conditions were regarded as unattractive, especially the atypical working time arrangements that were widespread. Employers complained about labor shortages, but while the trade union demanded higher wages and better working conditions, employers recruited immigrant workers who were more tolerant toward bad working conditions (NGG 1962).

Today the hotel industry is one of the economic sectors in Germany in which a significant proportion of workers receive low wages (62 percent). The working conditions typical of the industry, such as excessive working hours, frequent weekend and holiday work without extra pay, and unpaid overtime, remain another reason why such work holds little appeal for many workers. Although at least some of those employed in room cleaning receive standard wages, almost 90 percent of the room attendants in the hotel industry receive pay below the low-wage threshold. Given that it is proving extremely difficult to enforce collective wage agreements, large numbers of workers may not receive even this low standard wage.

The focus of this study is on how work and pay conditions for room cleaners in the German hotel industry have changed against the background of sustained structural transformation. Up to now, this sector has only rarely been studied, and very little is known about the working conditions of low-wage jobs in German hotels. Previous studies about the quality of hotel workers' jobs in the American hospitality industry conclude that workload and work instability have increased in housekeeping jobs and that very low wages are delivered for performing what is a back-breaking job. Even highly profitable hotels from the upscale segment of the market offer jobs with generally bad pay and working conditions. There is at least scattered evidence in the United States of a "high-road" strategy that, with the help of qualifications and innovative solutions, is pointing the way toward a brighter future for workers in "bad jobs" in the low-wage sector (Bernhardt, Dresser, and Hatton 2003). The North American hotel union HERE recommends increased staffing, equitable wages, humane workloads, reasonable quotas, and training initiatives to improve advancement opportunities (Spurgaitis 2006).

These results from the United States lead us to ask: What do jobs for room attendants in Germany look like under a different institutional setting?

THE SAMPLE AND THE METHODOLOGY

The research consists of eight case studies in city hotels that cater mainly to business travelers. The market segment was used as a selection criterion: the sample contains four hotels in the upscale market (four to five stars) and four hotels in the economy category (two to three stars). The differences between regional markets were taken into account by carrying out four case studies in locations with some of the highest occupancy rates in Germany and four in more peripheral areas. One case study was done in East Germany. Seven hotels belong to chains, and one is privately owned. The size of the hotels ranges from twenty-five to 770 rooms, and the number of employees (including external staff) from ten to more than 300. The upscale hotels are traditional and well established. The oldest hotel opened fifty years ago, the newest thirteen years ago. The economy hotels in the sample represent the new business. Three of them belong to new brands, and two to new chains on the German market. This selection is based on the hypothesis that varying contexts in different market segments influence the job quality of room attendants.

Interviews were carried out at each hotel with management (the hotel director or the human resource manager), frontline managers (housekeepers), room attendants, and—if such a person was on staff—works council representatives. A total of fifty-two interviews were carried out, of which twelve were with room attendants. To classify the results of the case studies more effectively, fifteen supplementary contextual interviews were carried out with employers' associations and trade unions at the national and regional levels, with a national housekeepers' network, with authorities responsible for combating illegal employment, with institutions that deal with occupational health and safety in the hotel industry, and with immigrants' organizations. Because six hotels in the sample had outsourced room cleaning in whole or in part to other firms, representatives and employees of these firms were included when possible.[2]

The following sections provide an overview of the market and the competition within the German hotel industry and discuss the influence of key institutions and industrial relations on pay and working conditions. We then look at firm strategies and the effect on job quality for room attendants on the basis of the case studies. The results are presented in the last section.

THE HOTEL INDUSTRY IN GERMANY

Historically, the American and German hotel markets have differed sharply in their developmental patterns. The first hotel chains and modern hotel management arose in the United States, and internationalization of the hotel trade began there. In Germany, the small, privately run hotel has traditionally dominated (Frei 2000, 68ff). While around two-thirds of hotels in the United States belong to chains, with independent hotels accounting for only 20 percent of bed capacity, 88 percent of hotels and similar establishments in Germany are individual firms or limited companies. Even today the average German hotel employs just nine people (Statistisches Bundesamt 2006a; Wein 2006, 591). But for some years far-reaching changes have been taking place in the German hotel market. One indicator of the change in the "classic" hotel industry (NACE 55.1) is the distribution of bed capacity according to business type, which shows a trend toward bigger businesses. The industry includes hotels with and without restaurants, guesthouses, and boardinghouses. The number of hotels climbed by 15.6 percent between 1995 and 2005, from 11,596 to 13,401, while the other types of hotel-related businesses became less significant (Statistisches Bundesamt 1996, 2006b). The bed capacity of hotels increased between 1993 and 2005 by more than one-third, to 951,990 (Spörel 1994, 460; Statistisches Bundesamt 2006b). Only 17 percent of German hotels have one hundred or more beds, yet they make up 53 percent of bed capacity (Deutscher Sparkassen und Giroverband 2003, 8). These developments are being driven by hotel chains and interfirm cooperation between independent hotels, which together cover more than 50 percent of large establishments. While some hotel chains have had a presence in the German market for a long time, chains and chain-related hotels have been expanding with increasing vigor since the 1980s.[3] International hotel companies like Accor and Marriott are the market leaders today. New business strategies, cultures, management techniques, and management fashions have left their marks on the industry. Many hotel chains compete through multibrand strategies. They offer domestic and foreign customers a standardized product, ranging from the low-budget to the luxurious, which can be marketed both nationally and internationally. A national classification system established by the German Hotel and Restaurant Association (Deutscher Hotel- und Gaststättenverband, or DEHOGA) enhances the transparency of the market and facilitates the product positioning of hotels.

The aggressive expansion of the hotel chains has encouraged a severe form of predatory competition, particularly in the centers of the hotel industry. Occupancy rates in the hotel trade have lagged behind the expanded capacity: between 1995 and 2005, those rates stood at between 32.2 and 36.6 percent (DEHOGA 2004, 40, table 2). DEHOGA complains that every night in German hospitality one million beds lie empty. Nonetheless, in 2005, 314 new hotel projects with a capacity of more than 30,000 rooms were being planned (IHA 2006, 19).

This expansion of capacity is bound up with a change in financing structures. From 1998 to 2003, the leasing model was the predominant operating model. The predominant type of investment was the open investment fund, with an average share of the hotel investment volume of around 60 percent. These funds typically work with a long-term investment plan and with lease contracts of fifteen years or more, which should guarantee a long-term and secure income. Recently the opening up of the country's financial market appears to be making itself felt: investment in the hotel industry has increased rapidly. The structure of investment has become more and more diversified and now includes private investors, private equity funds, and real estate investment trusts. The proportion of foreign investors jumped from 22 percent in 2003 to more than 90 percent in 2006 (Jones Lang Lasalle 2004, 2007). It is too early to get a clear picture of the consequences of this development for the industry at the corporate and firm level. But obviously the hotel companies' head offices are trying to get used to the fact that private funds expect a return on investment more quickly and at a significantly higher rate; this expectation will have an impact on the management culture in German hotels.

The Economic Situation

Business volume in the hotel industry in 2003 amounted to €14 billion (US$20 billion), or €44,300 (US$64,904) in sales per employee (Wein 2006, 592). While the American hotel industry has enjoyed very positive developments over the last ten years, it is evident that the German hotel industry has faced substantial growth problems over that period. After the turn of the millennium, hotels struggled with declining sales revenues. Many, particularly in the upscale sector, ensured a reasonable occupancy rate by cutting prices. A newly opened luxury hotel in Berlin, for instance, initially offered a price per night of €109 (US$160), while the local average was €131 (US$192). This strategy should be viewed in light of the fact that German hotel prices are already very low. According to one management consultant, these prices lag far behind average room prices in Paris (€277.17 [US$406.04]) and London (€267.57 [US$391.98]) (Marx 2005).

The German market differs markedly from markets in other countries in a number of ways. In international comparison, management consultants classify the German hotel industry as a "low performer." Personnel costs are regarded as high, investment as low and declining, capital commitment as highly constrained, and the return on investment as generally low (see Deloitte & Touche 2003; Deutscher Sparkassen und Giroverband 2002, 26; Wein 2006). In addition, in contrast to many other European countries, Germany subjects the hotel industry to the full amount of VAT, which stands at 19 percent.

EMPLOYMENT AND LOW WAGES

The expansion of capacity in the hotel trade since the 1980s initially boosted employment, but this "engine for jobs" began to splutter in the mid-1990s: from 1979 to 1993, jobs grew 37 percent, but from 1993 to 2003 the number of jobs fell by 10.3 percent (Statistisches Bundesamt 1996, 318). In 2004, 277,413 employees were working in the industry. Recently hotels have increasingly offered new jobs that are part-time, and mini-jobs have become especially widespread (table 5.1).

It is very obvious that hotels reacted to the economic problems that started in the mid-1990s with a change in labor use practices. The part-time jobs could not, however, make up for the losses of full-time jobs.[4] Moreover, part-time work is very much concentrated in mini-jobs.

Analysis of the employment characteristics of the hotel and restaurant industry using the BA employee panel shows that the share of women, part-timers, young employees below age twenty-five, unskilled employees, and migrant workers in the industry is higher than the average of the total economy. The most striking features of the industry is the strong segregation by gender and nationality, the polarization of working time patterns between full-time and marginal part-time, and the fact that the majority of employees are between thirty-five and fifty-four years old and 58 percent are unskilled (table 5.2).

Analyses using the Socio-Economic Panel (SOEP) show that low wages are widespread in the hotel and restaurant industry compared to the total economy. The highest risk of receiving low wages is concentrated among mini-jobbers (97 percent), similar to retail (see chapter 6). Not only do women and low-skill workers have a low-wage share above the total average, but many men, full-timers, and skilled employees in this industry receive low wages (table 5.3).

Although the share of low-skill jobs in the hotel and restaurant industry is above average compared to the total economy, hotel work in

Table 5.1 Employment in the Hotel Industry, 2004

	Total Employees	Full-Time Employees	Part-Time Employees	Exclusively Mini-Jobs
Hotel industry, 2004	277,413	69.9%	6.0%	24.1%
Difference, 1999 to 2004	+8.4%	+0.8	+16.2	+35.9
Total economy, 2004	31,326,848	70.9	13.8	15.3
Difference, 1999 to 2004	+0.6	−6.6	+17.6	+31.6

Source: Jaehrling et al. (2006, 116).

Table 5.2 Structural Employment Characteristics of the Hotel and Restaurant Industry, and of the Total Economy, by Occupation, 2003

	Hotel and Restaurant Industry	Housekeepers in Hotels and Restaurants	Total Economy
Gender			
Women	62.1%	95.5%	48.7%
Men	37.9	4.5	51.3
Nationality			
German	81.3	80.2	93.2
Non-German	18.7	19.8	6.8
Age			
Under twenty-five	26.7	10.4	13.8
Twenty-five to thirty-four	24.6	17.5	21.2
Thirty-five to forty-four	22.9	30.9	29.4
Forty-five to fifty-four	15.8	27.0	22.5
Fifty-five or older	9.9	14.1	13.0
Working time			
Full-time	51.3	56.0	71.8
Part-time	12.5	12.9	13.7
Mini-job	36.2	31.1	14.5
Education[a]			
Unskilled	33.9	57.2	16.3
Skilled	64.7	42.5	73.3
College or university	1.5	0.3	10.4

Source: BA employee panel; author's calculations.
Note: All employees covered by the social security system, including part-timers, marginal part-timers, and apprentices.
[a] Apprentices excluded.

Table 5.3 Distribution of Low-Wage Earners in the Hotel
and Restaurant Industry, by Employment
Characteristics, 2004

| | Low-Wage Shares | |
	Hotel and Restaurant Industry	Total Economy
Total employment	70.2%	22.1%
Full-time	58.4	13.7
Part-time	73.0	20.3
Mini-jobs (exclusively)	97.0	78.9
Skilled	66.6	21.9
Unskilled	82.4	47.2

Source: Jaehrling et al. (2006, 117).
Note: The low-wage shares for the economy as a whole shown here were also calculated with SOEP 2004, but the categories of employees included differ from the calculations in table 1.5. The main difference is that the calculations presented in chapter 1 exclude students and pensioners, whereas these groups are included in table 5.3.

Germany cannot be reduced to a low-skill story. The industry makes a considerable contribution to the German "skill engine": recently there were more than 100,000 apprenticeship training positions in the industry. The occupation Hotelfachfrau (specialist in the hotel business) is perennially one of the most attractive occupations in the last years, according to women (Berufsbildungsbericht 2006, 109, 134; Seibert 2007). At the same time, it is obvious that for many hotel workers being skilled provides no protection from receiving low wages.

High fluctuations in the numbers of all qualification groups are characteristic for the hotel and restaurant industry, for a number of reasons: the seasonal character of the work in parts of the industry, the high number of businesses that fail, and the career paths of qualified workers. Indeed, the industry has problems keeping its qualified employees. As a consequence of the industry's high turnover rate, the share of new workers hired from other occupations is higher than the average for the total economy (Hieming et al. 2005, 71).

As a location-bound industry, the hotel industry has a long tradition of using migrant work to cut costs. The share of migrant workers in the hotel and restaurant industry was 18.7 percent in 2003— nearly three times higher than for the economy as a whole. A special regulation of seasonal work in the hotel and restaurant industry allows employers to hire workers from other countries for a maximum period of four months. Recently the number of these seasonal workers has fluctuated around 18,000 to 19,000, most of them employed in the leisure sector of the industry. Employers must pay them according to the collective agreement, and their work allowances are controlled by a government agency. But this is only one type of migrant worker. Migrants' access to the German labor market depends on their legal status, which can range from having an unlimited work allowance to being a refugee with a very limited work allowance or no work allowance at all.

Despite the increase in hotel capacity, the number of room attendants liable for social insurance was reduced by the hotels. Between 1993 and 1996, room attendants' share in hotel employment fell to 28,220—a 12 percent decrease (see Parmentier, Schade, and Schreyer 1996, 425; 1998, 449).[5] This trend continued between 2000 and 2005, a period that saw a further 0.3 percent decrease.[6] In housekeeping, many hotels are no longer willing to act as employers and pay contributions to social security for room cleaning staff. Instead, they are increasingly falling back on external contractors.

The Context of Outsourcing Strategies

The basic approach in organizing housekeeping work is to adapt staffing to the fluctuation in demand. Many hotels shift the risk of fluctuating occupation and the employer function onto external contractors. They have been able to fall back on a hugely expanded range of services catering to the industry's specific needs for a number of years. An increasing number of competitors have crowded the market, setting in motion a downward spiral in the cost of cleaning services. This development is partly due to political factors. The 2003 reform of the Handwerksordnung (the law regulating the conduct of craft trades; see chapter 1) dramatically lowered the market entry barriers for people setting up a new business in the commercial cleaning market: nowadays, anyone may offer a cleaning service such as hotel room cleaning. As recently as 2003 there were 6,800 commercial cleaning firms in the market, but by 2005 there were already around 16,000 (*Rationelle Hauswirtschaft* 2005, 32). Among other reasons, the hotel market is attractive to new cleaning firms because, as early as the 1990s, 90 percent of the demand was being met in the commercial cleaning trade's traditional sphere of activity: hospitals, industrial plants, administrative buildings, public transport, and window cleaning (Deutscher Bundestag 2003, 5). Today, however, reputable firms in the Chamber of Crafts that pay standard wages and create skilled personnel are coming under massive pressure. The increased competition has caused dwindling margins and poor prices, which some hotels are reducing even further. "There is a miserable competition going on, and the hotels definitely contribute to it," said one cleaning firm owner (*Der Spiegel* 2007, 68).

Cleaning contractors in the hotel industry operate in a gray area when it comes to pay policy: it is not always clear whether they are covered by the universally binding wage agreement that applies to commercial cleaning. The fact is that cleaning contractors are already paying workers below the universally binding standard hourly wage for commercial cleaning of €7.87 (US$11.53). The 2004 pay round, moreover, for the first time ever, produced a wage cut for employees in the commercial cleaning trade. What is more, enforcing the standard wage is a hugely difficult task. In particular, cleaning contractors do not always adhere to the wage guarantee for employees on performance-related pay, laid down in the outline wage agreement for those employed by commercial cleaning firms.

As cleaning has increasingly been outsourced, the potential for illegal employment in the hotel industry has also increased, as one Chamber of Crafts representative confirmed: "We have seen extreme cases in which raids were carried out, and the people without work permits were being kept in the lousiest of lodgings like cattle." A high level of illegal work in the industry was also confirmed in our interviews with government agency representatives: "The hotel chains actually have realized that we keep an eye on them." Inspections carried out by the agency in the hotel and restaurant industry found evidence of possible violations in 25 percent of the establishments subjected to spot checks (Eichel 2004), though hotels were less likely to be affected than restaurants. These spot checks can have a range up to 10,000 establishments annually. Examples of illegal work include failure to pay the standard wage, offenses against the regulations covering the receipt of unemployment or social security benefits, social insurance fraud, violations of immigration law, and forms of organized crime. In reaction to negative headlines in the yellow press in early 2007 about the "starvation wages" being paid in hotel cleaning, the big hotel chains have contacted the government agency to discuss preventive measures.[7]

INDUSTRIAL RELATIONS: "COLLECTIVE BEGGING"

As chapter 1 has shown, low trade union density and coverage by collective agreements in private services contribute to a labor cost gap between the core industries of the German model and the private service sector. Even inside the private service sector, the hotel and restaurant industry is lagging behind. Labor costs in this industry were nearly stagnating for the last ten years (Horn et al. 2007). The trade union was never powerful enough to prevent low wages. The former head of the department for tariff policy at the trade union Gewerkschaft Nahrung-Genuss-Gaststätten (NGG) stated, when looking back on many years of bargaining in the industry: "Due to the weakness of the trade union some collective negotiations in the hotel and restaurant industry look like collective begging" (Pohl 2007, 64).

In the regulatory model anchored in the representation of collective interests, wages and working conditions are negotiated by comprehensive organizations that represent employers and employees, while works councils represent employees' interests at the firm level and make sure that the collective agreements are enforced. The bargaining arena in the hotel and restaurant industry is the regional level, with eighteen pay scale areas (Tarifgebiete). A "second wage round" at the establishment level to improve the collective wage agreements appeared in highly profitable establishments in the 1970s, but it is becoming very rare today. The wage drift in the industry has been negative for years (Deutsche Bundesbank 2004).

The parties to the wage agreement are the sectoral union NGG, which organizes the food and luxury food industry and the hotel and restaurant industry (Nahrung, Genuss, Gaststätten) and the members of the German Hotels and Restaurants Association (DEHOGA).[8] A low union membership of 5 percent limits the union's opportunities to achieve significant improvements. The reasons for this traditional union weakness are manifold: the small average establishment size; the employment structure, which employs a lot of women, young people, and migrants (many of them working part-time); the loss of jobs in East Germany; the discontinuity of interest representation on the shop floor due to high fluctuation; and the low visibility of the union at the shop-floor level. Not to mention that low-wage earners are motivated to save the membership fee by not joining.

Nevertheless, trade union representatives stated that room attendants were once one of the groups of hotel employees who were most likely to be in a trade union, because the women themselves had an awareness of problems: "One thing that was constantly being discussed was how many rooms the women had to clean in eight hours," said one NGG representative. "In firms with works councils, upper limits could be laid down. This spurred the women on to join the trade union."

Hotel chains are more likely to be covered by the collective wage agreement than independent private hotels because they are interested in maintaining a stable framework. Of course, this does not mean that all hotel chains abstain from using aggressive union-avoidance strategies.

One key factor affecting the job quality of employees at the level of the firm is the enforcement of collectively agreed wages and working conditions, along with other regulations on health and safety at work. This is strongly connected to the existence of works councils, the second pillar of representation in the German system of industrial relations. Works councils in the hotel industry, however, are few and far between. Union representatives estimate the current number of works councils in hotels at around two hundred.[9] In the past, the paternalistic management style in many small, family-owned hotels was a great barrier to collective action. Where the owner, family members, and only a few employees worked side by side, the most common way in which serious conflicts were resolved was the employee changing employers.

New Exit Options for Employers

The traditional system of negotiation governing wage setting and working conditions has also been influenced by organizational developments on the part of employers. In recent years, East German DEHOGA members in particular have begun to allow new members not to commit to the collective agreement, which was formerly an automatic aspect of membership, making negotiations at the level of the firm more important. The association explains this step by referring to the diminishing commitment (to collective norms), profound differences in the earning potential of small and large firms and thus their ability to finance the collectively agreed norms, and new firms' tendency not to join the association.

The large hotel chains are among the firms most likely to maintain their commitment to the collective agreement.[10] In case of conflict, the union must show that a firm is covered by the collective agreement, a requirement that greatly hinders the union's efforts to enforce health and safety laws, attain employees' demands, conclude new collective agreements, and have collective agreements declared generally binding.

Collectively Agreed Low Wages in the Hotel Industry

The proportion of low-wage work in the hotel industry, at nearly 62 percent, lies significantly above the average for the economy as a whole (BA employee panel 2003, author's analysis). This is not a new development. A low level of collectively agreed wages in the hotel and restaurant industry is not restricted to low-skill or entry-level positions. All qualification groups in this industry, both skilled and unskilled, traditionally receive wages below the level of comparable occupations in most other parts of the economy (Bispinck, Kirsch, and Schäfer 2003, 303; Pohl 1995, 144). The differentiation of basic wages by wage group is also rather low. The highest wage in a hotel and restaurant industry collective agreement exceeds the lowest wage by a factor of 2.05, compared to 2.55 in retail or 3.7 in public services (BMWA 2005, 111). It is a problem well known to hotel human resource managers that skilled employees leave the industry after a certain amount of time to earn more money in other parts of the economy.

With the generally lower wage level in the industry, room attendants, like the other hotel workers being paid below the basic rate of pay (Ecklohn), are at tremendous risk of receiving wages below the low-wage threshold. One consequence is that the share of employees in the hotel and restaurant industry who receive additional basic security benefits for job-seekers (Grundsicherung für Arbeitssuchende, also known as Hartz IV, one of the provisions of the Hartz reforms) is considerably above the average for the economy as a whole. Receiving these benefits in January 2007 were 7.5 percent of the employees in hospitality covered by the social security system and even 21.6 percent of mini-jobbers (BA 2007, 20).[11] Room attendants are categorized under the "housekeeper" occupational group (923) in the statistics. Almost 90 percent of these workers' wages lie below the low-wage threshold. Over time, the proportion of low-wage workers in this group has in fact increased.[12]

The collective pay agreements system also fails to protect room attendants from low wages. The lowest-paid workers in the seventeen wage areas receive anything from €887 (US$1,299) per month, or 35.6 percent of the median German full-time wage in Mecklenburg-West Pomerania, to €1,490 (US$2,183), or 59.8 percent of the median wage in Bavaria. In all wage areas, remuneration lies below the 2003 low-wage threshold of €1,661 (US$2,433). Room attendants in some wage areas (such as Hesse) who remain in their job for a long time may reach the basic wage group of skilled workers. Even then, however, their pay does not cross the low-wage threshold.

In some areas the NGG has in the past worked toward obtaining greater wage increases for the lower-wage groups, because some skilled workers receive payments from their employers above and beyond the collectively agreed figure. The union is no longer pursuing this strategy, however, because unionized skilled workers, according to trade unionists, are otherwise neglected. Pay policy is thus unlikely to produce tangible improvements in room attendants' wages in the future.

WORKING CONDITIONS

The introduction of the five-day week and the forty-hour week in the mid-1980s can be regarded as a milestone in the regulation of working conditions in the hotel industry, even though these regulations had occurred in manufacturing ten to fifteen years earlier (Pohl 1995, 173). In the 1960s the collectively agreed monthly working time of a chambermaid was still 208 hours. Today the collectively agreed monthly working time is 169 hours in most West German regions (38.5 a week) and 173 hours (40 hours a week) in most East German regions. A recent empirical study for the hotel and restaurant industry found that the actual average weekly hours worked is forty-two hours and that nonstandard working time arrangements—such as regular night work, work on weekends, and regular work with changing hours—are still widespread in the industry (Kümmerling and Lehndorff 2007). Current policy debates revolve around the issue of working hours. Employers are calling for a return to the forty-hour week in those West German wage areas with a shorter statutory working week (thirty-eight and a half hours) and a reduction in annual bonuses (vacation pay, Christmas bonus). Reducing these payments is intended to free up funds for discrete turnover- or performance-related payments.

An important lever for improving job quality was the instrument of generally binding collective agreements, which would otherwise not have been possible, owing to low union density (Pohl 1995, 125). Today this instrument is being used in framework agreements on employment conditions (Manteltarifverträge), mainly in West German tariff regions. Because of the principle of collective bargaining autonomy, wage agreements were excluded. But in 1999 the NGG changed its policy and called for a minimum wage because of the bad prospects for improving the situation for low-wage workers in the industry. The trade union had several reasons for changing its strategy: a trend toward uncontrolled decentralization in East Germany, including long periods without a new collective agreement; the position of many wage groups below the low-wage threshold; and massive problems in enforcing even the low level of wages and benefits. Also, the high unemployment rate had put the union in a defensive position because employees were more interested in keeping their jobs and were not willing to fight for better wages or working conditions.

Working conditions such as working hours, days off, vacation regulations, extra pay for working Sundays and night shifts, rules on dismissal, and annual bonuses are regulated by regional framework agreements on working conditions. There are regional differences, for example, in the regulation of extra pay for working Sundays and holidays, which employees in the hotel industry must frequently do. Only about one-third of collective agreements provide for extra pay. How great the holes in the system really are became evident only by accident when a collectively agreed, voluntary, national occupational pension scheme (the HoGa pension) was introduced in 2002. Contributions to this new payment were to be financed from a portion of holiday pay without spending extra money. When the scheme was implemented, it became apparent that around half of the small firms involved made no vacation payments at all, despite wage agreements, some of which were universally binding. Even representatives of the employers' association expressed surprise at the scale of this phenomenon.

In answer to increasing rationalization, the problems of Tayloristic work processes, and reform political approaches (the "humanization of work"), the improvement of job quality in the workplace became an important issue on the national political agenda during the 1970s and 1980s. In a project aimed at "reducing stress" in the hotel and restaurant industry, researchers and practitioners developed a lot of suggestions to improve job quality in the industry. Some of them were adapted on the establishment level or in collective agreements (Elbe and Pohl 1986). Today, however, this human resource–oriented approach has taken a back seat. The structural change of the market, new management strategies, and high unemployment have forced "better strategies" on to the defensive, while "cheaper strategies" dominate the political agenda. Instead of being a driving force for improving job quality, the NGG is limited to defending the status quo.

FIRM STRATEGIES AND JOB QUALITY: RESULTS FROM THE CASE STUDIES

The organizational structure has changed significantly in large hotels as a result of the pressure to cut costs and staff—away from a functional, highly hierarchical system featuring a high degree of specialization and the exercise of management on a number of levels and toward "lean" management, largely an import from the American hotel chains (see Winter 2004). The housekeeping division in large hotels, which includes room cleaning, is usually led by a head housekeeper supported by a number of assistants. Floor supervisors inspect the cleaned rooms. The work itself is carried out by the room attendants. Other housekeeper posts may exist to staff late or night shifts or to conduct training needs. The job content includes cleaning rooms as well as public areas such as the reception area and customer toilets. In smaller firms, the division has a flatter structure, with one housekeeper managing the room attendants. In practice, of course, there are deviations from this organizational model.

FIRM STRATEGIES

The spectrum of upscale hotels in the sample ranged from a seven-hundred-room hotel belonging to a listed global chain to a small, owner-managed luxury hotel operating in a niche with a high-quality strategy. At the level of the firm, differences in product positioning strategies were clearly apparent. While some hotels in the sample invested to achieve the highest star rating for their product, others preferred to do without a star in order to save on the increased staff costs involved and offer customers a better price. While the upscale chain hotels provided a standardized room product, the privately owned hotel offered very individual rooms in different sizes and designs, many furnished with antiques.

The two- and three-star hotels in the economy segment in the sample provided smaller, highly standardized rooms with less luxurious equipment. The new competitors hoped to take business away from the market leader by offering better value for the money. Their strategy was to integrate elements of quality competition into the price competition typical of this market segment by offering, for example, high-quality furnishings through a focus on design for around the same price of approximately €50 (US$73). "Lean" management, rigorous cost management, sometimes minimal staffing, and the use of technology to aid rationalization, such as check-in machines to reduce the time spent by employees at reception, were approaches they took to secure profits despite lower prices. To put it in slightly drastic terms, the newcomers were investing in furniture rather than people. The aim was to enhance the appeal of the hotel as a product while keeping labor costs strictly in check. The economy hotels, moreover, were moving from the urban margins, with their excellent transportation links (industrial parks, links to highways), and into the town centers.

The established hotels in the sample were making a profit, with one exception.[13] Their more recently established counterparts first had to gain a foothold in the market. In the large upscale hotels, occupancy rates were above the national average of around 60 percent in 2004 (IHA 2006, 8). Occupancy rates for the independent five-star hotel were below the average, but this establishment generated most of its turnover from its food and beverage business.[14] Among the economy hotels, only the well-established two-star hotel had an occupancy rate that was well above the average, while some of the newcomers' occupancy rates were below average.

The price and turnover trends characteristic of our case studies reflect those of the market as a whole: in the upscale sector, these trends are markedly less favorable than in the economy sector. The price pressure on hotels is enormous, particularly in hotel hotspots. The upscale hotels have responded by cutting prices. To get the pricing problem under control, the head offices are beginning to centralize pricing policy even further, leaving local managers with less room for maneuver.

Since personnel costs in the hotel trade make up around one-third of total costs, they are inevitably at the heart of cost-cutting measures (Wein 2006, 459). The hotels examined here were operating with a bare minimum of staff.[15] The scale of these adaptations is apparent only if we take a long-term view: one five-star hotel, for example, had half as many employees (350) as it had had in the 1970s (700). In one East German four-star hotel, staff numbers had fallen from 300 to around 100 over a period of six years. By cutting staff, flattening hierarchies, and changing how work is organized, costs have been reduced; chain hotels have to gear themselves toward industrywide and to some extent international benchmarking. One key element in cutting labor costs is the conversion of fixed costs into variable costs by means of external-numerical flexibility strategies.

Outsourcing as the Predominant Strategy for Promoting Flexibility

Housekeeping work, which is closely tied to occupancy, has proved particularly prone to outsourcing. It is considered low-skill work that requires no specific knowledge of the firm involved and is carried out in a clearly demarcated organizational unit. Outsourcing thus spares other divisions the need to make major changes to how they organize their work. In fact, some large chain hotels started contracting with other firms to clean rooms as early as the 1980s.

The head housekeepers are confronted with ever-dwindling budgets to ensure that rooms and public spaces are kept clean and maintained in good condition.[16] "'Budget' has become the magic word," said one head housekeeper in a four-star hotel. Outsourcing offers head housekeepers the chance to cope better with these budget limitations. The risk of outsourcing is that it will lead to a decline in the quality of cleaning, inspiring the hotel to take on a new service provider. That trend was confirmed in interviews with DEHOGA representatives, though no statistical data exist. At the same time, quality problems have led some hotels to take back the cleaning function: "This occurs partly in upscale chain hotels [and] partly in owner-managed hotels, where quality is a strong selling argument and the direct contact with guests is very close," said a DEHOGA representative.

Six of the eight hotels examined here had outsourced room cleaning entirely or in part to an external firm (see table 5.4). The upscale hotels preferred to retain a supervisory role: the work done by the ex-

Table 5.4 The Organization of Room Cleaning in the Case Study Hotels

Market Segment	Upscale				Economy			
	H1	H2	H3	H4	H5	H6	H7	H8
Location	Central	Central	Peripheral	Peripheral	Central	Central	Peripheral	Peripheral
In-house room cleaning	Partial	Partial	Complete	No	No	Partial	No	Complete
In-house housekeeper	Yes	Yes	Yes	Yes	No	No	No	Yes
Number of in-house room attendants	24	4	3	0	0	2	0	9
Number of external room attendants (average)	15	30	0	39	6 to a maximum of 14	4	14	0

Source: Author's compilation.

ternal firm was subject to additional checks by the head housekeeper and her assistants, which was explained as necessary to ensure quality. Two upscale hotels operated with a mixed system: they retained a supplementary core of internal room attendants. This was justified in terms of labor laws (the high degree of protection against unlawful dismissal and high separation costs) but also functionally (the hotel's own staff cleaned the VIP rooms).

The economy hotels no longer employed a housekeeper of their own after outsourcing. The supervisory role was taken over by the external firm or the hotel manager. The two hotels that continued to operate with their own staff explained this in terms of quality assurance and the value of experienced workers. Nevertheless, the manager of one of the hotels was under pressure from the chain to explain this decision.

Local management can now decide whether to outsource cleaning functions or keep them in-house only in cases where outsourcing decisions are not made centrally but through outline agreements at the firm level. Local management's primary motivation to opt for outsourcing is labor cost savings: costs related to the additional labor needed for holidays or to cover for employees who are ill or have quit and the costs of recruitment, induction, and training are all shifted onto the service provider. A second motivation is that outsourcing relieves local management entirely or in part of certain management tasks.

QUALIFIED WORKERS DOING LOW-SKILL WORK

Almost all housekeeping divisions in the case study hotels were staffed by women, ranging from the head housekeeper through the assistants and floor supervisors to the room attendants. This strict segregation according to gender is being ruptured to some extent by external firms because they employ a higher proportion of men in order to increase performance and meet the physical demands of the work. In all the West German hotels in the sample, the vast majority of room cleaning jobs were being done by migrant women. Alongside the large number of immigrant candidates for the jobs, the hotel managers interviewed mentioned that such women are more willing to put up with the working conditions. In East Germany, where migrant labor is scarce and unemployment is high, all the cleaners in the case study hotels were German. But here too an increasing number of workers from the new European Union member states are likely to move into such jobs in the future.

Since room cleaning is not a skilled occupation, theoretically employment opportunities are open to low-skill workers. The interviews with room attendants and external cleaners suggest that personal difficulties have led qualified people to take such jobs: the failure to move from an apprenticeship into a relevant job, unemployment, a marriage breakdown, migration. "It is nobody's wish to become a room cleaner," said the head housekeeper in a four-star hotel. Qualified women in particular opt for such work for want of alternatives. The German room attendants we interviewed had previously worked as a restaurant professional, a specialist in railway transport technology, and a qualified retail businesswoman. The immigrant room attendants included a teacher from Bosnia and an engineer from Afghanistan. We found that only Southeast Asian women identified with the occupation of room attendant, had relevant previous experience in their home country, and actively wished to clean rooms for a living.

The Nature of the Work and Performance Targets

"They only have to mop the floor." This comment from a human resource manager reflects the low prestige of the job of room attendant. From the point of view of a head housekeeper in a five-star hotel who is responsible for the results of the work—a clean room—the job looks a little different. Room attendants must understand the corporate culture of the hotel—especially what is expected in their behavior toward guests—and they must clean the rooms quickly, efficiently, and exactly according to the cleaning standards of the hotel. They must choose the correct cleaning techniques and equipment to avoid damaging expensive material like high-value furniture. And the head housekeepers must ensure that the cleaning team is motivated to do this job in the right way.

In all hotels, room cleaning is basically physically demanding and repetitive work. The vast majority of room attendants clean the rooms alone, with poor autonomy. To increase productivity and lower costs, the upscale hotels are increasing individual employees' workloads, not so much by increasing performance targets (rooms per shift) as by assigning more labor-intensive tasks, such as cleaning furnishings (such as mirror surfaces, shower units, and other amenities), or assigning other additional tasks (such as stocking the minibar) without giving workers more time to clean. As in the United States, upscale hotels in Germany compete by offering a luxurious ambience: sumptuous beds, more amenities that need daily tending, and lotions, soaps, and so on, that regularly need to be replaced. One hotel from our sample furnished the rooms with big mirrors and glazed showers that needed intensive polishing. The consequence was a greater workload for the cleaners.

Performance targets for room cleaning differed markedly between the hotel sectors in our sample. In the upscale sector, targets per full-time shift ranged from seven to eight rooms in the privately owned hotel to fifteen to seventeen rooms in the other upscale hotels. The difference can be put down to the fact that the private hotel offered very individual rooms (of different sizes, with individual and antique furnishings) and the rooms in the chain hotels were highly standardized.

External cleaners generally clean a larger number of rooms per shift. In the economy sector, the room attendants in the provincial three-star hotel cleaned fifteen rooms per full-time shift, compared to twenty-four rooms in the more simply furnished two-star hotels. The external cleaners in two-star hotels had to meet the same standard in only six hours.

"HARD WORK AND POOR PAY"

All the room cleaners we interviewed—both in-house and external, both those who received standard wages and those who received nonstandard wages—subjectively assessed their income as insufficient given the work they did: "hard work and poor pay" was the characterization of one room attendant in a four-star hotel. Additional income from a partner, such as a pension or earned income, was essential to covering basic needs. It was even more difficult for part-time workers to make ends meet. One single mother, a room attendant working twenty hours a week for an external firm, relied on supplementary payments from the Grundsicherung für Arbeitsuchende (means-tested basic security benefit, the so-called unemployment benefit). The inadequacy of a room cleaner's income continues even after she retires, since pension claims are based on this low income. Hotel managers and cleaning firm executives shared the same basic conviction that low wages are the norm in this sector. At the same time, they emphasized that within the low-wage economy it can by no means be taken for granted that the employer will in fact pay the agreed wage on time.

According to Michael Sturman (2006, 7), the "cost of cleaning is more a function of policy decisions (e.g., how many housekeepers to hire, how much to pay them, how much to train them), rather than of individual performance." Fifteen years ago, an American hotel manager stated that the switch from a fixed wage to piece rates—paying room cleaners per room within the context of cost-cutting strategies—improved productivity (Kirwin 1990). In Germany the parties to the wage agreement have so far adhered to the fixed wage rule for permanently employed room attendants.[17] The principle of "pay only for rooms" is widespread in commercial hotel cleaning firms. In-house room attendants receive a fixed wage in line with the collective agreement in their region. Whether or not a hotel is in the upscale or economy sector is not a decisive factor. At the time the survey was conducted, the room attendants in three hotels in North Rhine-Westphalia received a gross hourly wage of €7.38 (US$10.81) (€1,246 [US$1,825] per month). In line with the last pay round, their wages increased to €7.60 (US$11.13) (€1,284 [US$1,881] per month). The room attendants in a hotel in another collective bargaining region had reached the wage bracket for skilled workers (€9.97 [US$14.60] per hour, or €1,645 [US$2,410] per month) because they had been employed in the same job for a long time.

The pay regulations characteristic of the cleaning contractors are comparatively less transparent, since they are sometimes regarded as a trade secret. Only one cleaning firm paid the room cleaners in line with the universally binding collective agreement in the commercial cleaning trade, with fixed wages of €7.87 per hour.[18] The other service providers in the sample paid their cleaners per room cleaned. While the piece rates in the upscale sector are higher than in the economy sector, the amount of time spent cleaning is longer. As a result, wages in the upscale sector may be even lower than in the economy sector despite higher piece rates:

- In the East German four-star hotel, the external room attendants received €1.60 (US$2.34) for stay-over rooms and €1.72 (US $2.52) for checkout rooms. According to the cleaning firm, part-time workers (twenty hours a week) made between €480 (US

$703) and €700 (US$1,025) per month depending on individual performance.

- In the central five-star hotel, cleaners received piece rates of €3.00 (US$4.40) per room and cleaned an average of 2.25 rooms per hour. Most of the cleaners were refugees from non-EU countries. The number of hours they worked varied widely, depending on work permit regulations.

- In a provincial two-star hotel, the cleaners received €1.80 (US$2.64) per room and cleaned an average of four rooms an hour. They worked a fluctuating number of hours that depended on occupancy. No cleaner was working full-time.

Unavoidable operational disruptions, such as guests' delayed departure, cause employees on piece rates to work unpaid overtime. In one case, cleaners stated that while they had part-time contracts (for twenty hours), they were often at the hotel for thirty to forty hours until they had cleaned the requisite number of rooms. Room cleaners' income vulnerability stems not just from their low hourly wages but also from the variations in the number of rooms to be cleaned. The hotels pass fluctuations in occupancy rates on to the service providers, who in turn shift the risk to their employees.[19] The owner of a small cleaning firm said in an interview:

> The collective agreement has no bite. It is like this: The hotel pays us €4.50 (US$6.59) to clean a room. This includes the wage, material, gain. It can be figured out easily that there is not much left for the wage. The cleaners must be very speedy. But there is a difference between stay-over and checkout rooms. You can make four stay-over rooms in an hour. But we cannot guarantee the collectively agreed wage. . . . I have no influence on a declining occupation. . . . January, February, August, and December are weak months. "Weak" means twenty to thirty percent less.

Because the use of external firms is sharply reduced during such times, seasonal fluctuations in the business travel market can pose a significant income risk for external cleaners. Some of the service firms cover the core block of rooms to be cleaned by means of full- or part-time staff working year-round. Peak periods are covered by means of mini-jobs or by hiring unemployed people entitled to make a certain, limited amount of money.

The Employment Contract and Job Security

The vast majority of upscale hotels in the sample that continued to employ their own staff offered full-time room cleaning jobs because the volume of work was sufficiently large and any further fragmentation of the employer-employee relationship ran the risk of affecting quality. In the West German hotels, in line with the collective agreement, the standard working week for a full-time worker was thirty-eight and a half hours; in the East German hotel it was forty hours. A few part-time jobs were available in the form of evening work. Over the last few years, some hotels in our sample had switched to the strategy of taking on new workers on a fixed-term basis only. The time limits enable firms to adapt their stock of personnel more easily to their economic situation without expensive separation costs and increased screening opportunities.

Some of the room attendants who worked for old established hotels had been employed for decades and thus enjoyed a high degree of protection against dismissal. Social aspects of work may make room attendants more likely to stay in their jobs: many emphasized how important it was to be treated with respect "as a person." The cohesion of the housekeeping team appeared to be more important here than positive cooperation with colleagues from other divisions. Team spirit was sometimes bolstered by the fact that the room attendants were of the same nationality (such as the "Thai team") and could call upon friends to help out during peak periods.

In the smaller economy hotels, working conditions were often fragmented: students and part-timers (filling both midi-jobs and mini-jobs) worked at reception, external firms provided cleaners, and the manager was self-employed rather than a regular employee. The staff turnover rate among some of the external firms was more than 50 percent for the hotels studied here. One reason was the low commitment of the employees to this kind of work.

Working Hours and Work Organization

In the twenty-four-hour economy characteristic of the hotel industry, working hours constitute a key factor in job quality. The vast majority of regular room cleaning is carried out during the day shift, which is attractive for women with little children. Should rooms occasionally require cleaning at night, the night shift workers do this work in the larger establishments. Regulations on breaks are adhered to. Overtime is used very rarely as a means of enhancing flexibility because housekeepers regard it as impossible to ensure that quality standards will be met after eight hours of intense physical work. In hotels with a works council, head housekeepers need the approval of the works council to assign overtime work.

All hotels in the sample required their employees to work weekends. Room attendants' belief that they were being treated fairly in terms of how weekend and holiday work was distributed was a key factor in their level of contentment. Some of the regional collective agreements include regulations on the annual number of Sundays off (ten to fifteen a year). Room attendants could put in requests for Sundays off, which the head housekeepers did what they could to meet. However, head housekeepers took little account of workers' personal situations (such as having children to care for) because they didn't want to discriminate between room attendants in scheduling. This created problems for single mothers.

The room attendants were satisfied with their daily working hours and managed to reconcile their private lives with them. As a rule, the housekeeper made up the duty roster for the following week on Thursdays. As long as working hours matched the projected occupancy rate, they were very stable. But housekeepers made it very clear that they expected high flexibility from room attendants when it was needed, such as when guests booked a room with very little notice or when the hotel had "walk-ins" (customers who turn up with no notice at all). At times of crisis, all members of the hotel staff had to help out, from trainees to the manager.

Outsourcing often involves shifting working time instability onto the external staff and increases the employer's flexibility with respect to hours. While a head housekeeper needs the approval of the works council when she wants the internal staff to work overtime, this is not necessary in the case of external cleaners. The cleaning contractor is compelled to call in workers on their day off, bring in staff temporarily from other hotels, or even request personnel from other cleaning firms—that is, hand over profit to a third party—in order to avoid losing the contract. In small cleaning firms, even the owners themselves help out.

In the large hotel chains, modern forms of work organization, such as teamwork, multitasking, and total quality management, are becoming established in housekeeping. The room attendants generally clean and tidy the rooms alone and prefer to work this way. Only when a new employee is being trained does more than one cleaner ever clean a room.

The delegation of responsibility is a key component of the self-checker system. The room attendants not only clean the rooms but carry out final checks and thus reduce the burden on the supervisors and head housekeepers. For working with this system, the room attendants in one five-star hotel received a bonus of €100 (US$147). However, the level of quality to which the hotel aspired could not be achieved, so the system was modified again and the number of external cleaners increased. The most competent room attendants were made floor supervisors and assigned to wage group 6 (€10.32 [US$15.12] per hour, €1,733 [US$2,539] per month), which took them over the low-wage threshold. The less competent room attendants returned to room cleaning and lost their bonus and supervisory role. Most housekeepers found the self-checker system too demanding for room-cleaning staff and preferred traditional supervisory mechanisms.

Outsourcing has noticeably increased the intensity of supervision in the upscale sector. Room attendants were always subject to supervision. Now the use of technology has made it possible to quickly obtain data on the cleaning performance of individual employees. Total quality management systems make it possible to confront room attendants and external cleaners with detailed performance statistics, making it easier to supervise and guide employees' conduct. Increasing standardization thus also extends the potential for supervision (see the early contributions by Kramer and Seitz 1984, 100).

TRAINING AND CAREER DEVELOPMENT PROSPECTS

From a life-cycle perspective, it is an important characteristic of job quality whether there are stepping-stones that lead from low-wage jobs to better-paid positions. Training initiatives play a prominent role in "high-road" strategies for housekeeping workers in the United States—for example, providing training in vocational English language skills and basic skills (Auerhahn, Brownstein, and Zimmermann 2004; Bernhardt, Dresser, and Hatton 2003). The large hotel chains in our sample provided some human resource strategies, including company-based training and internal promotion programs, but it was mainly skilled frontline and administrative staff who benefited from these opportunities. Low-wage earners like room attendants or dishwashers did not take part in these programs. The qualifications for room cleaners were generally restricted to the introduction of new workers; occasionally they received ad hoc training if evidence of certain failings had begun to mount up. The amount of pay was unaffected by this training. Even in the bigger upscale hotels, we found no opportunities at all for cross-training that would have enabled staff to work in other departments. Management justified this training deficit by citing individual characteristics of the workers, like their lack of language skills, formal qualifications, or—even more—the "soft" skills (personal appearance, manner) needed to play a decisive role in hotel work.

In-house opportunities for further training are by their very nature closed to external cleaners. Training for external employees helps ensure quality and, from the employees' point of view, does not help them advance in their career but at best to hold on to their job. The amount of time spent training new cleaning staff indicates how simple the job is. Depending on the category of hotel, this training ranged from one week (economy sector) to several months (five-star hotel).[20]

The internal labor market even in larger hotels offered room attendants little prospect of advancing within the firm, owing to the flatness of the hierarchy. Vertical mobility in large hotels was limited to posts in the housekeeping division: floor supervisor, division manager, or assistant housekeeper. The posts of head housekeeper and most assistants were almost exclusively filled by qualified workers. Room attendants employed on a permanent basis sometimes benefited from outsourcing measures by taking on a supervisory role for their floor and being paid more. As hierarchies have been dismantled and outsourcing has taken off, it has become even more difficult for in-house room attendants to advance to a higher position.

Because qualified staff would be too expensive, the vast majority of cleaning firms in the commercial cleaning business take on workers who have no vocational training in professional cleaning. Interviewees in the sector saw the lack of language skills of many foreign cleaners, the low level of job commitment typical of the sector, and the high turnover rate as key barriers to workers gaining further qualifications. External cleaners may rise to the position of team leader in the cleaning firm. In the opinion of company owners, however, to advance further—to the post of project manager, for example—would require vocational training.

Representation Within the Firm

We encountered works councils only in the large hotels in the up-scale sector. Whether these helped improve working conditions in the housekeeping division depended on whether attention was paid to this subject. Following outsourcing, a hotel's works council loses the right to represent the cleaners. The most marked improvements for room attendants were achieved by the works council in a large five-star hotel in which employees from the housekeeping division were represented on the committee. This works council exercised its right to take part in the restructuring of room cleaning and, among other successes, negotiated with the management a shop-floor agreement to lighten the workload of older room attendants and those with health problems.

In the small hotels with fewer than twenty employees, the room cleaners had to represent their interests themselves vis-à-vis the housekeeper or manager-owner. The housekeepers claimed to uphold an open-door policy and expressed a desire to be responsive to their colleagues.

Of the cleaning firms in the sample, just one had a works council. The institutionalization of interests representation in this sector is hampered by the fact that the business structure is decentralized, there is very little contact between the scattered employees, and employees' commitment to the firm is negligible (see Wassermann 1999, 33ff). What is more, the many migrant workers employed in the industry generally have a very limited awareness—if any—of the German system of interest representation. In our case studies, we met employees who were unfamiliar even with the terms "union" and "works council."

Occupational Health and Safety

Studies on occupational health and safety issues in the American hotel industry show that a very high share of room attendants suffer from work-related pain (Parker and Krause 1999). Occupational medicine physicians stress that working in hotel room cleaning "is among the highest-stress jobs (on the body) in the services and production industries" (Yancey 2006). Also, in Germany room attendants are among the groups most at risk in hotel work: their work is very physically demanding and subject to specific dangers (see

Weiler 2003).[21] Again and again, interviewees in our study stated that new employees left, sometimes after a few days, because they were unable to endure the strain. Risk factors included frequently humid conditions, bad reactions to chemical cleaning substances, and the improper use of chemicals by, for example, employees with a poor grasp of German.

One basic problem with respect to occupational safety is that employees' difficulty dealing with the strain plays practically no role in the planning and furnishing of hotels. Since efforts to change the work environment generally come to nothing, occupational health measures focus on changing the body—by, for example, developing specific muscles through back exercises. Neither the hotels nor cleaning contractors in our case study, however, provided physical training for room attendants.

SUMMARY AND CONCLUSIONS

Is the cleaning of hotel rooms in Germany a good job? The results of this study suggest a negative answer (see table 5.5). In a market characterized by overcapacity, a downward trend in prices, and predatory competition, firms, all the way up to the upscale sector, are responding with cost-cutting strategies, which tend to focus on personnel costs. Downsizing and, especially, outsourcing are the main strategies pursued with respect to the cleaning function; outsourcing to external firms, however, threatens key aspects of employees' job quality. Regardless of market segment, room cleaning is a low-wage activity, makes great physical demands, and offers few opportunities, whether by means of vertical or horizontal mobility, to progress to a better job. The high demands placed on employees' availability the moment the company needs them and atypical working hours (weekends, holidays) are typical of the sector. Among external cleaners, payment at piece rates leads to unpaid working time and loss of income during periods of low occupancy. It is thus no surprise that it is mainly weaker groups within the labor market that do such work—immigrants, women, and those at risk of unemployment. Room cleaners with qualifications tend to assume that they will eventually have to leave the industry if they are to improve their situation.

In traditional hotels in the upscale sector, meanwhile, we can still find remnants of the old system: permanent employment contracts, full-time employment liable to social security contributions, collec-

Table 5.5 Summary of the Hotel Case Study Findings

	Upscale Market Segment	Economy Market Segment
Type of worker	Women, migrants	Women, migrants
Main strategy (housekeeping)	Lean staffing	Newcomers immediately externalize the cleaning function
	Mix of internal and external staff	
	Internal control (head housekeeper)	No internal head housekeeper
Working patterns	Stable working patterns for internal staff	Fluctuating working patterns for external staff
	Fluctuating working patterns for external staff	
Work organization	Physically demanding	Physically demanding
	Increased workload (more amenities, increased control)	High workload
Training and development	On-the-job training	On-the-job training
	Few internal advancement opportunities for internal staff	No internal advancement opportunities
	No opportunities for external staff	
Wages and benefits	Fixed wages for internal staff below the low-wage threshold	Monthly income fluctuates depending on the number of rooms to clean
	Wage increases and benefits according to the collective agreement	Exact wages and benefits of external staff often treated as firm secrets because firms compete by wages
	Pay per room for external staff	
	No overtime pay	No overtime pay
	Christmas allowance just for internal staff under a CLA	No Christmas allowance

Source: Author's compilation.

tively agreed (if low) wages with regular raises, some limited opportunities for advancement, and representation within the firm, which helps ensure that decent working conditions are maintained.

The case studies in the new hotel products being offered in the economy segment give us an idea of how hotel work could change in the future under the conditions of mainly price competition. These hotels are using the opportunities opened up by the fragmentation of employment relationships in a particularly offensive fashion. Complete outsourcing is the preferred strategy for dealing with room cleaning. Increased effectiveness and rationalization are being deployed to gain a price advantage. Money is being invested, but in furnishings rather than in labor-intensive customer service. As a result, those employed under the old system are better protected against the one-sided passing on of the risks brought about by employer-driven flexibility strategies.

But does the future of room cleaning jobs really belong to "low-road" strategies? Are there no alternatives? The prospects are much less predetermined than they look at first sight. That a room ends up "looking" clean does not mean that the work meets professional cleaning standards, especially in the bathrooms. Productivity in housekeeping is more than a matter of containing costs (Sturman 2006). It is already becoming apparent that the cost-cutting strategy of employing ever fewer staff from external firms to clean rooms, at ever lower costs, is threatening to become dysfunctional, particularly in the upscale sector: hotels are struggling with deficiencies in the quality of the cleaning. Behind the scenes, sometimes vehement discussions are taking place on how to proceed in the future.

The industry could begin by having new luxury hotels recruit permanent housekeeping staff with good language skills and publicize these German-speaking staff members as a distinctive quality feature. Also, outsourcing and quality cleaning are not necessarily mutually exclusive. Professionalizing room cleaning would make sense in the high-class hotels. In training workers specifically to deal with hotels, the cleaning firms have had to paddle their own canoe until now. The need for qualifications for room cleaners is apparent, for example, among cleaners who lack knowledge of chemicals, among those who lack the ability to organize and check their own work, and in the conduct of some toward customers. Overcoming such deficits and improving room cleaners' qualifications, however, would come only at a price, which hotels would be required to pay.

One important step has been taken toward ending the wage-dumping competition in room-cleaning jobs: improving conditions in these jobs has become an issue of public interest. Reports in the media about "starvation wages" in room cleaning in luxury hotels in early 2007 were a strong impetus for a national minimum wage debate. One concrete result of this debate was that in April 2007 a collective wage agreement for the hotel and restaurant industry at the regional level, covering 180,000 employees, was declared generally binding. Monthly pay for full-timers of €990 (US$1,450) is the new regional minimum wage. This political measure can be interpreted as a first step toward improving the situation of low-wage workers in hotels. The debate about a national minimum wage is still going on.

"She was a chambermaid, she had an insignificant situation with few prospects, she had dreams of a great future like any other girl, one can't stop oneself from having dreams." That is what Franz Kafka (1988, 377) wrote more than eighty years ago. At the beginning of the twenty-first century, there is new hope for Pepi's successors to step out of the shadow.

NOTES

1. The tasks of cleaning and tidying hotel rooms, making the beds, and changing the bed linen bring staff into contact with the guests' intimate sphere. As such, this work has also been referred to as "dirty work." The dividing line between the glamorous sphere of the frontline staff at the reception desk and in customer service and the back-of-house staff in housekeeping is marked, according to Yvonne Guerrier and Amel Adib (2000), not only by the visibility or invisibility of the tasks carried out as far as the guests are concerned but also by the distinction between "clean" and "dirty."

2. Additional interviews were carried out with four cleaning firms. Another such firm answered questions sent in written form.

3. In 1984 there were a mere 41 hotel chains, encompassing 1,068 hotels, on the market; by 2004, 111 chains were running 3,230 hotels (DEHOGA 2004, 42).

4. The only exception to this negative trend was a peak at the turn of the millennium.

5. The statistics include data for occupational code 923. Following a change to the statistics, data for the years after 1998 on the number of employees liable for social security contributions according to the occupational code 923 in hotels and guesthouses are no longer available.

6. These data are based on a different source—a special IAB analysis.

7. A female room attendant from a cleaning contractor who worked in a famous five-star hotel in Hamburg that demanded a standard rate of €350 (US$513) for a single room was receiving a net hourly wage of €1.92 (US$2.81). When she complained about the low wage, her employer dismissed her. It was this case that ignited a new nationwide discussion about the need for a minimum wage in Germany.

8. There are historical reasons why the NGG is organized this way—the food and food luxury industry and the hotel and restaurant industry—to represent employees in these industries.

9. One source from the 1990s (Wassermann 1999, 96) estimated that 7 percent of firms capable of sustaining a works council in the hotel and catering trade in fact had one.

10. Large hotel chains are more likely to maintain their commitment to the collective agreement for several reasons, including the legal security, the pacifying effect within the company (equal pay for equal work), and the benchmarking effect on the working conditions and wages of competitors. In small firms, the risk of legally deficient employment contracts is increasing as such firms break away from the collective wage agreement; employers may pay dearly for this decision should their case come to an industrial tribunal. As we learned in an interview with a DEHOGA representative, this is the reason why the employers' association rejects the idea of shifting the negotiation process entirely to the level of the firm.

11. This phenomenon is clearly linked to the service sector. From all employees receiving Hartz IV benefits, more than 80 percent work in the service sector (BA 2007, 20).

12. In 1980, 84.1 percent of low-wage workers in the industry earned wages below the low-wage threshold; this figure had risen to 88.3 percent by 2003 (BA employee panel and IAB employment subsample, author's calculations). Owing to changes in the economic structure, however, the figures may be compared only to a limited degree.

13. The exception was faced with expensive leases, which ate into the profits generated by the operational side of the business. This hotel was on target to achieve profitability in 2006.

14. The hotelier had affiliated with an international hotel consortium in the luxury sector, a move that enabled him to benefit from economies of scale without abandoning the firm's legal independence.

15. It is becoming almost impossible to cut costs, even sales costs, as long as leases are de facto fixed costs.

16. The investment costs for a room in a five-star hotel can quickly exceed €150,000 (US$219,722). In a two-star hotel, investment costs are between €50,000 and €60,000 (US$73,240 and US$87,888) per room (VÖB 2004, 65).

17. Even in the late 1970s—the heyday of the German model in the production industries—32 percent of those working in the hotel and restaurant industry received performance-related pay and a mere 12 percent could count on a guaranteed monthly cash wage (Kramer and Seitz 1984, 97). In the past, moreover, housekeeping jobs were sus-

ceptible to strategies based on intensifying the workload. Employers could thus take back the cost of wage increases.

18. In the recent wage round in the cleaning industry, the employers' association and the union agreed on an additional holiday allowance of €1.85 (US$2.71) per day off (see IG Bauen Agrar Umwelt website at http://www.igbau.de).

19. The exception is the service provider, which pays a fixed wage.

20. The induction of new room-cleaning staff is by no means limited to cleaning and tidying the rooms to a given standard. Moreover, the specific context in which the work is carried out also plays a key role: "Thinking in terms of service and being alert to customers' needs—you really have that drummed into you in the hotel industry," said one trainer.

21. In the housekeeping division, risks include injuries from using cleaning agents and handling infectious materials (syringes, waste, bed linen, towels) and sharp objects (such as glass shards, and so on), muscle strains from heavy lifting, carrying (such as moving beds), and performing awkward physical tasks (such as making beds), and psychological strain from interactions with customers (BGN 2006).

REFERENCES

Auerhahn, Louise, Bob Brownstein, and Sarah Zimmermann. 2004. "Jobs with a Future: Regional Growth Strategies and Strong Career Ladders for the Hospitality Industry." San Jose, Calif.: Working Partnerships USA.

Bernhardt, Annette, Laura Dresser, and Erin Hatton. 2003. "The Coffee Pot Wars: Unions and Firm Restructuring in the Hotel Industry." In *Low-Wage America: How Employers Are Reshaping Opportunity in the Workplace*, edited by Eileen Appelbaum, Annette Bernhardt, and Richard J. Murnane. New York: Russell Sage Foundation.

Berufsbildungsbericht. 2006. "Vocational Training Report." Berlin: Bundesministerium für Bildung und Forschung (BMBF).

Berufsgenossenschaft Nahrungsmittel und Gaststätten (BGN). 2006. "Alles aus einer Hand. Die BGN 10 ["Everything From One Source: The BGN 10"]. CD-ROM. Mannheim: BGN.

Bispinck, Reinhard, Johannes Kirsch, and Claus Schäfer. 2003. "Mindeststandards für Arbeits- und Einkommensbedingungen und Tarifsystem" ["Minimum Standards for Working and Pay Conditions and the Collective Bargaining System"]. Institute of Economic and Social research in the Hans Boeckler Foundation (WSI). Project report for the Ministerium für Wirtschaft und Arbeit des Landes Nordrhein-Westfalen (MWA). Düsseldorf, Germany.

Bundesagentur für Arbeit (BA). 2007. "Grundsicherung für Arbeitsuchende:

Anrechenbare Einkommen und Erwerbstätigkeit" ["Basic Subsistence for Job-Seekers: Allowable Income and Gainful Employment"]. Report of Statistik der BA, January 2007.

Bundesministerium für Wirtschaft und Arbeit (BMWA). 2005. "Tarifvertragliche Arbeitsbedingungen im Jahr 2004" ["Collectively Agreed Employment Conditions in 2004"]. Bonn, Germany: Bundesministerium für Wirtschaft und Arbeit.

Bundesverband Öffentlicher Banken Deutschlands (VÖB). 2004. "Beherbergungsgewerbe in Deutschland: Leitfaden für Immobiliensachverständige" ["The Hotel and Lodging Industry in Germany: Guidelines for Real Estate Specialists"]. VÖB-Kommission für Bewertungsfragen (Immobilien), September 2004.

Deloitte & Touche. 2003. "German Hotel Performance Continues to Decline as Average Room Rates Come Under Renewed Pressure." Accessed at http://www.hotelbenchmark.com/pressroom/pressreleases/27052003 Germany-EN.aspx.

Der Spiegel. 2007. "Vorindustrielle Ausbeutung" ["Pre-Industrial Exploitation"]. Der Spiegel 61(3): 68ff.

Deutsche Bundesbank. 2004. "Mehr Flexibilität am Arbeitsmarkt" ["More Flexibility in the Labor Market"]. Monthly report, September 2004.

Deutschen Hotel- und Gaststättenverband (DEHOGA). 2004. "Wir machen Branchenpolitik" ["We Make Industry Policy"]. Yearbook 2003–2004. Berlin: DEHOGA.

Deutscher Bundestag. 2003. "Antwort der Bundesregierung auf eine Grosse Anfrage der Abgeordneten Jürgen Klimke, Klaus Brämig und weiterer Abgeordneter der Fraktion der CDU/CSU. Auswirkungen der EU-Osterweiterung auf den Tourismus und die deutsche Tourismuswirtschaft." ["Federal Government's Response to a List of Questions Put by Jürgen Klimke, Klaus Brämig and Other Members of the CDU/CSU Parliamentary Party. Effects of the EU's Eastward expansion on Tourism and the German Tourism Industry"]. Deutscher Bundestag, 15. Wahlperiode, Drucksache 15/1267 vom December 15, 2003.

Deutscher Sparkassen und Giroverband. 2002. "Hotels, Gasthöfe, Pensionen, Hotel garnis" ["Hotels, Guest Houses, Bed and Breakfast Establishments"]. Industry reports of the Sparkassen-Finanzgruppe 38. Stuttgart, Germany: Deutscher Sparkassen Verlag.

———. 2003. "Hotels, Gasthöfe, Pensionen, Hotel garnis." ["Hotels, Guest Houses, Bed and Breakfast Establishments"]. Industry reports of the Sparkassen-Finanzgruppe 54. Stuttgart, Germany: Deutscher Sparkassen Verlag.

Eichel, Hans. 2004. Rede des Bundesministers der Finanzen Hans Eichel anlässlich der Zolljahrespressekonferenz am 27.2.2004 beim Zollamt Flughafen Köln/Bonn [Speech by Federal Finance Minister Hans Eichel on the occasion of the Customs Annual Press Conference on Feburary 27, 2004 at the Cologne/Bonn Airport Customs Office]. Accessed at http:// www.zoll.de.

Elbe, Annette, and Gerd Pohl. 1986. *Lernen und Handeln: Zur Verbesserung der Arbeitsbedingungen im Gastgewerbe* [*Learning and Acting: On the Improvement of Working Conditions in the Hotel and Restaurant Industry*]. Frankfurt am Main, Germany: Campus.

Frei, Illona. 2000. *Expansionsstrategien in der Hotelindustrie: Deutsche Hotelketten im internationalen Vergleich* [*Expansion Strategies in the Hotel Industry. German Hotel Chains in International Perspective*]. Hamburg, Germany: Dr. Kovac.

Gewerkschaft Nahrung-Genuss-Gaststätten (NGG). 1962. *Die Lage im Hotel- und Gaststättengewerbe: Vorschläge der Gewerkschaft Nahrung— Genuss—Gaststätten zur Neuregelung der Lohn- und Arbeitsbedingungen* [*The Situation in the Hotel and Restaurant Industry: Proposals by the Food and Allied Workers' Union on the Re-Regulation of Pay and Working Conditions*]. Hamburg, Germany: NGG.

Guerrier, Yvonne, and Amel Adib. 2000. "Working in the Hospitality Industry." In *In Search of Hospitality: Theoretical Perspectives and Debates*, edited by Conrad Lashley and Alison Morrison. Oxford: Butterworth-Heinemann.

Hieming, Bettina, Karen Jaehrling, Thorsten Kalina, Achim Vanselow, and Claudia Weinkopf. 2005. "Stellenbesetzungsprozesse im Bereich 'einfacher' Dienstleistungen" ["Recruitment Processes in 'Low-Skill' Services"]. Working paper 550. Berlin: Bundesministerium für Wirtschaft und Arbeit.

Horn, Gustav A., Camille Logeay, Sabine Stephan, and Rudolf Zwiener. 2007. "Preiswerte Arbeit in Deutschland: Auswertung der aktuellen Eurostat Arbeitskostenstatistik" ["Low-Cost Labor in Germany. Analysis of the Current Eurostat Labor Costs Statistics"]. Report 22. Institut für Makroökonomie und Konjunkturforschung (IMK).

IHA. 2006. "Hotelmarkt Deutschland 2006: Branchenreport des Hotelverbandes Deutschland." Berlin: IHA.

Jaehrling, Karen, Thorsten Kalina, Achim Vanselow, and Dorothea Voss-Dahm. 2006. "Niedriglohnarbeit in der Praxis: Arbeit in Häppchen für wenig Geld" ["Low-Wage Work in Practice: Small Chunks of Work for Little Reward"]. In *Mindestlöhne gegen Lohndumping: Rahmenbedingungen, Erfahrungen, Strategien* [*Minimum Wages Against Wage Dumping: General Conditions, Experiences and Strategies*], edited by Gabriele Sterkel, Thorsten Schulten, and Jörg Wiedemuth. Hamburg, Germany: VSA.

Jones Lang Lasalle. 2004. "Global Hotel Investment: Debt and Equity Environments." *Hotel Topics* 15(October).

———. 2007. "Deutscher Hotelinvestmentmarkt mit Rekordvolumen: An-teil ausländischer Investoren über 90%" ["Record Volumes Achieved by German Hotel Investment Market—Share of Foreign Investors Exceeds 90%"]. Press release. January 19, 2007.

Kafka, Franz. 1988. *The Castle*. Schocken Classics. New York: Schocken Books.

Kirwin, Paul. 1990. "A Cost-Saving Approach to Housekeeping." *Cornell Hotel and Restaurant Administration Quarterly* 31(3): 25–27.

Kramer, Andreas, and Dieter Seitz. 1984. "Arbeitsbedingungen und Rationalisierung im Gastgewerbe" ["Working Conditions and Rationalisation in the Hotel and Restaurant Industry"]. *WSI-Mitteilungen* 1984(2): 94–103.

Kümmerling, Angelika, and Steffen Lehndorff. 2007. "Extended and Unusual Working Hours in European Companies: Establishment Survey on Working Time 2004–2005." Dublin: European Foundation for the Improvement of Living and Working Conditions.

Marx, Gundula. 2005. "London—und dann der Rest der Welt" ["London—And Then the Rest of the World"]. *Allgemeine Hotel- und Gaststättenzeitung*, October 8: 5.

Parker, Eric, and Niklas Krause. 1999. "Job Quality in the Hospitality Industry: Findings from the San Francisco Housekeeping Study." Report to the Rockefeller Foundation. Washington: Working for America Institute.

Parmentier, Klaus, Hans-Joachim Schade, and Franziska Schreyer. 1996. "Berufe im Spiegel der Statistik: Beschäftigung und Arbeitslosigkeit 1985–1995" ["Occupations Reflected in Statistics. Employment and Unemployment 1985-1995"]. *Beiträge zur Arbeitsmarkt- und Berufsforschung* 60.

———. 1998. "Berufe im Spiegel der Statistik: Beschäftigung und Arbeitslosigkeit 1993–1997" ["Occupations Reflected in Statistics. Employment and Unemployment 1993-1997"]. *Beiträge zur Arbeitsmarkt- und Berufsforschung* 60.

Pohl, Gerd. 1995. *Humaner, sicherer, zufriedener: Handlungsfelder qualitativer Tarifpolitik: Das Beispiel der Gewerkschaft Nahrung—Genuss—Gaststätten* [*More Humane, More Secure, More Content: The Application of Qualitative Collective Bargaining. The Example of the Food and Allied Workers' Union*]. Hamburg, Germany: VSA-Verlag.

———. 2007. "Tariflose Zustände und Tariferosion: Erfahrungen aus dem Gastgewerbe" ["Non-Coverage by Collective Agreements and the Erosion of Collective Bargaining. Experiences from the Hotel and Restaurant Trade"]. In *Wohin treibt das Tarifsystem?* [*Where is the Collective Bargaining System Heading?*], edited by Reinhard Bispinck. Hamburg: VSA-Verlag.

Rationelle Hauswirtschaft. 2005. "Reinigungsleistung muss 'fairgütet' werden" ["Fair Pay for Cleaning Work"]. *Rationelle Hauswirtschaft* 10: 32.

Seibert, Holger. 2007. "Berufswechsel in Deutschland: Wenn der Schuster nicht bei seinem Leisten bleibt" ["Changing Occupation in Germany: When the Cobbler Doesn't Stay at His Last"]. *IAB-Kurzbericht* 17(1).

Spörel, Ulrich. 1994. "Inlandstourismus 1993: Ergebnisse der Beherbergungsstatistik" ["Domestic Tourism 1993: Results from Lodging Statistics"]. *Wirtschaft und Statistik* 6: 459–65.

Spurgaitis, Kevin. 2006. "Hotel Workers Rising." *Catholic New Times* 30(10): 5.

Statistisches Bundesamt. 1996. "Datenreport: Zahlen und Fakten über die Bundesrepublik Deutschland" ["Data Report: Facts and Figures on the Federal Republic of Germany Data Report 7"]. Wiesbaden/Bonn: Bonn Aktuell.

———. 2006a. "Umsatzsteuer" ["Value-Added Tax"]. Fachserie 14 Reihe 6. 2004. June 28, 2006. Wiesbaden: Statistisches Bundesamt.

———. 2006b. "Tourismus: Ergebnisse der monatlichen Beherbergungsstatistik" ["Tourism: Results of the Monthly Lodgings Statistics"]. Fachserie 6 Reihe 7.1. Dezember und Jahr 2005. February 2006. Wiesbaden, Germany: Statistisches Bundesamt.

Sturman, Michael C. 2006. "A New Method for Measuring Housekeeping Performance Consistency." Cornell Hospitality Report. *CHR Reports* 6(11).

Wassermann, Wolfram. 1999. "Diener zweier Herren: Arbeitnehmer zwischen Arbeitgeber und Kunde" ["Servants of Two Masters. Employees Between Employer and Customer"]. Münster: Verlag Westfälisches Dampfboot.

Weiler, Anni. 2003. "Branch Surveys on Working Conditions: Hotels and Restaurants." National report for Germany prepared for the European Foundation for the Improvement of Living and Working Conditions. Project 0262. Göttingen: Arbeitswelt—Working World (AWWW), Research and Consultation.

Wein, Elmar. 2006. "Gastgewerbe im Jahr 2003" ["The Hotel and Restaurant Industry in 2003"]. *Wirtschaft und Statistik* 6: 587–95.

Winter, Kay. 2004. "Die Aufbauorganisation von Hotelbetrieben" ["The Organisation Structures of Hotel Companies"]. In *Management in der Hotellerie und Gastronomie: Betriebswirtschaftliche Grundlagen* [*Management in the Hotel and Restaurant Industry*], edited by Karl Heinz Hänssler, with the help of Bernd Dahringer. Vol. 6., revised edition. München/Wien, Germany: Deutscher Fachverlag.

Yancey, Kitty Bean. 2006. "Hotel Housekeepers Create Luxury—But at a Cost." *USA Today*, April 27. Accessed at http://www.usatoday.com/travel/hotels/2006-04-27-housekeepers_x.htm.

CHAPTER 6

Low-Paid but Committed to the Industry: Salespeople in the Retail Sector

Dorothea Voss-Dahm

Reports on the Wal-Mart system do not sound at all unfamiliar to German ears. In Germany, as in the United States, large retail companies are growing primarily by squeezing out smaller retailers, and that growth is also being achieved by means of an approach to competition based on aggressive price cutting (Lichtenstein 2006). In 2004, 40 percent of sales in the German food retail trade were captured by discounters—that is, companies that offer mass-consumption goods at permanently low prices and on a self-service basis. Thus, the discount principle in its pure form is also known and in widespread use in Germany. In contrast to Wal-Mart in the United States, however, the discounters in Germany are not the largest German food retail chains. Rather, the German retail sector has many faces, not least because the two largest German retail companies, with their cooperative tradition and high share of self-employed traders, are not managed centrally but have instead introduced an element of decentralization into the world of retailing. Despite differences in organizational forms, however, German retail companies are also exploiting the advantages of integration into global value chains and modern information and communications technologies that allow real-time monitoring and control of goods management systems and stores.

The German and American retail sectors also have something in common when it comes to employment. In both countries, low wages are considerably more prevalent in the retail sector than in the economy as a whole (Holgate 2006). There are significant differences, however, in the employment structure. More than half of retail workers in Germany are part-timers, many of them employed in marginal part-time jobs called "mini-jobs," whereas in the United States the share of full-timers is much higher. There are also considerable differences in the level of institutional support for employment relationships. More than three-quarters of all employees in German retailing have completed a two- or three-year vocational training course, whereas American retail workers have little formal training. Another difference is that, in Germany, the basic working and employment conditions, such as pay and working time, are regulated by industry-wide collective agreements. Moreover, employees in Germany enjoy a higher level of social protection than their counterparts in the United States. In Germany all part-time and full-time employees in jobs subject to social insurance contributions are covered by the social security system. In the United States, in contrast, only one-third of retail trade workers have medical insurance and receive employer-sponsored retirement benefits (Carré, Holgate, and Tilly 2006).

Institutions introduce certain limiting factors into the employment system in the retail sector, and firms and employees use these constraints to guide them in shaping employment relationships. But do these institutions exert a substantial influence on job quality throughout the retail trade? For example, how do low wages in German retailing fit in with occupational labor markets? Is sound vocational training not an entrance ticket to jobs with good working and employment conditions? And how can it be that the structure and level of remuneration are regulated at the industry level by the social partners and yet considerable income differences exist? These questions can also be put in a different way: does the situation in the German retail trade suggest that the legal anchoring of labor market institutions is not sufficient and that those institutions must also wield considerable power and influence in order to create good working and employment conditions?

THE SAMPLE AND THE METHODOLOGY

Twelve case studies were carried out in eight retail companies. Of these eight companies, four are food retailers and four electrical goods retailers. All the companies are leading companies in their sector in terms of market power and should be regarded as full-range retailers, since the product ranges they carry are broad and deep. Thus, our sample does not include retail formats like discounters and specialist retailers operating small outlets. The target occupations studied were sales activities on the selling floor and at checkouts. In the course of the case studies, we conducted guided individual interviews with sixteen managers at the head-office or store level, four works councillors, and fifty employees. In the employee interviews, we emphasized questions about career biographies, job profiles, and working conditions. At the end of the interviews, the employees were given a questionnaire with thirty-eight questions on work content and job evaluation, each with a five-digit scale for the response. Two case studies were carried out in East Germany, and all the others were in West Germany. Background discussions were held with five trade union representatives and three representatives of the employers' association. To acquaint ourselves with the latest technological developments, we went on guided visits of retail stores in which new technology was being piloted.

The chapter is organized as follows. Differences in pay and the reasons for these differences are outlined in the next section. That discussion is followed by a section in which I present the argument that the vocational training system in the retail trade is a very stable factor in the German retail employment system. Then I investigate the question of whether technological developments constitute a threat to the skill profile of German retail workers, which is relatively high by international standards. Next, I focus on the task profiles of employees in frontline activities, paying particular attention to work organization in retail stores. The results are summarized in the final section.

PAY STRUCTURE, PAY SYSTEMS, AND PERSONNEL COST REDUCTION

Low-wage work is widespread in both the American and German retail sectors. In 2004, 42 percent of all retail workers in the United States—considerably more than in the economy as a whole (28 percent)—were paid an hourly rate below the low-wage threshold of $9.12 (defined in accordance with the OECD standard of two-thirds of the median income in the economy as a whole) (Holgate 2006). In Germany the share of low-wage workers in the retail trade is the same as in the United States. However, since the share of low-paid workers in the German economy as a whole (22 percent) is lower than in the United States, retail workers in Germany are even more adversely affected by low pay in relative terms than their American counterparts.

Our analyses show that the share of low-wage employment in German retailing varies a lot by employment form and size of firm. Thus, mini-jobbers are frequently paid lower wages than full-time and part-time workers in jobs subject to social security contributions. Similarly, rates of pay in small and medium-sized retail companies are frequently below the low-wage threshold, while wages and salaries in large retail companies are regulated by collective agreements, which set a lower limit on the price of labor. The example of the food retail chains shows, however, that personnel costs can be reduced even if the collectively agreed wage and salary structure is maintained— namely, by reducing the volume of labor required through part-time work.

Pay Structure

The data on retail earnings show that actual wage levels vary considerably depending on employment form (see table 6.1).

The high share of low-wage earners in mini-jobs is particularly striking: 86.8 percent of all retail workers in such jobs are low-wage earners, with a gross hourly rate of less than €9.83 (US$14.38) in West Germany and €7.15 (US$10.46) in East Germany. In essence, the legal regulations governing marginal part-time work provide a subsidy for this particular employment form, since those working in such jobs pay no income tax or social security contributions (see chapter 1), although, according to the regulations, they are entitled to the same rate of pay as those in fully insurable jobs. As can be seen from table 6.1, however, the statutory regulations are frequently circumvented, which explains the considerable difference in pay between marginal part-time workers and those subject to income tax and social security contributions. Our sample includes a number of employers who pay the collectively agreed rates only to employees in fully insurable jobs, while paying lower rates to those in mini-jobs. In these firms, therefore, the hourly labor cost of marginal part-time employees is lower than that of workers subject to income tax and social security contributions. This obviously makes increasing the number of mini-jobs at the expense of fully insurable jobs attractive to employers seeking to reduce labor costs. In companies in which employees' interests are strongly represented, however, it has proved possible either to prevent the use of mini-jobs altogether or at least to monitor developments closely to ensure that a differentiated pay policy is not put in place. One works councillor summed up the situa-

Table 6.1 Low-Wage Work and Employment Structure in
the Retail Sector, by Employment Form, 2004

	Share of Low-Wage Earners	
	In the Economy as a Whole	In the Retail Sector
Employment form		
Full-time	13.7%	34.4%
Part-time	20.3	28.5
Marginal part-time	78.9	86.8
Sex		
Men	14.4	27.7
Women	30.2	47.1
Total	22.1	42.0

Source: Jaehrling et al. (2006, 117).
Note: The low-wage shares for the economy as a whole were also calculated with
SOEP 2004, but the categories of employees included differ from the calculations in
Table 1.5. The main difference is that the calculations presented in chapter 1 exclude
students and pensioners, whereas these groups are included in table 5.3, since these
groups form a substantial share of marginal part-time employees.

tion quite succinctly: "If we don't ensure that those in mini-jobs are
also paid the collectively agreed rate, then they'll gradually devour
us."

Analysis of full-timers' pay shows that the share of low-wage work
in retail food chains (NACE 52.11) and in electrical retailing (NACE
52.45) is considerably lower than in the predominantly small outlets
of specialist food retailers (NACE 52.1) (table 6.2). This suggests that
collectively agreed rates of pay exert a strong influence in the first
two sectors and that such regulation does not exist in the specialist
food retail trade.

Evidently, therefore, interfirm differences in pay levels run along
the line dividing the large retail groups from small and owner-operated retail businesses.[1] This finding is further supported by information gathered during the employee interviews. One worker employed in a part-time job reported that she earned the same as a
friend of hers working full-time in a bakery. Another worker employed by a company bound by the collective agreement to work
twenty hours a week actually earned more than in her previous job,
in which she worked thirty hours per week as a salesperson in a
franchise outlet.

Table 6.2 Low-Wage Work in the Retail Trade, by Occupation and Sector, Full-Timers Only, 2003

	Share in Total Retail Employment	Share of Full-Time Employees with Low Wages[a]	Share of Sales Staff[b] (Full-Time Only) with Low Wages[a]	Share of Checkout Operators[c] (Full-Time Only) with Low Wages
Retail trade		33%	42%	35%
Food retail chains	24.0%	28.6	41.1	26.4
Specialist food retailers	8.2	62.5	74.6	100
Electrical retailing	3.3	26.5	23.7	48.8

Source: Special evaluation of BA employee panel, author's calculation.
[a] The low-wage threshold is defined as two-thirds of median gross monthly earnings. The low-w threshold is €1.736 per hour West Germany and €1.309 in East Germany.
[b] Sales staff as defined in ISCO 682.
[c] Checkout operators as defined in ISCO 773.

COLLECTIVELY AGREED PAY SYSTEMS

The collectively agreed structure and the level of remuneration for dependent employees in the retail trade are laid down in pay agreements negotiated at the sector level. The collectively agreed retail pay structure is differentiated in two regards. First, a distinction is made between white collar and manual workers, with different regulations applying to the two categories. Second, pay levels for white collar employees vary depending on position and number of years' retail experience. Consequently, in addition to the differentiation *between* firms already described, the pay structure in the German retail trade is characterized by a high level of differentiation *within* firms.

The relevant pay scale in the context of our research is pay scale 1 (G1), since this is the scale to which sales staff, cashiers, and checkout operators—in other words, the vast bulk of retail workers—are allocated. The basic rates of pay on G1 are €8.41 (US$12.31) per hour (gross monthly pay of €1,372 [US$2,008]) in the first year of retail work and €12.30 (US$18.00) per hour (gross monthly pay of €2,006 [US$2,936]) by the sixth year (pay agreement of North Rhine-Westphalia, the largest collective bargaining area in Germany in terms of employee numbers). Those employees who have completed a vocational training program in a relevant occupation are allocated to the point on the scale for workers with three years' experience immediately on completion of their training. Thus, the collectively agreed pay structure based on vocational qualifications and number of years' experience puts the hourly rate for untrained sales assistants in their first year of retail work below the low-wage threshold of €9.58 (US$14.02) (West Germany). If they spend longer in the job and complete a course of vocational training, however, they will be able to work their way up the pay scale and move beyond the low-wage threshold.

The collective pay agreement lays down the foundations of the payment structures, but other legal provisions and collective agreements also play a part in determining pay levels. A clause in the collective pay agreement provides for the payment of a supplementary allowance of €51.13 (US$74.82) per month to salespersons on pay scale G1 if they take on additional tasks or are deployed in several different areas of operation. Another clause provides for the payment of a stress allowance of €25.56 (US$37.40) per month for cashiers and checkout operators. The outline collective agreement stipulates the regular weekly working time (thirty-seven and a half hours in North Rhine-Westphalia) and the premium payments for late-night opening and Saturday work (20 percent), additional hours (25 percent), night work (55 percent), Sunday working (120 percent), and working on public holidays (200 percent). The collective agreement on exceptional payments fixes the level of holiday and Christmas bonuses at 50 and 62 percent, respectively, of gross pay for the relevant months.

Collective agreements regulate basic work and employment conditions. However, what impact do they have in practice? Until the year 2000, all collective agreements in the retail trade were generally binding: the collectively agreed rates of pay applied to all workers, regardless of whether their employer was a member of the employers' associations or the worker was a member of the trade union. The generally binding nature of collective agreements eliminated wages as a competitive factor—that is, it was not possible, at least under the prevailing law, to differentiate between firms in terms of the remuneration element of the employment relationship. Employers regarded this situation as politically outdated, however, and used their right of veto to halt the process of declaring collective agreements generally binding. Since then, wages have been a central factor in competition. Employers who are either not members of the employers' association at all or in a special membership category (ohne Tarifbindung) that means they are not bound by multi-employer collective agreements no longer have to pay collectively agreed wages and salaries.

According to information derived from the IAB establishment panel, which contains representative data on coverage by collective agreement among firms and employees, 36 percent of establishments and 55 percent of all employees in the wholesale and retail trade (NACE 5) in West Germany in 2005 were covered by a collective agreement (Kohaut 2007). The figures for East Germany were 15 percent and 30 percent, respectively; clearly, coverage by collective agreement is considerably lower in East Germany than in West Germany. This represents a sharp decline of the coverage rate: within just two years (2003 to 2005), the share of employees covered by collective agreements decreased by 8 percent in West Germany and by 4 percent in East Germany (Ellguth and Kohaut 2004). As far as integration into the industrial relations system is concerned, the vast majority of stores in our sample represent the stable core of the sector. Of the twelve stores we investigated, eight adhered to the collective agreement (of which six had a works council and two did not), and four did not (one of which had a works council while three did not). In the eight stores covered by the collective agreement, all the allowances and premium payments listed earlier were paid, whether because the works councils saw to it that the collective agreements were adhered to or because the employers adhered scrupulously to the provisions of the collective agreements in order to prevent the establishment of a works council.

But what pay system was in use in the four stores not bound by collective agreements? There were in fact divergences from the collectively agreed standards: in premium payments (no allowances were paid for working at particular times, no overtime premiums were paid); in Christmas and vacation bonuses, which, if paid at all, depended on company profitability; in weekly working time, which was forty hours in the firms not bound by collective agreements; and, finally, at least in the electrical retail sector, in payment systems, which combined fixed and variable elements.

Part-Time Work as a Cost Reduction Strategy

Part-time work is a characteristic of retail employment. This is true of both Germany and the United States, but it is even more prevalent in

Table 6.3 Employment Structure of the Retail Trade in
the United States and Germany, 2003

	U.S. Retail Trade	German Retail Trade	German Food Retail Chains	German Electrical Retailing
Full-time	72%	49%	34%	77%
Part-time	28	25	40	8
Marginal part-time	—	26	26	15

Source: Holgate (2006), based on U.S. Current Population Survey (CPS); BA employee panel; author's calculations.

Germany. In 2004, 28 percent of retail workers in the United States were part-timers, and in frontline activities the share was as high as 42 percent (Carré, Holgate, and Tilly 2006). In Germany in the same year, the part-time rate in retailing was significantly higher, at 51 percent; half of these part-timers were in jobs subject to social insurance contributions, while the other half were employed in mini-jobs (table 6.3).

In the interviews in food retail stores, a high part-time rate was seen as an essential condition for dealing successfully with the considerable flexibility requirements of the retail trade. This view is also reflected in the part-time rate, which at 66 percent is particularly high in food retail stores. In many food retail stores, full-time employment is more or less a management preserve, with frontline operations entrusted almost exclusively to part-timers. And indeed, the part-time strategy gives firms a high degree of flexibility in staff deployment even with restrictive staffing levels. Fragmented working time and employment units are more maneuverable and more likely to leave "productivity-enhancing holes" in personnel cover than employment relationships with long working times. And yet, combined with the great importance of cost reduction strategies in retail companies (Ernst & Young 2004), the flexibility argument advanced by food retailers could also be interpreted as a "Trojan horse" intended to conceal efforts to push through labor cost reductions: the part-time strategy enables companies to reduce labor costs by reducing the volume of labor, and thus it can be seen as one way of reducing labor costs without cutting wages.

A strategy based on fragmentation operates in the retail food chains, where women account for 78 percent of the workforce. Obviously, this is not the case in electrical retailing, where 63 percent of the workforce is male and 77 percent work full-time. Thus, the part-time work strategy adopted by the food retail chains is wholly consistent with the influence of the German welfare state on women's labor market participation (Jany-Catrice and Lehndorff 2005). In Germany women's paid work is largely shaped by an underdeveloped system of child care, a social security system in which women's entitlement to health and, in some cases, old-age insurance benefit is derived from their husbands, and a taxation system in which second household incomes are subject to a high marginal tax rate (see chapter 1). These are all so many incentives for women to keep their labor supply at a low level, which is why the German welfare state is characterized in one well-known typology as "conservative" (Esping-Andersen 2000). Against this background, retail companies experience no difficulty in filling part-time vacancies; furthermore, the high level of unemployment in Germany also serves to keep female workers' resistance to reductions in contractual working hours low as a rule.

Clearly cost reductions in food retail chains, at least with respect to fully insurable jobs, are being achieved by reducing the *volume* of labor used rather than reducing the *price* per unit of labor used. The channeling of employers' strategies in this direction rather than others is supported by the two institutional pillars of wage formation in the German employment model. First, firms that are bound by collective agreements do not have the option of reducing labor costs by cutting wages. Second, the workplace representation of employees' interests, which is enshrined in the Works Constitution Act, tends to channel employers' decisions in the same direction. The act gives works councils full rights of codetermination on matters of pay determination at the establishment level, but works councils have no power to decide on staffing levels. Thus, both these pillars of the industrial relations system are engineered in such a way as to preclude competitive strategies aimed at achieving cost reductions by reducing wage levels. The system does, however, have an exposed flank— namely, the opportunities it offers firms to adopt competitive strategies that seek to achieve cost reductions by reducing the volume of labor deployed.

The result of the part-time work strategy adopted in the retail trade in general and by the food retail chains in particular is that employees are not necessarily working for low hourly rates of pay, even though their actual monthly earnings are low. For women in particular, retail work scarcely provides a living wage; at best they earn just a second income. Some of our interviewees, particularly female employees in East Germany, openly expressed their resentment of this situation. It would be an exaggeration, however, to suggest that skilled part-timers have been leaving in droves, thereby damaging retail companies by increasing the turnover rate and the costs associated with it and taking away company-specific know-how. Clearly the combination of a high level of occupational loyalty, mainly female workforces, and the social protection for "housewives" provided by the German welfare state produces enormous scope for implementing a regressive personnel policy. Occupational loyalty ("this is the occupation I trained for"), the socialization that takes place during training ("but my colleagues are here"), and the option of taking on an alternative role outside the labor market (mother, housewife), which can have a stabilizing effect during periods of uncertainty, may compensate for any trends toward insecurity and devaluation, since occupational loyalty and a possible alternative role act as a "secondary mode of integration" (Kraemer and Speidel 2005). In combination with the openings offered by the industrial relations system, these factors provide a stable basis for retail firms to implement their part-time work strategy with a view to reducing costs.

Pay Determination at the Firm Level

The relevance of pay determination at the firm level goes beyond considerations of income policy, since the monetary incentive system also reflects the performance policy goals that firms are pursuing (Marsden 1999). Pay determination at the firm level differs from sector to sector of the retail trade. In food retailing, sales personnel are generally paid a flat rate for the job; pay related to profitability or performance is not widespread. The situation in electrical retailing is different: in all four of the companies we investigated, the pay systems for sales staff included profitability- or performance-related elements.

In two electrical retail companies covered by collective agreements but with no works councils, all the allowances and bonuses provided for in the industry collective agreement were paid. Bonuses over and above those stipulated in the collective agreement were negotiated in bilateral discussions between management and sales staff; these discussions were not institutionalized, and there was no entitlement to these additional bonuses, which, according to one store manager, could amount to as much as 25 percent of the collectively agreed basic pay. In this system, each salesperson's negotiating skills had a significant influence on the level of individual bonuses.

The situation was different in another electrical retailer that was no longer bound by multi-employer collective agreements since the employer had changed its employers' association membership category. But this retailer did have a works council, which made use of its right to full codetermination in matters of pay determination according to the Works Constitution Act. Since the retailer had declared itself no longer bound by the industry collective agreement, management and the works council had been in negotiations over a new pay system. Management was seeking to introduce profitability- and performance-related pay elements on top of the basic wage, to be funded by a sum made available by management for the increase in weekly working time from thirty-seven and a half to forty hours. As the negotiations proceeded, it became clear how difficult it was to weight the individual parameters of the variable pay elements. Some areas of the product range generated high sales for the company but with low margins, whereas others generated high profits with low sales volumes. Another problem arose out of the question of who was responsible for fixing the monthly sales target, which had to be reached in order to trigger payment of the maximum variable pay element. A third problem was the weighting of profitability- and performance-related pay elements. Whereas the profitability-related pay elements rewarded the performance of each department and the store as a whole (that is, groups), individual performance-related pay rewarded individuals.

According to information provided by representatives of the employers' association and the trade union, the fourth case study firm, an electrical goods retailer, was typical of specialist, owner-operated retail outlets. In this firm, which was not bound by collective agreements and had no works council, the fixed pay element for sales staff amounted to only two-thirds of the collectively agreed wage. According to the owner, a pay system of this kind reflected the performance principle, without which an independent retailer could not operate in a low-margin environment: "With the right attitude to performance, our employees can earn the collectively agreed wage of €2,000 (US$2,923). Anyone unable to achieve that, firstly, has a problem himself, and secondly, is the wrong person for the company in the long run."

This comparison shows that the *principles* underpinning the pay systems in the various electrical retailers are not substantially different from each other. However, the *level* of the fixed pay elements differs considerably depending on whether a collective agreement has been implemented or a firm has a works council that can prevent or limit attempts to reduce them. Thus, collective agreements and workplace codetermination exert a ratchet effect that does not come into play in firms that are not bound by collective agreements and have no workplace representation of interests.

OCCUPATIONAL IDENTIFICATION AS THE BASIS OF RETAIL WORK

The evidence presented up to this point shows that low wages are indeed paid in the retail trade and that the prevalence of low-wage work varies depending on retail format and employment form. In this section, we show that this pay structure and human resource strategies very obviously based on occupational identification are not mutually exclusive.

THE DUAL VOCATIONAL TRAINING SYSTEM

One distinctive characteristic of the German retail trade is certainly the high share of skilled workers. In 2002, 81 percent of retail workers had completed a course of vocational training. The average skill level in the retail trade was thus even higher than in the economy as a whole: the overall share of workers with a vocational qualification was 73 percent in the same year. Correspondingly, the share of university graduates in the retail trade was extremely low at 2.7 percent. The share of low-skill workers in retailing, at 16.3 percent, was about the same as that in the economy as a whole (16.7 percent).

At 47 percent of all employees in retail trade, salespersons constitute the sector's largest occupational category. The retail sector's training policy is based on this clearly dominant occupational category. In 2005 around 8 percent of all new training contracts in Germany were concluded in retail companies and in the two most important training occupations in the retail trade—namely, trained retail sales assistant (two-year training course) and trained retail salesperson (three-year training course) (BIBB 2006). Despite a decline in total employment in retailing, the number of newly concluded training contracts has not declined in the last fifteen years.

The fundamental reorganization of the curricula for the two training occupations by the tripartite vocational training system, which was completed in 2004, also shows that employer and employee representatives regard vocational training as fundamentally important to the future of the industry. The thoroughgoing overhaul of the content of vocational training programs has made particular allowance for the pronounced differentiation of the industry by retail formats. In the previous training programs, "advice and sales" occupied a central position in both the two- and three-year courses. In the new training regulations, this topic is just one of several opportunities for extension and specialization. Similarly, bookkeeping has become a marginal topic in both occupational profiles, while operational controlling now occupies a much more prominent position.

THE VALUE OF VOCATIONAL TRAINING IN THE EYES OF THE ACTORS

All the case study firms were active in training, and the vocational training principle was not questioned by management at any of them. But all our interviewees with human resource responsibilities emphasized that work tasks in retailing are not homogeneous in terms of their skill requirements. In the food retail business, for instance, they stressed that, in order to work as shelf stackers or checkout operators, employees need virtually none of the knowledge or skills acquired during the training program. Rather, these activities should be characterized as semiskilled.

Even when delivering a fundamentally positive assessment of initial vocational training, managers stressed that vocational training can indeed be a prelude to a successful career, since trainees acquire basic knowledge about business processes and customer and sales psychology and products, as well as certain technical skills (such as cutting techniques). At the same time, however, they emphasized that even the best vocational training is of little benefit if certain fundamental personal qualities, such as willingness to work and a talent for selling, are absent. And occupational experience plays such a fundamental role that the owner of three supermarkets declared: "We could teach the purely technical stuff in a year, but trainees have not learned everything there is to learn after two years or even after three years. Skilled workers need a certain amount of experience, both of life and work. That is, competencies that have to be acquired over time."

The complex relationship between initial training and the requirements of retail work is evident from employees' statements as well. When asked in the employee questionnaire to respond to the statement: "I can make good use in my daily work of what I learned during my training," 60 percent of workers in food retailing and 47 percent in electrical retailing agreed. This can be interpreted as an indication that the knowledge and skills acquired during initial training are more relevant to the requirements of everyday work in food retailing than in electrical retailing. Of the workers in electrical retailing we interviewed, 53 percent agreed "to some extent" or gave no response at all, compared with 23 percent in food retailing; however, 17 percent of food retail workers disagreed with the statement. The high share of disagreement among food retail workers may suggest that the knowledge acquired during training is not applied in daily work, that is, that more knowledge and skills are imparted than are actually needed. The most frequent response given by electrical retail workers—"to some extent"—suggests that the basic skills acquired during training are not sufficient to deal with the requirements of work in electrical retailing, and in fact considerable importance is attached to product and sales training in electrical retail stores.

Internal Labor Markets: Promotion Opportunities

In all the firms investigated, the institutionally rooted vocational training system is used not only for the training of skilled workers but also for the recruitment of managerial staff. Managers in retailing are typically not college or university graduates but rather have completed a course of career advancement training following their initial training program. The institutional framework for promotion to managerial status is constituted by the regulations governing the two relevant vocational training certificates: retail manager (Handelsfachwirt), which is the equivalent of the master craftsman (Handwerkermeister) in craft trades or the qualified foreman (Industriemeister) in manufacturing industry, and assistant retail manager (Handelsassistent). Both career advancement programs provide the qualifications required for the positions of store and department manager, and the first also provides qualifications for those wishing to go into business on their own. Both sets of regulations were thoroughly modernized in 2005 and adapted to the demands now made of managerial staff (Malcher and Paulini-Schlottau 2005).

In some case study companies, trainees for vocational training were selected with a view to possible future recruitment as managers. These were companies that either were expanding rapidly or, as in the case of two of the food retailers organized along cooperative lines, were facing the imminent retirement in the next few years of many of the independent retailers who were members of the buying group, without appointed successors. This is also why some companies have changed the recruitment criteria for initial training places. First, preference is given to school-leavers with higher-level qualifications; in an applications situation that favors employers, lower secondary school pupils (Hauptschüler) stand little chance of being offered a training place when most places are given instead to intermediate secondary school pupils (Realschüler) with good grades and, increasingly, to upper secondary school pupils with the Abitur. Second, the gender segmentation that is apparent with regard to promotion opportunities begins as early as the selection process for training places. Whereas frontline activities, at least in food retailing, are performed primarily by women, managerial positions in retail stores are occupied predominantly by men. Thus, the more companies make potential recruitment for management positions a criterion for allocating initial training places, the more disadvantaged female applicants become in the search for training places. This is clearly illustrated by the example of an owner-operated supermarket in which there were seventy-five applicants for two training places and a female-male applicant ratio of 80:20, although efforts were made to obtain a balanced gender mix in the allocation of training places.

In our interviews with young workers who had recently completed their vocational training, no systematic difference in the attitudes of men and women to promotion could be discerned. Some female employees did complain, however, that they had to express their interest in one of the few places in the company's career advancement training program much more aggressively than their young male colleagues, and in some cases without success. Clearly many—again, mostly male—managers, on whose recommendation places on the program are awarded, are of the opinion that investment in women's career advancement is a waste of resources. One store manager justified this view in the following terms: "Women with higher-level vocational qualifications disappear anyway at some point." In a way, the demands made of managerial staff in the retail trade are themselves a barrier that leads to the segmentation of vertical promotion ladders by gender. According to both workers and managers, the preconditions for internal promotion are a willingness to work long hours (forty-five or more hours per week) and geographical mobility. In large retail companies in particular, and in an industry with a very high part-time rate, these demands cannot be justified in terms of business processes. Moreover, while these demands do not explicitly exclude women, they are undoubtedly at odds with many women's preferences and are therefore a very effective way of indirectly preventing women from advancing their careers within a female-dominated industry.

Gender segregation in internal promotion is obviously not a phenomenon confined to Germany; it is confirmed by reports on the denial of internal promotion to female employees of Wal-Mart in the United States as well (Rosen 2006). Gender segregation is also reflected in pay differences between men and women, the so-called gender pay gap. This gap is considerably wider in the German retail trade, where it stands at 30 percent, than in retailing in the United States, where it stands at 13 percent (Carré, Holgate, and Tilly 2006; Hinz and Gartner 2005). However, it is scarcely imaginable in Germany that retail companies could have actions brought against them because of discrimination against their female employees, as has happened to Wal-Mart in the United States. The unequal distribution of opportunities between men and women working in retailing is not a matter for public debate in Germany.

OCCUPATIONAL LABOR MARKETS

German retailers employ vocationally qualified staff, and the large companies at least provide further training programs for (male employees) seeking promotion. These facts suggest that firms are likely to adopt personnel policies based on company loyalty and commitment. And in fact labor turnover in the firms we investigated was low. Labor turnover was not regarded as a personnel policy problem at all, which is why these retail companies did not even measure this figure. The level and structure of labor turnover in the retail labor market also point to the dominance of stable employment relationships and of an occupational labor market: labor turnover in the German retail trade is close to that in the national economy as a whole (Kalina and

Voss-Dahm 2005). The structure of mobility revealed by an activity-based analysis clearly shows that, at least for sales personnel in fully insurable employment, a change of *employer* is not necessarily associated with a change of *occupation*. During the observation period (1999 to 2003), 50.4 percent of those who took up new jobs as salespersons were already working as salespersons. Thus, sales personnel are more likely to remain "faithful" to the occupation for which they initially trained than employees in the economy as a whole (50.4 percent, compared with 44.1 percent). However, the picture is different in the case of marginal part-time employment, since two-thirds of new recruits to mini-jobs have no current experience in retailing or as salespersons. This is an indicator of an unstructured or unspecific labor market in which workers can perform their duties after a short induction period and are easily substitutable.

The labor turnover rate in the retail trade is close to that in the economy as a whole. To that extent, it is a "normal" sector. However, international comparison reveals certain differences. Our own analysis of the European Labor Force Survey (2001) shows that the share of German retail workers with job tenure of more than ten years, at 30 percent, is higher than in other European countries. (The corresponding figure for France is 27 percent, for Denmark 13 percent, and for the United Kingdom and Netherlands 20 percent.) Thus, in domestic terms the German retail trade has a "typically German" pattern of mobility, but in international terms interfirm mobility is low.

DO MODERN INFORMATION AND COMMUNICATIONS TECHNOLOGIES LEAD TO DESKILLING?

"Lean retailing" is the catchword that encapsulates the technological challenges facing the retail trade (Abernathy et al. 2000; Christopherson 2001). The logic behind lean retailing is that production processes should be managed from the end of the supply chain, that is, from the point of sale, following the principle of just-in-time production. The aim of lean retailing is to maximize economies of scale, which requires close links between retailers and manufacturers. The retail trade, which enjoys privileged access to up-to-date information on consumers' purchasing behavior, works with manufacturers on logistics systems that are known as efficient consumer response (ECR) systems (Bieber et al. 2004). Modern checkout systems constitute the technological core of the innovation, since it is at the checkout that data on the type and volume of goods sold are recorded and passed on to manufacturers, which use the data to calculate production volumes. Currently, however, it is RFID (radio frequency identification of products) technology that is keeping the retail trade on tenterhooks, since this technology, which can be used to track and monitor individual products by means of radio antennae, holds out the promise of much quicker and more efficient distribution processes than those achievable with the current technological possibilities.

With regard to changes in the employment system, these technological developments raise the following questions. Will the standardization and automation of distributive processes have an effect on work organization? Will the only effect be to reduce the volume of work, or is deskilling an inevitable consequence of the increasing dominance of lean retailing? Thomas Bailey and Annette Bernhardt (1997) and Bernhardt (1999) answer these questions unambiguously. Drawing on the results of studies of the American retail trade, they argue that the dominant Wal-Mart model is based on the twin pillars of high performance and low wages. In this context, "high performance" refers quite explicitly *not* to a particular approach to personnel policy but rather to the objective of effective process organization based on high investment in technology. Thus, the thrust of this argument is that the increasing use of technology in work processes leads inevitably to the deskilling and devaluing of work.

It is not only technological developments that can be interpreted as attacks on the skill structure of the German retail trade; the same applies to the principle of self-service, which is widespread in German retailing. Thus, the question of whether or not the German retail trade needs vocationally qualified workers is being raised on both sides of the value-added chain, making it doubly pressing. An answer is provided by Martin Baethge (2001, 98) when he discusses the (assumed) difference between the manufacturing and service sectors:

> Recent developments in service reduction and standardization suggest there is a difference between manufacturing and services that has skill implications. It was only during the shift from craft to mechanized mass production that the standardization of manufacturing processes led to the destruction of skilled work; subsequently, it was mainly simple routine activities that were eliminated by technical rationalization, while the skill requirements of many of the remaining activities actually increased.

Against the background of retail workers' changing activity profile, it is now being argued that the production of services in the German retail sector is following the skill trajectory outlined for the manufacturing industry: while technology is reducing simple routine activities, the introduction of highly complex technical systems is at the same time either raising skill requirements for the remaining jobs or even changing the requirements altogether, although they remain tailored to the intermediate skill level.

Lean Retailing in Practice

To substantiate this argument, we examine those operational areas in our sample of firms affected by technological change to ascertain how work requirements and work intensity have changed. The main areas of operations involved are the goods management systems and the checkout systems.[2]

Modern goods management systems were in use in all the firms we investigated. Merchandise planning systems may be either fully automatic or manual. With fully automatic systems, which were used in two of the firms we investigated, sales recorded at the checkouts trigger new orders, which are put in automatically without human intervention. However, employees stressed that merchandise planning continues to exist as an operational area. The master file data must be updated when demand for a particular item falls or rises, and it makes sense to reduce or increase the size of the order for that item. The master file data also must be amended when new articles are listed, when an eye-catching secondary display is planned for seasonal goods (such as bakery products at Christmas), when special promotions require temporarily higher stocks, or when goods must be removed from the system because of damage or perishability, particularly in the fresh goods department.

In reality, however, even regular updating of master file data in a fully automatic merchandise planning system is no guarantee that goods management processes will proceed smoothly, since all such systems are prone to disruptions. This seems to be true independently of the country, since the same is reported from Wal-Mart in the United States (Rosen 2006). Consequently, employees must actively search for and eliminate errors. The order volume can be wrong, for example, if an item is put through the checkout with an incorrect EAN number, if the order is incorrectly filled in the warehouse, or if the item is entered on the store's stock list with the incorrect EAN number in the incoming goods department. All in all, fully automatic merchandise planning systems save on labor, since goods are ordered automatically. As a consequence, merchandise planning is still an area of operations for skilled workers with departmental responsibilities who, apart from exceptional items, regularly update the master file data. One employee clearly felt that the changeover to fully automatic merchandise planning had deskilled her when she remarked: "I regret the fact that I don't put in the orders anymore. I feel that I'm not being used anymore, that I no longer have any responsibility."

In contrast, manual merchandise planning systems, which were used in the other two food retailers we investigated, require continuous work on the shelves. The bar codes of items on the shelves are scanned by employees using MDE devices (mobile data acquisition). The device, in which the current goods inventory is stored, calculates an order volume, which employees accept or adjust depending on the anticipated sales volume. In this way, stocks are continuously monitored, so that faulty inventories cannot go undetected for long. Responsibility for individual sections of the product range is evenly distributed among the workforce, and each employee has his or her own area of responsibility. This ensures that flows of goods (from sales via orders to shelf stacking) are always monitored by the same person, who is able to develop a feeling for the items that are selling well and those that are selling badly. Owing to the fixed allocation of responsibilities and the regularity with which stocks are monitored, employees have a good knowledge of the goods in their particular sections. What is surprising is that stock management duties are not allocated only to employees at a certain level of the management hierarchy or only to workers in fully insurable employment or with a certain level of experience. Some firms give responsibility for certain sections of the product range to trainees or marginal part-time employees, albeit only for small inventories.

Checkout scanning systems were in use in all the companies we investigated. Although checkout scanners allow for sophisticated analysis of goods management systems, the registration operation still ties up a considerable share of a store's labor resources. New technology will change this. When RFID replaces bar codes one day and every product is fitted with an RFID chip, customers will go through a gate and the goods in their carts or baskets will be registered in a fraction of a second. Then checkouts as the retail trade's "bottleneck" will no longer be the most complex and sensitive area of personnel planning. However, these are all dreams for the future. The technical problems associated with fixing RFID chips to products and then reading them have not yet been solved, and the microchips are still too expensive to be used on all products.

Obviously spurred by imminent but not yet achievable rationalization gains in the checkout area, one company was pursuing a different strategy at its checkouts. The various steps of the standard checkout procedure had been separated: scanning was done as always by checkout operators, but bills were paid by customers at self-service payment stations. The introduction of payment stations had not only eliminated the checkout procedure as an area of activity but also had a strongly rationalizing effect on the activities upstream and downstream of the traditional checkout procedure. All activities, some of them labor-intensive—such as distributing change to checkout operators, closing the cash accounts, and preparing the paper money for the bank—were eliminated completely because the payment stations automatically balanced the day's cash and recycled change.

Another way of organizing the scanning and payment procedure involves the use of NCR self-scanning stations at which customers scan their own purchases and make cashless payments. Although customers carry out both parts of the checkout procedure themselves, the assistance of checkout personnel continues to be required. One reason lies in the legislation governing the sale of goods such as tobacco and alcohol. The other is the need for staff to be present to assist in the event of malfunctions and to prevent theft. The work of checkout staff at the NCR self-scanning stations differs from standard checkout work in that it is passive rather than active and is carried out standing up rather than sitting down. The self-scanning systems have a labor-saving effect, since one checkout operator can keep an eye on four stations simultaneously. Thus, the rationalization effect is three-quarters of the staff employed on conventional checkouts.

Lean Retailing Equals Deskilling?

In the light of all the technological changes that either have already been introduced or are in the offing, is there little hope left for a core workforce in the German retail trade with a broadly based skill profile? This question must remain unanswered for the time being: despite the tempting rationalization gains, lean retailing is unlikely to be implemented in its pure form because of the heterogeneity of the retail trade. Rather, lean retailing will have to develop in conjunction with particular competitive strategies and particular corporate organizational structures.

Companies that base both their competitive strategy and their organizational structure on lean retailing principles take the "purchasing" stage of the value-added chain as the starting point for defining their commercial function and seek to optimize their position in procurement markets. As a consequence, the head office has considerable power and authority to achieve economies of scale, while the individual stores are merely a downstream stage in the value-added process whose function is to distribute the goods. As a result, the local market situation is of little importance—that is, the specificities of local or regional demand play no role in decisions about the product range. The same applies to employees' specialist knowledge and skills.

A competitive strategy that aims to achieve economies of scope constitutes an alternative production principle. Companies adopting such a strategy take the sales side as the starting point for defining their business activities. As a result, their head offices act as service providers for the individual stores; it is not unusual for the stores to be legally independent units, while their managers are self-employed traders who buy their goods from purchasing cooperatives or associations. Alternatively, the managers may be minority shareholders with a stake in the company's capital stock. Product policy is not determined centrally; rather, decisions on the structure and volume of goods on offer are taken locally and then brought together at the central level. Departments are organized as cost and profit centers and are accountable to the next highest level in the organizational structure, not for what they do but for how successfully they run their operations. Within these structures, sales personnel at the store level have opportunities to play an active part in determining product ranges and prices. As a consequence, job content is more broadly defined than in companies with more centralized organizational structures.

Both organizational forms were observed in the companies we investigated, and in approximately equal proportions. However, no company can completely avoid one production principle or the other, and as a result hybrid forms predominate. In decentralized companies, for example, the predominant product range policy is one in which a core range is supplied through the head office; this core range is then supplemented by local purchasing that takes into account the specific structure of local demand. This is the purchasing strategy that has been adopted by the market leaders in the German food and electrical retail sectors, and it is implemented by means of manual merchandise planning systems in which skilled workers play an active role. So are these firms using a technology that is inferior to fully automated systems? Hardly, at least not according to the managers of the stores in question: "There will never be an automatic merchandise planning system in this company." Or: "We want to retain control over what goods we stock. In this area, standardization and automation are utterly unimportant to us." These statements indicate that the choice of technology also reflects the power relationship between the corporate head office and the individual stores and that corporate decisions on the use of this or that technological system are influenced by more factors than just the rationalization gains to be achieved (Christopherson 2006). The same applies to checkout systems, since not all stores aspire to self-service at the checkouts. Some stores have offset reductions in staffing levels on the sales floor with high-quality personal service at the checkout, provided through the deployment of long-standing, experienced checkout personnel.

Conversely, in those stores in which fully automatic merchandise planning systems are in use, it is clear that such systems reduce the volume of work required and thus have a draining and deskilling effect on the jobs of many salespersons. Practical experience shows, however, that retailing may well be prey to the same fallacy that has already been identified in manufacturing—namely, that complex production systems can be completely managed by technology. Consequently, human coordination and management competencies in the sphere of error prevention and elimination, particularly in highly complex distribution processes, are likely to gain in importance in the future. Finally, the example of a full-range retailer that operated such a merchandise planning system shows that reductions in the personnel required for routinized tasks do not necessarily lead to deskilling in the store as a whole: compared to other food retailers, this company was making a very considerable investment in its employees' product knowledge and sales skills.

In all the interviews, it became more than clear that making full use of employees' commercial and business competencies is an element not of a luxury strategy but rather of a strategy that has profitable sales rather than merely volume sales as its goal. If products with good profit margins are correctly placed, well-informed employees focus on selling products with high margins, or competent service creates a high level of customer loyalty, the level of profit a retailer achieves may be higher than if stock turnover is reasonably high but margins are low. At the same time, a strategy in which employees' commercial competencies are disregarded can be costly if a store that has no "right of veto" is supplied with products that do not sell, resulting in high inventories or employees spending their time dealing with customer complaints.

In sum, there can be no doubt that labor-saving technological advances have already considerably reduced the volume of work in retail companies and will reduce it still further in the future. It must be emphasized, however, that salespersons' activity and job requirement profiles are shaped by employers' competitive strategies, corporate organizational principles, and technological shape. Empirical evidence can in no sense be said to indicate that deskilling is inevitable across the board. What David Autor, Frank Levy, and Richard Murnane (2003, 132) demonstrate in their account of the introduction of information technology in an American bank also applies to the German retail trade—namely, that technological determinism is to be rejected. Rather, management decisions play "a key role . . . in determining how tasks are bundled into jobs, with potentially significant implications for skill demands." Thus, one option open to the modern German retail sector is to produce its services by taking advantage of the presence of a vocationally qualified workforce. At the same time, it is clear that a vocational training system has to exist as an institutional precondition if this option is to be developed.

FLEXIBILITY REQUIREMENTS AND WORK ORGANIZATION

The retail sector is rightly characterized as a service industry that, because of daily, weekly, and seasonal fluctuations in demand, has to cope with high flexibility requirements. And yet developments in the case study companies make it clear that these requirements are not immutable and can be influenced to a large extent. For example, flexibility requirements can be reduced if customers carry out the scanning and payment procedure themselves and if they serve themselves on the sales floor. Furthermore, the distributive processes can be optimized in such a way as to make them more predictable, particularly with regard to the punctuality of deliveries. Nevertheless, if retailers wish to maintain specialist customer advice services and a high level of service at the checkouts and counters, then their flexibility requirements increase, confirming the statement that high demands are placed on the system of work organization in retail companies. Personnel deployment must be adjusted to match customer flows and product-related fluctuations in workloads if a high level of labor productivity is to be achieved.

It would seem reasonable to assume that employers make use of the skills of vocationally qualified workers within a broad labor deployment strategy based on functional flexibility. The empirical evidence clearly shows, however, that this is not the case, either in food or in electrical retailing. Rather, the main form of work organization observed in the case study stores is based on the organizational principle of functional integration within teamwork.

FUNCTIONAL FLEXIBILITY: PERSONNEL DEPLOYMENT ACROSS DEPARTMENTS

In all the stores we investigated, trainees were the only group for whom a labor deployment strategy based on functionally flexible work across all departments had been put in place. The reason was simply that the training regulations stipulated that trainees had to be deployed in all departments within the store. In one specialist electrical store, it was the trainees who, under the supervision of different managers, put products on display in the morning before the store opened. In a supermarket, it was the trainee who provided cover for the various peaks in workload that occurred over the course of the day. In the mornings, he helped the specialist personnel stack the fruit and vegetable counter; later he took incoming goods deliveries to the sales floor, and in between he opened up a second or third checkout if required.[3]

FUNCTIONAL INTEGRATION WITHIN TEAMWORK: PRODUCTIVITY THROUGH WORK ENRICHMENT

In all the stores investigated, most of the employees were responsible for their own area of work as part of a heightened division of labor, but cooperated with each other within the department team when it came to dealing with customers and other routine activities.

There are various degrees of cooperation within teams, depending on the working times of the workers concerned. If a company's personnel policy is based on fragmentation and the specified volume of working time is very closely matched to individual areas of activity, there will be little spare time for cooperation within the team. One example would be the employee in a mini-job who has full responsibility for the shelf containing the whole range of products from two suppliers: she orders goods, checks the sell-by dates, and keeps the shelf clean and stocked with product. On the other hand, there are more opportunities for cooperation within teams in the electrical retail sector, where most workers are full-timers. Long shop opening hours can also reduce teamwork if the members of a department team work staggered schedules and are unable to speak to each other directly. There is a strong link between the degree of teamwork and a store's hierarchical structure. In two of the stores we investigated in particular, it was clear that a cut in the number of department managers had been associated with an increase in department size. With the merging of departments, department teams had increased in size, which in turn had increased the pool of employees able to cover for each other. The importance of teamwork is also revealed by analysis of our employee questionnaires. Seventy-seven percent of employees in food retailing and 71 percent of those in electrical retailing agreed with the statement "Discussions with colleagues help me to do my job well." At the same time, supervisors did not seem to be particularly active in monitoring their subordinates' work, since the statement "My work is monitored daily by supervisors" was answered in the negative by 23 percent of electrical retail workers, while 53 percent answered "to some extent." The share of negative responses, at 40 percent, was even higher in food retailing, while the share of those answering "to some extent" was 30 percent.

A work organization system based on teamwork, however, combined with the delegation of responsibility for certain segments of the product range, has another effect on individual employees. A store manager said: "I can put pressure on the permanent workers. They have the basic knowledge for me to be able to discuss particular developments, objectives, and plans with them. They have a background in retailing and know what it's all about." And an employee in an electrical retail store declared: "The company provides the core range, but I don't have to take it. I could even sell condensed milk here, provided it sold well." Both statements make clear that work enrichment within teamwork not only reflects a "high involvement" policy but also constitutes an attempt to make active use of employees' professional awareness to optimize work processes (Lehndorff and Voss-Dahm 2005).

This strategy is not compatible with close monitoring by supervisors as part of a mode of work organization based on command and control. One alternative is a control strategy based on objective constraints, which is implemented by means of business performance indicators. In a strategy of this kind, the broad communication of such indicators, such as the sales, profits, stock levels, or inventories to be achieved within a given period, is accorded considerable importance. A predetermined share of labor costs in total sales or profits is used as a basis for controlling staffing levels in each cost center; any increase in that share leads to a reduction in the volume of available working time.

The setting of targets and the allocation of fixed resources make employees' work capacity the principal variable in operational processes. The more successfully employees are induced to adopt the required approach to selling or to search out opportunities for rationalization on their own initiative, the quicker the targets will be achieved (Voss-Dahm 2003). It is reported that cost targets exert a fundamental influence on working conditions in Wal-Mart stores as well, with managers coming under particular pressure (Rosen 2006). Finding themselves constantly squeezed, managers in both the United States and Germany can do little other than pass this pressure on to their staff. There would seem to be a difference, however, in how they go about doing this. The American reports suggest that the pressure on Wal-Mart employees is heightened as a result of direct instructions from management; German retail workers, on the other hand, internalize the cost and performance targets communicated via the corporate hierarchy and convert them into concrete actions more or less autonomously. It is more than debatable, however, whether a more "democratic" distribution of information about the restrictive conditions would make any difference to the actual strains and stresses to which employees are subject.

The consequences for employees in the companies we investigated are mixed. On the one hand, 81 percent of the employees we questioned agreed with the statement "I feel responsible for my department"; at the same time, in response to the statement "Sales targets are a source of pressure," 40 percent chose the response "agree completely or agree," while 26 percent chose "to some extent" as their answer or gave no answer at all. Employees' explanations of why they chose their particular answers also reflect this ambivalence. On the one hand, the fact that employees' competencies are becoming an integral part of business processes was welcomed: "Responsibility is always associated with stress, but with positive stress." On the other hand, this was also associated with specific pressures: "The figures are still going around in my head in the evening, and I worry about that. I find it disturbing that I can't switch off. Then I start thinking about the people at work. And after that I find myself going over the next day's routine in my head." Some employees obviously have alternative coping mechanisms: "After twenty-five years' work experience, one gets used to organizing oneself. Doing a number of things at the same time is actually motivating."

FUNCTIONAL DIFFERENTIATION AND OUTSOURCING

The strategy of functional integration within team-based work is the dominant but not the only flexibility strategy adopted by the companies we investigated. In many cases, particularly in the food retailing sector, it was complemented by functional differentiation of activities. The aim of this strategy was systematically to categorize activities on the basis of their skill requirements and then to separate out simple activities from those with higher skill requirements. The simple tasks were allocated primarily to employees in marginal part-time jobs, who were almost exclusively engaged in operating the checkouts or stacking the shelves. This strategy was also justified in terms of productivity considerations: "The productivity of people with short working times is simply higher. After five to six hours, an individual worker starts to run out of energy and slow down, while two workers can get through a lot of work in four hours each."

Now it is commonly assumed that it is the flexible peripheral workforce that shoulders most of the temporal flexibility burden, while the core workforce remains largely spared. This is correct as far as the scheduling of working time is concerned, since marginal part-time employees work on the checkouts primarily in the evenings and on weekends. The labor strategy for this segment does not, however, require the peripheral workforce to be temporally flexible; in fact, workers in mini-jobs often have particularly regular schedules, since these jobs are often filled by women with families or by high school and university students who are subject to time constraints because of family responsibilities or their school or university schedule. The expectation of temporal flexibility would make it difficult if not impossible to recruit workers in this category (Voss-Dahm 2000). Consequently, it is primarily workers in fully insurable employment who are expected to have a more flexible attitude toward their working hours—to cover for colleagues who are ill or on holiday and to step in when workloads increase unexpectedly. This is obviously the price they have to pay for more stable employment relationships, and it is wholly consistent with the closer integration of their competencies into stores' business processes, as outlined earlier.

Outsourcing, broadly defined as a strategy adopted by firms seeking to externalize risk and cost pressures, was not at all widespread in the case study stores. One of them used temporary workers in the butchery department as a means of dealing with seasonal fluctuations. In two other cases, a small proportion of the goods were put on the shelves by an outside contractor, although the cost of the service amounted to only about 1 percent of turnover. It is reasonable to suppose that, in the retail trade, mini-jobs, particularly those paid below the collectively agreed rate, serve as the functional equivalent of cost-driven outsourcing. However, mini-jobs have two decisive advantages. The store manager who declared, "Shelf stacking is a core function in retailing—I want to know *who* is touching the products and *how* they are being handled," was alluding to the fact that outsourcing leads to a loss of direct control over the function concerned, which can lead to problems with quality. One statement that points in this direction stressed the monitoring costs associated with the outsourcing of shelf stacking: "The contractor's people sometimes don't know what's new and what's old product. So they just put the new product back into the storeroom. We always have to have somebody keeping an eye on them."

PROSPECTS FOR THE GERMAN RETAIL TRADE

The traces of the institutional environment are readily perceptible in German retail companies. The vocational training system and collective agreements on pay and working conditions capable of being applied across the whole industry can be seen as a pair of institutions that give the employment system in the German retail trade a high degree of stability. Employees commit themselves to a training program and long-term careers in the sector not least because the income situation and working conditions are predictable because they are enshrined in industrywide collective agreements and are clearly also acceptable. Retail companies benefit from this situation—first, because labor turnover is not an operational problem for them, and second, because trained workers with many years of retail experience can be granted considerable scope to exercise their own discretion, making it possible to delegate responsibility. In this context, a vocational qualification is in fact an admission ticket to a job with well-protected working and employment conditions. We argue that this is true even if the effects of modern technology are taken into account, since we observed no general trend toward deskilling in the case study companies under the influence of lean retailing.

What was once an industrywide and stable system, however, is developing increasing numbers of cracks and losing its stability as a result. Collective agreements laying down minimum standards for pay and working conditions have less and less binding power in the industry. Faced with intense competition, small retailers in particular are increasingly deciding not to apply collective agreements. As a result, considerable downward pressure is being exerted on wages. Furthermore, the share of low-wage earners among mini-jobbers is particularly high. Consequently, these employees are attractive to employers for cost reasons. So long as this particular employment form exists, it must be assumed that it will continue to act as one of the forces driving the increase in low-wage work in the retail trade.

True, the large German retail companies remain within the vocational training and industrial relations systems. If German retailers were to make greater efforts, however, to achieve their growth, profit, and cost targets by adopting low-wage strategies, professional standards and with them the sector's entire institutional stability could go into a tailspin. Thus, the declining importance of collectively agreed pay rates in German retailing and the low wages paid to mini-jobbers could in the long term turn out to be the gateway to the reduction of standards at many levels. Competitive pressures would then have caused the collapse of two important institutions that once played a key role in protecting working and employment conditions.

NOTES

1. An intermediate position is occupied by those retailers organized along cooperative lines, a group to which three of the eight companies in our sample belong. These retailers, together with the networks of independent retailers that have joined together to form buying groups, represent the Mittelstand of the German retail sector: the medium-sized businesses that are often said to form the core of the German productive system and that have always enjoyed special protection of their status (Wortmann 2004). The independent retailers organized in these ways are collectively the owners of the wholesale business from which they are required to obtain the goods they sell. As far as their personnel policies are concerned, however, these independent retailers are not bound by any particular directives or instructions, and therefore personnel policy, including pay determination, varies a lot between independent retailers within cooperative lines.

2. The following remarks relate in particular to the food retailers we investigated. Modern technology is also used by electrical retailers, of course; however, stock turnover in consumer durables is obviously not as high as in daily consumer goods, which is why technology does not have the central importance even in large electrical retail companies that it has in the food retail sector.

3. The discounter's employment policy was one of the topics discussed in interviews with trade union representatives and representatives of the employers' association. According to our interviewees, work organization in discount stores is characterized by functionally flexible labor deployment combined with low staffing levels. The few individuals who work almost exclusively full-time at some discounters move from the checkouts to the sales floor and from goods reception to the shelves, depending on workload; in the evenings they sweep the yard. Although discounters do pay the collectively agreed rates—and some actually pay in excess of those rates—they require in return that workers accept full responsibility for all the work that has to be done. This blanket responsibility for all work processes generally gives rise to high or even very high volumes of overtime, for which discounters do not pay extra. As a result, actual hourly pay rates are low. Discounters are usually members of the employers' association and adhere to the collectively agreed standards, but they do everything they can to prevent the establishment of works councils at the local level. As far as training is concerned incidentally, discounters are firmly rooted in the German model. Their training rate is not generally lower than that of other retail companies, and when it comes to the training of store

managers in particular, the discounters make use of the training and further training system that is firmly institutionalized throughout the sector (see Haman and Giese 2005).

REFERENCES

Abernathy, Frederick, John Dunlop, Janice H. Hammond, and David Weil. 2000. "Retailing and Supply Chains in the Information Age." *Technology in Society* 22(1): 5–31.

Autor, David H., Frank Levy, and Richard J. Murnane. 2003. "Computer-Based Technological Change and Skill Demands: Reconciling the Perspectives of Economists and Sociologists." In *Low-Wage America: How Employers Are Reshaping Opportunity in the Workplace*, edited by Eileen Appelbaum, Annettte Bernhardt, and Richard J. Murnane. New York: Russell Sage Foundation.

Baethge, Martin. 2001. "Qualifikationsentwicklung im Dienstleistungssektor" ["Skill Development in the Service Sector"]. In *Die grosse Hoffnung für das 21. Jahrhundert? Perspektiven und Strategien für die Entwicklung der Dienstleistungsbeschäftigung* [*The Great Hope for the 21st Century? Prospects and Strategies for the Development of Service Employment*], edited by Martin Baethge and Ingrid Wilkens. Opladen, Germany: Leske und Budrich.

Bailey, Thomas, and Annette Bernhardt. 1997. "In Search of the High Road in a Low-Wage Industry." *Politics and Society* 25(2): 179–201.

Bernhardt, Annette. 1999. "The Future of Low-Wage Jobs: Case Studies in the Retail Industry." Working paper 10. New York: Institute on Education and the Economy (IEE).

Bieber, Daniel, Heike Jacobsen, Stefan Naevecke, Christian Schick, and Franz Speer. 2004. "Innovation der Kooperation: Auf dem Weg zu einem neuen Verhältnis zwischen Industrie und Handel?" ["An Innovative Approach to Cooperation. Towards a New Relationship between industry and commerce?"]. Berlin: Edition Sigma.

Bundesinstitut für Berufsbildung (BIBB). 2006. "Datenblätter zur Situation der beruflichen Ausbildung" ["Data Sheets on the Vocational Training Situations"]. Internetdokumentation. Bonn: BIBB.

Carré, Françoise, Brandynn Holgate, and Chris Tilly. 2006. "What's Happening to Retail Jobs? Wages, Gender, and Corporate Strategy." Paper presented to the annual meeting of the International Association for Feminist Economics and the Labor and Employment Relations Association. Boston, Mass., January 5-8, 2005.

Christopherson, Susan. 2001. "Lean Retailing in marktliberalen und koordinierten Wirtschaften" ["Lean Retailing in Liberal Market and Coordinate Economies"]. In *Aldi oder Arkaden? Unternehmen und Arbeit im europäischen Einzelhandel* [*Aldi or Arkaden? Companies and Work in the European Retail Trade*], edited by Hedwig Rudolph. Berlin: Edition Sigma.

———. 2006. "Challenges Facing Wal-Mart in the German Market." In *Wal-Mart World*, edited by Stanley D. Brunn. New York: Oxon.

Ellguth, Peter, and Susanne Kohaut. 2004. "Tarifbindung und betriebliche Interessenvertretung: Aktuelle Ergebnisse aus dem IAB-Betriebspanel" ["Collective Agreement Coverage and the Workplace Representation of Interests: Current Results from the IAB Establishment Panel"]. *WSI-Mitteilungen* 2004(8): 450–54.

Ernst & Young. 2004. "Händler am Scheideweg: Chancen und Risiken auf dem Weg aus der Krise" ["Retailers at the Crossroads. Opportunities and Risks on the Way Out of Crisis"]. Heilbronn/Düsseldorf, Germany: Ernst & Young.

Esping-Andersen, Gøsta. 2000. *Social Foundations of Postindustrial Economies.* Oxford: Oxford University Press.

Haman, Andreas, and Gudrun Giese. 2005. "Schwarzbuch Lidl" ["Lidl Black Book"]. Berlin: Ver.di Dienstleistungsgewerkschaft.

Hinz, Thomas, and Hermann Gartner. 2005. "Lohnunterschiede zwischen Frauen und Männern in Branchen, Berufen, und Betrieben" ["Differences in Men's and Women's Pay in Industries, Occupations and Firms"]. Discussion paper 4/2005. Nürnberg, Germany: Institut für Arbeitsmarkt- und Berufsforschung (IAB).

Holgate, Brandynn. 2006. Unpublished calculations based on the U.S. Current Population Survey and Current Employment Statistics. Boston, Mass.: Center for Social Policy, University of Massachusetts.

Jaehrling, Karen, Thorsten Kalina, Achim Vanselow, and Dorothea Voss-Dahm. 2006. "Niedriglohnarbeit in der Praxis—arbeit in Häppchen für wenig Geld" ["Low-Wage Work in Practice: Small Chunks of Work for Little Reward"]. In *Mindestlöhne gegen Lohndumping: Rahmenbedingungen, Erfahrungen, Strategien* [*Minimum Wages Against Wage Dumping: General Conditions, Experiences, Strategies*], edited by Gabriele Sterkel, Thorsten Schulten, and Jörg Wiedemuth. Hamburg, Germany: VSA.

Jany-Catrice, Florence, and Steffen Lehndorff. 2005. "Work Organization and the Importance of Labor Markets in the European Retail Trade." In *Working in the Service Sector: A Tale from Different Worlds*, edited by Gerhard Bosch and Steffen Lehndorff. London: Routledge.

Kalina, Thorsten, and Dorothea Voss-Dahm. 2005. "Fluktuation und Mobilität im Einzelhandel: Analysen auf Basis von Auswertungen des Beschäftigtenpanels der Bundesagentur für Arbeit" ["Turnover and Mobility in the Retail Trade: Analyses Based on Evaluations of the Federal Labor Agency's Employee Panels"]. Working paper. Gelsenkirchen, Germany.

Kohaut, Susanne. 2007. "Tarifbindung und tarifliche Öffnungsklauseln:

Ergebnisse aus dem IAB-Betriebspanel 2005" ["Coverage by Collective Agreement and Derogation Clauses: Results from the IAB Establishment Panel"]. *WSI-Mitteilungen* 2007(2): 94–97.

Kraemer, Klaus, and Frederik Speidel. 2005. "Prekarisierung von Erwerbsarbeit: Zum Wandel eines arbeitsweltlichen Integrationsmodus" ["The Growing Precariousness of Paid Work: the Changing Mode of Integration into the World of Work"]. In *Integrationspotentiale einer modernen Gesellschaft* [*The Potential for Integration in a Modern Society*], edited by Wilhelm Heitmeyer and Peter Imbusch. Wiesbaden, Germany: VS Verlag für Sozialwissenschaften.

Lehndorff, Steffen, and Dorothea Voss-Dahm. 2005. "The Delegation of Uncertainty: Flexibility and the Role of the Market in Service Work." In *Working in the Service Sector: A Tale from Different Worlds*, edited by Gerhard Bosch and Steffen Lehndorff. London: Routledge.

Lichtenstein, Nelson. 2006. "Wal-Mart: A Template for Twenty-first Century Capitalism." In *Wal-Mart: The Face of Twenty-first-Century Capitalism*, edited by Nelson Lichtenstein. New York: New Press.

Malcher, Wilfried, and Hannelore Paulini-Schlottau. 2005. "Handelsfachwirte und Handelsfachwirtinnen: Eine Fortbildung mit Aufstiegsoption" ["Diploma in Wholesale and Retail Management: An Advanced Training Program with Promotion Prospects"]. *Berufsbildung in Wissenschaft und Praxis* 2005(4): 40–44.

Marsden, David. 1999. *A Theory of Employment Systems: Micro-Foundations of Societal Diversity*. Oxford: Oxford University Press.

Rosen, Ellen Israel. 2006. "How to Make More Out of a Penny." In *Wal-Mart: The Face of Twenty-first-Century Capitalism*, edited by Nelson Lichtenstein. New York: New Press.

Voss-Dahm, Dorothea. 2000. "Service-Sector Taylorism and Changing Demands on Working Time Organization: The Example of the Retail Trade." Paper presented to the international conference "The Economics and Socioeconomics of Services: International Perspectives." Lille/Roubaix, France, June 2000.

———. 2003. "Zwischen Kunden und Kennziffern: Leistungspolitik in der Verkaufsarbeit des Einzelhandels" ["Between Customers and Indicators: Performance Policy in Retail Sales Work"]. In *Dienstleistungsarbeit: Auf dem Boden der Tatsachen: Befunde aus Handel, Industrie, Medien und IT-Branche* [*Service Work: Grounded in Fact. Findings from Retailing, Manufacturing, the Media and the IT Industry*], edited by Markus Pohlmann, Dieter Sauer, Gudrun Trautwein-Kalms, and Alexandra Wagner. Berlin: Edition Sigma.

Wortmann, Michael. 2004.: "Aldi and the German Model: Structural Change in German Grocery Retailing and the Success of Grocery Discounters." *Competition and Change* 8(4): 425–41.

CHAPTER 7

Summary and Conclusions

Gerhard Bosch and Claudia Weinkopf

G ermany has long been noted for its well-balanced income structure. Between the 1980s and the early 1990s, the share of low-paid workers actually declined, albeit only slightly, against the general international trend. In most OECD countries, including the United States, income inequality increased, particularly in the 1980s (CBO 2006; OECD 1996, 1997). However, the trend has now reversed. Since the mid-1990s, low-wage work has been rising in Germany, whereas in most other EU-15 countries, and in the United States as well, the share of low-paid workers has fallen. In the year 2000, low-wage work in Germany actually exceeded the EU average for the first time (CBO 2006; European Commission 2004, 168).

The object of this study has been to analyze the ways in which low-wage work is evolving in the economy as a whole and in certain industries and why it has increased in Germany. In summarizing the key findings, we begin by outlining the most important results of our data analysis of the evolution of low-wage work and of the economic and institutional causes of this evolution. We then compare the findings of the case studies in various industries. The heated debate triggered by the political reactions to the rapid increase in low-paid occupations in Germany is the subject of the final section.

THE INCREASE IN LOW-WAGE
EMPLOYMENT AND ITS CHANGING FACE

Low-wage work in Germany has not only substantially increased in the last years but also has changed its structure. Wages have been differentiated in a downward direction, and within the low-wage sector a very low-wage sector is emerging. It is remarkable that the expansion of low-wage work in Germany has not improved the employment chances of the low-skilled. Three-quarters of the low-wage earners are skilled—a higher proportion than in the past and also much higher than in most other countries. While low-wage work was more evenly distributed over the economy in the past, it is now more concentrated in some employment forms and in small and medium-sized companies with no works councils or collective agreements. Low-wage work is moving from the center to the periphery of the labor market.

To reach these surprising results we analyzed two sets of data. The Federal Employment Services' employee survey is by far the most extensive dataset available, and it can be used even for highly differentiated analyses (for example, of individual occupational groups). Any analyses based on it, however, are necessarily restricted to full-time workers, since the dataset contains no precise figures on part-timers' working times. The Socio-Economic Panel (SOEP), on the other hand, makes it possible to include part-timers. Because of the considerably smaller number of cases, differentiated sector and occupation analyses are possible only to a limited extent. In accordance with international conventions, all wages below two-thirds of the median wage are designated low wages. Because of the considerable differences in wages between East and West Germany, we used the different median wages in the two parts of the country as a basis for calculating the shares of low-wage work.

While the share of low-paid full-time employees in West Germany fell from 15.3 percent in 1980 to 13.8 percent in 1993, it increased rapidly after the mid-1990s, reaching 17.3 percent by 2003. Following reunification, the wage distribution in East Germany was considerably more egalitarian than in West Germany. Mainly owing to high unemployment and a significantly lower rate of coverage by collective agreements, since 1996 the share of low-wage work in East Germany has been higher than in West Germany, and the gap continues to grow. In 2003 the low-wage share accounted for 19.5 percent in East Germany and for 17.7 percent in Germany as a whole. In contrast to countries with a minimum wage or higher union density, the wage dispersion in Germany extends a long way downward. One and a half million workers (around 5 percent of the population) earn less than €5 (US$7.32) per hour—less than one-third of the median wage—and 876,000 workers earn less than €4 (US$5.85) per hour. If we include part-timers, the share of low-wage work, at 20.8 percent in 2004, was more than three percentage points higher than among full-timers. Part-timers are at much greater risk of being paid a low wage than full-timers.

As in other countries, younger people, women, non-nationals, and persons with lower skill levels are disproportionately affected. Compared with 1980, it is noticeable that the shares of low-wage workers among West German full-timers have risen in all groups. Particularly high increases are found among non-nationals (from 14.1 percent in 1980 to 26.6 percent in 2003), among low-skill workers (from 22.6 percent in 1980 to 29.8 percent in 2003), and among those under age twenty-five (from 33.5 percent in 1980 to 42.3 percent in 2003). The largest increase is among university graduates, whose share of low-wage work doubled between 1980 and 2003, albeit from a very low initial level of 1.8 percent to 3.7 percent. Women constitute the only exception: at 31.9 percent, their share of low-wage work in 2003 was somewhat lower than it was in 1980 (36.3 percent).

A comparison of the structure of low-wage work in Germany and the United States reveals some significant differences. For example, skill level and pay are less closely related in Germany. It is true that almost one in three of those without a vocational qualification are low-wage earners; however, more than three-quarters of all low-wage workers in Germany have a higher-level qualification (a vocational qualification or university degree). In contrast, around 70 percent of low-wage workers in the United States have no qualifications at all or at best graduated from high school (Appelbaum, Bernhardt, and Murnane 2003; CBO 2006, 18), which means that their level of education and training is below that of someone who has completed a vocational training program in Germany. This striking difference in the skill profile of low-wage workers in the two countries is undoubtedly attributable in part to the persistently high level of unemployment in Germany, which increases the pressure even on well-qualified workers to accept low-wage work. It should also be noted, however, that the number of poorly qualified workers in Germany is relatively low by international standards because of the highly developed vocational training system.

Also noteworthy is the fact that the share of low-paid workers among part-timers is much higher than it is among full-timers. The share of those in insurable part-time employment in Germany (with gross monthly earnings greater than €400 [US$585], that is, above the earnings threshold for mini-jobs) is more than six percentage points above the level of full-timers (21 percent compared to 14.6 percent). Regulations on equal pay and status in labor and social law as full-time employed might have reduced but not abolished the inequalities of treatment. Regulations on equal treatment of marginal part-timers (mini-jobbers) are definitely not enforced. More than four-fifths of mini-jobbers are low-wage earners.

As in other countries, good employment forms are being squeezed out by bad ones in Germany. Low-wage work used to be distributed more evenly over the economy as a whole; in recent years, however, it has migrated to the margins of the labor market. Low-wage work is increasingly being shifted into marginal part-time jobs, temporary agency work, and, as a result of outsourcing, areas with low levels of coverage by collective agreement, weak trade unions, and few works councils. The share of low-paid workers in large firms has declined, but it has increased significantly in small firms. In firms with more than five hundred employees, the share of low-wage workers fell from 4.5 percent in 1980 to 3.2 percent in 2003. In firms with fewer than twenty employees, on the other hand, the share of low-wage workers rose from 33.6 percent to 36.4 percent during the same period. It has also fallen in the core areas of the economy with high rates of coverage by collective agreements, strong unions, and works councils, while it has increased in the new service industries in particular.

On the margins of the labor market, not only are hourly rates lower, but nonwage labor costs too are below the level in the core areas of the labor market. The share of nonwage labor costs is considerably lower in small firms and low-wage industries, where only the legal minimum is usually paid. In many cases, the aim of outsourcing is not—or not solely—to reduce hourly wage rates, but also to cut nonwage labor costs. There are limits, however, on the extent to which nonwage labor costs in Germany can be reduced. In the German welfare state model, income from work employment is linked to statutory benefits. Wages have to be paid not only for the work actually done but also for certain periods when no work is done (for example, during four weeks of vacation and around ten public holidays and up to six weeks annually for illness). Additionally, with the exception of mini-jobs, contributions have to be paid to the statutory social insurance funds, together with any collectively agreed or voluntary benefits. These contributions give rise to entitlement to certain benefits in the event of illness, accident, need for nursing care, unemployment, or old age.

As a result of these wage-linked benefits, working and employment conditions in Germany, particularly those of low-paid workers, differ significantly in quality from those in the United States, where the hourly or monthly wage gives rise, for certain groups, to considerably fewer entitlements to benefits. The main difference between the two countries lies less in the level than in the distribution of nonwage labor costs. In the United States a considerable proportion of labor costs—37 percent in the year 2000—are attributable to nonwage labor costs (EBRI 2006), compared with 43.3 percent in Germany. In the United States, however, many social benefits (such as holiday and sick pay) are not legally regulated. The National Compensation Survey shows that low-paid and part-time workers are frequently excluded from social benefits. For example, only 76 percent of workers in the United States are entitled to paid holidays, and only 57 percent receive sick pay. Among employees earning less than $15 per hour, these shares are even lower, at 67 percent and 46 percent, respectively; the figures for part-timers are 37 percent and 22 percent (U.S. Department of Labor 2006).

Only in some areas of activity does this shifting of low-wage work in Germany lead to the physical relocation of jobs. In many cases, workers continue to work at the same physical location as before, but for a different employer (such as a subcontractor or temp work agency). Cooperative relations within the workplace frequently do not change either, or only slightly. Invisible institutional barriers are erected between different jobs or occupations, however, to facilitate the payment of lower wages. Moreover, these barriers frequently reduce the opportunities for moving into better-paid jobs. This increasing segmentation of the German labor market has also reduced upward mobility to better-paid jobs. For young, well-qualified workers, upward mobility is still relatively high, since quite a few of them are employed in low-paid jobs for only a brief transitional period. After a short search period, they are able to move into better-paid jobs, usually with a different employer. For others, however, a spell of low-wage work is no longer a transitional period of employment.[1] This applies to women even more than to men. It is obvious that temporary agency workers, marginal part-timers, and workers employed in outsourced jobs are less likely than in the past to be part of the recruitment pool for jobs in the primary segment of the labor market.

Not all low-wage earners are poor. They might have property or live with other earners in a household. Nevertheless, the growth in low-wage work, together with high unemployment, has been the major reason for the increase in the share of poor households in Germany since 1991, with the figure now being slightly above the European average. At the same time, households' income mobility has declined, suggesting that poverty is becoming firmly entrenched.

REASONS FOR THE INCREASE IN LOW-WAGE WORK

The low level of income inequality, relative to other countries, that characterized the German employment and production system until the mid-1990s is attributed in the literature largely to the German economy's particular product portfolio—its so-called diversified quality production (Streeck 1991)—and to high productivity levels. One precondition for this was the existence of "patient capital" and its concern with long-term returns. The "patience" of capital was the result of the stable company ownership that arose out of the close financial links among large joint-stock companies and between the companies and their house banks, the high share of family-owned companies, and the great importance of public enterprises. The emphasis on high-quality production was supported by high investment in research and development, cooperation between engineers and skilled workers thoroughly trained under the dual vocational training system, and German companies' gradual specialization in the high-price, high-quality segments of their product markets. Labor markets were dominated by long-term contractual relationships, which were the result of a high level of dismissal protection, high investment in vocational training for the core workforce, and close cooperation between capital and labor based on industrywide collective agreements and codetermination exercised on supervisory boards and through works councils. The high level of job security guaranteed by the regulations on dismissal protection and codetermination encouraged the development of "productivity coalitions" set up to assist with the modernization of vocational training and corporate reorganization.

The analyses of the German model that concentrate almost exclusively on the export-oriented segments of the country's manufacturing sector pay little attention to the low-skill manufacturing and service jobs that are investigated in our study and that even in the German model's heyday were characterized by below-average rates of pay. It was implicitly assumed that the structures and configurations of actors observed in Germany's export industries could be taken as representative of the system as a whole. This assumption was justified to some extent. A high level of union density, particularly in the public sector and in areas predominantly or partially funded out of the public purse, ensured that even low-skill employees were relatively well paid. Thus, publicly owned firms were protected from short-term market pressures in much the same way as manufacturing firms were sheltered by the availability of patient capital. Furthermore, the dual vocational training system was not confined to craft trades and manufacturing but encompassed virtually all service industries as well. As a consequence, virtually all industries in Germany have a significantly higher share of well-trained skilled workers than is the case in most other OECD countries. Traditionally, many of these skilled workers were paid more than unskilled and semiskilled employees in the same industry.

This sometimes overly optimistic characterization of the German employment system has often overlooked the fact that low-wage work is not in any sense a new phenomenon in Germany. In contrast to their counterparts in the Scandinavian countries, German trade unions were not strong enough and not sufficiently centralized to pursue a solidaristic wage policy that would have led to lasting reductions in wage differentials, both between industries and between men and women. Pay bargaining took place largely at the industry level. True, the unions succeeded in reducing regional differences in pay within individual industries and in extending the improvements in pay and benefits obtained in the "pacesetter" industries to weaker sectors. There remained considerable differences, however, between the core industries in the export sector and the services associated with them, on the one hand, and many consumer and social services, on the other. Because of its industry-level collective agreements, which were mostly not declared generally binding—as such agreements were in France and in the Netherlands—and the lack of minimum standards for wage setting applicable across industries, even the traditional German model was always vulnerable to a widening of wage differentials.

Widening wage differentials were also due to the fact that the German welfare state, and in particular the considerable subsidies it allocates to the single male breadwinner, restricted and fragmented the female labor supply. Gøsta Esping-Andersen (1990) saw Germany as an exemplar of the conservative welfare state that had failed to implement such reforms. In this model, women in particular derive their social security entitlements from their husbands' employment, and the state offers strong incentives for them either to remain out of the labor market or to accept marginal part-time jobs. While female participation rates in most developed industrialized countries rose, in Germany they remained very low for a long time. The Scandinavian countries had reformed their welfare states and were able to open up new areas of employment in social services, particularly in child and other care services and education. With the increase in female labor market participation, the failure to reform the welfare state in Germany proved to be the gateway for the increase in poorly paid marginal part-time jobs. Initially this attracted little attention from politicians, since well-paid male workers, and indeed many women themselves, expected only a second income rather than a living wage.

Thus, even in the past the German employment model consisted of two different submodels: a fairly egalitarian production (or manufacturing) model and a dual-economy model with greater social inequality. The dominance of the production model kept the second model hidden for a long time, but, as a dormant alternative (Crouch and Farrell 2002), it had the potential to become dominant if conditions changed. The production model's dominance was based not only on the similar governance structures that existed in many largely public-service activities but also on several labor market conditions: high economic growth and low unemployment, which increased the bargaining power of workers even in industries with lower union densities; a relatively low female participation rate; and an underdeveloped service sector.

The 1990s saw the conjunction of all the conditions required to call into question the dominance of the egalitarian German production model. Those conditions arose out of the historically unique combination of international political developments that led to German reunification, the EU-driven deregulation of national governance structures in important service industries, the restructuring of the institutions of the German model at the national level, and the growing importance of the service sector, with its high shares of female workers.

The key factors that have encouraged the rise in low-wage work since the mid-1990s are the low level of economic growth compared with other OECD countries and rising unemployment, which has intensified competition in the labor market and put pressure on wages, particularly in the lower segments. The most important triggers of the growth crisis were the political and economic measures introduced in connection with reunification. As a result of the transfer of West German institutions to East Germany, the reforms of the West German employment and production system that had been debated in the 1980s came to a halt for about ten years, which led to a considerable innovation backlog. The currency reform led to a considerable revaluation of the East German mark, and East German enterprises, with their antiquated products and technologies, became uncompetitive overnight. Finally, West Germany to this day must transfer around 3 percent of its GNP to East Germany to finance reconstruction and manage the consequences of high unemployment. These transfers have also hindered growth because they have been funded by increases in taxation and social security contributions and reductions in public investment in infrastructure and education. In this exceptional situation, the restrictive financial policy required to keep government debt down to the level stipulated in the Maastricht criteria and at the same time to fund extensive tax-cutting programs has merely exacerbated these effects.

Simultaneously, corporate governance structures have changed. The old "Germany plc" is breaking up and is increasingly being replaced by a financial capitalism concerned with maximizing short-term returns. The impetus for this came from the opening up of the markets of former state monopolies in areas such as energy, telecommunications, transport, and health to private providers, a move forced by EU regulations. This was accompanied by a strategic reorientation on the part of the banks, which withdrew from their role as long-term providers of finance to industry in order to concentrate on the more profitable business of investment banking free of their ties to individual companies. The lucrative disposal of their industrial holdings was facilitated by the SPD-Green coalition government's decision to exempt from taxation the capital gains accruing from the sale of shares. In many public institutions (such as hospitals) and public contracts (for example, the awarding of contracts for construction projects), the introduction of new corporate cost reduction strategies led to the establishment of governance structures similar to those in the private sector.

Although governance structures have also been changed in the Scandinavian and Benelux countries and in France, this has not led to as great an increase in low-paid work in those countries as in Germany. Certainly none of them has had to cope with an external economic shock of the magnitude of reunification. However, their institutions also provide better protection against wage competition driving pay to the bottom. Generally binding collective agreements, which are widespread in France and the Netherlands, or strong trade unions, which ensure a high level of coverage by collective agreement in the economy as a whole, have taken wages out of competition and prevented the competition between firms bound by collective agreements and those not so bound that has increasingly determined the evolution of pay in Germany since the mid-1990s. Wage competition developed first in East Germany, where the West German collective bargaining system had been able to gain only a partial foothold because of the precarious economic situation of most businesses and the high unemployment rate, and then it spread to West Germany as well. The dormant social inequality model gradually gained ground because of the absence of universal minimum standards of pay.

The increase in low-paid work in Germany takes a number of very diverse forms, ranging from the outsourcing of certain activities to firms not bound by collective agreements and the substitution of regular employment by precarious employment forms, particularly mini-jobs and temporary agency work, to a reduction in collectively agreed standards for categories of employees facing competitors not bound by collective agreements. Through the deliberate deregulation of certain employment forms, particularly temporary agency work and mini-jobs, the abolition of income-related unemployment assistance for the long-term unemployed, and a tightening of the reasonableness criteria, the state has increased the options available to employers seeking to reduce wage levels. The high level of dismissal protection has slowed down the pace of outsourcing, so that in many areas there are now dual wage structures with different rates of pay for the same occupation. However, this is merely a transitional phenomenon. Those employees who benefit from dismissal protection and are paid higher wages are being replaced when they leave by workers who are less well-paid. Another reason why this has not affected the whole of the German production system is that the German companies that lost their competitiveness in the early 1990s have now reformed their traditional hierarchical structures, which were geared to a functional division of labor. By putting in place a sort of German version of lean production based on a high level of functional flexibility—achieved by deploying well-trained workers with a broad range of skills, and on a high level of numerical flexibility—it has proved possible to stabilize internal occupational labor markets, albeit for a core workforce much reduced by the outsourcing of many activities. These changes have been supported by the modernization of vocational training and the extension of works councils' rights of codetermination. This corporate reorganization and the competitiveness regained as a result of relatively low wage settlements have enabled Germany's "diversified quality production" segment to achieve new export records.

Despite all the structural changes, the well-paid middle classes in Germany have remained in such a strong position that many households continue to adhere to the traditional single male breadwinner model in which women are expected to earn only a second income. This presumably is the reason why, despite rising educational levels among women and their increasing career-mindedness, the institutions that support the conservative family model have been able to survive for so long. Even today they still have a considerable following in the major political parties and among voters. That model was deliberately strengthened further by the SPD-Green coalition government in 2003 when it significantly raised the earnings threshold for mini-jobs, which can be held without loss of the advantages of the splitting system used to calculate married couples' tax liability or loss of derived social security entitlements. Changes are being introduced slowly, with the expansion of child care facilities and the introduction of all-day schools and a parental allowance after the birth of a child, following the Swedish model. These new measures remain inadequately funded, however, since the bulk of family transfers are still being used to support the old "housewife model" of marriage. Even now, virtually no politician in either of the two main parties dares to question the splitting tax system, which provides the largest subsidy for the traditional family model, amounting to some €21 billion (US$31 billion) per year. The initial measures aimed at reforming the conservative family model have not yet had any visible effect on the female labor supply.

The possibility cannot be excluded, however, that these measures will mark the transition to a new family and service model, one no longer based on women's role as second-income earners. It is as yet unclear whether a new dormant model of an egalitarian service economy, along Scandinavian lines, or an Anglo-Saxon model with a dual economy is emerging. The outcome will depend not only on family policy but also, and above all, on future pay and collective bargaining policies. German policymakers do not yet seem to have a clear master plan for the breakup or stabilization of the current German employment system. True, the trend toward deregulation has been dominant in recent years, but at the same time the core institutions of labor and social legislation have remained relatively stable.

PAY AND WORKING CONDITIONS IN THE INDUSTRIES AND OCCUPATIONS UNDER STUDY

What may appear occasionally in a general analysis of the German employment system as a marginal phenomenon is brought into the limelight in the industry studies, as if viewed through a magnifying glass. Precisely because low-paid work has increased markedly in certain industries and occupations, relatively small percentage changes in the economy as a whole conceal considerable changes in certain segments of the labor market; moreover, these changes cannot be fully captured statistically because of outsourcing and the transfer of jobs to other sectors. Unfortunately, changes over time in the industrial classifications used by statisticians make it more difficult to analyze developments in industries and occupations over a longer period. For this reason, the basis for comparison in table 7.1 is just the period between 1999 and 2003. However, even that short four-year period saw the shares of low wages increase, in some cases considerably. Whereas in 2003 the share of low-wage work among full-time employees was 17.7 percent in the economy as a whole, in the target occupations the shares were considerably higher. If we focus on the developments in Germany as a whole (right column in table 7.1), we see that these shares range from 24.5 percent for nursing assistants up to even 90.8 percent for cleaning staff in hotels. The relatively moderate rise of 1.1 percentage points in low-wage work in the economy as a whole between 1999 and 2003 contrasts with the considerable increases in most of the target occupations, where levels were frequently already high before. The increases were particularly marked among nursing assistants (7 percentage points), hospital cleaning staff (6.9), hotel housekeepers (4.6), and meat producers (3.8). In the other occupations under study, the share of low-paid workers remained relatively stable at a high level. In the retail trade,

Table 7.1 Development of the Share of Low-Wage Workers in the Case Study Occupations, 1999 to 2003

Industry and Occupation	West		East		Germany	
	1999	2003	1999	2003	1999	2003
Food, tobacco (NACE 15, 16)	31.3%	34.3%	41.0%	45.9%	33.1%	36.6%
Producer of meat products and sausage (BKZ 402)	31.8	34.8	33.5	40.4	32.2	36.0
Manufacturer of sugar, confectionary goods, or ice cream (BKZ 433)	39.0	40.2	(22.6)	(19.7)	35.9	35.5
Retail (NACE 52)	32.7	33.1	35.4	34.9	33.2	33.4
Sales assistant or sales clerk (BKZ 682)	42.0	41.5	48.4	46.8	43.4	42.6
Cashier (BKZ 773)	37.4	36.8	(23.5)	(27.5)	35.1	35.2
Hotel and restaurant (NACE 55)	69.5	72.0	63.6	65.5	68.1	70.5
Other guest attendant (BKZ 913)	84.2	82.0	75.2	78.4	82.7	81.3
Housekeeper (BKZ 923)	82.9	88.3	75.7	75.9	81.6	86.2
Cleaning staff (BKZ 933)	92.6	91.7	88.0	86.4	91.8	90.8
Health (NACE 85)	21.4	23.5	16.5	19.4	20.3	22.6
Nursing assistant (BKZ 854)	19.3	25.3	9.3	21.3	17.5	24.5
Cleaning staff (BKZ 933)	37.1	43.3	23.4	32.3	34.5	41.4
Total economy	16.3	17.3	17.5	19.5	16.6	17.7

Source: BA employee panel; authors' calculations.
Note: Numbers in brackets are based on a small number of cases and should be interpreted with care.

this is probably attributable to the increasing use of marginal part-time workers, who are not included in these statistics, and in the confectionary industry to automation and the physical relocation of jobs.

It should also be noted that an analysis based solely on industries and occupations within a specific industry gives only a partial view of reality, because in most of the industries under study the outsourcing of jobs is becoming increasingly important—particularly cleaning jobs in hotels and hospitals, but also call center jobs and (at least partially) food-processing jobs. In some cases, wage differentials between the original industries and those to which the jobs have been outsourced are an important driving force for outsourcing, but they are not the prime motive in every case. Differences in nonwage labor costs or employment conditions also play a role, as do employers' efforts to make costs more variable and to shift capacity utilization risks to subcontractors. The example of hotel cleaning services providers shows that some subcontractors are even able to shift the risks to employees, who in some cases no longer receive a fixed wage but are paid according to actual workloads and performance.

Both factors are obviously playing an important role in the rapidly increasing use of temporary agency workers in Germany. On the one hand, temporary work agencies take on the risk of fluctuating workload distributions; on the other hand, they have a particularly high share of low-wage workers (71.5 percent of all employees; see the category "labor recruitment and provision of personnel" in table 1A.1).[2] However, in the industries and occupations under study, temp agency work tends to play a somewhat subordinate role. Outsourcing to small and medium-sized subcontractors that have no works councils and collective agreements, substantially lowering nonwage benefits, and increasing the use of mini-jobs are the dominant strategies for flexibilization and cost reduction, even though these strategies may vary in form (see table 7.2).

Besides these general trends, our case studies reveal very divergent developments in individual areas, which have to do with the differing degrees to which firms are rooted in the traditional employment system as well as with differences in corporate strategy:

- By far the widest wage range and variation in other employment conditions was observed in *call centers*, owing in large part to the diversity of tasks carried out by the employees and the fact that call centers are found in many different industries. A lack of reli-

Table 7.2 The Predominant Strategies in the Case Study
Industries to Cut Wages and Increase
Flexibility

Industry	Temp Agencies	Outsourcing	Mini-Jobs
Food	+	++ (including posted workers)	–
Retail	–	–	++
Hotels	–	++	+
Hospitals			
Nursing assistants	–	–	–
Cleaners	–	++	++
Call centers	–	++	–

Source: Authors' industry and company case studies.
++: very important; +: relevant; –: is used only seldom or not at all

able data, however, makes it impossible to put a figure on the share
of low-paid workers among call center staff or to track its evolution over time. Nevertheless, since external service providers typically pay lower wages, it can be assumed that the growing share of
external service providers goes along with the increase in low-
wage work.

• In the *hospital* sector, shares of low-paid workers have increased
only recently, as a result of new budgetary regulations and the introduction of low pay grades, one of the products of concession
bargaining. Although the overall increase in low-wage work in the
sector between 1999 and 2003 was relatively modest at 2.3 percentage points, the target occupations were affected to a considerably greater extent. However, the shares among nursing assistants
in particular remain relatively low compared with the other occupations under study, probably because pay levels in health care occupations, despite some recent deterioration, are still relatively
high. The situation is different with cleaning jobs: pay rates have
been reduced considerably in the new collective agreements covering these jobs in order to avoid outsourcing.

• The "front-runner" by far in the low-pay stakes is *hotel room cleaning*, where the share of low-paid workers now exceeds 90 percent.
Although these jobs have always been very low-paid, the share of

low-wage workers has increased even further. This is very likely attributable not only to increasing competition from subcontractors, who often pay even lower rates, but also to the increasing difficulty of ensuring adherence to existing collective agreements.

- In the *retail* trade, the shares of low-paid workers among the occupations investigated are also relatively high, at over 40 percent; however, these shares seem to be lower in the case studies, because they focused on larger companies bound by collective agreements. In these companies, the main strategy for reducing wage costs is to cut the volume of labor deployed through the increasing use of regular and marginal part-time workers (work intensification). Mini-jobbers are also frequently paid lower rates than other employees.

- In the *food-processing* industry—the only manufacturing industry in our study—the share of low-wage workers at the industry level is also relatively high, at 36.6 percent, and it has risen over time. The shares of low wages in the occupations investigated evolved in different ways between 1999 and 2003. In meat processing there was a clear increase, whereas the share of low-paid workers in confectionary declined slightly. Moreover, the overall figures conceal differing trends in East and West Germany. One fundamental reason for these divergent developments must lie in differences in the conditions for enforcing collectively agreed standards, as well as in increasing automation in the confectionary industry, which is associated with a decline in low-paid jobs.

In many establishments in various industries, outsourcing and wage cuts have been slowed down by the right of continuance enjoyed by workers already employed (Bestandsschutz) and by some other regulations that make it difficult for companies to circumvent existing collective agreements. However, such regulations are effective primarily in larger firms with strong trade unions and employee representative bodies. In small and medium-sized firms, only a weakened form of dismissal protection applies, and there are often no works councils to protect employees from redundancies or deterioration in employment conditions.

In all the industries investigated, we observed increased cost pressures and an intensification of competition, both of which put wages under considerable pressure. Some of the causes are common to the various industries, while others are industry-specific. Thus, in the hospital sector it is primarily changes in the financial regulations and the precarious position of the social insurance funds that are putting wage levels under pressure, while in the other industries changed market conditions are playing a greater role. The extent to which these changed conditions are reflected in pay levels also depends on the strength of the trade unions and workplace representative bodies in the industry and in the companies. In retailing and the hotel industry, for example, there have not yet been any real reductions in collectively agreed wage rates; in other sectors, however, such as hospitals, utilities, and financial services (the two subsectors in which call center case studies took place), new agreements with lower pay grades have been concluded—sometimes along with the introduction of new low-wage groups. Elsewhere, it is becoming increasingly difficult to conclude any collective agreements at all, as in the meat-processing industry. In addition, there are industries in which collective agreements certainly exist but their actual binding power is declining, as in the hotel industry in East Germany. In virtually all industries, additional benefits, such as bonuses and the Christmas allowance, as well as working and employment conditions, such as the collectively agreed weekly working time, are also under considerable pressure.

Differences in job quality between the companies investigated depend in part on whether or not the companies are bound by collective agreements and have bodies representing workforce interests. Even in those sectors and firms in which trade unions and works councils are able to influence wages and employment conditions, however, they often find themselves, under pressure from employers, in a catch-22 situation: either they succeed in maintaining wages and employment conditions at relatively high levels for their own members, running the risk that companies will look for loopholes and outsource certain services to providers not bound by collective agreements at all or at a lower level—or they accept concessions for their own industry or company in order to secure jobs or, in the best case, even win some back. Similar choices characterize the internal bargaining process for certain categories of employees. For example, many works councils agree to pay cuts for marginal part-timers if they are able, in exchange, to obtain improvements (or at least the maintenance of existing standards) for the core workforce.

In some industries, however, corporate strategy plays a not unimportant role in determining job quality. This is particularly evident in the call centers, where we observed considerable differences between the various companies with respect not only to pay but also to the use of subcontractors and fixed-term employment contracts. Despite considerable cost pressures, most of the companies investigated relied on employees of long standing with relatively high skill levels who provided the basis for a high level of functional flexibility. Similar tendencies could also be observed in some hospitals, which preferred to recruit more highly qualified staff rather than nursing assistants because they could be deployed more flexibly in a context of an overall decline in staffing levels.

POLICY IMPLICATIONS

It has become clear that wages in Germany, particularly in what already tend to be low-paid occupations, have been exposed to increasing fragmentation and strong downward pressures because collectively agreed standards have been persistently eroded and the state has not yet laid down any legal minimum wage standards. Instead, by extensively deregulating temporary agency work and changing the regulations governing mini-jobs in such a way as to encourage employers to make increasing use of them, the German government has removed more of the restraints on low pay, thereby encouraging its expansion and putting wage levels as a whole under pressure. This trend is reinforced by the fragmentation of the female labor supply by the traditional German welfare state. The initial steps to address this fragmentation have until recently been rather hesitant and to some extent contradictory.

In the past, minimum wage standards could be enforced at the industry level because of the high level of coverage by collective agreements in Germany. Moreover, because of the favorable employment situation, many firms not bound by collective agreements used the collectively agreed pay rates as reference points. As a result, wages in Germany were largely taken out of competition. State "interference" in the form of statutory minimum wages was rejected by both unions and employers as an encroachment on their right to engage in free collective bargaining. The developments and upheavals that have taken place since the 1990s, however, have resulted in a considerable increase in low-wage work since the middle of that decade. One reason is that coverage by collective agreement is declining and a change of attitude in the employers' associations has made it difficult to have collectively agreed standards declared generally binding on all companies in a particular industry. Thus, it is particularly easy for employers to exploit pay differentials between industries and categories of workers in Germany, both because coverage by collective agreements has declined (unlike in Denmark) and, in contrast to France, the United Kingdom, the Netherlands, and even the United States, there is no legal minimum wage to set a generally binding lower limit on wages.

The question of whether the expansion of low-wage work in Germany should be regarded as a problem or a welcome development—even one that should be supported politically and that could help to cut unemployment—continues to be hotly debated in both political and academic circles. Widely differing views on the need for political action have been expressed. Among the advocates of a further expansion of low-wage work, two basic positions can be discerned:

1. Some—among them the German Council of Economic Experts (Sachverständigenrat 2006)—are calling for a significant reduction in unemployment benefit II in order to increase the incentive to accept low-paid work. At the same time, they argue, the amount of earned income that is disregarded when the level of benefit is calculated should be increased, particularly for jobs with longer working times. As a result, wages should fall sharply, boosting the demand for low-wage jobs. People who, despite these measures, are still unable to find work will have to work on public job creation programs if they are to retain their entitlement to the basic security benefits.

2. Others argue that the level of transfer payments should remain unchanged but that the demand for low-wage jobs should be stimulated by offering subsidies. The state should reduce wage costs in the lower income segment by paying wage cost subsidies or meeting the cost of social insurance contributions, thereby making low-wage work more attractive for both employers and employees. These so-called combi-wages (Kombilöhne) have been the subject of many different proposals. The most wide-ranging ones call for permanent subsidies for all low-wage jobs, while others argue that such subsidies should be paid for limited periods only and restricted to certain target groups (such as young or older workers).

Combi-wage schemes are popular in all political camps, since they promise high employment levels combined with social equalization for the low-paid. What frequently goes unheeded, however, is the fact that a number of different combi-wage schemes have already been tried in the course of various political programs at both the federal and state levels and that, according to the subsequent evaluations, their employment effects have at best been meager. The same also applies to model calculations, which have shown that extending such schemes nationwide would be very expensive and that significant positive net employment effects could hardly be expected, since many regular jobs would be replaced by subsidized jobs (Jaehrling and Weinkopf 2006).

Furthermore, a nationwide, means-tested combi-wage, which is used to top up low market incomes, has already been introduced, more or less by the back door, in the form of unemployment benefit II. Approximately one in five of those in receipt of this basic allowance (more than one million people in June 2006) are employees receiving the benefit as a supplement to their earned income. The total number of employees who are entitled to such top-up payments but do not claim them is estimated to be significantly higher (Becker 2006).

It is only since the number of people claiming top-up benefits started to rise and some recent studies (including the initial results of our own analyses; see Bosch and Kalina 2005; Kalina and Weinkopf 2006a, 2006b) showed that the extent of low-wage work in Germany is already quite considerable by international standards that the need for a minimum wage has been increasingly debated. The arguments advanced in favor of a minimum wage include the need, first, to prevent poverty even among those in full-time employment, and second, to eliminate wage dumping. Without a binding lower limit on wages, employers can rely on the state, with its basic security benefits, to underwrite the deficit if they continue to pay low wages or even cut wages further.

One major factor in changing attitudes toward the idea of a minimum wage has been a shift of opinion in the German trade union movement. In the past, unions were very reluctant to abandon their opposition to legal minimum wages because to do so would have represented a break with the tradition of negotiating wages themselves. The relatively powerful trade unions in the manufacturing sector, in particular, also feared that their frequently above-average wage levels would come under pressure if a lower legal minimum wage was introduced. For this reason, they argued instead for the generalization of industry-level minimum standards. On the other hand, the trade unions in the service sector, in which wage levels have traditionally in some cases been considerably lower, were finding it increasingly difficult to agree to acceptable minimum standards in collective bargaining. Against this background, service-sector unions were the first to start campaigning for a statutory minimum wage. For many years, this lack of consensus within the trade union movement provided successive governments with a ready-made excuse to kick the issue into the long grass, particularly since the expansion of low-wage work was widely regarded as necessary to reduce unemployment. It was not until 2006 that the unions affiliated with the German Trade Union Confederation (DGB) brought themselves to make a joint demand for a statutory minimum wage. They are now demanding a national minimum wage of €7.50 (US$10.97) gross per hour (about 50 percent of the German full-time median wage).

In the political sphere, opinions are still divided. The new federal government agreed in its coalition agreement of November 2005 to investigate the necessity of introducing minimum wages; on the conservative CDU/CSU side in particular, however, majority opinion is against such a move. Opponents of a minimum wage are broadly supported by most academic economists in Germany, who point to negative employment effects without taking into account the diversity of the findings produced by empirical studies carried out abroad (see Bosch and Weinkopf 2006). The clearly divergent views held by economists in many other countries are also simply ignored or even deliberately concealed. The campaign launched in 2006 by hundreds of economists in the United States with the slogan "Raise the minimum wage—hard work deserves fair pay" (EPI 2006) would still have been completely unthinkable in Germany at the time. On the Social Democrat (SPD) side, the federal minister with competence in this area recently came out in favor of industry-level arrangements that could be declared generally binding by a political decision of the ministry. In 2007 the government agreed to declare collective agreements on minimum wages in low-wage industries as generally binding. However, one important precondition for this would be that employers and trade unions reach a prior agreement on minimum standards. In a not inconsiderable number of industries, however, either employers are pushing for reductions in collectively agreed standards or there are no standard national agreements that could be declared generally binding, as is clear from the industry chapters in this volume. Therefore, the coalition agreement supports the introduction of minimum wages in some industries, like temp agencies, cleaning, postal services, and electricians, but does provide lower thresholds in the high number of industries without national collective agreements.

In the employers' camp—where opinion has, with the exception of the construction industry, traditionally been against a minimum wage—attitudes have also changed, at least in the employers' associations in some of the industries most affected (such as contract cleaning and temporary agency work). Employers in these industries are increasingly discovering the advantages of minimum wages as a means of eliminating wage dumping and are now calling for generally binding minimum wages at the industry level, modeled on the arrangement that already pertains in the construction industry. The idea is that, to circumvent the blocking tactics of the employers' associations' umbrella organization on the collective bargaining committee, a simplified procedure should be adopted, whereby minimum wages would be introduced by a decree issued by the Ministry of Labor based on the European posted workers directive. A further advantage of this strategy would be that such minimum standards would also apply to foreign companies operating in the German market.

Overall, it can be concluded that political attitudes toward a minimum wage are shifting. According to recent polls, a large majority of Germans are in favor of a minimum wage. At the beginning of 2007, these poll results persuaded the SDP, which in 2006 had pronounced itself in favor of a combination of combi-wages and generally binding collective agreements, to come out in support of a minimum wage. Against this background, cautious attempts are also being made to change tack within the CDU.

The apocalyptic arguments advanced by many German economists, who predicted a dramatic collapse in employment levels if a minimum wage was introduced, have lost a great deal of credibility, particularly as a result of the positive British experiences and the studies by David Card and Alan Krueger (1995), which have received considerable attention. There are other reasons why opinion has shifted in favor of a statutory minimum wage. First, a minimum wage is the only way of ensuring fair competition between German nationals and non-nationals following the eastward expansion of the EU. Second, the sharp increase in subsidies for low-wage work following the introduction of unemployment benefit II has made people recognize that the welfare state must be protected from abuse by employers offering poor employment conditions. Third, and finally, many people's sense of justice has been offended by the considerable increase in earnings and wealth at the top end of the labor market and the simultaneous reduction in wages at the bottom end. The not-unjustified concern that a minimum wage could have negative consequences in East Germany, with its fragile employment situation, remains as a counterargument. This concern can be allayed only by a sustained economic upturn.

We regard the introduction of a national statutory minimum wage in Germany to be urgently necessary to prevent a further increase in low and very low wages, since the conditions for the implementation of effective industry-level minimum wages exist in only a few industries. Furthermore, our empirical studies have shown that there is a particular need for action with regard to the regulation of special employment relationships, particularly temporary agency work and mini-jobs; the above-average rate of low pay in these jobs puts pressure on the pay and job quality of other employment relationships as well.

As far as temporary agency work is concerned, current developments suggest that the government went too far in 2003 with its extensive deregulation of pay and lifting of the restrictions on the length of time for which temp agency workers can be deployed. The equal pay regulation promoted as compensation for the relaxation of many of the restrictions on temporary agency work has in practice been invalidated by the exceptions for which the law provides. It does not apply if temporary work agencies base their rates of pay on collective agreements that have been concluded for the sector as a whole. By concluding several collective agreements with extremely low starting wages, the Christian trade unions have so weakened the DGB unions' bargaining position that the collectively agreed rates in the temp agency sector are significantly lower than those in the industries that traditionally make extensive use of temp agency workers (Weinkopf 2006). Furthermore it is now possible in Germany— unlike in most other countries—to deploy temp agency workers in a company without any time restrictions. The low rates of pay and the possibility of long-term deployment obviously create major incentives for employers to make increased use of temp agency workers or even to set up subsidiaries themselves in which the lower temp agency pay rates can be applied.

It is obviously very difficult to implement legal minimum standards, such as continued payment of wages in the event of sickness, in mini-jobs, which now account for almost one-fifth of all employment relationships in Germany. For this reason, and also because these employment relationships are growing at the expense, to some extent, of insurable jobs, the special treatment granted to mini-jobs should, in our view, be reviewed as a matter of urgency. This urgency is all the greater since the subsidies granted to marginal part-time employees are paid without any regard whatsoever for target groups or examination of need. Furthermore, it is obvious that employers frequently take advantage of these subsidies in order to reduce wage rates, although this infringes the German Part-Time Work and Temporary Employment Act (Teilzeit- und Befristungsgesetz), which expressly prohibits any discrimination against part-time employees. To reduce the incentives to fragment employment, either the equal treatment regulation must be effectively enforced or the special treatment accorded to mini-jobs (exemption from income tax and social security contributions) must be abolished. Both measures could give employees in sectors with particularly high shares of marginal part-time jobs a better chance of earning a living wage, despite relatively low hourly rates, by increasing the number of hours they work.

We regard the modernization of the welfare state as another priority task to reduce low-wage work. The German welfare state is still largely geared to the single male breadwinner model and no longer accords with the labor market behavior of most couples. The "splitting" system of taxation for married couples, the mini-jobs, and the persistence of derived entitlement to social security benefits for spouses influence the labor supply of married women in particular in such a way that they are frequently prepared to accept marginal part-time and low-paid jobs with limited social protection. This is further reinforced and encouraged by the continued inadequate provision of public child care facilities and all-day schools, particularly in West Germany.

Last but not least, one particular challenge facing Germany is to make sustained increases in its investment in education and training. The main objective in doing so must be to achieve significant reductions in the share of people without a vocational training qualification, which is currently rising again. Despite the high share of workers with formal qualifications in low-paid work, a good level of education or training remains the best protection against low pay, poor job quality, and unemployment.

NOTES

1. Such transitions are the focus of the so-called transitional labor market theory (Schmid 1993).
2. The share of low-wage workers among temps may actually be even higher, because no distinction can be made in this category between the temp agency's core workforce (placement and administrative staff) and the temps who are sent to work in other companies.

REFERENCES

Appelbaum, Eileen, Annette Bernhardt, and Richard J. Murnane. 2003. "Low-Wage America: An Overview." In *Low-Wage America: How Employers Are Reshaping Opportunity in the Workplace*, edited by Eileen Appelbaum, Annette Bernhardt, and Richard J. Murnane. New York: Russell Sage Foundation.

Becker, Irene. 2006. "Armut in Deutschland: Bevölkerungsgruppen unterhalb der Alg II-Grenze" ["Poverty in Germany: Population Groups Below the Threshold of Unemployment Benefit II"]. Social Justice Project working paper 3. Frankfurt, Germany: Johann Wolfgang Goethe Universität.

Bosch, Gerhard, and Thorsten Kalina. 2005. "Entwicklung und Struktur der Niedriglohnbeschäftigung in Deutschland" ["Development and Structure of Low-Wage Employment in Germany"]. In *Institut Arbeit und Technik: Jahrbuch 2005* [*Work and Technical Institute: Yearbook 2005*]. Gelsenkirchen, Germany: Institut Arbeit und Technik (IAT).

Bosch, Gerhard, and Claudia Weinkopf, with the help of Thorsten Kalina. 2006. "Mindestlöhne auch in Deutschland?" ["Statutory Minimum Wage in Germany Too?"] Expert's assessment on behalf of the Friedrich Ebert Foundation. Bonn, Germany: Gesprächskreis Arbeit und Qualifizierung.

Card, David, and Alan B. Krueger. 1995. *Myth and Measurement: The New Economics of the Minimum Wage*. Princeton, N.J.: Princeton University Press.

Congressional Budget Office (CBO). 2006. "Changes in the Low-Wage Labor Markets Between 1979 and 2005." Washington: CBO.

Crouch, Colin, and Henry Farrell. 2002. "Breaking of the Path of Institutional Development? Alternatives to the New Determinism." EUI working papers SPS No. 2002/4. Florence: European University Institute. Badia Fiesolana/San Domenico (FI).

Economic Policy Institute (EPI). 2006. "EPI on the Minimum Wage" and "Hundreds of Economists Say: Raise the Minimum Wage," *EPI-News*, October 27. Accessed at http://www.epi.org/epinews/epinews2006 1027.html.

Employee Benefit Research Institute (EBRI). 2006. *EBRI Databook on Employee Benefits*. Washington: EBRI. Accessed at http://www.ebri.org/publications/books/index.cfm?fa=databook.

Esping-Andersen, Gøsta. 1990. *The Three Worlds of Welfare Capitalism*. Cambridge: Polity Press.

European Commission. 2004. *Employment in Europe 2004*. Luxembourg: European Commission.

Jaehrling, Karen, and Claudia Weinkopf, with the help of Bettina Hieming and Bruno Kaltenborn. 2006. "Kombilöhne: Neue Wege, alte Pfade, Irrweg?" ["Wage Subsidies—New Ways, Old Paths, Wrong Track?"]. Expert's assessment on behalf of the Friedrich Ebert Foundation. Bonn, Germany: Gesprächskreis Arbeit und Qualifizierung.

Kalina, Thorsten, and Claudia Weinkopf. 2006a. "Einführung eines gesetzlichen Mindestlohnes in Deutschland: Eine Modellrechnung für das Jahr 2004" ["Introduction of a Statutory Minimum Wage in Germany: A Model Calculation for 2004"]. In *Institut Arbeit und Technik: Jahrbuch 2006* [*Institute for Work and Technology: Yearbook 2006*]. Gelsenkirchen, Germany: Institut Arbeit und Technik (IAT).

————. 2006b. "Ein gesetzlicher Mindestlohn auch in Deutschland? Modellrechnungen für Stundenlöhne zwischen €5,00 und €7,50—und wie machen es die anderen?" ["A Statutory Minimum Wage in Germany? Model Calculations for Hourly Wages between €5 and €7.50—And How Is It in Other Countries?"]. Report 2006-06. Gelsenkirchen, Germany: Institut Arbeit und Technik (IAT).

Organization for Economic and Cooperative Development (OECD). 1996. *Employment Outlook*. Paris: OECD.

————. 1997. *Employment Outlook*. Paris: OECD.

Sachverständigenrat. 2006. *Widerstreitende Interessen—ungenutzte Chancen: Jahresgutachten des Sachverständigenrates 2006–2007*. [*Conflict of Interest—Missed Opportunities, Annual Report of the German Council of Economic Experts*].Wiesbaden, Germany: Sachverständigenrat.

Schmid, Günther. 1993. "Übergänge in die Vollbeschäftigung: Formen und Finanzierung einer zukunftsgerechten Arbeitsmarktpolitik" ["Transitions to Full Employment. Forms and Funding of a Labor Market Policy Fitting for the Future"]. WZB Discussion paper 93-208. Berlin.

Streeck, Wolfgang. 1991. "On the Institutional Conditions of Diversified

Quality Production." In *Beyond Keynesianism: The Socioeconomics of Production and Employment*, edited by Egon Matzner and Wolfgang Streeck. London: Edward Elgar.

U.S. Department of Labor. 2006. "National Compensation Survey: Employee Benefits in Private Industry in the United States." Washington: U.S. Department of Labor (March).

Weinkopf, Claudia. 2006. "Mindestbedingungen für die Zeitarbeitsbranche? Expertise im Auftrag des Interessenverbandes Deutscher Zeitarbeitsunternehmen (iGZ)" ["Minimum Standards for the Temporary Agency Industry?"]. Gelsenkirchen, Germany: Institut Arbeit und Technik.

Index